D1232053

INTERNATIONAL COMMODITY CONTROL:
A CONTEMPORARY HISTORY AND APPRAISAL

HF
1428
.G64
1984

CROOM HELM COMMODITY SERIES
Edited by Fiona Gordon-Ashworth, Bank of England

URANIUM: A STRATEGIC SOURCE OF ENERGY
Marian Radetzki, Institute for International Economic Studies,
Stockholm

TIN: ITS PRODUCTION AND MARKETING
William Robertson, University of Liverpool

INTERNATIONAL COMMODITY CONTROL 1929-1980
Fiona Gordon-Ashworth, Bank of England

COMMODITY MODELS FOR FORECASTING
AND POLICY ANALYSIS
Walter C. Labys and Peter K. Pollak

The author, formerly of the University of Southampton, now works
at the Bank of England. The views expressed in the book are those of
the author and do not reflect those of the Bank of England.

International COMMODITY CONTROL

A Contemporary History and Appraisal

Fiona Gordon-Ashworth

CROOM HELM
London & Canberra
ST. MARTIN'S PRESS
New York

© 1984 F. Gordon-Ashworth
Croom Helm Ltd., Provident House, Burrell Row,
Beckenham, Kent BR3 1AT
Croom Helm Australia Pty Ltd, 28 Kembla St,
Fyshwick, ACT 2609, Australia

British Library Cataloguing in Publication Data

Gordon-Ashworth, Fiona
    International commodity control.
    1. Raw materials − Prices   2. Price
    regulation   3. Commodity control
    I. Title
    338.5'2   HF1051
    ISBN 0-7099-1148-3

All rights reserved. For information, write:
St. Martin's Press, Inc., 175 Fifth Avenue, New York, NY 10010
First published in the United States of America in 1984

Library of Congress Cataloging in Publication Data

Gordon-Ashworth, Fiona.
    International commodity control, 1929 to 1977.

    Bibliography: p.
    Includes index.
    1. Commodity control − History − 20th century. 2. Inter-
national economic relations − History − 20th century.
    I. Title.
HF1428.G64   1984   382'.4   81-48262
ISBN 0-312-41994-5

Printed and bound in Great Britain

CONTENTS

TABLES AND FIGURES

Tables

Figures

To my husband, Christopher

EDITORIAL STATEMENT

This study is the third in the Croom Helm Commodity Series. The aim of the Series is to advance the understanding of issues relating to the production and marketing of primary commodities. Most volumes in the Series, including the first two - Uranium by Marian Radetzki and Tin by William Robertson - concentrate on analysing the essential properties, production and trade of a single commodity. The present study, in contrast, and the fourth, Commodity Models by Walter C. Labys and Peter K. Pollack (forthcoming), are wider in compass. Although differing markedly in content, it is envisaged that all volumes in the Series will share a similar form and direction, so that they may be useful for reference purposes. Similarly, each of the studies is to set the subject of commodity production firmly within the framework of the changing international economic environment and will include a prospects section. It is hoped, in consequence, that some light may be shed on the future profile of commodity production and trade and that the Series will be broad in its appeal. For, as implied by Gamani Corea in the Preface to the current volume, the issues arising from primary commodity production and trade are far-reaching and may no longer be considered of exclusive interest to producers in developing countries.

Fiona Gordon-Ashworth
Series Editor
April 1983

PREFACE

The collapse in commodity prices has been one of the manifestations of the present world economic crisis. It has had its repercussions on the capacity of the developing countries to service their external debts and to sustain the level of their imports and, hence, on the international financial and banking system and the flow of world trade. The commodity situation has, in fact, been an important dimension of the downward spiral in world economic activity.

This experience underlines once more the importance of international action to deal with commodity problems. Recent evidence suggests that commodity prices tend to fluctuate even more sharply than before in response to changes in the demand for industrial products, due partly to the altered climate of expectations. These fluctuations have, therefore, a greater effect on overall price movements in the industrialised countries, rendering more difficult the task of macro-economic management.

The importance of providing greater stability to commodity markets has for long been recognised. This objective was, indeed, an important part of the approaches to post-War systems building. Up to now, however, there has been a failure in implementation. The concepts embodied in the Havana Charter were never realised. In 1976, at the fourth session of UNCTAD in Nairobi, the issue was revived once more, leading to the adoption by governments of the Integrated Programme for Commodities. But once again there has been a lag in implementation. Despite the comprehensive framework provided by the Programme, there is still an inadequate record of actions to impart strength and stability to commodity trade.

The practical efforts to achieve this goal, however, have been numerous and cover a long period of time. Since 1976, in particular, a large number of preparatory meetings, and even negotiations, have taken place for an impressive number of specific products. It is opportune, therefore, to draw the lessons of this experience, to analyse the causes of failure or slow progress, and to understand the concerns of the various actors in the negotiating process -producers as well as consumers. Out of this might emerge useful pointers for future progress.

The present volume is indeed a valuable contribution towards this need. It brings together the various strands that make up the story of international commodity negotiations since their inception over six decades ago. It is also rich in its analysis of recent developments. The author has many pertinent remarks to make regarding some of the negotiations initiated in UNCTAD and, although one need not agree with all her observations, one values the constructive views of a critical outsider. Dr. Gordon-Ashworth, with her background of academic teaching and international banking, has

provided a perceptive analysis. I hope it would be a stimulus not only
to further research but to effective actions in this very critical area.

Gomani Corea
Secretary-General
United Nations Conference on Trade and Development
31 March 1983

NOTE

1. References to Countries

Changes have occurred in the names of several countries in the period covered by this study. Such countries are referred to by their present (1983) name as far as possible: for example, Thailand (Siam until 1939), Indonesia (Netherlands East Indies until 1945) and Zaire (the Belgian Congo until 1960 and the Democratic Republic of the Congo from 1960 to 1972). The classification of countries used in the study accords to that of UNCTAD, the details of which are provided in the notes to Table 1:6.

2. Measurements and Currencies

Unless otherwise specified, tons refers to long tons, billions to American billions (a thousand million) and dollars to US dollars.

3. Abbreviations

For ease of reference, abbreviations used in the text refer to commonly accepted forms. These include:

ACP	the African, Caribbean and Pacific group of countries granted special trading relations with the EEC
AIEC	Association of Iron Ore Producing Countries
ASSIMER	International Association of Mercury Producers
CACM	Central American Common Market
CAP	(EEC) Common Agricultural Policy
cif	cost, insurance and freight
CIPEC	Conseil Intergouvernemental des Pays Exportateurs de Cuivre
CMEA	Council for Mutual Economic Assistance (Comecon)
EEC	European Economic Communities
EFTA	European Free Trade Association
FAO	(United Nations) Food and Agriculture Organization

fob	free on board
GATT	General Agreement on Tariffs and Trade
IBA	International Bauxite Association
IBRD	International Bank for Reconstruction and Development (World Bank)
ILO	International Labour Office
IMF	International Monetary Fund
ITO	International Trade Organization
LAFTA	Latin American Free Trade Assocation
LTA	Long Term Arrangement regarding International Trade in Cotton Textiles
MFA	Arrangement regarding International Trade in Textiles or Multi-Fibre Arrangement
n.a.	not available
NIEO	New International Economic Order
OECD	Organization for Economic Co-operation and Development
OPEC	Organization of Petroleum Exporting Countries
STABEX	EEC-administered scheme of compensatory finance
UK	United Kingdom
UNCTAD	United Nations Conference on Trade and Development
US	United States (of America)
USSR	Union of Soviet Socialist Republics

FOREWORD

'Another damned, thick, square book!
Always scribble, scribble, scribble!
Eh! Mr Gibbon?'

(William Henry, Duke of Gloucester, 1745-1805)

There have been two periods in which interest in international commodity control has blossomed: the first, during the 1930s, was stimulated by a dramatic fall in the prices of primary commodities. The second, during the 1970s, was associated with sharp movements in such prices and the adoption by UNCTAD of its Integrated Programme for Commodities in 1976. It was the first period and a study of the importance of international commodity control for one country, Brazil, which first awakened my interest in the subject. It has been developments in the second which have confirmed that interest and suggested that the current investigation was worth pursuing.

There are several reasons, in brief, why it seemed appropriate to attempt a comprehensive and analytical appraisal of international commodity controls, from their origins in the 1920s to their widespread acceptance as an important element in international trade policy in the 1970s. First, international commodity controls have been a sufficiently recurrent theme in trade policy to merit an economic history in their own right. Secondly, those engaged or likely to be engaged in the production of and trade in primary commodities may find a study of this type of interest in appraising the strengths and weaknesses of such controls in the past and in assessing their prospects for the future. Thirdly, it is hoped that policy-makers may find this study a helpful tool in providing an historic and analytic framework in which to consider contemporary commodity policy.

As perhaps is often the case with a study such as this, the contents have proved to be something of a 'moving frontier'. The subject is large and any attempt to reduce it to manageable proportions has meant, of necessity, a selective appraisal rather than a blow-by-blow account. It is hoped, nevertheless, that the study may fill a gap and prove useful for reference purposes by covering all of the international commodity agreements, together with examples of cartels, within an historic, economic and institutional framework. It is hoped, furthermore, that the Conclusion and Appraisal section may enable the reader to bring to current developments some of the lessons arising from past experience of international commodity controls.

In the course of researching and writing this book many organisations and individuals have been very helpful to me. It is not possible to mention them all by name. However, special thanks go to Christopher Platt for the idea, Gamani Corea for sparing the time to write the Preface, Chris Wright and Jan Hedges for their work on commodity prices and Pen Kent, for encouraging the venture. Valuable comments on various draft sections of the text were received from Andrea Boardman of Gill & Duffus, colleagues at the Bank of England (particularly those on Groups I, III, 6, 7 and 10 in the International and Territorial Divisions), Robert Greenhill, Alistair MacBean, Tin Nguyen, William Robertson, Leelananda da Silva and Richard Woodhams. I am grateful also to the following organisations for their assistance in supplying data: the Economist, F.O. Licht, GATT, Gill & Duffus, the International Cocoa Organization, the International Coffee Organization, the International Institute for Cotton, the International Rubber Study Group, the International Tea Committee, the International Tin Council, the International Wheat Council and UNCTAD.

I have also benefited from a very supportive family. I am indebted first and foremost to my husband, Christopher, for all his ideas, help and encouragement. I should also like to thank my mother and mother-in-law, for looking after Luke so well, and my sister, Elspeth, for her work on statistics.

Finally, I should like to mention Gill Cox, who deciphered several drafts of the book and whose excellent typing allowed it to be completed.

I am, of course, solely responsible for the views expressed in this study.

Fiona Gordon-Ashworth
April 1983

PART I: THE ECONOMIC AND INSTITUTIONAL FRAMEWORK OF
INTERNATIONAL COMMODITY CONTROL

1:   PRIMARY COMMODITY TRADE AND ASSOCIATED PROBLEMS

'No nation was ever ruined by trade.'

(Benjamin Franklin, Essays)

1. General

A commodity, by definition, is an item suitable for trade. As such, it can assume many different forms and characteristics which render it suitable to be bought and sold for commercial purposes. It may, for example, be a staple or leading article in world trade or a minor article, an article produced mainly for export purposes or one produced principally for domestic consumption, an article with many types or forms or an article distinguished by its homogeneity, an article produced by many countries in every continent or one produced by only a few countries within limited climatic belts. It is important at this stage, therefore, to define the commodity terms of reference used in this book.
    This study is concerned with attempts to regulate trade in primary as opposed to manufactured goods at the international as opposed to national level. Primary commodities are defined in this context as goods in or near to their first stage of transformation and manufactured goods will be considered only when they add to an understanding of primary commodity control. (Examples include the case of cotton textiles and of synthetic rubber.) International commodity controls have assumed two main forms: formally negotiated and published agreements between governments or producer associations known as international commodity agreements; and cartels, arrangements between producers or traders organised to

3

reduce or defeat competition and to control the production or distribution of a commodity to their common advantage. Some form of controls has probably applied to most primary commodities at some stage in their history. However, at the international level their application has been limited to a dozen or so conspicuous examples. It is these which form the central object of this enquiry. The most clearly articulated have been those applied to tin, wheat, sugar, rubber, coffee, cocoa, tea and olive oil in the form of international commodity agreements. These are considered on an individual basis in Part III. Raw material cartels, in contrast, although more numerous, have been less public in their terms of operation so that discussion in Part III relies on an illustrative appraisal rather than a blow-by-blow account of six major examples of cartel-styled action. These cover crude petroleum, copper, mercury, bauxite, uranium and iron ore. Reference is also made in the Conclusion and Appraisal Section to those commodities for which international controls have been proposed as a future course of action.

The purpose of this chapter is to set the commodities considered in subsequent chapters in their economic context. How important, for example, have been such commodities in terms of total world trade? Which countries or country-groups specialised in trade in such commodities? And what problems may be considered special or peculiar to primary as opposed to manufactured goods? The account which follows aims to answer these questions by providing first a snapshot view of the composition of primary commodity trade in two years, 1938 and 1977, the former near to the beginning and the latter near to the end of the time span covered by this book; secondly, an insight into the parties participant in such trade; and, thirdly, a brief assessment of several of the problems considered to be special to primary commodities. For a more detailed economic history of the periods covered, readers are referred to the large specialist literature available.(1)

2. The Composition of Primary Commodity Trade in 1938 and 1977

1938 and 1977, the years chosen for this snap-shot view of world primary commodity trade, share two important characteristics: both followed a pronounced world recession; and, for both, a reliable and detailed breakdown of world trade is available which permits a comparative analysis to be made. At the same time, it should be recognised that such a snap-shot view cannot provide a substitute for a more detailed account, particularly since commodity definitions vary and only one currency is used for valuation purposes. For this purpose, as outlined above, recourse is needed to some of the more specialist histories which are available.

The entry-point to world trade data for 1938 is the League of Nations survey of world trade published in 1942. This aimed to assist

Table 1:1 : The Value and Volume of World Trade,
1928, 1935, 1937 and 1938

	IMPORTS			
	1928	1935	1937	1938
Value				
(new) $ (millions)	60,080	21,042	28,171	24,583
£ sterling (millions)	7,291	4,271	5,695	5,027
Prices (1928 = 100)				
$	100	70	79	75
£ sterling	100	69	78	75
Quantum (1928 = 100)	100	85	100	91
	EXPORTS			
Value				
(new) $ (millions)	55,223	19,025	25,409	21,917
£ sterling (millions)	6,702	3,861	5,137	4,482
Prices (1928 = 100)				
$	100	68	78	74
£ sterling	100	68	76	73
Quantum (1928 = 100)	100	85	100	91

Source: League of Nations, The Network of World Trade (League
of Nations, Geneva, 1942, II.A.3), p. 16.

in an understanding of the functioning of the world trading system in order to avoid 'the disruption of trade and accentuation of the depression to which commercial policies pursued in the '30s led ...'(2)

The survey of commodity data was part of a broad account of the 60 per cent decline in the US dollar value, and the 9 per cent decline in the volume, of world exports between 1928 and 1938 (Table 1:1). In this period trade in foodstuffs experienced the most pronounced decline compared with a smaller decline in manufactured goods and, notably, in other raw materials. Throughout the years in question, manufactured goods represented less than 40 per cent of the value of world trade.(3)

Table 1:2 : The Value of Exports of Major Primary Commodities in 1938 (millions of $)

Commodity	Value of Exports	Rank in Sample
Cotton	600	1
Coal	530	2
Crude Petroleum	448	3
Wheat	442	4
Wool	435	5
Petroleum	394	6
Tobacco	359	7
Sugar	340	8
Copper	325	9
Butter	304	10
Gas and Fuel Oil	298	11
Rubber	287	12
Coffee	263	13
Beef, Lamb and Mutton	222	14
Maize	220	15
Pork	216	16
Tea	202	17
Rice	197	18
Iron Ore	149	19
Silk	124	20
Wheat Flour	127	21
Tin (metal)	123	22

Source: League of Nations, The Network of World Trade (League of Nations, Geneva, 1942, II.A.3), p. 30.

The twenty-two leading primary commodities in world trade in 1938, representing 30 per cent of the total value of world trade, are itemised in Table 1:2. The table reveals that crude petroleum, wheat, sugar, copper, rubber and coffee, of the commodities considered in this study, ranked among the thirteen leading primary commodities in value terms in 1938. In contrast, tea, iron ore and tin were of far less importance and other commodities considered in

Table 1:3 : The Value of Exports of Major Primary Commodities in 1977 (millions of $)

Commodity	Value of Exports	Rank in Sample
Crude Petroleum	145,161	1
Petroleum Products	42,760	2
Coffee	12,918	3
Coal, coke and briquettes	10,907	4
Pearls and precious and semi-precious stones	9,972	5
Gas, natural and manufactured	9,293	6
Meat, chilled and frozen	9,291	7
Wheat, unmilled	7,987	8
Wood	7,810	9
Sugar and Honey	7,612	10
Copper	7,292	11
Oilseeds, Nuts and Kernels	7,282	12
Animal Feed[a]	7,074	13
Maize	6,171	14
Ores[b]	6,163	15
Fruit	6,157	16
Fish	5,959	17
Rubber	5,228	18
Iron Ore	4,911	19
Cotton	4,717	20
Vegetables	4,664	21
Cocoa	4,231	22

Notes: a excludes unmilled cereals
         b ores and concentrates of non-ferrous base metals

Source: UNCTAD, Handbook of International Trade and Development Statistics: Supplement 1980 (UNCTAD, New York, 1980, TD/STAT.9), Table 4.3 A.

subsequent chapters, namely cocoa, olive oil, mercury, bauxite and uranium, did not feature in the League's survey.

If a similar table is constructed for 1977, rather different results emerge although, coincidentally, the twenty-two leading commodities also covered about 30 per cent of world trade (Table 1:3). Perhaps the most striking development was the rise of crude petroleum to the position of the unrivalled primary commodity in world trade, a development closely associated with price movements considered in Chapter 14. A second point of interest was the displacement of cotton from its rank as the leading primary commodity, a move associated with the sluggish growth of the cotton trade compared with that of other commodities. (The changing structure of the world cotton trade is considered briefly in Chapter 2.) It may also be noted that of the commodities which form the central object of this study, wheat, sugar and copper retained their ranks among the top eleven of commodities traded in 1977, coffee substantially enhanced its position, rising from thirteenth to third place, and cocoa was also included in the sample. In contrast, rubber fell from twelfth to eighteenth place. Iron ore remained a commodity of medium importance and tin, tea and olive oil did not rank in the sample. (Bauxite and uranium were not itemised separately.)

It is perhaps surprising that cotton and coal, both important commodities in 1938 and 1977, did not become the objects of major international commodity controls throughout the period. Conversely, tin and olive oil, both relatively minor items in world trade, each formed the object of such action. It may be concluded, in consequence, that no correlation existed between the importance of a primary commodity in world trade and the incidence of international commodity control measures.

3. Participation in Primary Commodity Trade since the 1930s

During the 1930s, the UK and her colonies were by far the most important trading group in world trade (Table 1:4). Similarly, this group of countries was the most important exporting entity of the twenty-two commodities included in the League's survey, leading (exporting over half) world exports of wool, rubber, tea and tin and exporting over 30 per cent of the value of world exports of wheat, butter, beef, lamb and mutton, rice and wheat flour (Table 1:5). Other colonial powers, in contrast, played a far less significant role: the Netherlands Overseas Territories, for example, exported less than half of the commodities itemised and played a major part only in the export of petroleum, gas and fuel oil and, to a lesser extent, rubber and tea; the French Overseas Territories were major exporters only of rice of the commodities considered. Similarly, Continental Europe led the export only of butter, pork and iron ore although its exports

Table 1:4 : The Share of Major Economic and Political Groupings of World Trade, 1928, 1935 and 1938 (percentage of total $ value)[a]

	IMPORTS			EXPORTS		
	1928	1935	1938	1928	1935	1938
WORLD	100	100	100	100	100	100
British Commonwealth[b]	29.8	31.7	32.7	27.2	27.5	26.7
France and her overseas territories	7.8	9.4	7.2	7.9	8.1	6.1
Netherlands and her overseas territories	4.5	4.5	5.1	4.7	4.7	5.2
Belgium, Belgian Congo (Zaire) and Rwanda-Urundi	2.6	3.1	3.3	2.7	3.2	3.5
Italy and her overseas territories	3.4	3.5	3.1	2.5	2.4	2.6
Spain and her overseas territories	1.7	1.5	0.7	1.3	1.1	0.5
Portugal and her overseas territories	0.5	0.7	0.6	0.3	0.4	0.4
United States and her overseas territories[c]	13.0	11.0	9.6	16.3	12.6	14.7
All other countries	36.7	34.7	37.7	37.1	40.2	40.3

Notes: a Totals may not sum due to rounding

  b The British Commonwealth, the largest of the groupings, included the UK, Ireland, Australia, Canada, New Zealand, the Union of South Africa, India and Burma and other colonies and territories under protectorate or mandate.

  c The overseas territories included in this table are the Philippines, the Panama Canal Zone, Guam and Samoa, Alaska, Hawaii, Porto Rico and the Virgin Islands.

Source: League of Nations, Network of World Trade (League of Nations, Geneva, 1942, II.A.3), derived from p. 19.

of coal and tobacco exceeded 30 per cent of the world total. The US, in contrast, did not export over half of any of the commodities considered although its participation in world exports of cotton, crude petroleum, tobacco and maize exceeded 30 per cent of the

Table 1:5 : Exports of Major Primary Commodities in 1938 by Major Export Grouping (percentage share of the export of each commodity by value)

Commodity	Continental Europe	British Dominions and Colonial Empire	UK and Ireland	Latin America	US	Netherlands Overseas Territories	French Overseas Territories	Rest of World[a]
Cotton	2.8	20.8	-	13.0	37.3	-	0.3	25.7
Coal	45.7	2.3	34.5	-	10.6	0.2	0.7	6.0
Crude Petroleum	1.1	1.6	-	65.4	25.0	1.8	-	5.1
Wheat	17.4	38.9	-	13.3	17.6	-	3.6	9.0
Wool	9.7	64.4	4.1	19.1	-	-	1.4	1.4
Petroleum	10.2	13.5	1.0	3.0	31.0	29.2	-	12.2
Tobacco	33.7	6.4	-	4.7	43.4	5.6	0.6	5.6
Sugar	10.6	20.9	3.8	35.6	0.9	7.4	3.5	17.4
Copper	16.9	28.3	0.6	21.5	27.8	-	-	5.9
Butter	53.9	40.5	3.6	1.0	0.3	-	-	0.7
Gas and fuel oil	6.4	5.7	1.0	5.7	18.8	40.9	-	21.5
Rubber	-	61.7	-	1.7	-	25.8	6.3	4.5
Coffee	0.8	3.4	-	85.6	-	2.7	4.2	3.4
Beef, lamb and mutton	6.3	41.9	0.9	49.1	0.5	-	-	0.4
Maize	10.9	6.4	-	25.9	43.2	-	7.3	6.4
Pork	63.0	19.9	6.5	1.9	7.9	-	-	0.9
Tea	-	73.8	-	-	-	15.3	-	10.4
Rice	7.6	48.7	-	1.0	4.1	-	0.5	23.4
Iron ore	77.9	8.7	-	2.7	1.3	-	15.2	2.0
Silk	6.5	-	-	-	-	-	7.4	93.5
Wheat flour	23.6	33.1	7.1	3.1	18.1	-	3.1	11.8
Tin	26.6	50.4	9.8	0.8	-	4.9	0.8	7.3

Note: a   May not sum to 100 due to rounding.

For the country coverage, see Table 1:4.

Source: League of Nations, The Network of World Trade (League of Nations, Geneva, 1942, II.A.3).

total.   Latin America, finally, played an important role in world exports of crude petroleum and coffee and exported over 30 per cent of world exports of sugar, beef, lamb and mutton.

With the independence of many former colonial countries, the formation of new trading groups such as the European Economic Communities (EEC) and the more leading role played by the US, the post-Second World War environment of primary commodity trade departed from its comparatively simple pre-War model.   The institutional and political development of this new environment is considered in Chapter 3.   In terms of international trade, the changes led to new categories of country groupings being adopted, two based on income levels - 'industrialised' or 'developed' countries (terms used interchangeably in this study), that is, countries for whom manufactured goods were the most important exports, and 'developing countries', that is, countries for whom primary commodity exports tended to predominate - and a third, 'centrally-planned' or 'socialist' economies, based on political organisation and including countries such as China and the USSR.   For the latter, intra-country or intra-bloc trade was more important than international trade.   Within each grouping, sub-divisions were formed as patterns of growth diverged or new trading groups emerged. Examples of the former include the oil-exporting country grouping, which emerged following the oil price rises of the 1970s, its counterpart, the oil-importing grouping, and the group of industrialising developing countries known as the 'fast growing exporters of manufactures' or 'newly industrialising countries'. Examples of new trading groups include the EEC and the European Free Trade Association (FFTA).   The contributions of the main groupings to world trade, together with a breakdown of their members, is provided in Table 1:6.   The definitions used in this table will form the basis for subsequent reference in the remainder of this study.

As the table indicates, the post-War period was characterised by the rapid growth in the value of world trade and the consolidation by developed countries of their pre-eminent position over it.   The share of world trade of the latter, for example, rose from 61.1 per cent of exports and 65.3 per cent of imports in 1950 to 65.8 per cent and 70.4 per cent respectively in 1979 with increased trade between developed countries of manufactured goods a major explanatory factor.   The shares of developing countries, in contrast, fell - from 30.8 per cent of exports and 26.7 per cent of imports in 1950 to 25.0 per cent and 20.1 per cent respectively in 1979 - whilst that of centrally planned countries, although rising slightly - from 8.1 per cent of exports and 7.8 per cent of imports in 1950 to 9.3 per cent and 9.5 per cent in 1979 - remained modest.   Much of the increase in the value of world trade was accounted for by price movements: between 1960 and 1979, alone, for example, the value of exports from

Table 1:6 : The Value of World Imports and Exports in 1938, 1950, 1960, 1970, 1975, 1977 and 1979 (millions of $)

	1938	1950	1960	1970	1975	1977	1979
IMPORTS (cif)							
TOTAL	23,700	63,700	135,200	328,600	908,000	1,162,700	1,679,300
Developed Countries	17,900	41,600	89,100	237,600	614,200	795,600	1,182,900
EEC	-	19,480	44,460	115,740	298,170	384,940	598,260
EFTA	-	4,100	9,730	25,150	62,340	78,000	110,400
Developing Countries	5,800	17,000	30,000	56,300	189,700	251,500	336,900
Centrally Planned Countries of Eastern Europe	-	4,000	13,900	31,700	92,100	105,900	140,500
Centrally Planned Countries of Asia	-	1,000	2,200	3,000	9,300	9,700	19,000
EXPORTS (fob)							
TOTAL	21,100	60,700	128,300	315,300	876,900	1,129,000	1,635,900
Developed Countries	15,200	37,100	85,700	224,900	578,400	730,400	1,075,800
EEC	-	16,160	41,630	111,780	295,330	377,620	571,090
EFTA	-	3,340	7,840	20,690	52,980	65,380	98,090
Developing Countries	5,900	18,700	27,600	57,000	212,900	291,100	408,700
Centrally Planned Countries of Eastern Europe	-	4,140	13,000	31,000	78,300	99,200	136,100
Centrally Planned Countries of Asia	-	790	2,040	2,380	7,190	8,640	15,270

12

Notes and Sources to Table 1:6

The 1938 data is derived from United Nations, Statistical Yearbook 1960 (United Nations, New York, 1960), pp. 386-87. For this year, the term developed countries refers to Canada, the US, countries in Western Europe, Japan, Australia, New Zealand, the Union of South Africa; and developing countries to the difference between the total and that of developed countries. Data for subsequent years is derived from UNCTAD, Handbook of International Trade and Development Statistics: Supplement 1980 (UNCTAD, New York, 1980, TD/STAT. 9); in some years the data do not sum to the world total. The country classifications used are as follows:

Developed Countries

The US, Canada, the EEC (Belgium, Denmark, France, the Federal Republic of Germany, Ireland, Italy, Luxembourg, the Netherlands, the UK) EFTA (Austria, the Faeroe Islands, Finland, Iceland, Norway, Portugal, Sweden, Switzerland), Greece, Spain, Yugoslavia, Gibraltar, Israel, Japan, Australia, New Zealand and South Africa.

Centrally Planned or Socialist Countries of Asia

The People's Republic of China, Mongolia, the Democratic People's Republic of Korea and Vietnam.

Centrally Planned or Socialist Countries of Eastern Europe

Albania, Bulgaria, Czechoslovakia, the German Democratic Republic, Hungary, Poland, Romania, the USSR.

Developing Countries

All countries in Africa, Asia, America and Oceania not specified above.

In addition to these broad headings, UNCTAD also uses the following sub-divisions:

Petroleum Exporting Countries

Countries for which petroleum and petroleum products accounted for over 50 per cent of total exports in 1974. These were Algeria, Angola, Bahrain, Brunei, Ecuador, Gabon, Indonesia, Iran, Iraq, Kuwait, Libyan Arab Jamahiriya, Nigeria, Oman, Qatar, Saudi Arabia, Trinidad and Tobago, United Arab Emirates and Venezuela.

Fast Growing Exporters of Manufactures or Newly Industrialised Countries

Countries whose exports of manufactures amounted to more than $800 million in 1976 and grew at an average rate of more than 20 per cent per annum during the period 1967 to 1976. These were Argentina, Brazil, Hong Kong, Korea, the Republic of Mexico and Singapore.

Least Developed Countries

Afghanistan, Bangladesh, Benin, Bhutan, Botswana, Burundi, Cape Verde, the Central African Republic, Chad, Comoros, Ethiopia, Gambia, Guinea, Haiti, Lao People's Democratic Republic, Lesotho, Malawi, Maldives, Mali, Nepal, Niger, Rwanda, Samoa, Somalia, Sudan, Uganda, United Republic of Tanzania, Upper Volta, Yemen and Democratic Yemen.

13

developed countries rose over twelvefold and those of developing countries over fourteenfold compared with volume rises which were only four and threefold respectively.(4)

The declining share of world trade accounted for by developing countries may be explained in terms of the slower growth of primary, as opposed to manufactured, exports on which the former depended for the bulk of their export earnings. The division of world trade by broad commodity class in 1960, 1970 and 1979 is shown in Table 1:7.

Table 1:7 : Primary Commodities as a Percentage of the Total Value of Exports of Developing and Industrialised Countries, 1960, 1970 and 1979

(Percentage Shares)	1960	1970	1979
Developing Countries			
Total Primary Commodities	88.0	75.7	74.4
Primary Commodities excluding Petroleum	62.3	46.7	22.9
Petroleum	25.7	29.0	51.5
Manufactured Goods	11.7	22.2	24.6
Other	0.3	2.1	1.0
Developed Countries			
Total Primary Commodities	33.0	25.6	25.0
Primary Commodities excluding Petroleum	29.0	22.2	19.0
Petroleum	4.0	3.4	6.0
Manufactured Goods	65.7	72.8	73.3
Other	1.3	1.6	1.7

Source: IBRD, Commodity Trade and Price Trends (IBRD, Johns Hopkins University Press, Baltimore, 1981), pp. 2-3.

It has been suggested further that the prices of the primary commodities in which developing countries specialised declined relative to those of manufactured goods after the Second World War. Such commodities included crude petroleum, coffee, jute (of which developing countries exported over 90 per cent of the total value in 1977); cocoa, tin, tea (of which developing countries exported over 80 per cent in the same year); rubber, bananas, copra, coconut oil, groundnut oil, sisal, tobacco, bauxite and manganese ore (of which developing countries led (accounted for over 50 per cent) world exports). It should be noted in this context that although developing countries depended more than developed countries on primary exports as a source of income, the latter dominated primary commodity trade, despite the independence of many former colonies, and led the export of a number of commodities including coal, wheat, maize, wool, copper, iron ore, nickel and zinc.

4. Problems Associated with Primary Commodity Trade

Two of the problems associated with primary commodity trade have already been mentioned in passing. The first, the perceived declining terms of trade of developing countries, is an important one since it acted as a pervasive influence on international commodity policy since the 1960s when it was articulated by Prebisch in his role as first Secretary General of the United Nations Conference on Trade and Development (UNCTAD), the organisation established with the brief of considering development and trade issues (Chapter 2). However, whereas most writers agree that a sharp drop in the terms of trade of primary products took place in the 1930s, there is considerable disagreement on the trend since the Second World War. Assessments have varied markedly depending both on the time period considered and on the method of calculation used. For example, assessments excluding either the Korean War price boom of the early 1950s or the sharp commodity price rises of the mid-1970s produce very different results from those which include such periods. Similarly, as Table 1.7 may imply, the results for oil-exporting and oil-importing countries vary markedly and make any blanket statement concerning the general trend in the terms of trade of developing countries subject to hazard. It is sufficient to note here, therefore, that the question is by no means clear cut. Using one of the more simple measures available (the unit value of exports divided by the unit value of imports), the terms of trade appear to have worked against developing countries between 1960 and the mid-1970s and to have improved until the end of the 1970s, with oil price rises a major influence. If oil-exporting countries are extracted from the calculation, the terms of trade of the remaining developing countries may be judged to have followed a similar course to that of developed countries in the same period, namely a slight improvement to 1970 followed by a slight deterioration. Full data is not yet available for the 1980 to 1982 period but the evidence suggests that the terms of trade worked against developing countries in the face of a collapse in the prices of many of the primary commodities they exported.(5)

The second problem mentioned above was that of the high degree of dependence of developing countries on primary commodities as a source of income and their consequent susceptibility to reductions in income from that source. This vulnerability was enhanced in many cases by the greater concentration of the export portfolios of developing countries compared with those of their industrialised country counterparts.

15

In 1977, for example, twelve developing countries relied on only one (primary) commodity for 90 per cent or more of the value of their exports (of which seven relied on crude petroleum, two on petroleum products, two on coffee and one on copper); ten for 80 per cent or more (of which two relied on crude petroleum, two on petroleum products and two on sugar); eight for 70 per cent or more, thirteen for 60 per cent or more, and seventeen for 50 per cent or more. Crude petroleum and petroleum products together were responsible for the dependency of twenty-three of the countries on one commodity for 50 per cent or more of their export earnings, coffee for six, oilseeds, sugar and honey and fruit and nuts for four each, cotton and fish for three each and copper, cocoa and iron ore for two each. In contrast, only one developed country, Iceland, depended on one commodity (fish) for 50 per cent or more of its export earnings. Similarly, whereas sixty-one developing countries exported less than thirty-three products and ten exported seven items or less, these conditions applied to only one developed country, the Faeroe Islands, which exported nine commodities.(6) It should be noted, however, that developed countries displayed a reverse dependence in terms of their import requirements for a number of commodities. Examples are considered in the case of the US strategic stockpile in Chapter 3.

A third problem, associated strongly with the second, was that of the greater instability of primary as opposed to manufactured commodity prices which, it is claimed, has created special problems for developing as opposed to developed countries. The degree of cyclical instability in primary commodity markets has been the object of extensive enquiry.(7) Measurement of variations in prices has depended amongst other things on the time period considered and on the currency in which prices are observed. An indication of the variations in price movements over time for the main primary commodities considered in this study is provided in Table 1:8. The degree of divergence between the index of the most and the least volatile of the prices of the commodities considered in the table was far more pronounced in the post-Second World War period than between 1901 and 1951. Although the average level of volatility is similar in the first two periods considered, 1901 to 1951 and 1952 to 1972, it increased markedly when the mid-1970s are included in the calculation. If a comparison is made of developments between the latter two periods, the most pronounced change related to coffee prices which became much less volatile between 1965 and 1981. In contrast, tin, wheat, rubber, tea and sisal prices became more volatile although on balance the degree of instability decreased in the sub-period 1973 to 1981 (Table 1:8). Sugar stands out as the commodity with the most unstable prices on average during the periods covered - an instability which increased after 1973 - followed by cocoa and sisal, rubber, copper and tin.

16

Table 1:8 : Volatility Indices of Dollar Primary Commodity Prices (mean absolute percentage deviation from an exponential time trend calculated over the stated periods)

Commodity	1901-1951	1953-1972	1965-1981	1973-1981
Tin	14	8	20	17
Wheat	16	5	19	20
Sugar	15	33	37	48
Rubber	21	13	22	19
Coffee	14	17	5	5
Cocoa	17	23	25	27
Tea	9	6	17	17
Copper	13	21	21	22
Iron Ore	n.a.	8	12	11
Jute	16	12	13	14
Sisal	16	18	33	31

Note: n.a. denotes not available

Sources: United Nations, Instability in Export Markets of Under-Developed Countries (United Nations, New York, 1952, II.A.1), pp. 4-6, J.R. Behrman, International Commodity Agreements: An Evaluation of the UNCTAD Integrated Commodity Programme (Overseas Development Council, no place ref., October 1977), p. 55 and C.B. Wright and J.L. Hedges, 'Price Stability in Commodity Markets' (Bank of England unpublished working paper, October 1982, quoted with permission).

Finally, if the volatility indices are calculated of real (inflation-adjusted) commodity prices for the same commodities for the sub-periods 1965 to 1972 and 1973 to 1981, different results are obtained. As indicated in Table 1:9, whereas dollar prices in these two periods showed no clear trend, real commodity prices, in contrast, displayed a tendency to become more variable.

The impact of commodity price instability has been hotly debated. Until the early 1960s, for example, it was generally accepted that such instability caused particular problems for developing countries, by destabilising their income and tax proceeds and creating stop-start conditions for development. Since then, however, a number of studies have questioned these assumptions and one recent study went so far as to suggest a positive relationship between export price instability and economic growth. The uncertainty surrounding the impact of commodity price instability is

17

Table 1:9 : Volatility Indices of Real Primary Commodity Prices, 1965-1972 and 1973-1981 (mean absolute percentage deviation from an exponential time trend calculated over the stated periods)[a]

Commodity	1965-1981	1965-1972	1973-1981
Tin	13	11	15
Wheat	14	7	21
Sugar	38	24	51
Rubber	18	20	16
Coffee	19	9	28
Cocoa	23	19	26
Tea	11	6	15
Copper	19	18	20
Iron Ore	7	6	8
Jute	12	13	11
Sisal	29	25	32

Note: a   annual observations deflated by the world export price of manufactured goods

Source: C.B. Wright and J.L. Hedges, 'Price Stability in Commodity Markets' (Bank of England unpublished working paper, October 1982, quoted with permission).

important since price stabilisation has formed a recurrent objective of international commodity controls (Chapter 4). From the evidence available it seems reasonable to suggest broadly that price instability does not lead necessarily to revenue instability for developing countries. In Behrman's survey, for example, only sisal, of four commodities classified as displaying high price instability in the 1953 to 1972 period (Table 1:8), also led to highly unstable revenue receipts. Conversely, wheat, deemed to be subject to low price stability in the time span covered, produced a high degree of revenue instability.

Nonetheless, price stabilisation is considered to be a desirable goal in its own right as a means of lessening the inflationary impact of sharp upward movements in the prices of primary commodities. As Reynolds has pointed out, however, the impact of unstable commodity prices has varied markedly from country to country making any generalised statements difficult to substantiate.(8)

Finally, mention may be made of a fourth problem associated exclusively with primary as opposed to manufactured products. This may be summarised briefly as the concern articulated by a Club of Rome statement at the beginning of the 1970s that global mineral reserves would soon be depleted if demand for them continued to grow at the prevailing rate. Subsequent discoveries of new sources of supply lessened the impact of the proposals by the Club of Rome that the exploitation of all non-renewable resources should be subject to more selective control. However, the distinction between renewable and non-renewable resources remained an important element in international commodity discussions, with crude petroleum a conspicuous example of a commodity whose controls were to an important degree governed by the desire of producers to protect their assets of non-renewable resources.(9)

5. Conclusion

This chapter has attempted to highlight some of the key economic factors bearing on the history of international commodity controls. These may be distinguished as follows: the decreasing importance of trade in primary commodities in terms of total trade flows after the Second World War; the fragmentation of pre-War patterns of commodity trade, dominated as they were by developed countries with the UK playing the leading role, and their replacement by a growing number of often newly independent countries; and a greater awareness, resulting partly from this combination of factors, of the special problems associated with primary commodity trade. Mention should also be made, finally, of the dramatic changes which took place in the monetary and economic environment of the 1970s which further complicated the already complex framework in which primary commodity trade was conducted.

The key feature which characterised the 1970s compared with the preceding two decades was the increasing instability of the world economy. After two decades of rapid and fairly orderly growth, it became necessary in the 1970s to adjust to higher levels of inflation, the realignment of currencies following the collapse in 1971 of the fixed exchange rate system drawn up at Bretton Woods in 1944, the 1972 to 1974 world food crisis, the 1973 to 1974 quadrupling of oil prices, and the deceleration of growth in oil supplies. As noted in more detail in subsequent chapters, the oil price hike represented a shift in world income equal in magnitude to about two per cent of world output and led to a short, sharp recession in 1974 to 1975 as the major industrialised countries adopted generally deflationary policy responses. The recovery from this recession, which was hesitant and uneven between countries, was stymied in 1979 when oil prices doubled, inflation accelerated and exchange rates and interest rates became unusually volatile. The growth in output of industrial countries, which had averaged 4 per cent per year between 1976 and 1979, fell to 1 per cent in 1980 and 1981 in the face of increasingly restrictive financial policies.

Table 1:10 : The Growth of World Trade 1963-1981
(percentage changes from the preceding year)

| | Volume | Unit Value | |
		US Dollar Terms	SDR Terms
Average 1963-1972[a]	8.5	3.0	2.0
1973	12.5	22.5	11.5
1974	4.5	38.5	37.5
1975	-4.0	9.5	8.5
1976	11.0	1.5	7.0
1977	5.0	8.5	7.5
1978	5.5	10.0	2.5
1979	6.5	18.5	15.0
1980	2.0	19.5	19.0
1981	0.0	-1.5	9.0

Note: a   compound annual rate of change

Source: IMF, World Economic Outlook: A Survey by the Staff of
           the International Monetary Fund (IMF, Washington, 1982),
           p. 149.

The impact of these developments varied markedly from
country to country with oil importing or exporting status a new
important variable. In terms of international trade after 1973 the
result was an increase in growth in value and a decrease in volume
(Table 1:10) compared with the 1963 to 1972 period. This led to
growing competition for available markets together with a greater
preparedness on the part of governments to introduce measures to
protect domestic markets. For non oil-exporting developing
countries as a group, the need to finance growing balance of
payments deficits led to a rapid rise in levels of debt and debt service
which, with the high level of interest rates after 1979, placed a
number of such countries in a liquidity squeeze.(10)
        It is beyond the scope of this study to enter into a detailed
analysis of the implications of all of these major developments of the
1970s and early 1980s. For the purposes of international commodity
trade, however, the division of countries between oil-importing and
oil-exporting categories was a critical one, and oil-related balance of
payments imbalances in their turn generated an increased emphasis
on the part of developing countries on the need for a new
international economic order (NIEO) in which they should obtain a
greater level of transfers of resources. At the same time, the

greater preoccupation of policy-makers in developed countries with reducing inflation generated a stronger interest in international commodity control as a means of preventing sharp movements in primary commodity prices. The political and institutional background to these issues is discussed in more detail in Chapters 2 and 3.

Notes

1   For examples see G. Curzon, Multilateral Commercial Diplomacy (Michael Joseph, London, 1965), C.P. Kindleberger, The World in Depression, 1929-1939 (Allen Lane, London, 1973), P. Bairoch, The Economic Development of the Third World since 1900 (Methuen, London, 1975), H.J. Habakkuk and M. Postand (eds.), The Cambridge Economic History of Europe, vol. 6 (Cambridge University Press, Cambridge, 1965) and W. Ashworth, A Short History of the International Economy since 1850 (Longman, London, 1975). For two general bibliographies on commodities see United Nations, Commodities: A Select Bibliography 1965-1975 (United Nations, New York, 1975) and V.L. Sorenson, International Trade Policy: Agriculture and Development (Michigan State University, Michigan, 1975).

2   League of Nations, The Network of World Trade (League of Nations, Geneva, 1942, II.A.3), Preface.

3   The League Report used the Brussels Classification of world trade of 1913 which included refined mineral oils among raw materials. Under foodstuffs were included factory-produced goods such as refined sugar, canned meats and vegetable oils. The Report noted that the more detailed classification of world trade prepared by the League of Nations Committee of Statistical Experts in 1935 was available only for twenty-five countries and covered a limited range of years. See League of Nations, International Trade Statistics, 1938 (League of Nations, Geneva, 1939, II.A.21).

4   See for example IBRD, Commodity Trade and Price Trends (IBRD, Johns Hopkins University Press, Baltimore, August 1981), Table 3, for the volume increases.

5   For these measures of the terms of trade see UNCTAD, Handbook of International Trade and Development Statistics: Supplement 1980 (UNCTAD, New York, 1980, TD/STAT.9), p. 50 and IBRD, Commodity Trade and Price Trends, pp. 8-9.

6   UNCTAD, Handbook of International Trade and Development Statistics, derived from Table 4.3 (D) and Table 4.5. The ten countries exporting seven items or less were Oman, Qatar, the Libyan Arab Jamahiriya, Brunei, the Falkland Islands, Tuvalu, Tonga, Rwanda, Gambia and Comoros. See also P.T. Bauer and B. Yamey, The Economics of Under-developed Countries (Cambridge University Handbooks, Cambridge, 1957).

7   Early examples of the debate on the terms of trade include League of Nations, Industrialisation and Foreign Trade (League of Nations, Geneva, 1945) and United Nations, Commodity Trade and Development (New York, 1953, E.2519, II.B.1). The former concluded that the terms of trade moved against primary commodities between 1878 and 1938 to a significant degree; the latter, that they revealed no clear trend. In addition see W.W. Rostow, 'The Terms of Trade in Theory and Practice', Economic History Review, vol. III (1950). Further examples include J.D. Coppock, International Economic Instability (McGraw-Hill, New York, 1962), A. Maizels, Exports and Economic Growth of Developing Countries (Cambridge University Press, Cambridge, 1968), G. Myrdal, An International Economy: Problems and Policies (Routledge & Kegan Paul, London, 1956), G. Haberler, International Trade and Economic Development (National Bank of Egypt, Cairo, 1959), Commonwealth Secretariat, Terms of Trade Policy for Primary Commodities (Commonwealth Secretariat, London, 1976), P.T. Ellsworth, 'The Terms of Trade between Primary Producing and Industrial Countries', Interamerican Economic Affairs (Summer 1956), G.K. Helleiner, (ed.), A World Divided: the Less Developed Countries in the International Economy (Cambridge University Press, Cambridge, 1976) and N. Kaldor, 'Stabilizing the Terms of Trade of Underdeveloped Countries', Economic Bulletin for Latin America, vol. 8, no. 1 (March 1963). On the general subject of commodity price movements see S. Caine, 'Instability of Primary Product Prices: A Protest and A Proposal', Economic Journal, vol. 44 (September 1954), C.A. Enoch and M. Panić, 'Commodity Prices in the 1970s' Bank of England Quarterly Bulletin (March 1981) and C. Tisdell, 'Price Instability and Average Profit', Oxford Economic Papers, vol. 22 (1970).

22

8   For examples of early work on the impact of export price instability on growth see P.T. Bauer and F.W. Paish, 'The Reduction of Fluctuations in the Incomes of Primary Producers', Economic Journal (December 1952), United Nations, Instability in Export Markets of Underdeveloped Countries (United Nations, New York, 1952, II.A.1) and T. Viner, 'Stability and Progress: The Poorer Countries' Problems' in D.C. Hague (ed.), Stability and Progress in the World Economy (London, 1958). For pioneering studies of the 1960s see A.I. MacBean, Export Instability and Economic Development (Allen & Unwin, London, 1966) and Coppock, International Economic Instability. Subsequent studies include G.F. Erb and S. Schiavo-Campo, 'Export Instability, Level of Development and Economic Size of Less Developed Countries', Oxford Bulletin of Economics and Statistics, vol. 31 (May 1969), R.F. Emery, 'The Relation of Exports to Economic Growth', KYKLOS, vol. 20 (1967), B.F. Massell, 'Export Instability and Economic Structure', American Economic Review, vol. 60 (September 1970), J.T. Thoburn, Primary Commodity Exports and Economic Developments: Theory, Evidence and A Study of Malaysia (John Wiley & Sons, London, 1977) and S. Noys, 'Fluctuations in Export Earnings and Economic Patterns of Asian Countries', Economic Development and Cultural Change (July 1973).

The recent study was M. Kreinin and S. Finger, 'A New International Economic Order: A Critical Survey of its Issues', Journal of World Trade Law, vol. 10 (1976). See also A.I. MacBean and D.T. Nguyen, 'Commodity Concentration and Export Earnings Instability: A Mathematical Analysis', Economic Journal, vol. 90 (1980), J.R. Behrman, International Commodity Agreements: an Evaluation of the UNCTAD Integrated Commodity Programme (Overseas Development Council, no place ref., October 1977) and P.D. Reynolds, International Commodity Agreements and the Common Fund: A Legal and Financial Analysis (Praeger Publishers, New York, 1978), p. 38. Behrman has suggested that the US could gain $15 billion over the course of a decade from a reduction in inflation if prices of the ten core commodities were stabilised.

9   The Club of Rome described itself as 'an invisible college', designed to 'foster understanding of the varied but interdependent components - economic, political, natural, and social - that make up the global system'. It grew from a meeting of thirty individuals from different disciplines in Rome in April 1968. The Club initiated a project, the Project on the Predicament of Mankind, designed to 'examine the complex problems troubling men of all nations . . .' The results of the first phase of research of the Project were published in Club of Rome, The Limits to Growth (Potomac Associates Book, Earth Island Ltd, London, 1972). For subsequent work on the subject see J.E. Tilton, The Future of Nonfuel Minerals (The Brookings Institution, Washington, 1977), C. Nappi, Commodity Market Controls (Lexington Books, Lexington, Mass., 1979), pp. 26-30, M. Chisholm, Modern World Development: A Geographical Perspective (Hutchinson & Co., London, 1982), Chapter 4, C. Freeman and M. Jahoda (eds.), World Futures: The Great Debate (Robertson, 1978), G. Manners, 'Our Planet's Resources', Geographical Journal, vol. 147 (1981), S.R. Eyre, The Real Wealth of Nations (Arnold, 1978) and W.W. Rostow, The World Economy: History and Prospect (Macmillan, London, 1978).

10   For one consideration of many of the problems faced by developing countries in the face of developments after 1979, see IBRD, World Development Report 1982. The IMF devoted considerable attention to the impact of what it called persistent stagflation. It noted in Annual Report on Exchange Arrangements and Exchange Restrictions 1982, summarised in IMF, 'IMF Survey' (IMF, Washington, 16 August 1982), that the prevailing slump in trade was a cause rather than an effect of increasingly restrictive trade practices which if unchecked could result 'cumulative contractionary effects on world trade and growth and result in the loss of the momentum toward the liberalization of members' exchange and trade systems . . .'

2: THE DEVELOPMENT OF INTERNATIONAL POLICY CONCERNING COMMODITIES

'With the development of the new conception of the possible role of buffer stocks ... the problem of intergovernmental commodity regulation is clearly entering a new phase.'

(International Labour Office, 1943)

1. General

Any attempt to isolate with precision the earliest examples of international commodity control measures is fraught with definitional difficulties: mercantilism in its most applied form, for example, offers perhaps the clearest example of the rigid control of trade between colony and metropolis; and even the evolution of the most-favoured-nation concept of trading relationship during the nineteenth century could be interpreted as a form of commodity control. Within the definitional terms of this study, however, international attempts to regulate systematically trade of certain commodities on a multi-lateral basis did not emerge until after the First World War.(1) This followed the distortion of pre-War patterns of trade on a geographic basis and of the composition of trade by commodity sector. In 1919, for example, at the first session of the International Labour Office, the question of trade in raw materials was raised as a problem for discussion. However, no body was established specifically to monitor international trade developments although the League of Nations was given a brief involving certain limited surveillance responsibilities. The League's Economic and Financial Committees, for example, established statistical and reporting facilities and during the 1920s, as raw material and industrial cartels proliferated, issued warnings regarding the dangers inherent in increasingly restrictive trade practices. However, their views appear to have been little heeded and for the most part trade matters were the subject of bi-lateral rather than international negotiations in that period.(2)

An exception was the World Economic Conference held in Geneva in 1927. The agenda of the Conference was far broader than the debate only of trade issues. However, in the event, trade policy featured prominently in discussions and in its Final Report, the Conference recommended that international commodity agreements should be formed between parties interested in the same commodities in order to permit a 'more methodical organization of production', a 'reduction of costs by means of a better utilization of existing equipment' and the more 'rational grouping of undertakings'. It was hoped that the negotiation of such agreements would prevent artificial rises in prices regarded as detrimental to the interests of producers and consumers alike.(3)

There is little to suggest, in practice, however, that the policies prescribed by the 1927 Conference were acted upon by governments in their response to the Depression. Instead, following the lead of the US with its imposition of the protective Hawley Smoot Tariff on imports in 1930, country after country sought to protect their domestic producers against foreign competition and to regulate existing trading relations.(4) A League of Nations Monetary and Economic Conference was held in London between 1932 and 1933 to discuss the crisis of the contraction of world trade and plummetting commodity prices and the question of international commodity agreements was raised again as a potential policy response. As a result, a sub-committee was appointed to consider their possible formation. A subsequent report, accepted by the Committee, laid down that international commodity agreements should have as their primary purpose the increase in the purchasing power of producers of raw materials. The method espoused for realising this increase was to raise the wholesale prices of the exports of such producers to a 'reasonable' and 'fair and remunerative' level, based on an assessment by a commodity organisation in which consumers and producers were represented on equal terms. The report specified in addition that, in order to work effectively, such agreements should be supported by the introduction of parallel and complementary domestic legislation. The report conferred official approval on international commodity agreements as instruments of trade policy although circumscribing the terms of operation under which they were acceptable.(5)

Protective trade policies were strongly deplored internationally despite their widespread adoption. The League of Nations, for example, came out strongly against protectionism on the grounds that it led inevitably to over-production;(6) it recommended instead international commodity agreements as a means of increasing the

25

volume of world trade, provided that such schemes were regulated by governments and included adequate consumer representation. The object of such schemes, it was specified further, should be 'to reduce stocks to a normal level, to maintain them at that level, and to maintain a fair and equitable price for reasonably efficient producers'. Existing schemes, it was posited, might also be improved by the introduction of international buffer stocks operated by the governments of the interested producing and consuming countries and designed to correct 'excessive movements in price, particularly in the upward direction'. In contrast, cartels, agreements operated simply for and on behalf of producer interests, did not qualify for League approval as a means of achieving the same end result.(7)

In practice, the conclusions stemming from the 1933 Conference and subsequent work by the League of Nations, emphasising as they did the preferability of internationally negotiated rather than nationally imposed measures to deal with the economic problems of the 1930s, were not in general translated into policy. International commodity agreements were formed for tin, wheat, tea, rubber and sugar but this reflected in large part the initiative of specialised producer interests or their governments. At the national level, new forms of restrictive trade practices were commonly introduced such as quantitative controls on imports, currency restrictions and higher tariff barriers. Where trade preferences already existed, as in the case of the British Empire, they were often strengthened or defined more clearly and direct subsidies were provided at the national level to support many industries. Overall, protectionist national policies prevailed over the co-ordinated international response which had been hoped for by discussions at the international level.(8)

It was the advent of war in 1939 which brought international commodity control into a new and more comprehensive phase. Although the Munich agreement in 1938 had led to rearmament and the stockpiling of strategic materials, it was the disruption of normal trading patterns which started with the German invasions in Europe of May 1940 and escalated in December 1941 with the entry of US into the conflict, which had the most pronounced impact on international commodity trades. The disappearance of a large part of the European market, increased demand for shipping for military reasons and the German submarine campaign led to increasing shortages in major consuming centres whereas stocks of primary products built up, in contrast, in many primary producing countries. To address the problem of uneven and short supplies, governments and their agencies became active in direct buying operations; the US Commodity Credit Corporation, for example, engaged in the purchase of entire crops. As the disruption caused by war increased, the Combined Food Board, the Combined Raw Materials Board and the Combined Production and Resources Board of the Allied Powers took

26

over the reins of many aspects of international commodity marketing and rationing was introduced for a number of key commodities to allocate available supplies.(9)

Despite the direct controls introduced on commodity trade and marketing, the question of how best to regulate international commodity markets did not disappear entirely from the international agenda. Instead the subject was discussed, albeit in general terms, at the war-time meetings of the Ministers of Foreign Affairs of the American Republics and by the Inter-American Conference of Agriculture of 1942. The latter, for example, went so far as to endorse the formation of international commodity agreements 'wherever applicable' to assist in the solution of the problem of surplus commodity production.(10) The United Nations Food and Agriculture Conference of 1943, which met to discuss ways of improving the distribution of food and other agricultural products, also addressed the question of international commodity control. It concluded that international commodity arrangements were a suitable device to promote the expansion of world economic growth and recommended that an international organisation should investigate the feasibility of establishing such arrangements and the form that they should take to deal with the functional disorders of international commodity trade. In addition, several of the international agreements which had been established in the inter-War period were continued during the War, albeit in substantially modified form.(11)

The War also brought to the fore the views of Keynes in his advisory capacity to the UK Government. Probably the first true advocate of international and integrated commodity controls, Keynes had written on the subject of the control of raw materials as early as 1920 when his observations on the boom conditions of the years 1919 to 1920 led him to the conclusion that, while there was 'some continuous improvement in the daily conditions of the life of the masses of the population, society was so framed as to throw a great part of the increased income into the control of the class least likely to consume it'.(12) Keynes opposed the producer cartels of the 1920s and the international commodity agreements of the 1930s as overly restrictive, especially in respect of output. He proposed instead a comprehensive plan for the introduction of international controls on a range of raw materials to be administered by a general council, on which producers and consumers were equally represented, and which was to be funded by an international clearing union. Buffer stocks were cited as the preferred control mechanisms and the initial coverage suggested was for maize, sugar, coffee, cotton, wool, rubber and tin.(13)

Whereas Keynes envisaged that world trade, development and monetary policy should be considered in an integrated fashion, events conspired to create a post-War system in which development and monetary policy were considered through separate channels and in which a formal organisation for the consideration of trade policy failed to materialise. As a result, any student of the development of post-War thinking on international commodity control is obliged to consider the question by examining a variety of sources. An important statement of principle underlying post-War negotiations, however, was that laid down by the Allied Powers in the Atlantic Charter of 1941. This stated that these nations were desirous of securing 'the fullest collaboration between all nations in the economic field, with the object of securing for all improved labour standards, economic advancement, and social security'. This would involve access, on equal terms, for all nations 'to the trade and to the raw materials of the world . . .'(14)

These principles were re-affirmed in the United Nations Charter of June 1945 which aimed to promote the solution of 'international economic, social, health, and related problems' together with 'Higher standards of living, full employment and conditions of economic and social progress and development'(15). A United Nations Economic and Social Council (ECOSOC) was established together with functional and regional commissions with the brief of making studies of, and reports and recommendations on, world co-operation in the fields of economic, social, cultural and humanitarian questions. Later, independent international organisations were formed in co-operation with the United Nations to take on a range of specialised functions. The most important of these in the context of this study were:

the Food and Agriculture Organization (FAO), established in October 1945, with the objective of raising standards of living, of improving efficiency in the production and distribution of food and agricultural products and of improving conditions for rural populations;

the International Bank for Reconstruction and Development (IBRD), established in December 1945, to facilitate investment, to further the balanced growth of international trade and to maintain equilibrium in the balances of payments of its members;

the International Monetary Fund (IMF), also established in December 1945, in order to promote stability and international co-operation in the fields of trade and monetary exchange; and

the General Agreement on Tariffs and Trade (GATT), a multi-lateral trade agreement designed to negotiate rules and standards for the conduct of international trade, concluded in October 1947.(16)

It was contemplated that GATT should form just one part of an International Trade Organization (ITO) which would take on responsibility for international trade policy. However, the latter never came into being as a result of conflict between those who supported free trade and those reluctant to abandon national freedom on trade policy. The principles which were to have governed its operations were published in the Havana Charter of 1948 and remained the essential force guiding subsequent international commodity negotiations. It is therefore worth considering briefly the terms of the Charter here.

In essence, the Havana Charter prohibited agreements between governments or private enterprises leading to price-fixing, the allocation of market shares or collusion in the promotion of export restrictions. In concert with pre-War trade policy, international commodity agreements were permissible exceptions to these general principles provided that they were designed to encourage the expansion of consumption, the stabilisation of prices and the relief of problems caused by the existence of burdensome surpluses. The conditions governing the acceptable operation of such agreements were clearly spelt out: they should be negotiated at public conferences open to both consumers and producers of the commodity in question; they should last for a maximum of five years; and their operations should be jointly administered by producer and consumer interests.(17)

Finally, mention should be made of the United Nations Conference on Trade and Development (UNCTAD), a body established in 1964 with the function of encouraging international trade, particularly between countries at different levels of development and with different social and economic systems. Although UNCTAD emerged in part as an attempt to fill the gap created by the aborted ITO, it came to represent a dynamic new form of international institution by providing a focus for the debate on relations between developed and developing countries. This led, amongst other things, to the negotiation of the Integrated Programme for Commodities of 1976 which brought the question of policy on commodities to the very centre of international trade policy.

The proliferation of post-War channels of policy and debate on international trade and commodity issues provided a direct contrast to the comparatively simple pre-War pattern. It reflected the desire of major countries, led by the US, to avoid a repetition of the problems of the 1930s which were associated with over-protection, and the general hope that a liberalisation of trading relations could provide a firm basis for growth and development. A detailed account of post-War progress in pursuit of these broad goals is beyond the scope of this study. However, an appraisal of those aspects of international policy which have applied directly to trade and commodity issues is essential in order to understand the manner in which international commodity controls evolved in practice. Such an institutional and political framework, in turn, is incomplete without reference to the role played by the emergence of new trading blocs and to the important influence of the US in the formulation of international policy on commodities. The remainder of this chapter will be devoted therefore to constructing a more detailed post-War framework. Consideration will focus principally on the operations of GATT and UNCTAD, the organisations involved most directly in the structural questions of world trade, although a brief outline is included also of the responses of the IMF and IBRD in respect of commodity-related issues. Chapter 3 will then complete the framework for this study by examining the role played by new trading blocs and the US since 1945.

2. GATT
a. General Principles

GATT is the obvious starting point for discussion since, until the establishment of UNCTAD in 1964, it provided the principal forum for the debate and negotiation of rules and standards for the conduct of international trade. GATT, a multi-lateral treaty, was signed in October 1947 between twenty-three (largely developed) countries; by the early 1980s, its membership had risen to eighty-five contracting parties. A permanent secretariat was established to provide for collective supervision although contracting parties remained the essential guiding forces in subsequent negotiations and discussions.

Although the Agreement was a long and complex document, it rested on a few fundamental principles and aims. The first, embodied in the 'most-favoured-nation' clause, was that trade should be conducted on the basis of non-discrimination between signatories and that all contracting parties should be bound to grant each other treatment as favourable as that given to any country in the application of import and export duties and charges. Permitted exceptions to be 'most-favoured-nation' principle included members which had formed a customs union or free trade area and cases where anti-dumping duties had been imposed. Traditional colonial and other preferences, similarly, were permitted with no commitment required for their dismantlement. The second basic principle governing GATT's operations was that protection should be conferred on domestic industries only through customs tariffs. The levels of such tariffs were to be negotiated between participant countries and bound items were to be listed in published tariff schedules. Quantitative restrictions on trade were prohibited except to alleviate balance of payments difficulties. A third basic tenet was that participants should consult with each other in respect of their trade policy with a view to reducing generally tariffs and other barriers to trade.(18)

b. Trade Negotiations to the Kennedy Round

Between 1947 and 1961 five conferences were held under GATT's auspices with a view to effecting general reductions in tariff levels. However, although these conferences secured substantial reductions in trade barriers on industrial products, it was recognised that they had little impact in respect of barriers to trade in agricultural products. Part of the explanation for this divergence in treatment lay in the introduction of various waivers in the 1950s which reduced the applicability of GATT's provisions to agricultural products and contributed to a growing disenchantment with GATT by countries such as Denmark and New Zealand, whose main interest was in agricultural exports. A second factor was that the mechanics of tariff bargaining tended to focus attention on goods traded by the major industrialised countries, whose key common interests were industrial products.(19)

The failure of GATT to bring primary products fully within its regulatory ambit did not escape attention. As early as 1958 the Haberler Report, prepared by a panel of experts commissioned by GATT, stressed that the needs of producers of primary products, and particularly those of developing countries, were different to and distinct from those of producers of manufactured goods and that existing rules and conventions concerning commercial policy were in general unfavourable to developing countries. It suggested that, as a result, developing countries had valid reasons for making a rather freer use of trade controls than their industrialised country counterparts. Finally, it recommended that general stabilisation policies operated by developing countries should be supplemented with measures to stabilise particular commodity markets. In this context, international commodity agreements were considered to be an acceptable form of conduct, particularly when they allowed for the equal representation of importing and exporting countries. The Report recommended that such schemes should not be unduly ambitious in seeking to raise price levels and endorsed the buffer-stock mechanism as preferable to schemes based on long-term contracts or on export quotas. In addition, it proposed that serious attention should be paid to the possibility of 'close co-operative action between a number of otherwise independent national buffer-stocks covering a commodity or group of commodities'.(20)

Although GATT conducted an annual review of trends and developments in international commodity policy and endorsed international commodity agreements (both in general and in specific terms), it was not until 1965 that a new chapter was added to the Agreement under which developed countries became committed to 'positive efforts designed to ensure that less-developed contracting parties secure a share in the growth in international trade commensurate with the needs of their economic development.'(21) In this context, a new principle was adopted that developed countries would not expect developing countries to reciprocate commitments to reduce or to remove tariff and other trade barriers and that 'more favourable and acceptable conditions of access to world markets' should be provided for them. The chapter specified in addition that measures should be devised where appropriate to stabilise and improve conditions in world markets for the primary exports of developing countries in order to enable them to attain 'stable, equitable and remunerative prices' and to provide them with expanding resources for economic development.(22)

The new chapter thus formalised the principles regarding international commodity agreements which had been laid down in the Havana Charter. It did not, however, include positive new policy measures such as the promotion of negotiations on specific commodities or the reduction of tariff barriers on specified tropical products. Instead, the main focus of GATT's activities continued to be a broad-brush attempt to secure a general reduction in the level of tariffs. The Kennedy Round of negotiations, for example, between 1964 and 1967, aimed to secure tariff reductions across the board and applicable to all products. Although little success was achieved in respect of agricultural products, the tariff concessions achieved by the major participants for dutiable non-agricultural products were substantial, averaging slightly more than 35 per cent and covering $20 billion of world trade. Some progress was also made on non-tariff issues with the agreement of an anti-dumping code.(23)

c. The Tokyo Round

Following the conclusion of the Kennedy Round in 1967 it was decided to prepare for a more comprehensive programme of trade negotiations. However, it was not until the Tokyo Declaration of September 1973 that formal agreement was reached on their terms of reference. The Declaration established that developed countries should negotiate on the basis of reciprocity but should not expect from developing countries contributions inconsistent with their individual financial, trade or development needs.(24) Ninety-nine countries, both GATT and non-GATT members, accounting for nine-tenths of world exports, were involved in the Tokyo Round which was far more extensive and comprehensive than any undertaken before and designed 'not only to reduce or eliminate tariff and non-tariff barriers to trade in agricultural as well as industrial products, but also to shape the multilateral trading system and international trade relations into the 1980's and beyond'.(25) Negotiations were guided by the Trade Negotiations Committee, consisting of representatives of all ninety-nine countries. However, the responsibility for detailed bargaining fell to seven negotiating groups covering tariffs, non-tariff measures, the 'sectoral approach' to negotiations, safeguards, agriculture, tropical products and improvements to the international framework for the conduct of world trade. Unlike the Kennedy Round, developing countries played a prominent role in the Tokyo Round discussions.(26)

Whereas the Kennedy Round reduced tariffs by a fixed percentage regardless of how high or how low they were set initially, the Tokyo Round attempted not only to reduce but also to bring closer together ('to harmonise') tariffs charged by different countries. As a result of these cuts, the weighted average tariff on manufactured products in the world's nine major industrial markets declined from 7.0 to 4.7 per cent, representing a 34 per cent reduction in customs receipts; concessions in agriculture resulted in the decline of the weighted average tariff for developing countries from 8.1 per cent to 7.1 per cent although most tariff action on agricultural products of interest to developing countries was taken in the form of improvements to the Generalized System of Preferences or under the tropical products negotiations.(27) The former, negotiated under UNCTAD's auspices, is discussed in more detail below. The latter, a priority under the Tokyo Declaration, took place between 1976 and 1977 and consisted of tariff and non-tariff concessions applied to a broad range of products - agricultural, raw materials, minerals, semi-manufactures and manufactures - of which developing countries were producers and actual or potential exporters. Concessions eventually covered 2,930 of 4,400 dutiable items.(28)

Other features of the Tokyo Round which are of interest in a discussion of international commodity controls were the series of agreements or codes aimed at reducing non-tariff barriers and bringing them under more effective international discipline. The Code on Subsidies and Countervailing Duties, for example, aimed to ensure that the use of subsidies did not harm the trading interests of another party and that countervailing measures did not provide an unduly restrictive influence on international trade relations. Other codes drawn up under the Round included an Agreement on Technical Barriers to Trade, which was designed to limit the trade restricting impact of government regulations and testing schemes relating to them, an Agreement on Import Licensing Procedures, which specified the acceptable uses of such procedures, an Agreement on Government Procurement, drafted with a view to securing greater competition in the government procurement market, and a revision of the Anti-Dumping Code, negotiated under the Kennedy Round, to provide more preferential treatment for developing countries.(29)

Finally, of interest to any student of international commodity matters were the Arrangements concerning Bovine Meat and Dairy Products negotiated by the Agriculture Committee of the Tokyo Round. The former had as its aim the promotion, expansion, liberalisation and stabilisation of international trade in meat and livestock and covered beef, veal and live cattle. It established within GATT an International Meat Council empowered to evaluate developments in the world meat market and to provide for regular consultation on matters concerning international trade in bovine meat, including bi-lateral agreements on trade reached under the Round itself. The Arrangement, which entered into force on 1 January 1980, replaced the International Meat Consultative Group established by GATT in 1975. The International Dairy Arrangement, secondly, continued the work of the Arrangement on Dairy Products negotiated under GATT and the OECD in the mid-1970s, which established minimum prices for skimmed milk and whole milk powder. These gentlemen's agreements were subsumed into the International Dairy Arrangement of 1 January 1980 which was given the function of expanding and liberalising world trade in dairy products, of achieving greater stability in such trade in order to avoid surpluses, shortages and undue fluctuations in prices, and of providing better opportunities for developing countries to participate in the expansion of world trade in dairy products. The Arrangement covered all dairy products although three separate protocols set out provisions, including minimum prices, for international trade in milk powders, milk fats, including butter, and certain cheeses. An International Dairy Products Council was established within GATT to review the functioning of the Arrangement and to evaluate developments in the world dairy market.(30)

The similarities between the Arrangements for Bovine Meat and Dairy Products and the international commodity agreements discussed in Parts II and III of this study are readily apparent. The motivating factor for the Arrangements under GATT was the perception that the commodities in question were subject to unwelcome fluctuations in respect of supplies and prices and the Councils of each were empowered to alert participants to any potential problems with a view to identifying (unspecified) remedies. However, meetings of the Councils were to be held only twice a year and it fell to the GATT Secretariat to pursue a detailed monitoring function of the markets concerned. A further point of difference between the Arrangements under GATT and fully fledged international commodity agreements was that the former were only one aspect of GATT's far broader range of activities concerning trade issues, including tariff and non-tariff measures, and did not apply simply to the producers and consumers of the commodity concerned but to all GATT signatories; in contrast, international commodity agreements were independent of any international institution, apart from those specialised agencies set up specifically to administer the agreements, and were drafted to cater for the peculiar needs of the individual commodities concerned. Perhaps on account of the broader coverage, neither of the GATT Arrangements specified detailed economic provisions or administrative guidelines in contrast to most of the international commodity agreements. It is interesting, furthermore, that GATT chose to regulate two primary product groups which were dominated by developed rather than by developing country producers. The reason for this may have been the awareness of the wide variety of restrictive trade practices and marketing arrangements which had been imposed on these groups in the past. Developed countries probably also found GATT a more convenient forum for discussion than UNCTAD, the alternative, which was associated with the commodity policy needs of developing countries. It is worth noting that, despite the GATT Arrangement, meat as a product group was included in UNCTAD's Integrated Programme for Commodities (discussed below) as a commodity suitable for an international commodity agreement. However, discussions on this subject under UNCTAD's auspices were reported to have been slow not least because they coincided with discussions on the Arrangement for Bovine Meat held by GATT.(31)

The breadth of coverage of the Tokyo Round and its detailed provisions militate against drawing any firm conclusions on its importance and impact at this early date. In November 1980, GATT's own Committee on Trade and Development sought to explore the post-Tokyo Round situation with regard to tropical products by commissioning a case-by-case examination. Results from its preliminary studies emphasised that 'important progress' had been made in respect of trade liberalisation but underlined the fact that a wide variety of treatment was applied from country to country, not only for the same commodity but also for different types of the same commodity at different stages in its processing. A good example of this phenomenon was provided by the case of coffee which was given duty-free access by Sweden, the US and Norway, subject to low duties in Canada and Australia and to a wide range of duties in other markets. Higher duties were levied on imports of roasted and instant coffee in a large number of developed countries than on raw or unroasted coffee. A further complicating feature was that certain countries, such as those of the EEC, permitted duty-free entry for coffee from special preferential sources. Similar diverse results were found in the case of tea, rubber, olive oil and cocoa.(32)

It seems clear that, although the detailed results are yet to be fully appraised, the Tokyo Round made less progress on agricultural than on industrial trade barriers, an outcome which was fully consistent with the greater leniency of GATT in respect of restrictive actions in the agricultural as opposed to the industrial sector in general and which inspired the GATT Summit of 1983 discussed below. This point was recognised by the IMF in their World Economic Outlook Survey of 1982. The Survey also pointed to a combination of factors, including the persistence and deepening of international recession, increased unemployment levels and a lessening of confidence in internationally negotiated policies, which had increased demands on governments for the pursuit of independent industrial and commercial policies (see also Chapter 1). In 1982, for example, an estimated $ 60 billion of trade was blocked outside GATT's rules by a number of devices ranging from gentlemen's agreements to embargoes. One estimate suggested that a 50 per cent reduction by the OECD area of barriers for ninety-nine agricultural commodities would increase the earnings of fifty-six developing countries by a substantial 11 per cent. The positive achievements of the Tokyo Round in reducing some tariff levels and in providing international codes of conduct for certain aspects of trading activity have thus to be set against contrary influences, such as moves toward bi-lateral and tri-lateral negotiations, particularly in the case of sectoral problems. The claim made for the Round that it provided a focus for resisting new protectionist forces does not seem to have been justified by subsequent events, at least in the short-term.(33)

d. The Summit Meetings of the early 1980s

Prolonged international recession at the beginning of the 1980s seemed also to push some of the focus of discussion on international trade and development issues to summit meetings between the major industrialised countries. Examples included the Ottawa Summit of July 1981, that held in Cancun, Mexico in October 1981 and the GATT Ministerial Summit of November 1982. These meetings were inspired in part and the Cancun Summit proposed by the report of the Independent Commission on International Development Issues chaired by Willy Brandt, which emphasised the need for discussion 'at the highest level' as a matter of emergency on relations between developed and developing countries. The report made a number of recommendations on lines very similar to those expressed by the United Nations in its resolution calling for a new international economic order (NIEO) in 1974 (discussed below). These included: long-term programmes to assist the poorest countries of the world; an increase in food production in developing countries; a larger volume of food aid; greater participation by developing countries in commodity processing, marketing and distribution; action to stabilise commodity prices at remunerative levels including greater efforts to conclude international commodity agreements; effective rules of conduct regarding the activities of transnational corporations; a reform of the international monetary system; and an increase in development finance.(34)

Whereas the Brandt Report covered similar ground to the NIEO, the summit conferences which it inspired did not. The Ottawa Summit, for example, brought forth commitments of only a general nature: 'to support the developing countries in the efforts they make to promote their economic and social development within the framework of their own social values and traditions', 'to increase access to [developed countries'] markets', 'for accelerated food production in the developing world', for 'liberal trade policies' and 'to resist protectionist pressure'.(35) Much time was spent in debating the economic problems currently facing industrialised, rather than developing, countries such as the rising levels of unemployment, inflation and public financing requirements and the level of interest rates. The Cancun Summit, similarly, although including developing country participants, was essentially led by developed country interests. It addressed four main topics, food, trade, energy and finance, and concluded that there was a need for an energy affiliate to the World Bank, to channel funds for investment in energy production in developing countries, and for a rationalisation of United Nations' food agencies. Critics drew attention subsequently to the discrepancy between President Reagan's address on the virtues of free trade and the negotiation of the Multi-Fibre Arrangement which defined a framework of bi-lateral agreements between importing and exporting nations. (See below.)(36)

One of the off-shoots of the Ottawa Summit was the convening in November 1982 of a GATT Ministerial Summit with a view to bringing agriculture back into the discipline of GATT. Various proposals were tabled for discussion, including a freeze on agricultural subsidies, the introduction of reduced tariffs for tropical products and the establishment of a specialised GATT committee to deal with agriculture. In the event, however, the meeting foundered, with the major point of discord the call by the US for the EEC to reduce substantially its level of farm subsidies. Although the meeting agreed to make determined efforts to ensure that trade policies and measures were 'consistent with GATT principles and rules' and to resist protectionist pressures, it provided no new means for doing so. In the words of the Australian delegation, the final communiqué represented 'a papering over of the real issues'. The immediate outcome was not confined, however, to mild disillusionment with GATT as a negotiating forum. The failure of the EEC to adhere to US demands resulted in the threat that the US would subsidise its own farm exports in retaliation (Chapters 7 and 8.) Far from engendering a liberal framework for negotiation, then, the GATT Summit served rather to accentuate existing chinks in GATT's administrative armour.(37)

e. The Arrangements on Textiles

There remains to mention, finally, the major and perhaps most controversial example of exemption to GATT's rules on non-discrimination: the Arrangements on textiles negotiated from 1962. Although the Arrangements applied to manufactured rather than to primary products, they were of considerable importance both as examples of the regulation of trading relations between developed and developing countries in respect of one sector and also for those countries, such as the US, India, Brazil and Pakistan, which combined both the agricultural and the manufacturing aspects of cotton production. They therefore merit a brief consideration here.

The Arrangements had their roots in the major structural changes which took place in the world cotton textile industry in the course of the twentieth century. These included the declining importance of textiles in manufacturing output (from 19 to 8 per cent, for example, in the US between 1913 and 1959), a strong trend towards import substitution in textiles by new competing developing country producers and a decline in the levels of world trade in textiles and clothing. This, together with the emergence of alternative fibre and synthetic products, had the most pronounced impact on those countries such as the UK, France, Germany and the US which had traditionally enjoyed large surpluses in textile goods. Until the mid-1960s only Japan, Hong Kong, the Philippines and Taiwan of the new producers posed much of a challenge to these countries in their domestic markets and it was concern regarding the impact of a flood of cheap imports in the future which led the US and the UK to negotiate bi-lateral agreements of import regulation with their main suppliers in the 1950s. In 1961, a Short Term Arrangement on Cotton Textiles was negotiated under GATT and this was expanded in scope and lengthened in duration to form the Long Term Arrangement regarding International Trade in Cotton Textiles (LTA) in 1962.(38)

The LTA sought to address the problems (in developed countries) caused by the disruption of the market for cotton textiles from imports (from developing countries) by 'special practical measures of international co-operation' to assist in any necessary adjustment process. Participants agreed to relax restrictions on imports of cotton textiles and to expand access to their markets in proportion to specified quota provisions. However, where imports caused or threatened to cause disruption, consultations were to be carried out with a view to indicating 'the specific level at which . . . exports of such products should be restrained'.(39) The LTA thus organised and legitimised the introduction of quantitative restrictions on trade prohibited otherwise under GATT and provided a regulatory framework for the major industrialised countries to impose quota restrictions on cotton textile imports. The US imposed its first quota restrictions in 1961 and by 1972 it had introduced restrictions against thirty suppliers. As a consequence both of protective measures and of technical innovation, the surplus of industrialised countries in the trade in international textiles rose between 1963 and 1973 while the net balance with developing countries remained roughly the same with a share of only 18 per cent of world exports. However, developments in the clothing industry, primarily in man-made fibres, worked in the opposite direction and the rise in clothing exports from developing countries was precipitous -from $240 million in 1962 to $3,800 million in 1973. Not surprisingly, when the LTA came to be re-negotiated in 1973, the US, which had been a major market for developing country clothing exports, pressed for a broader agreement covering not only cotton textiles but also man-made fibres and wool.(40)

The Arrangement regarding International Trade in Textiles (known as the Multi-Fibre Arrangement or MFA) which resulted from the re-negotiations introduced a Textiles Surveillance Body to supervise the terms of the Arrangement.(41) The aims and mechanisms of the MFA were similar to those of its predecessor. However, its coverage was broader and extended to man-made fibres and wool. In general, the MFA was considered to have been more favourable than the LTA in respect of the interests of developing countries. Quotas, for example, were to be increased by 'not less than' six per cent a year and a flexible provision permitted the transfer of quotas between categories and between years.

The conditions under which the MFA operated were very different to those prevailing during the life of the LFA. The severity of the world recession in the mid-1970s led to a dramatic decline in the demand for textiles and clothing which created in its turn a strong lobby from traditional producers, notably those in the EEC, for waiver provisions. These were secured in 1977 by a protocol which allowed 'jointly agreed reasonable departures' from the terms specified in the Arrangement. The US, for example, reached agreement with its principal suppliers allowing a growth rate of below 6 per cent. The number of curbs imposed by industrialised countries was reported to have increased substantially rather than to have decreased under the terms of the Arrangement.(42) As a result of increasing doubts regarding the purpose and efficacy of the Arrangement, it was re-negotiated only after considerable debate at the end of 1981. The parties agreed to co-operate fully in dealing with problems of circumvention and the level of permitted import growth was retained at 6 per cent per year except in special circumstances if market disruption occurred. In essence, the 1981 Arrangement had little new to offer and, in the words of one commentator, was a 'standstill agreement' which fully satisfied the wishes of neither the developed, nor the developing, countries concerned.(43)

f. Conclusion

Several general conclusions can be drawn from the operations of GATT since its formation in 1947.(44) First, GATT enshrined the principle of the most-favoured-nation concept but permitted a number of important exceptions such as the existence of customs unions and the Textile Arrangements. Secondly, GATT was successful in liberalising world trade in certain manufactured goods but was generally more lenient in respect of the agricultural sector. Its influence in resisting protectionist pressure was also weakened at the end of the 1970s by an increase in tri-lateral and bi-lateral negotiations on trade matters between the major industrialised countries and at the beginning of the 1980s by the failure of the 1982 GATT Summit to achieve any progress on liberalising world trade in agriculture. Finally, although GATT recognised formally in 1965 that developing countries should not be expected to reciprocate commitments to reduce or to remove tariff and other trade barriers and explicitly endorsed international commodity agreements on Havana Charter lines as a means of stabilising the export receipts of developing countries, it did not itself initiate action in furtherance of these objectives. The Bovine Meat and Dairy Products Arrangements under the Tokyo Round applied essentially to exports in which developed countries led production; the Textile Arrangements, similarly, reflected the concern of developed countries to avoid disruption in markets in which they had been traditionally the leading producers. It is not surprising in these circumstances that developing countries should look to a new forum in which to press their views and further their policy objectives. This forum, UNCTAD, is the natural next subject for discussion.

3. UNCTAD
a. General Principles

The establishment of UNCTAD in 1964 followed a resolution by the United Nations General Assembly in 1962 calling for more detailed work in the fields of trade and development. The conference leading to the creation of UNCTAD as a permanent institution specified that the new organisation should be responsible for creating 'an international trading environment that would facilitate the growth of developing countries and not thwart it'. From the first, then, UNCTAD was concerned more directly with the needs of developing as opposed to developed countries. The philosophy underlying its activities in the first decade of its life owed much to Raúl Prebisch, the first Secretary-General, whose main thesis was that the terms of trade of developing countries were in secular decline (Chapter 1) and that a broad range of policies was required to bring about a solution to the serious structural problems which such countries faced. Prebisch's policy prescriptions included commodity price support policies, the rescheduling of developing country debt, greater market access for exports from developing countries and compensatory finance for shortfalls in their export earnings.(45) In its first decade of operation, it was market access (the Generalized System of Preferences), however, which formed the main focus of UNCTAD's negotiating activities. From the mid-1970s, this focus broadened to an attempt to bring an integrated approach to the range of problems facing developing countries in the pursuit of a New International Economic Order (NIEO) in which their interests were more effectively represented. Each of these phases will be considered in turn.

b. The Generalized System of Preferences

Whereas GATT was concerned with securing a general liberalisation of world trading relations, UNCTAD aimed to improve the access of products, both primary and manufactured, from developing countries to developed country markets. UNCTAD's call for a 'generalized system of non-reciprocal non-discriminatory preferences' for developing countries reflected both a disenchantment with the development strategies based on import substitution espoused during the 1950s and early 1960s and the perception that negotiations under GATT were not tailored to meet the special needs of developing countries.

In principle the concept of 'generalized preference' was a simple one: developing countries were to be granted a degree of preference not less than the most-favoured-nation tariff accorded by developed countries under GATT. In practice, however, negotiations held under UNCTAD's auspices between 1964 and 1975 resulted in a system that was neither generalised nor non-discriminatory. Twenty-four countries introduced sixteen different schedules of provisions whose terms were both complex and variable. The US scheme, for example, excluded all OPEC members; other schemes applied import quota limitations after which the most-favoured-nation tariff was paid; others set individual country limits; and others excluded certain items such as textiles, petroleum and some tropical products, such as coffee, cocoa and bananas.(46) The variety and complexity of the different schedules meant that they were difficult to interpret, to establish eligibility and to administer: their existence therefore did not necessarily result in greater market access on a product basis.

From the mid-1970s the main thrust of tariff policy for developing countries shifted back to GATT from UNCTAD with the hope that the Tokyo Round would go further toward meeting the goal of improved access. In the event, the Tokyo Round added a further complex stratum to what was already a highly complicated series of tariff schedules applying to goods from developing countries. As outlined above, most tariff action on agricultural products of interest to developing countries was taken by improving the terms of the Generalized System of Preferences which already existed under UNCTAD. Given the expectations raised, it was with some disappointment that the Group of 77 (developing countries)(47) noted at the fifth UNCTAD conference (UNCTAD V) in 1979 that tropical products of interest to developing countries had been virtually excluded from the Round despite the separate negotiations on tropical products.(48) It was the perceived failure of negotiations under both GATT and UNCTAD to achieve notable improvements in the terms of trade of developing countries which added urgency to UNCTAD's integrated approach in pursuit of the NIEO.

c. Trade and Development Policy

Whereas GATT adopted a generally passive approach to issues such as international commodity agreements and world trade in primary commodities, UNCTAD's interest in them was active from the first. In 1964, for example, Prebisch proposed a range of direct commodity control measures for certain products, decreased price support by developed countries on commodities competing directly with developing country imports and international commodity agreements aimed at linking the prices of primary commodities with those for manufactured goods. As a matter of general policy, the first UNCTAD conference (UNCTAD I) resolved to deal with commodity issues on a case-by-case basis and created a Commission on Commodity Arrangements and Policies. This approach was continued at the second UNCTAD conference in 1968 (UNCTAD II), where attention centred on drawing up a draft policy agreement on commodity arrangements and on encouraging the promotion of international commodity price stabilisation measures. At the third UNCTAD conference in 1972 (UNCTAD III) intensive inter-governmental consultations on commodity issues were commissioned.(49)

In parallel moves, the Group of 77 met in Lima in 1971 and formulated a Programme on trade and development issues which formed the basis for discussion at the Sixth Special Session of the United Nations held in April 1974.(50) On the grounds that the negotiations resulting from UNCTAD III had failed to resolve the questions of market access for goods from developing countries and commodity price instability, the General Assembly adopted resolutions calling for the establishment of a New International Economic Order (NIEO) to 'redress existing injustices' and 'to make it possible to eliminate the widening gap between the developed and the developing countries'. The NIEO was to be effected by a seven-pronged Programme of Action consisting of:

1   an Integrated Programme for Commodities (the Integrated Programme), designed to stabilise and to raise commodity prices and to increase the export earnings of developing countries;
2   debt rescheduling or forgiveness for the poorest developing countries;
3   increased official aid with a target of 0.7 per cent of developed countries' gross national product;
4   improved access for developing countries to the Special Drawing Rights (SDRs) of the IMF;
5   improved status for developing countries at the IMF and the IBRD;
6   a code to govern the transfer of technology and to bring an increase in the level of such transfers;

42

7   and national sovereignty over property with the right to
nationalise without necessarily observing legal conventions on
compensation.

Not surprisingly, the resolutions were supported by most developing
countries whereas most developed countries abstained; the UK, the
US, Germany, Belgium, Luxembourg and Denmark all opposed the
resolution.(51)
In its first draft, the NIEO Programme thus envisaged that
wealth transfer and improved earning capacity for developing
countries would be achieved through the broad channels of debt
relief, aid, improved financing facilities and the transfer of
technology in addition to higher income resulting from commodity
trade.   In practice the Integrated Programme and its associated
Common Fund to finance buffer stock activity came to represent the
main thrust of subsequent action, at least until early 1983.
From the United Nations General Assembly, the focus of debate
on the NIEO shifted back to UNCTAD with the fourth conference
(UNCTAD IV) in Nairobi in May 1976. In the months preceding the
conference, preparatory meetings were held by the various interest
groups concerned. The Group of 77, for example, issued a statement
in Manila in February 1976 (the Manila Declaration) re-affirming the
Group's commitment to a restructuring of international trade and
output to increase the participation of developing countries in both
and to improve their terms of trade. A new Programme of Action
was proposed, covering a wide range of topics and based firmly on the
NIEO Declaration and Programme.   A detailed section on
commodities advocated that the Integrated Programme should aim to
improve the terms of trade of developing countries by supporting
commodity prices at levels which were 'remunerative and just to
producers and equitable to consumers' and by expanding developing
countries' exports of both primary and processed products. In order
to achieve these objectives, the Programme recommended the
establishment of a Common Fund for the financing of international
commodity stocks, the harmonisation of stock policy, the indexation
of the prices of commodities exported by developing countries to the
prices of manufactures imported from developed countries and the
promotion and support of processing and diversification activities in
developing countries. A further section of the Programme dealing
with finance advocated that the IMF should undertake a review of its
compensatory financing facility in order to permit greater flexibility
in the calculation of the terms under which long-term assistance at
low interest rates could be provided.(52)
The position paper submitted by major industrialised countries
(known as Group B), in contrast, dealt exclusively with the subject of
commodities and came out in favour of the negotiation of
international commodity agreements; pricing arrangements, stock

43

provisions, long-term contracts, undertakings on market access and supply and export quotas were considered to be the acceptable mechanisms. Group B also favoured improved market access and 'systems' to stabilise export earnings.(53) The socialist countries supported international commodity agreements 'of a new type which took into account the special features of current conditions'. These were to include 'a mechanism for controlling price policies practised by transnational corporations', measures to combat inflation, export quotas and multi-lateral commitments on commodity supply and purchase, and rules for 'full effective state control by developing countries over the activity of foreign capital'.(54)

Even a brief survey such as this of the background to UNCTAD IV reveals both the concentration of attention on commodity-related issues and the wide range of views concerning the most appropriate way of achieving the policy objectives laid down by the General Assembly in the NIEO Programme. This was reflected in the outcome of the conference whose most positive achievement was the adoption of a resolution on the Integrated Programme. The resolution synthesised (albeit imperfectly) the aims of the various interest groups: objectives were couched in general terms of improving the terms of trade of developing countries, increasing their export earnings, achieving stable conditions in international commodity trade, seeking improved market access for, and reliability of supply of, primary products, diversifying output in developing countries and expanding domestic processing of primary goods. The commodity coverage of the Integrated Programme was established as bananas, bauxite, cocoa, coffee, copper, cotton and cotton yarns, hard fibres and products, iron ore, jute and products, manganese, meat, phosphates, rubber, sugar, tea, tropical timber, tin and vegetable oils, including olive oil and oilseeds. Agreement was also reached in principle on the need for a Common Fund and for a series of preparatory meetings to be held with a view to negotiating new international commodity agreements.(55)

From its role at the periphery of international trade policy before 1964, international commodity control had thus by 1976 been brought to its centre with international commodity agreements, particularly those using some form of stock policy, the most clearly defined points of agreement. Despite the general enthusiasm with which it was greeted the Integrated Programme represented a broad statement of intent rather than a detailed portfolio of practical measures to be followed. Considerable ambiguity surrounded many of its terms of reference and it is not surprising in these circumstances that events moved forward only slowly in advancement of its aims. By the fifth UNCTAD conference in 1979 it was noted formally that little progress had been made on the Integrated Programme and that a more urgent approach was needed. Governments were urged to expedite their negotiations on individual international commodity agreements, particularly those for perishable commodities which had been neglected in the past, and to 'exert all necessary efforts' to ensure that negotiations on the Common Fund were completed as soon as possible.(56)

The proposed Common Fund had been debated at several conferences prior to UNCTAD V with agreement being reached on its 'fundamental elements' in March 1979. Under the terms of this agreement, the Fund was to be established as a 'new entity and an effective and financially viable institution' to 'facilitate the conclusion and functioning of international commodity agreements and arrangements . . . particularly on commodities of special interest to developing countries'. It was to consist of two sections ('windows'), the first designed to finance buffer and internationally co-ordinated national stocks and the second to finance measures other than stocking such as those concerned to provide research and development, productivity improvements and unspecified measures 'designed to assist . . . vertical diversification'. It was further stated that the financial resources of the Fund should consist of direct government contributions of $400 million for the first 'window', and a target of $350 million for the second (of which $280 million was to be in the form of voluntary subscriptions), held in separate accounts.(57) As a result of a further conference based on the 1979 draft, agreement was reached on the form to be taken in June 1980.

The most outstanding features of the document setting out the terms of reference of the Common Fund were its length (sixty-two pages and fifty-eight articles), its complexity (with detailed provisions concerning membership, capital, organisation and management, the suspension of, and withdrawal from, operations, status and arbitration) and the reliance it placed on stock policy as the desirable control mechanism to be used to regulate trade in ten (cocoa, coffee, copper, cotton, rubber, jute, sisal, sugar, tea and tin) of the eighteen 'core' commodities contained in UNCTAD's Integrated Programme. It will be necessary to judge the potential of the Fund to fulfil claims made for it as 'a single landmark against the vast background of the New International Economic Order' (by the Group of 77) against the appraisal of past experience with stock policy in international commodity agreements provided in Parts II and III. From the onset, however, support for the Fund from member signatories was far from whole-hearted. By the March 1982 deadline for ratification, for example, only twenty-two countries had even signed the Agreement.(58)

d. Conclusion

In contrast to GATT, UNCTAD's most clearly identifiable achievement was in providing a forum for the discussion of trade and development issues with specific reference to the needs and concerns of developing countries. In practice, specific initiatives were limited in number, with the Generalized System of Preferences and the Common Fund the most obvious products of a considerable volume of discussion. It was the existence of UNCTAD and its concern with the terms of trade of developing countries which pushed commodity policy to the forefront of international trade discussions during the 1970s. And, as implied in the preface, the increasing interest in international commodity agreements as instruments of trade policy has provided a strong reason for this examination of how international commodity controls have worked in the past. This may in turn suggest the lessons that past experience has to offer for the future.

4. The IMF

Unlike GATT and UNCTAD, the IMF's central concern was to promote stability and international co-operation within the existing world system of trade and monetary exchange. However, its function of making funds available to countries with balance of payments difficulties, with a view to permitting the maintenance of liberal trading policies whilst 'necessary domestic adjustments' were made, was expanded in a number of ways from the late 1960s. This reflected both the changing mood of policy-makers to commodity trade and problems, under the combined influence of UNCTAD and the special sectoral problems of the 1970s, and the IMF's awareness that a more flexible approach was needed than available under existing IMF facilities. The following offers only a brief outline of the measures introduced since ample primary and secondary material on the facilities is available elsewhere.(59)

The first notable example of the expansion of IMF facilities was the compensatory finance scheme introduced in 1963 and liberalised in 1966 and 1976. This provided an additional credit facility to that already available under IMF rules to assist members in meeting short-term balance of payments difficulties arising from commodity price fluctuations and attributable to circumstances beyond the member's control. The facility was intended to benefit developing countries and in particular to countries dependent for export earnings on only a few commodities. The funds available depended on the IMF's calculation of the short-fall in export earnings which was based in the first instance on a comparison with actual exports on a five-year moving average basis with repayment essentially short to medium-term in nature. In 1975 the terms of access to the scheme were liberalised and a more flexible method of calculation of export shortfalls was introduced. A substantial increase in the use of the facility followed.(60)

A second example was the provision in June 1969 of a buffer stock facility designed to assist members participating in international commodity agreements to finance buffer stocks associated with such agreements. The facility was introduced following a joint study by the IMF and the IBRD on the question of commodity stabilisation and provided that members could draw up to the equivalent of 50 per cent of their IMF borrowing quota allowance. The function of such borrowings was to help to offset balance of payments problems rather than to attempt artificially to raise prices. In practice, little use was made of the scheme owing to the dearth of international commodity agreements with buffer-stock mechanisms. However, limited purchases were made in connection with the tin and sugar agreements.(61)

A third example of the response of the IMF to problems relating specifically to commodities was the introduction in mid-1974 of an oil facility under which governments in balance of payments difficulties relating to the oil price rises of the mid-1970s could borrow at relatively low rates of interest. The scheme was financed from a special fund of $7 billion provided by oil-producing countries. According to one authority on the subject, the low degree of conditionality attached to the loans encouraged a high proportion of eligible countries to use the facility.(62)

Finally, the IMF introduced in 1981 a food financing facility. This provided financial assistance for members encountering balance of payments problems produced by 'an excess in the cost of their cereal imports ... presumed to be reversible within a very few years'. The aim was to prevent cereal consumption levels from falling in the face of surges in import costs caused by factors essentially beyond the control of members, such as a temporary decline in domestic production or a sharp rise in import prices. It was introduced in response to the perceived needs of low-income countries and integrated with the assistance already available under the IMF's compensatory financing facility.(63)

In general, the introduction of the IMF's financing facilities regarding export shortfalls, buffer stocks, oil and cereals was welcomed in principle. However, developing countries criticised the rigidity with which policy was applied in the case of the first three examples. The food financing facility has also been criticised on the technical grounds that there could be occasions when the shortfall data provided 'a wholly misleading picture of a country's need for assistance'. In general, the IMF measures did not seek to address structural problems facing raw material producers but rather to provide contingency aid in what were regarded as short-term balance of payments crises.(64)

5. The IBRD

Finally, a brief mention is needed of the activities of the IBRD in respect of commodity issues. The IBRD was established in 1945 to make loans to governments and private enterprises for 'productive purposes', associated initially with post-War reconstruction. However, with the formation of its affiliates, the International Finance Corporation in 1955 and the International Development Association in 1960, the IBRD's functions were extended to include the provision of development finance. The International Finance Corporation, for example, was established to provide loans on flexible terms to finance projects in developing countries and the International Development Association, similarly, was given the function of financing development projects. It was only gradually that the IBRD expanded the volume of its lending - from $250 million per year in the early 1950s, for example, to $600 million in 1964. With the succession of Mcnamara as president in 1968, however, a new vigour was injected into the Bank's operations and lending increased dramatically - to over $2 billion a year by the end of the 1960s and to $6 billion in 1975.

It was the expansion of IBRD lending and the increase in project evaluation which accompanied it which is of interest to this consideration of international commodity control. Until the 1960s, the IBRD's lending policies concerning primary commodities were based on a general assessment of the demand outlook and staff studies sought to highlight potential problem areas. A 1958 report, for example, pointed to the problematic conditions of over-supply in the coffee market and effectively forestalled further IBRD-financed investment in coffee in the near-term. It was only in 1961, however, that formal guidelines were laid down regarding directional lending. These concerned sugar and recommended that the IBRD should finance the expansion of sugar production only in net importing countries in order not to exacerbate the problem of persistent surplus. In 1969, the case-by-case approach of the IBRD to commodity-project finance was translated into general guidelines. These favoured projects which aimed to reduce over-production by encouraging diversification. In addition, the IBRD adopted the procedure of consulting specialist international commodity organisations in order to assess the advisability of new projects. In 1973 the IBRD went further and limited investment which would lead to an increase in the production of commodities, such as coffee, tea and cocoa, for which demand was considered to be relatively inelastic. Exceptions were permitted where there were limited alternative opportunities, where long-term prospects were favourable or where an international commodity agreement was in force.(65)

Several points of interest emerge from even a brief review of IBRD policy such as this. First, increased attention on development issues and the expansion of the IBRD's resources from the 1960s corresponded to similar moves in other fora, such as UNCTAD and the IMF. Secondly, the IBRD continued to channel a large proportion of its development lending to primary production despite a sharpening of awareness of the problems associated with such production, including over-dependence on a few commodities as a source of export earnings and the perceived decline in the terms of trade of commodities against manufactured goods. Some attempt was made in the 1970s to encourage diversification and to assess the long-term prospects for primary commodities considered for IBRD lending. It remains to be seen from the commodity-by-commodity analysis in Part III whether the IBRD achieved its aim of discouraging over-production, particularly of the tropical beverages.

Notes

1   Exceptions included minor attempts to form international cartels for zinc and currants. See J.W.F. Rowe, Primary Commodities in International Trade (Cambridge University Press, Cambridge, 1965), pp. 121-22 and League of Nations, Economic Committee, Consideration on the Present Evolution of Agricultural Protectionism (League of Nations, Geneva, 1935, II.B.7).

2   International Labour Office, First Annual Meeting (International Labour Office, Geneva, 1919), pp. 134-44 and 237-39 and E. Luard, International Agencies: The Emerging Framework of Interdependence (Macmillan, London, 1977), pp. 195-96.

3   League of Nations, The World Economic Conference, Geneva, 1927, Final Report (League of Nations, Geneva, 1927, CEI 44 (1); I 46a, Section 5, Subsection IV.

4   League of Nations, Commercial Policy in the Post-War World (League of Nations, Geneva, 1945, II.A.7), pp. 56-7, Ibid., Commercial Policy in the Interwar Period: International Proposals and National Policies (League of Nations, Geneva, 1942, II.A.6), which gives a good account of the 'new protectionism' of 1933-1936, and Luard, International Agencies, p. 196.

5   League of Nations, Monetary and Economic Conference, London, 1933 Report of the Economic Commission of the London Monetary and Economic Conference on the Work relating to the Coordination of Production and Marketing (League of Nations, Geneva, 1933, C.435, M. 220, 1933, II. Conf. M E 22 (1)), Section A.

6   See for example League of Nations, The Course and Phases of the World Economic Depression (League of Nations, Geneva, 1931, II.A.2).

7   League of Nations, Report of the Committee for the Study of the Problem of Raw Materials (League of Nations, Geneva, 1937, A.27, II.B), Section 4, sub-section 4.

8   League of Nations, Commercial Policy in the Interwar Period, Luard, International Agencies, pp. 196-98 and Chapter 5. See also J.W.F. Rowe, Markets and Men (Cambridge University Press, Cambridge, 1936).

9   P. Einzig, Economic Warfare 1939-1940 (Macmillan, London, 1941), Chapter xv, J. Hurstfield, The Control of Raw Materials (HMSO, London, 1953), A.R. Prest, War Economics of Primary Producing Countries (Cambridge University Press, Cambridge, 1948) and International Labour Office, Studies in War Economics (International Labour Office, Montreal, 1941). See also W.N. Medlicott, The Economic Blockade (HMSO, London, 1959), which offers a thorough account of the war-time blockade on a regional basis and E. Roll, The Combined Food Board: A Study in Wartime International Planning (Stanford University Press, Stanford, 1956), which provides a good account of the Board's operations.

10   'Resolution Adopted by the Second Meeting of Ministers of Foreign Affairs of the American Republics' (21 - 30 July 1940), 'Resolutions Adopted by the Third Meeting of Ministers of Foreign Affairs of the American Republics' (15-28 January 1942) and 'Resolutions of the Second Inter-American Conference on Agriculture' (6-16 July 1942), in International Labour Office, Intergovernmental Commodity Agreements (International Labour Office, Montreal, 1943), pp. 139-46, referred to hereafter as ILO, Intergovernmental Commodity Agreements.

11   'Extracts from the Section Reports and Final Act of the United Nations Conference on Food and Agriculture (18 May - 3 June 1943), in ILO, Intergovernmental Commodity Agreements, pp. 146-48 and Chapters 6 and 10 of this study for examples of war-time agreements.

12   J.M. Keynes, The Economic Consequences of the Peace (Macmillan, London, 1920), p. 3.

13   J.M. Keynes, 'The Control of Raw Materials by Government', The Nation and the Athenaeum, vol. XXXIX (June 1926), no. 10, pp. 267-69, Ibid., 'The International Control of Raw Materials', Journal of International Economics, no. 4 (1974) (UK Treasury Memorandum of 1942), Ibid., 'The Policy of Government Storage of Foodstuffs and Raw Materials', Economic Journal, vol. 48 (1938) and H. O'Neill, A Common Interest in a Common Fund (United Nations, New York, 1977), pp. 14-16.

14   'The Atlantic Charter' (August 1941), Articles 4 and 5 in Keesing's Publications Ltd, Treaties and Alliances of the World (Keesing's Publications Ltd, Bristol, 1968), p. 7. The Charter was signed initially between Roosevelt and Churchill on 14 August 1941 and later adopted by the twenty-six Allied nations on 1 January 1942.

15   'The Charter of the United Nations' (26 June 1945), Article 55 in Keesing's, Treaties and Alliances of the World, pp. 8-11.

16   The regional commissions of ECOSOC were the Economic Commission for Europe, 1947, The Economic Commission for Asia and the Far East, 1947 (replaced in 1974 by the Economic and Social Commission for Asia and the Pacific), the Economic Commission for Latin America, 1948, the Economic Commission for Africa , 1958 and the Economic Commission for Western Africa, 1974.

17   The sections of the Havana Charter relating to commodities are reproduced in L.N. Rangarajan, Commodity Conflict: The Political Economy of International Commodity Negotiations (Croom Helm, London, 1978), Appendix I. See also C.P. Brown, The Political and Social Economy of Commodity Control (Macmillan, London, 1980), Chapter 1 and A.I. MacBean and P.N. Snowden, International Institutions in Trade and Finance (Allen & Unwin, London, 1981), Chapter 1 for useful accounts of the background to the still-born ITO.

18   'General Agreement on Tariffs and Trade' (HMSO, London, 1948, Cmd. 7258), GATT, Documents relating to the First Session (HMSO, London, 1948, Cmd. 7376), GATT, 'What it is: What it does' (GATT, Geneva, October 1977) and GATT, 'GATT Information' (GATT, Geneva, February 1981).

19   The conferences were held in 1947 In Geneva, in 1949 in Annecy, France, in 1951 in Torquay and in 1956 and in 1960/61 in Geneva. The first was considered to have succeeded largely due to the enthusiasm of the US. On the waivers, introduced largely at the instigation of the US, see S. Golt, 'World Trade and the Developing Countries' in H.G. Johnson (ed.), The New Mercantilism (Basil Blackwell, Oxford, 1974), pp. 24-5. The fact that the application of GATT's rules on quantitative restrictions and tariffs did little to break down trade barriers on agricultural products was recognised officially in GATT, The Role of GATT in relation to Trade and Development (GATT, Geneva, March 1964). The impact of GATT's actions has been discussed extensively elsewhere. See for example Curzon, Multilateral Commercial Diplomacy: GATT, K.W. Dam, The GATT: Law and International Economic Organization (University of Chicago Press, Chicago, 1970) and J. Fawcett, International Economic Conflicts: Prevention and Resolution (Europea Publications Ltd, London, 1977) which provide good general accounts.

20   GATT, Trends in International Trade: A Report by a Panel of Experts (GATT, Geneva, 1958). The Report also recommended that buffer stocks should not be based on any rigid price formula.

21   GATT, Part IV: Trade and Development (HMSO, London, 1965, Cmnd. 2618), Article XXXVI.

22   Ibid., Articles XXXVI and XXXVII.

23   GATT, 'What it is: What it does', pp. 5-6, R.E. Baldwin, <u>Non-Tariff Distortions of International Trade</u> (Allen & Unwin, Washington, 1971), p. 1, and J.W. Evans, <u>The Kennedy Round in American Trade Policy</u> (Harvard University Press, Cambridge, Mass., 1971). The limited concessions made concerning the exports of developing countries during the Dillon Round, which preceded the Kennedy Round in 1960-61, are discussed in J.M. Finger, 'GATT Tariff Concession and the Exports of Developing Countries: United States' concessions at the Dillon Round', <u>Economic Journal</u>, vol. 84 (September 1974).

24   For the text of the Declaration see GATT, <u>GATT Activities in 1973</u> (GATT, Geneva, 1974).

25   GATT, <u>GATT Activities in 1978</u> (GATT, Geneva, 1979), p. 12.

26   GATT, <u>GATT Activities in 1979</u> (GATT, Geneva, 1980).

27   Ibid., pp. 18-20.

28   Full details are available in GATT, <u>GATT Activities in 1976</u> (GATT, Geneva, 1977) and Ibid., <u>GATT Activities in 1978</u>.

28   Of the 2,930 items covered, approximately 940 were implemented in the initial 1976 to 1977 phase of the negotiations.

29   A general account of codes introduced is to be found in GATT, <u>GATT Activities in 1979</u>, pp. 20-6 and Ibid., <u>GATT Activities in 1978</u>, pp. 29-43.

30   GATT, <u>GATT Activities in 1978</u>, pp. 44-8.

31   In 1977, for example, developing countries produced only 11.4 per cent of fresh, chilled and frozen meat exports. See UNCTAD, <u>Handbook of International Trade and Development Statistics</u>. Argentina and Brazil were the only developing producers of any importance in terms of the value of their international trade in these products. Meat and dairy products have been the object of extensive national policies, particularly in developed countries. In the UK, for example, beef production was encouraged by a system of guaranteed prices and in Australia a Meat Board was established as early as 1935 to supervise the issuing of export licences. Other policies of importance have been the EEC's system of customs duties combined with variable levies, quantitative restrictions on beef imports imposed by the US at the beginning of the 1970s and trading agreements between the UK and the Commonwealth. See also Agricultural Adjustment Unit, University of Newcastle, <u>Stability and the Beef Market</u> (Agricultural Adjustment Unit, Newcastle, 1970) and W.G. Tomek and W.W. Cochrane, 'Long-run Demand: A Concept and Elasticity Estimate for Meat', <u>Journal of Farm Economics</u>, vol. 43 (August 1962). The publications of the (UK) Meat and Livestock Commission also offer excellent coverage of developments in the international meat market.

32   These reports covered a wide range of products which come under the general title of GATT, Committee on Trade and Development, 'Tropical Products: Information on the Commercial Policy Situation and Trade Flows'. Of particular interest for the purpose of this study are 'Coffee and Coffee Products' (12 March 1981), 'Oilseeds, Vegetable Oils and Oilcakes' (3 July 1981), 'Cocoa and Cocoa Products' (13 March 1981), 'Rubber and Rubber Articles' (10 July 1981), and 'Tea and Instant Tea' (13 March 1981). There were substantial variations in the levies for bulk green, black, instant and packed teas.

33   IMF, <u>World Economic Outlook: A Survey by the Staff of the International Monetary Fund</u> (IMF, Washington, 1982), pp. 135-37, W.R. Cline, N. Kawanabe, T.O.M. Kronsjo and T. Williams, <u>Trade Negotiations in the Tokyo Round: A Quantitative Assessment</u> (The Brookings Institution, Washington, 1978), pp. 2-3, and IBRD, <u>World Development Report 1982</u> (Oxford University Press, New York, 1982), p. 33. Forty-seven semi-protectionist deals were reported in <u>Financial Times</u>, 15 November 1982, quoting a

'secret' GATT report. The impact of the reduction of agricultural barriers was estimated in an International Food Policy Research Institute Study, quoted in Financial Times, 17 August 1982.

34 North-South: A Programme for Survival: The Report of the Independent Commission on International Development Issues under the Chairmanship of Willy Brandt (Pan Books, London, 1980). The recommendations are summarised in Annexe 1 of this book.

35 The declaration resulting from the Ottawa Summit was published in Financial Times, 23 July 1981.

36 See for example the Guardian, 24 October 1981, and the Wall Street Journal, 31 December 1981. The Guardian described the Cancun summit as 'a rather expensive form of encounter group therapy'.

37 See, for instance, Financial Times, 15 November 1982 and for the GATT Declaration ensuing from the Summit, Ibid., 30 November 1982.

38 The literature on these subjects is copious. See for example GATT, A Study on Cotton Textiles (GATT, Geneva, 1966) which provides a useful historical account, United Nations Industrial Development Organization, Textile Industry (United Nations, New York, ID /40/ 7, E.69), R. Burford Brandis, A Short History of US Textile Import Quotas (American Textile Manufacturers' Institute, Washington, 1974) and G. Shephers, Industrial Adjustment and Intervention: Textiles and Clothing in Britain and Germany (University of Sussex, Brighton, 1979). For the LTA see GATT, 'Long-term Arrangement regarding International Trade in Cotton Textiles' (GATT, Geneva, 1963).

39 'Long-term Arrangement regarding International Trade in Cotton Textiles', Preamble and Articles 1-3.

40 B. Bardan, 'The Cotton Textile Agreement 1962-1972', Journal of World Trade Law, vol. 7, no. 1 (January: February 1973) and D.B. Keesing and M. Wolf, Textile Quotas against Developing Countries (Trade Policy Research Centre, London, 1980).

41 'Arrangement regarding International Trade in Textiles' (GATT, Geneva, 1974).

42 The GATT Surveillance Body, for example, reported this to be the case in 1980, with most of the restrictions applied by the EEC, Sweden, the US, Austria, Canada and Finland.

43 Keesing and Wolf, Textile Quotas against Developing Countries, Chapter 3, GATT, 'Extension of Multifibre Arrangement Agreed' (GATT, 1304, December 1981) and 'GATT: Third Multifibre Arrangement', Journal of World Trade Law, vol. 16, no. 2 (March:April 1982).

44 A more detailed appraisal of developments in GATT to 1975 may be found, if required, in R.E. Hudoc, The GATT Legal System and World Trade Diplomacy (Praeger Publishers, New York, 1975). See in particular Chapter 18, which covers the EEC and the Tokyo Round.

45 UNCTAD, Proceedings of the First Session of UNCTAD, Geneva (United Nations, New York, 1964, 64.II.B.11 E/Conf. 46/141) and UNCTAD, Report of the Secretary General: Towards a New Trade Policy for Development (United Nations, Geneva, 1964, E/Conf. 46).

46 Brown, The Political and Social Economy of Commodity Control, p. 290 reported that the USSR and Australia started their schemes in 1965 and 1966 respectively; the EEC, Japan and Norway in 1971; Austria, Finland, New Zealand, Switzerland, Bulgaria, Czechoslovakia and Hungary in 1972; Canada and Sweden in 1974; and the US and Poland in 1975. UNCTAD was not the first group advocating the generalized system of preferences. Other schemes submitted were included in United Nations, Economic

Commission of Europe, Economic Survey of Europe, 1960 (United Nations, Geneva, 1961) and I.M. Rom, UNCTAD and the Problem of Preferences for Exports of Manufactures from Developing Countries (Tel Aviv Export Institute, Tel Aviv, November 1965).

47   The designation stemmed from a Joint Declaration by seventy-seven developing countries at UNCTAD I, Proceedings of the Third Session of UNCTAD, Santiago de Chile, 13 April to 12 May 1972 (United Nations, New York, 1972, TD/180, E.73.II.D.4).

48   UNCTAD, 'Report of the United Nations Conference on Trade and Development on its Fifth Session held at the International Convention Center, Philippines, 7 May to 3 June 1979' (mimeo, UNCTAD, Geneva, 1979, TD/268/Add. 1), p. 11. On the complex comparative schedules of the Generalized System and the Tokyo Round see UNCTAD, The Generalized System of Preferences and the Multilateral Trade Negotiations (United Nations, New York, 1978, TD/B/C.5/52 Rev. 1 E.78.II.D.6). This was preceded by several other detailed studies by UNCTAD. See for example UNCTAD, Operation and Effects of the Generalized System of Preferences: Selected Studies submitted to the Seventh Session of the Special Committee on Preferences for its Third Review (United Nations, Geneva, 1974, TD/B/C.5/15, E.78.II.D.2).

49   UNCTAD, Report of the Secretary General: Towards a New Trade Policy for Development, pp. 117-22, Ibid., Proceedings of the First Session, Ibid., Proceedings of the Second Session and Ibid., Proceedings of the Third Session (United Nations, New York, 1972, TD/180, E.73.II.D.4). See also UNCTAD, Final Act (HMSO, London, 1964, Cmnd. 2417), pp. 39-40, which summarises the proposals on commodities.

50   UNCTAD, Proceedings of the Third Session, pp. 373-404.

51   United Nations, 'Programme of Action on the Establishment of a New International Economic Order', Resolution A/RES/3202 (S-VII) (16 May 1974) and 'Declaration on the Establishment of a New International Economic Order', Resolution 3201 (S-VI) (1 May 1974) in Resolutions Adopted by the General Assembly during its Sixth Special Session (United Nations, New York, 1974, A/9559). See also J.R. Vastine, 'United States International Commodity Policy', Law and Policy in International Business, vol. 9, no. 2 (1977), Brown, The Political and Social Economy of Commodity Control, Chapter 3 and H.G. Grubel, 'The Case Against the New International Economic Order', Weltwirtschaftliches Archiv, band 113, heft 2 (1977).

52   'Manila Declaration and Programme of Action', in UNCTAD, Proceedings of the UNCTAD Fourth Session, Nairobi, 5 - 31 May 1976 (United Nations, New York, 1977, TD/218, E.76.II.D.10), Annex V.

53   UNCTAD, Official Records of the General Assembly, Thirty-first Session, Supplement No. 15 (UNCTAD, Geneva, 1976, A/31/15).

54   'Position Papers submitted by Bulgaria, Byelorussian Soviet Socialist Republic, Cuba, Czechoslovakia, German Democratic Republic, Hungary, Mongolia, Poland, Ukrainian Soviet Socialist Republic and Union of Soviet Socialist Republics' in UNCTAD, Proceedings of the UNCTAD Fourth Session, Annex VIII. See in particular Section III.

55   UNCTAD, Proceedings of the UNCTAD Fourth Session, Resolution 93 (IV).

56   UNCTAD, Report of the UNCTAD on its Fifth Session, Part 1, Resolution 124 (V). This urged members 'to continue to exert the requisite political will with a view to bringing about the establishment of the Common Fund as a key instrument in attaining the agreed objectives of the Integrated Programme for Commodities'.

57   'Fundamental elements of the Common Fund' re-printed in G. Goodwin and J. Mayall (eds.), A New International Commodity Regime (Croom Helm, London, 1979), pp. 71-5. The resolution was adopted at the Final Plenary Session of the United Nations Negotiating Conference in Geneva on 20 March 1979.

58 UNCTAD, 'Agreement establishing the Common Fund for Commodities' (mimeo, UNCTAD, Geneva, 1980, TD/IPC/CF/CONF/24), Ibid., 'Report of the United Nations Negotiating Conference on a Common Fund under the Integrated Programme for Commodities on its fourth Session, 5 - 27 June 1980' (UNCTAD, Geneva, 1980, TD/IPC/CF/CONF/26), pp. 29 and 5. In the words of the Group of 77, 'It would be premature for the international community to proclaim a triumphant success and rest on its laurels' (p. 29). The deadline for ratification was extended to September 1983. In January 1983 less than half of the 90 countries needed had ratified and Malaysia, the world's leading exporter of rubber, tin, palm oil and tropical timber, a prime initiator of the Fund, reported that it was unlikely to do so on account of its disenchantment with international commodity agreements and its view that the Fund was too small to be effective.

59 Keesing's, Treaties and Alliances of the World, p. 19. See, for example, G.C. Abbot, International Indebtedness and the Developing Countries (Croom Helm, London, 1979).

60 IMF, Compensatory Financing of Export Fluctuations (IMF, Washington, 1963), L.M. Goreux, Compensatory Financing Facility (IMF, Washington, 1980), M.G. de Vries, The International Monetary Fund 1966-71 (IMF, Washington, 1976), Chapters 14 and 15 and Reynolds, International Commodity Agreements and the Common Fund: A Legal and Financial Analysis p. 13 and Chapter 8.

61 de Vries, The International Monetary Fund, Chapter 15 offers a good account of IMF experience with this provision to 1975 and an account of the Tin Agreement borrowings.

62 A good summary of the oil facility is provided in E.M. Ainley, The IMF: Past, Present and Future (University of Wales Press, Bangor, 1979).

63 IMF, IMF Survey (IMF, Washington, 8 June 1981), pp. 165 and 177.

64 C. Green and C. Kirkpatrick, 'The IMF's Food Financing Facility', Journal of World Trade Law, vol. 16, no. 3 (May:June 1982).

65 Keesing's, Treaties and Alliances of the World, p. 19. S. Singh, J. de Vries, J.C. Hulley and P. Yeung, Coffee, Tea and Cocoa: Market Prospects and Development Lending (IBRD, US, 1977), pp. 14-18, L.B. Pearson, Partners in Development (Praeger Publishers, New York, 1969), IMF and IBRD, The Problem of Stabilization of Prices of Primary Products (IMF and IBRD, Washington, 1969) and B.S. Hurni, The Lending Policy of the World Bank in the 1970s: Analysis and Evaluation (Westview Press, Colorado, 1980).

3: THE ROLE OF NEW TRADING BLOCS AND OF THE US
SINCE 1945

'All nations share an interest in ending the friction which
characterizes the issue of raw materials.'

(Henry Kissinger, US Secretary of State, 1975)

1. General

Thus far our discussion of the post-War development of international
commodity policy and trade has dealt in broad institutional terms and
in a way which has tended to divide the world simply into 'developed'
and 'developing' country groups. It is clear, however, that such a two
dimensional approach offers an incomplete background to the often
intricate influences which have played on the implementation of
international controls. This section aims to trace, therefore, some of
the other factors which assist in the interpretative process, notably
the emergence of new trading blocs and of the US as important
influences on international commodity policy. It is of necessity brief
and confines its attention to the impact on commodity trade and
policy of these new developments. Some examples of the range of
specialist studies available elsewhere are provided in the notes at the
end of the chapter.(1)

2. The Loosening of Colonial Ties

Chapter 1 revealed the dominant position held by colonial trading
blocs in world commodity production and trade before 1945. This
influence extended to the formulation of policy on commodities in
which individual colonial powers had a vested interest. Thus the UK

56

and the Netherlands led initiatives for international controls on tin
and rubber and coordinated producer arrangements on tea. The UK
was also instrumental in arbitrating the case of the copper cartel in
West Africa during the 1930s. These controls were facilitated by the
existence of a network of colonial administrative apparatus and by
the comparatively limited number of participants involved.
Similarly, the colonial trading links of the UK assisted in the
operation of the Combined Raw Materials Board during the Second
World War.

The gradual loosening of colonial ties after the War had a
number of important consequences for commodity control measures.
In general, the increasing number of nations complicated the
negotiation of international commodity policy for simple numerical
reasons. The complication was enhanced when an expansion of the
production of a commodity was seen as a central and often politically
sensitive element in national development plans. Specific examples
included the expansion of rubber production in Malaysia between 1956
and 1975 and, more recently, the stimulation of cocoa production in
the Ivory Coast. In this context, conflicts of interest often arose
between countries anxious to preserve their market share and newer
producing countries intent on expanding the volume of their exports.
A second important outcome was that the de-centralisation of
control from colonial power to newly independent nation was often
accompanied by a discontinuity in the stance of commodity policy
and of the machinery used to implement it. Where the machinery of
colonial controls were retained - marketing boards, commodity
associations and so on - it was often subject to changes in personnel
and in methodology which in the early stages at least probably
weakened the degree of control exercised.

However, the loosening of colonial ties did not mean the
complete abandonment of special relationships between ex-colony
and former colonial power. The legacy of close links was often
carried forward in the form of special trading preferences. The UK
model of preferences, first introduced in the 1930s and re-worked in
the system of Commonwealth preferences after the War, was a
notable example. Its most conspicuous manifestation was the
Commonwealth Sugar Agreement of 1951 which conferred on
Commonwealth countries a market for a fixed amount of sugar at a
price generally above that prevailing on the 'free' world market.
(Chapter 8 discusses this question in more detail.)(2) Similarly, the
EEC provided for the continuation of close trading links between its
members and their former colonies, notably those of the French. The
Yaoundé Convention of 1963 was a major example of this and allowed
the entry of exports from eighteen African countries on the same
basis of gradual elimination of duties as applied within the EEC.
Certain tropical products were allowed duty-free entry.(3)

57

Yaoundé, modified in 1969, was an important precursor of the Lomé Convention of 1975 (Lomé I). Under Lomé I, most products originating from forty-six African, Caribbean and Pacific (ACP) states (which included the British Commonwealth as a result of the entry of the UK into the EEC) were to be imported duty-free provided that the treatment applied to such products was not more favourable than that applied among the member states themselves. In addition, ACP states were eligible to an EEC-administered scheme of compensatory finance, STABEX, which applied initially to twelve agricultural commodities and iron ore on which their economies were considered to be dependent and affected adversely by fluctuations in price and volumes traded. In the event of a shortfall in the value of the exports of one of the eligible products - itemised in the first instance as groundnuts, cocoa, coffee, cotton, coconut, palm oil and kernels, skins and leather, bananas, tea, raw sisal, wool and iron ore with cloves, gum arabic, mohair, vanilla, wood, pyretheum and ylang-ylang added to the list in 1977 - of 7.5 per cent or more against a reference ('trigger') level, an eligible country could apply for compensation in the form of a grant or an interest free loan to make good the shortfall.(4) The Lomé Convention was re-negotiated between 1979 and 1980 with an extension in the list of products eligible under STABEX (to include, for example, rubber, cotton seeds and oil cake) and a reduction in the trigger thresholds to 6.5 per cent in general and to 2 per cent for the least-developed, landlocked and island ACP countries. A new agreement was also drawn up to cover mineral exports including copper, cobalt, phosphates, manganese, bauxite, aluminium, tin and iron ore (except for ore from sites already being worked, which continued to be covered by STABEX for five years).(5)

Views on the relative merits and flaws of the Yaoundé and Lomé Conventions vary markedly with proponents commending them as a positive gesture in the advancement of trading relations between the EEC and developing countries and critics pointing out that financial resources available under the schemes declined in real terms in their years of operation, that they discriminated against non-ACP developing countries and that in practice a country could have a shortfall in earnings for a range of eligible products but fail to obtain compensation either because the commodity was below the prescribed dependency threshold or because the trigger threshold was not met. On balance, it is difficult to state positively that the ACP share of total EEC trade was substantially affected by the Conventions: under Lomé I, at least, trade between the two groups remained roughly in balance and, if oil is excluded, the EEC sustained a large and increasing trade surplus. Overall there appears to have been a general tendency for Lomé countries to lose rather than to gain market shares for their exports to the EEC.(6)

3. The Formation of New Trading Groups
a. The EEC

Although the EEC continued to base its trading preferences and financial aid to a significant degree on past colonial ties, of far greater import for international commodity trade and policy was the evolution of the EEC itself as an important trading entity and agricultural commodity producer. Formed by the merger of the executives of three parents in 1967 - the European Coal and Steel Community (1952), the European Economic Community (1957) and the European Atomic Energy Community (1957) - the EEC (also known as the EC) aimed amongst other things to secure 'an enduring and closer union between European peoples' by means of the formation of a customs union between participants and the development of common policies on agriculture, transport, labour mobility and other important sectors of the economy. The customs union involved the gradual abolition of import or export levies between members, the introduction of a common tariff on imports from non-Community countries and the abolition of all quantitative import, export and similar restrictions between members.(7)

The EEC's most obvious achievement in pursuit of these goals was the elimination of intra-EEC tariffs on industrial products and the adoption of the Common External Tariff, accomplished simultaneously in 1968, a year and a half ahead of the target date set. The EEC also emerged as a negotiating group of some importance in its own right at the global level. In the Kennedy Round of tariff negotiations, for example, the EEC was instrumental in pushing for the coverage of a wider range of products and in resisting policies on agricultural products which might have worked counter to the Common Agricultural Policy (CAP), then in the process of negotiation. Similarly, the EEC entered the Tokyo Round with a precisely documented policy strategy which included proposals for tariff reductions of 25 to 50 per cent, for international co-operation on agricultural products such as butter, maize, milk powder, rice, sugar, wheat and meat and for markets of certain essential raw materials to be stabilised by encouraging international commodity agreements. It was successful in achieving at least part of these objectives (Chapter 2).(8)

The EEC's agricultural policy also had an important bearing on world commodity trade and far-reaching policy implications for the operation of the international wheat and sugar agreements. The aim of EEC agricultural policy as expressed in the Treaty of Rome was to increase agricultural productivity, to safeguard an adequate standard of living for the agricultural population, to stabilise agricultural markets and to assure adequate supplies at fair prices to consumers.(9) As originally contemplated, the CAP was designed to rationalise and to modernise European agriculture in order to allow improvements in productivity, a greater security of supplies and more stable prices. In practice, the structural aspects of EEC farm policy fell prey to political debate on where the burden of adjustment should lie and how the reforms should be financed. The focus of policy switched instead to the negotiation of common pricing structures for major agricultural commodities at levels which would not only assure but also raise farm incomes.

The apparatus of the EEC's pricing policies on agricultural products has already been the object of detailed study.(10) It is sufficient to note here that the machinery was extremely complicated and varied from one product to another. For cereals, for example, the first product group to be covered in 1967, a 'target price' was set on an annual basis consisting of the price which the product was expected to achieve in the part of the EEC where cereals were in shortest supply - Diusburg in the Ruhr Valley. A 'threshold price' was then calculated for various import points so that the target price was maintained. On the basis of the threshold price an import levy was established to prevent import prices from falling below the threshold price. If target prices led to excess supplies, an 'intervention' (guaranteed minimum) price was introduced at which the EEC would buy cereals in order to maintain prices. Export subsidies could also be paid to exporters. The price support systems for pigmeat, eggs and poultry, in contrast, did not provide guaranteed prices or large scale support buying and target prices were maintained by means of minimum import prices, import levies and export subsidies. In the case of beef and vegetables, thirdly, a more simple system of fixed tariff was introduced although a variable levy could be applied to make good the difference between the duty paid import prices and the threshold price. Minimum prices operated for other commodities such as sugar beet, potatoes, peas and field beans, whilst production aids (a direct payment to the producer based on the quantity produced and the area sown) were available for others. Only sugar, however, was subject to production quotas and minimum stock levels (to ensure normal supplies equal to 10 per cent of the basic production quota of each sugar producer).(11)

It is apparent from even a brief review such as this that the introduction of such an extensive system of farm supports had serious implications for EEC and non-EEC producers and consumers alike. A general feature of the CAP in practice was that it encouraged the over-production of certain commodities and then transferred part of the burden of excess supplies to the world market by means of subsidising exports. The most obvious examples of this phenomenon in terms of commodities covered by international commodity agreements were wheat and sugar. In the case of the former, the existence of a heavy programme of price subsidies probably lessened the chances of the economic provisions of the 1971 Wheat Agreement being activated during the 1970s and of a new agreement with economic provisions being negotiated thereafter (Chapter 7). In the case of the latter, subsidised EEC sugar production and a fairly detailed network of regional controls on sugar output and prices operated in counterpoint to the policies pursued by the international sugar agreements of the 1970s. Not surprisingly, the EEC failed to participate in these agreements although in 1983 it was reported to be considering joining a new sugar agreement (Chapter 8).

The impact of the CAP was also strong in other important respects -it has been suggested, for example, that it served to raise agricultural prices within the EEC more than would otherwise have been the case and that its rising share of the EEC Budget to 70 per cent of expenditures in the late 1970s deflected resources from other equally worthy areas. However, it is with the international implications of EEC policy that this study is concerned and in this context it is important to note that its 'spill-over' effect increased substantially during the course of the 1970s with the expansion of EEC membership. In the early 1980s, as noted in Chapters 2, 7 and 8, this led to increasing friction between the EEC and the US.

b. Other Examples in Europe and Latin America

In contrast to the EEC, other trading blocs formed after the Second World War had little direct impact on international commodity policy. The European Free Trade Association (EFTA), for example, established in 1960, was essentially a commercial arrangement on free trade in industrial goods, a reaction to the establishment of the EEC. Unlike the EEC, it covered only a limited number of agricultural goods and provided no detailed framework for agricultural policy. Its main focus was on the elaboration of rules of origin and of customs procedures and it made few demands either on domestic structural policies or on the conduct of trading relations outside the union.(12)

The Latin American Free Trade Association (LAFTA), also formed in 1960, was similarly limited in economic scope and aimed to eliminate trade barriers between participants over a twelve year period. Although signatories agreed to attempt to 'coordinate their policies of agricultural development and the exchange of agricultural produce ...', this aim was not translated into specific policy measures and progress on the reduction in tariff barriers was also slow owing to the cumbersome item-by-item basis on which negotiations were conducted. By 1968 intra-group trade accounted for only a tenth of the total and during the 1970s the Association, except for Andean Pact countries, was largely passive.(13) It was disappointment with the progress of LAFTA which prompted the formation of the Andean Pact between Bolivia, Colombia, Chile, Ecuador and Peru in 1968. The Pact aimed to secure a liberalisation of intra-Pact trade and joint planning of major industrial investments. However, even this much less comprehensive agreement than LAFTA ran into difficulties at a relatively early stage with the departure of Chile in 1976 due to disagreement regarding foreign investment policy.(14)

A further American example of attempts at forging international trading policies was provided by the Central American Common Market (CACM), established in principle in 1960, the outcome of several previous treaties, and followed in 1964 by a Central American Central Banks System which was responsible for coordinating the monetary policies of member countries. The CACM aimed to secure the liberalisation of intra-group trade although, at the time of its foundation, tariffs on 95 per cent of tariff items of intra-group trade had already been abolished and a common external tariff covered about 97 per cent of the remainder.(15)

c. The CMEA and others

Examples of emergent trading groups formed in Asia and Africa after the Second World War reveal, similarly, a concentration of attention on policies of tariff reduction and the general liberalisation of intra-group trading relations rather than the forging of common policies on commodity trade and development.(16) The same result emerges from an examination of the socialist bloc of countries despite their far greater political importance and economic muscle. It is for the latter reasons that some mention must be made of the Council for Mutual Economic Assistance (CMEA), formed in 1949 with Bulgaria, Czechoslovakia, Hungary, Poland, Romania and the USSR as founder members. Discussion will be limited, however, to highlighting those aspects of CMEA trade and policy which have been of importance in respect of the broader international framework.

The CMEA was founded in 1949 but it was not until 1959 that a charter was issued defining its main policy objectives and that the function of the Council was broadened to deal explicitly with economic matters. The task set the CMEA was 'to continue developing all-round economic co-operation on the basis of the consistent implementation of the international socialist division of labour in the interests of building Socialism and Communism in their countries . . .' It was to achieve this objective by planned economic development and, specifically, by the co-ordination of members' policies to permit the 'most rational use of their natural resources and acceleration of the development of their productive forces'. In practice, the degree of co-ordination before 1975 was limited and applied principally in the form of bi-lateral arrangements on trade between member countries. From 1976, however, provision was made for a more comprehensive programme of cooperation in terms of five-year economic plans.(17)

62

The CMEA did not result in a substantial expansion of intra-group trade. On the contrary, only 49.1 per cent of CMEA trade was with member countries in 1980 compared with 72.0 per cent in 1960 and the shares of both developed and developing countries increased. The relative importance of CMEA trade in world terms was also not large - less than a tenth of the total - a fact which partly reflected the CMEA's underlying philosophy of encouraging self-sufficiency; exports, notably of agricultural and mineral products, were traded in order to obtain hard currency to purchase goods not produced within the CMEA area.(18)

The CMEA did not participate actively in international trade negotiations under GATT since tariffs had virtually no function within the CMEA area; imported commodities, for example, were usually sold at the same price as comparable domestic goods, any difference being equalised by offsetting taxes and subsidies. Its role within UNCTAD was generally supportive of the interests of developing countries and of the concept of international commodity agreements to promote development. However, the policies pursued within the CMEA, which tended to encourage the disposal of surplus agricultural and mineral products abroad and to incorporate prices based not on the cost of imported goods but on predetermined formulae, did not in practice further developing country aims since they were often no less protectionist than those pursued by industrialised countries. On occasion they worked directly against the avowed objectives of international commodity agreements. Examples, considered in more detail in subsequent chapters, include the sales by the USSR of substantial quantities of tin in the late 1950s, which served to depress world prices, and large USSR purchases of wheat following a crop shortfall in 1972/73, which acted to increase existing shortages.(19)

It was the indirect rather than the direct impact of CMEA trade policies which thus bore most strongly on the operation of post-War international commodity controls. In addition to the general economic strategies of the CMEA, mention must also be made here of the strong political as opposed to economic motivation which guided policy decisions. In 1961, for example, the USSR intervened directly in international commodity relations by providing a market denied by the US to Cuban sugar. This resulted in the USSR taking up the slack of US demand for Cuban sugar by long-term contracts at terms which were often much above the prevailing world price. These purchases added to existing uncertainties within the world sugar market since the USSR occasionally re-sold a proportion of the sugar abroad.(20)

4. The US
a. General

A discussion of the importance of political factors in the negotiation of international policy after the War leads on naturally to an assessment of the role played by the US. Although the US is in technical terms a national rather than a regional trading group, the central role it played in the evolution of the Organization for Economic Co-operation and Development (OECD) and as a major commodity producer and trader in its own right mean that it cannot be excluded from this appraisal of important influences on the development of international commodity policy.

It was the passage of the (US) Trade Expansion Act of 1962, which conditionally sanctioned the abrogation of US tariff rates (on the assumption of an enlarged EEC), which provided the impetus for the Kennedy Round in 1964. Similarly, the (US) Trade Act of 1974, by reviving presidential authority to implement tariff cuts, facilitated the Tokyo Round of trade negotiations. The US also participated actively in discussions concerning international commodity finance and development assistance under the auspices of the IMF and GATT. US policy on international commodity issues, in contrast, was less explicitly stated and varied considerably over time and from commodity to commodity. Whereas the US expressed outright hostility to rubber and coffee controls between the Wars, in 1952 a government commission called attention to the disadvantages of commodity price fluctuations and came out in favour of international commodity agreements which used multi-lateral contracts or buffer stocks as mechanisms. In 1954, this view was modified in turn by the results of another government enquiry which concluded that extensive resort to international commodity agreements would not necessarily solve the problem of price instability and might instead introduce rigidities which would impair the elasticity of economic adjustment considered fundamental to economic progress.(21)

Although in general the US did not come out strongly in favour of international commodity agreements, it supported such agreements in cases where there was a strong US producer interest. The key examples were the wheat agreements of the 1950s. The US played an active role both within and outside these agreements by stock withdrawal at the national level. Another factor inducing the US to enter international commodity agreements was the over-ruling of economic by political considerations. The most notable case was the 1962 Coffee Agreement. US adherence, which had been withheld in strenuous terms during the 1950s, resulted from its new perception that Western hemispheric security would be improved by the stability of coffee trade and prices.

However, it was only in the 1970s that the US conducted a detailed review of its commodity policy following the move of international commodity issues to the centre of trade policy discussions. Following an initiative led by Kissinger, who had condemned the NIEO, the US agreed to negotiate international commodity agreements on a 'case-by-case' basis as part of its approach to the gamut of issues raised in the Tokyo Round. It stated that the aim of such agreements should be to ensure adequate supplies rather than to raise prices and that efforts to mobilise capital investment in raw materials should be urgently pursued. These views represented a significant change in policy; the more generally sympathetic attitude of the Carter Administration toward international commodity agreements led to US participation in the 1977 Sugar Agreement (Chapter 8). With the accession of the Reagan Administration, in contrast, and its commitment to the virtues of 'free market forces', US support for international commodity agreements weakened considerably and, as outlined above, tri- and bi-lateral negotiations on trade became increasingly popular. In this context, US participation in discussions to secure a renewal of the 1971 Wheat Agreement were unenthusiastic whilst US refusal to accede to the 1980 Cocoa Agreement cast doubt over the future of an agreement which excluded the major importing country.(22)

In addition to its prominent role in the formulation of international tariff and commodity policy, the influence of the US was also felt keenly in respect of national agricultural and strategic stockpile policy. Although far from unique or even unusual in terms of the evolution of national policies on these subjects after the Second World War, the experience of the US merits separate consideration here on account of the scale of operation and the large spill-over effect on world markets for certain of the commodities in question. What follows is a brief introduction to the principles which have guided the evolution of US agricultural policy, on the one hand, and strategic stockpile policy, on the other. Further consideration of the control mechanisms used is provided in Chapter 5 and of the influence of US national policy on a commodity-by-commodity basis, notably in respect of sugar and wheat, in Part III.

b. Agricultural Policy

Between 1945 and the early 1970s the philosophy underpinning US agricultural policy was that the farm sector constituted a weak and declining part of the economy 'beset by endemic economic problems that could only be kept within socially tolerable bounds by extensive public support programmes'.(23) These problems were deemed to be the fruits of increases in output which exceeded increases in demand and led to excess capacity, a secular deterioration in the terms of trade of the agricultural sector and low and unstable returns to labour, capital and managerial resources engaged in agriculture. The main thrust of public policy in respect of agriculture was therefore that income should be re-distributed to farmers, that market stability should be enhanced and that the necessary process of farm and rural adjustment should be facilitated. As a result, attention focussed on agricultural policies dealing with production levels, marketing arrangements and farm gate prices rather than on the interests of consumers. The role of the US as a leading agricultural producer in global terms was largely disregarded.(24)

Within these general terms of reference, however, the stance of policy shifted markedly over time. Following a decade of comparatively high support prices in the 1950s, which led to the accumulation of large government stocks and necessitated the use of export subsidies, import restriction and rigid production controls, the 1960s witnessed a general lowering of price supports toward market levels and subsidy schemes to induce producers to diversify their mix of products. It was the transformation of the US from net importer of agricultural commodities to net exporter, notably for grains and oilseeds, from 1963, together with the increasing integration of US agriculture in the world economy, which conspired to bring about a shift in agricultural policy during the 1970s. From a concentration on farm income support in the 1950s and 1960s, attention turned instead to a greater concern for price stability and for the security of world food supplies in an increasingly inter-dependent world economy. As a result, rigidly fixed price supports were used less frequently and deficiency payments, under which the government made up the difference between a guaranteed price and the average price, became a more favoured control mechanism. Similarly, from 1977 greater attention was paid to policies of crop diversion with the ascendant assumption that market forces should play a greater part in the determination of national agricultural policy.

To sum up, US agricultural policy shifted from a narrow preoccupation with domestic farm output in the 1950s to an increased awareness by policy-makers of the external effects of national farm policies in the 1970s.(25) As noted above, under the Carter Administration this increasing awareness was translated into greater US support for international commodity agreements; under the Reagan Administration, in contrast, tri- and bi-lateral negotiations on trade were frequently used, with a recent example, the pressure brought to bear on the EEC to pursue policies which do not conflict with the US farm policy stance.

c. The Strategic Stockpile

A strategic stockpile was established in 1946 with a view to providing for the acquisition and retention of stocks of materials within the US in order to prevent 'a dangerous and costly dependence . . . upon foreign nations for supplies . . . in times of national emergency.'(26) It was administered by the General Services Administration on the basis of the estimated potential requirements of the US and its principal allies; every material in the stockpile was subject to review on a regular basis to determine its strategic importance. Prior to 1959, the stock was to be sufficient for a five year war; thereafter, the general requirement was that it should meet the needs of a three year war. As a result, successive administrations after 1959 authorised sales of surplus stocks from the stockpile (although in 1975 it was estimated that there were nineteen commodities, including bauxite, rubber and tin, for which supplies in the stockpile were surplus to requirements).(27) Commodities on which the US depends on imported supplies to a large degree include chromium ore, bauxite, tin, manganese, nickel, zinc and tungsten.

It was purchases and sales from the strategic stockpile together with the uncertainty surrounding them which was of importance to international commodity trade. The case of tin, which provides perhaps the clearest example over a long time span, is considered in Chapter 6. More recently, the announcement by President Reagan of plans to purchase unspecified quantities of defence-related materials considered to be in short supply in the stockpile - to be financed from sales of excess materials including tin -offered a further vivid illustration. Uncertainty surrounded not only the volume and timing of the sales but also even the commodities to be covered by them. The impact of this and other announcements, in sum, was to add a further uncertain element to commodity markets already subject to a range of unpredictable influences.(28)

5. Conclusion

Perhaps the most important point to emerge from this analysis of the role of new trading blocs and of the US in international commodity trade and policy since 1945 is that international controls had and continue to have many counterparts and alternatives at the regional and national levels. The examples included of trading preferences, farm support policies, regulated pricing systems and national stockpiles all have parallels elsewhere which underline the multiplicity of influences bearing on international commodity markets. In this context, the task of policy-makers in searching for solutions to the range of problems faced by primary commodity producers (outlined in Chapter 1) has been arduous in the extreme and mined with many problem areas. It remains for subsequent parts of this study to consider the tools at the policy-makers' disposal and their success or failure in carrying out stated policy objectives.

Notes

1   For references on each theme discussed see subsequent footnotes.

2   See for example, Commonwealth Economic Committee, A Review of Commonwealth Agriculture (Commonwealth Economic Committee, London, 1952), C.B. Hoover (ed.), Economic Systems of the Commonwealth (Duke University Press, Durban, 1962), D.J. Morgan, The Official History of Colonial Development (Macmillan, London, 1980) and H.J. Harvey, Consultation and Co-operation in the Commonwealth (Oxford University Press, London, 1952).

3   The eighteen countries covered were Burundi, Cameroon, the Central African Republic, Chad, Congo (Kinshasa), Congo (Brazzaville), Dahomey, Gabon, Upper Volta, the Ivory Coast, Madagascar, Mali, Mauritania, Niger, Rwanda, Senegal, Somalia and Togo. The Convention was also extended to Surinam, the Netherlands Antilles and French overseas territories and departments.   D. Swann, The Economics of the Common Market (Penguin, Middlesex, 1970), p. 162 pointed out that the association did not enable associates to expand their exports to the EEC more rapidly than to the developing world as a whole. Between 1958 and 1967 their exports increased by 47 per cent whereas that of the developing world as a whole increased by 68 per cent. It should be noted that under the Treaty of Rome a provision was made for association with other countries; two countries taking advantage of this provision were Greece (1962) and Turkey (1964). Under the modified Yaoundé Convention provision was made for the common external tariff on some tropical products to be suspended, thus reducing the degree of preference conferred on associated countries.   See also B. Balassa (ed.), European Economic Integration (North-Holland Publishing Co., 1975) and P. Coffey, The External Relations of the EEC (Macmillan, London, 1976).

4   See EEC, Official Journal of the European Communities, vol. 19, L.25 (30 January 1976).   STABEX was funded by making more resources available to the European Development Fund.   See Commission of the European Communities, 'Lomé Dossier', The Courier, no. 31 (March 1975).   The amount of funds involved under STABEX was less than 4 per cent of the 1973 EEC import value of the commodities involved. See also K.P. Treydte, 'The Stabilization of Export Earnings: Two Years' Experience in STABEX', Intereconomics, vol. 11/12 (1977) and C.C. Twitchett, A Framework for Development: The EEC and the ACP (Allen & Unwin, London, 1981), Chapters 2 - 6.

5   C.H. Kirkpatrick, 'Lomé II', Journal of World Trade Law, vol. 14, no. 4 (July:August 1980), EEC, 'Background Report: Lomé II: Terms of the New Convention' (EEC, London, September 1979, ISEC/B33/79) and Twitchett, A Framework for Development, Chapter 6.

6   Kirkpatrick, 'Lomé II' and MacBean and Snowden, International Institutions in Trade and Finance, pp. 167-71.   Twitchett, A Framework for Development, p. 133 stressed that Lomé was not a response to the NIEO debate but a legacy of colonialism whose strength might fade as colonial ties lessened.

7   The quotation is taken from the Treaty of Rome which established the European Economic Community. See Keesing's Treaties and Alliances of the World, pp. 44-5.

8   A.M. El-Agraa (ed.), The Economics of the European Community (Philip Allan, Oxford, 1980). A considerable volume of work has been conducted on the impact of EEC tariff policy.   Macbean and Snowden, International Institutions in Trade and Finance, for example, concluded that with the conspicuous example of agriculture, it was difficult to point to increased Community trade diversion notwithstanding the international troubles of the 1970s. Other studies have reached different and varying conclusions. See for examples B. Balassa, 'Trade Creation and Trade Diversion in the European Common Market', Economic Journal, vol. 77 (March 1967), Ibid., 'Trade Creation and Trade Diversion in the European Common Market: an Appraisal of the Evidence', The Manchester School, vol. XLII, no. 2 (1974) and D.G. Mayes, 'The Effects of Economic

Integration on Trade', Journal of Common Market Studies, vol. 17, no. 1 (September 1978).

9   Keesing's, Treaties and Alliances of the World, p. 44.

10 'Proposals for the Working-out and Putting into Effect of the Common Agricultural Policy in Application of Article 43 of the Treaty establishing the European Economic Community' (EEC, Brussels, 1960), Memorandum on Reform of Agriculture in the European Communities (European Communities Information Service, London, 1968), G. Hallett, The Economics of Agricultural Policy (Basil Blackwell, Oxford, 1981), Chapter 15 and R. Fennell, The Common Agricultural Policy of the European Community (Granada, St Albans, 1979).

11 El-Agraa, The Economics of the European Community, Chapter 7, Macbean and Snowden, International Institutions in Trade and Finance, pp. 159-60, T. Josling, Burdens and Benefits of Farm-Support Policies (Trade Policy Research Centre, London, 1972) and T. Heidhues, T.E. Josling, C. Ritson and S. Tangermann, Common Prices and Europe's Farm Policy (Trade Policy Research Centre, London, 1978).

12 Keesing's, Treaties and Alliances of the World, pp. 54-7, V. Pertot, International Economics of Control (Oliver and Boyd, Edinburgh, 1972), pp. 140-41 and M.A.G. van Meerhaeghe, A Handbook of International Economic Institutions (Martinus Nijhoff, The Hague, 1980), Chapter 9. The countries who founded EFTA were the UK, Austria, Sweden, Switzerland, Denmark, Norway and Portugal. EFTA, The European Free Trade Association: Structure, Rules and Operation (EFTA, Geneva, 1976) provides a good over-view of the organisation and its activities. See also F.V. Meyer, The European Free Trade Association: An Analysis of 'The Outer Seven' (Praeger Publishers, New York, 1960) and V. Curzon, The Essentials of Economic Integration: Lessons of EFTA Experience (Macmillan, London, 1974).

13 Keesing's, Treaties and Alliances of the World, pp. 118-19, S. Dell, A Latin American Common Market? (Oxford University Press, London, 1966) and Macbean and Snowden, International Institutions in Trade and Finance, pp. 184-85.

14 R. Vargas-Hidalgo, 'The Crisis of the Andean Pact: Lessons for Integration Among Developing Countries', Journal of Common Market Studies, vol. 17, no. 3 (March 1979) and Macbean and Snowden, International Institutions in Trade and Finance, pp. 186-87.

15 van Meerhaeghe, A Handbook of International Economic Institutions, pp. 11-12. Members were Costa Rica, El Salvador, Guatemala, Honduras and Nicaragua.

16 Examples include the Association of South-East Asian Nations, formed in 1967, which provided for the gradual lowering of mutual trade restrictions between Indonesia, Malaysia, the Philippines, Singapore and Thailand; the Economic Community of the West-African States, established in 1975, which aimed to establish a customs union between certain West African countries within fifteen years; and the Arab Common Market, which became effective from 1965 and provided for the removal of tariffs and quantitative restrictions on intra-territorial trade. See for example B. Bracewell-Milnes, Economic Integration in East and West (Croom Helm, London, 1976) and P. Taylor and A.J.R. Groom, International Organization: A Conceptual Approach (Francis Pinter, London, 1978).

17 Keesing's, Treaties and Alliances of the World, pp. 92-3. This includes a summary of key clauses of the CMEA Charter from which the quotations are taken. See also van Meerhaeghe, A Handbook of International Economic Institutions, Chapter 7 and M.Kaser, Comecon: Integration Problems of the Planned Economies (Oxford University Press, London, 1967).

18 IBRD, Commodity Trade and Price Trends, pp. 12-13. The share of industrialised countries, for example, rose from 18.7 per cent in 1960 to 32.6 per cent in 1980. As Kaser, Comecon: Integration Problems of the Planned Economies, pp. 12-17 pointed

out, the priority of CMEA policy was on heavy industry rather than agriculture and light industry. See also J.M.P. van Brabant, Bilateralism and Structural Bilateralism in Intra-CMEA Trade (Rotterdam University Press, Rotterdam, 1979) and J.S. Garland, Financing Foreign Trade in Eastern Europe: Problems of Bilateralism and Currency Inconvertibility (Praeger Publishers, New York, 1977).

19 Rangarajan, Commodity Conflict, pp. 141-44 and see Chapters 6 and 7.

20 See Chapter 8, N.G.M. Watts (ed.), Economic Relations between East and West (Macmillan, London, 1978) and C.M. Friesen, The Political Economy of East-West Trade (Praeger Publishers, New York, 1976).

21 A useful summary of US tariff policy is provided by F.V. Meyer, International Trade Policy (Croom Helm, London, 1978), Chapter 3. See also W.B. Kelly (ed.), Studies in United States Commercial Policy (The University of North Carolina Press, Chapel Hill, 1963), United Nations, Commodity Trade and Economic Development (United Nations, New York, 1956), US, Commission on Foreign Economic Policy, Report to the President and the Congress (The Randall Commission) (US Government Printing Office, Washington, 1954) and S.D. Cohen, The Making of the United States International Economic Policy (Praeger Publishers, New York, 1977).

22 G.P. Shultz and K.W. Dam, Economic Policy beyond the Headlines (W.W. Norton, New York, 1977), Chapter 7 and Goodwin and Mayall, A New International Commodity Regime, pp. 116-22.

23 T.K. Warley, Agriculture in an Interdependent World: US and Canadian Perspectives (Canadian-American Committee, C.D. Howe Research Institute, US, 1977), p. 9. This appraisal offers a perceptive summary of the issues.

24 The agricultural policy of the US in this period has been the object of detailed research, both on a general and on a commodity-by-commodity basis. For examples see G.E. Brandow, 'American Agriculture's Capacity to Meet Future Demands', American Journal of Agricultural Economics, vol. 56, no. 1 (December 1974), J.P. Gittinger, North American Agriculture in a New World (Canadian-American Committee, US, 1970) and P. Bidwell, Raw Materials: A Study of American Policy (Harper, New York, 1958).

25 For a recent perceptive account see G.E. Schuh, 'US Agriculture in an Interdependent World Economy: Policy Alternatives for the 1980s', in D.G. Johnson (ed.), Food and Agricultural Policy for the 1980s (American Enterprise Institute for Public Policy Research, Washington, 1981) and G.M. Meier, 'US Foreign Economic Policies', in P. Duignan and A. Rabushka (eds.), The United States in the 1980s (Croom Helm, London, 1980).

26 US, 'Strategic and Critical Materials Stockpiling Act' (1946), quoted in B.O. Szuprowicz, How to Avoid Strategic Materials Shortages (John Wiley & Sons, New York, 1981), p. 223.

27 F. Kottke, The Promotion of Price Competition Where Sellers are Few (D.C. Heath, Lexington, Mass., 1978) and W. Schneider, Food, Foreign Policy and Raw Material Cartels (National Strategy Information Center, New York, 1976), pp. 40-2.

28 US, Federal Preparedness Agency, The Strategic and Critical Materials Stockpile (General Services Administration Fact Sheet, Washington, October 1976), Schneider, Food, Foreign Policy and Raw Material Cartels, Chapter 4 and US, Council on International Economic Policy, Special Report: Critical Imported Materials (Washington, December 1974). For the 1981 increase to the stockpile see Financial Times, 14 March 1981 and Ibid., 4 June 1981. The US proposed to sell all of the silver in its stockpile, for example, and to buy cobalt, chromium, manganese, titanium and other materials. Total stockpile goals in 1981 in value terms were $20.7 billion compared with existing holdings of $14.9 billion of which $6.8 billion were surplus to requirements.

PART II: THE MECHANICS OF COMMODITY CONTROL

Introduction

Part I was concerned with establishing the institutional, political and economic framework within which international commodity control measures have been formulated. Part II attempts to examine the frequency, the aims and the mechanics of these controls as they have been adopted in international commodity agreements and international cartel arrangements. As indicated in Chapter 3, there has been a considerable overlap and inter-dependence between controls at the international and national levels since every form of control measure adopted internationally has depended on supporting domestic measures. Separate consideration is given also to domestic measures, such as tariffs and subsidies, alternative rather than complementary to international controls since, in practice, these have dominated trade policy throughout the period considered.

The aim of this section is to provide an illustration rather than a catalogue of the range of tools which have been at the policy maker's disposal. It is hoped that this will permit a more balanced assessment of past and present experience of international commodity controls. This in turn may be suggestive of viable courses of action for the future.

4: INTERNATIONAL CONTROLS

> 'Exports ... from the producing countries shall be regulated in order to restore equilibrium between supply and demand'.
>
> ('International Tea Agreement, 1933-1938')

1. International Commodity Agreements
a. Frequency and Commodity Coverage

There have been thirty-nine international commodity agreements which accord to the definition given in Chapter 1, of which the first was the 1931 Tin Agreement and the latest to be implemented, the 1980 Cocoa Agreement. (The Jute Agreement of October 1982 is not included in this chapter since full details were not available.) In terms of commodity coverage, tin has been the object of the most regular agreements throughout the period with a total of ten, wheat ranked second, with a total of eight, most of which were negotiated after the Second World War and sugar, third, with a total of six agreements. Although olive oil has been subject to only three agreements, these were revised at intervals to provide continuous coverage since 1956. Of the other commodities, there have been four for tea (albeit limited in range and participation) and three each for coffee and cocoa. Rubber was the object of pre-War but little post-War control until 1979. Coffee agreements date from the 1960s. And cocoa agreements date only from the 1970s.

In terms of date of introduction, the 1930s witnessed eight international commodity agreements covering five commodities, the Second World War only one new agreement, the 1942 Tin Agreement (although coffee was the object of an Inter-American Agreement,

72

Table 4:1: International Commodity Agreements[a]

Commodity	Pre-1939	Second World War	1945 -49	1950s	1960s	1970 to August 1982	Total
Tin	3	1	-	1	2	3	10
Wheat	1	-	1	3	2	1	8
Sugar	1	-	-	2	1	2	6
Rubber	1	-	-	-	-	1	2
Coffee	-	-	-	-	2	1	3
Cocoa	-	-	-	-	-	3	3
Olive Oil	-	-	-	1	1	1	3
Tea	2	-	1	1	-	-	4
Total	8	1	2	8	8	12	39

Note: a   The dates and key features of the agreements are provided in the Appendix.

Source: For full sources on the international commodity agreements, see the Bibliography, Section I.

wheat of a draft agreement and sugar of an extension to the 1937 Agreement), the 1945 to 1949 period witnessed only the 1948 Tea Agreement and the 1949 Wheat Agreement and the 1950s, eight agreements. There followed the fairly regular renewal of the main tin, wheat, sugar and olive oil agreements so that of eight agreements of the 1960s, only one, the 1962 Coffee Agreement, broke new ground in terms of commodity coverage. In contrast, there have been twelve international commodity agreements since 1970, negotiated and distributed evenly in time, with cocoa and rubber added to the ranks of commodities covered. Attempts were made also to negotiate international agreements for tea, copper, jute, iron ore, tropical timber and cotton and discussions continue on the possibility of negotiating other agreements under UNCTAD's Integrated Programme (see the Conclusion and Appraisal).

It is interesting to note that except for wheat all of the commodities for which there have been international agreements were included in UNCTAD's list of 'core' commodities* and that, of

---

*   As outlined in Chapter 2, these included: bananas, bauxite, cocoa, coffee, copper, cotton and cotton yarns, hard fibres, iron ore, jute and jute products, manganese, meat, phosphates, rubber, sugar, tea, tropical timber, tin and vegetable oils (including olive oil and oilseeds).

these, developed countries have led the export (more than half the market) of only wheat and olive oil. In contrast, developing countries have been important exporters of sugar and natural rubber and have dominated exports of coffee, tea, cocoa and tin. Wheat, sugar and coffee stand out as commodities major in value terms in world trade for which there have been several international commodity agreements. In terms of commodities attracting a strong degree of dependence, six developing countries in 1977 were dependent for over half of the value of their export earnings on coffee, four on sugar and two on cocoa (Chapter 1).

b. Aims

The stated aims of international commodity agreements have fallen into two categories: those with direct links to commodity production and trade, the 'economic' provisions; and those which have touched on broader issues. It is the first category which is of most importance for this Chapter. However, in order to set the economic aims in a wider perspective, mention will be made also of the second category of objectives. In both cases, it should be stressed, expectations have tended to be great as to what can be achieved. The performance of the agreements in meeting their objectives will be considered in Part III and in the Conclusion and Appraisal.

With the exceptions of the olive oil agreements (which aimed to reduce fluctuations in supplies), every international commodity agreement has had as a major objective the balancing of the supply of the commodity with the demand for it. The 1933 Tin and 1934 Rubber Agreements and the war-time Tin Agreement of 1942 also included as an aim the absorption of surplus stocks and, similarly, the 1933 Wheat Agreement and the 1962 and 1968 Coffee Agreements specified the need to avoid burdensome surpluses. After the War, there was an increasing emphasis on encouraging the greater consumption of, or trade in, the commodity in question, an aim included in most of the sugar, wheat, coffee and olive oil agreements. However, only the olive oil agreements specified the securing of standard grading as a policy objective and only a few agreements, such as the tin agreements and the 1979 Rubber Agreement, stated the need to promote more efficient ('economic' or 'improved') production methods.

The stabilisation of the price of the commodity has also been a recurrent policy goal. It was included as an objective in each of the tin, coffee, wheat and cocoa agreements, the 1934 and 1979 Rubber Agreements and the sugar agreements since 1953. Many of the agreements specified further that the prices achieved should be 'reasonable' and 'remunerative to the efficient producer' and almost all of the post-War agreements stressed that the resultant price should be 'fair' (also without definition) to the consumer. Most of the post-War agreements also specified a price range within which the agreement should operate or minimum and maximum prices which were acceptable.

A further economic aim included in international commodity agreements was that of increasing the export earnings of producers. This objective followed close on the heels of UNCTAD I in 1964 and was incorporated in subsequent tin, coffee, sugar and cocoa agreements and in the 1979 Rubber Agreement. The sugar agreements and the 1979 Rubber Agreement also emphasised the need to increase market access for developing country producers for the product concerned.

The broader issues addressed in the objectives of the agreements included matters relating to labour and the role of commodity earnings as a means of enhancing development prospects. Whereas the pre-War agreements were in general tacit on these subjects, a number of post-War agreements, such as the tin and coffee agreements, included as a general aim the prevention or alleviation of unemployment or, in the case of the coffee agreements, the need to maintain existing levels of employment. A mix of post-War agreements - the tin agreements from 1960, the 1953 Sugar Agreement and its successors, the 1956 Olive Oil Agreement, the 1979 Rubber Agreement and the cocoa agreements - also stressed the need for fair labour standards with little further explanation. A few others, notably the 1953 and 1958 Sugar Agreements and the coffee agreements, included as an objective the maintenance of the purchasing power of producers or exporters.(1)

General statements on the need to foster reconstruction and development were spasmodic; the 1975 and 1980 Cocoa Agreements, for example, stated that increased export earnings for producers would contribute 'the necessary incentive for a dynamic and rising rate of production' and 'provide such countries with resources for accelerated economic growth and social development . . .'(2) The inclusion of specific policy statements on this subject featured most prominently in agreements relating to commodities such as tin, cocoa, and rubber in which developing countries dominated production. From 1959, the wheat agreements also stressed the need to increase the consumption of wheat and wheat-flour in order to improve health and nutrition and to foster economic development.

The aims of international commodity agreements were thus variable with the main emphasis on balancing supply with demand. In general, objectives were not only ambitious but also, in several cases, ill-defined. The adjudication of a 'fair' price for an 'efficient' producer exemplifies the type of definitional problem involved. Similarly, the constitution of 'fair labour standards' was never clearly spelt out and depended on a large number of variables which the agreements could not and did not make any attempt to control. Finally, the wisdom of price stabilisation as a goal has itself been subject to considerable debate with some arguing in favour of revenue rather than price stabilisation as a more important policy goal (Chapter 1). The shift in the debate has been reflected in the greater emphasis of agreements since the 1960s on increasing the export earnings of primary producers.

c. Regulatory Techniques
(1) General

The regulatory techniques used in international commodity agreements have also varied markedly between commodities and, to a lesser extent, in respect of the controls employed for the same commodity. The most common form of control mechanism has been some form of quantitative restriction on exports, used in conjunction with either international or national stock policy. This was a common element in the tin agreements, the 1934 Rubber Agreement, most of the sugar agreements and the cocoa agreements. In several cases, for example, the 1942 Tin Agreement, the 1934 Rubber Agreement, the sugar agreements to 1958 and the coffee and cocoa agreements, provision was made for export and/or stock policies to be combined with some form of domestic production controls. Another common feature of the agreements was the conferral on participants of a preference, either implicit or explicit, with regard to markets or to supplies. The wheat agreements, for example, were designed to ensure that trade with parties outside the agreements was conducted on terms which were no more favourable than those within them, a procedure mirrored in most of the sugar, coffee and cocoa agreements. A further repeated mechanism was the inclusion of measures relating to consumption, both those designed to promote increased consumption and trade (for example, those contained in the olive oil agreements) and those which aimed to encourage alternative end-uses (such as those in the cocoa agreements). The 1962 and 1968 Coffee Agreements also included, unusually, precise recommendations and financial facilities for diversification away from coffee production to alternative crops.
        The remainder of this section offers a brief and non-technical outline of the features which have distinguished the regulatory techniques outlined above. In several cases, such as export and production controls and stock policy, these techniques were common also to the cartels considered in Part 2 of this chapter.

(2) Export Quotas

The export quota specifies limits as to the quantity of a commodity which a member is authorised to export. It has only a secondary effect on prices through the quantitative effect on supply and demand. As Pertot has pointed out, there are no essential differences between the economic effects of various types - global or specific, autonomous or bi-lateral - of quotas.(3) However, export quotas have been considered generally to be a legitimate instrument of trade policy, particularly when used in international commodity agreements, in contrast to the less favourable status of import quotas, notably under GATT.

The terms governing the operation of export quotas have varied from agreement to agreement. In the tin agreements, for example, they have tended to be introduced when the price of tin fell below the targeted price scale and were used in conjunction with buffer stock operations. In the 1972 and 1975 Cocoa Agreements, in contrast, export quotas were established each year on the basis of an estimate of world net import demand and stocks and constituted the principal control instrument used. Critical to the operation of export quotas was their distribution - usually based on an historical assessment of national export levels - and the accuracy of the forecasts on which they were based. Exports were usually permitted outside of the terms of the agreements to meet special needs or in the form of aid and donations. The 1967 Grains Arrangement and the 1971 Wheat Agreement, for example, included specific provisions for aid commitments.

In order for some measure of policing to be introduced regarding the operation of export quota schemes, many of the agreements required that the countries should take 'appropriate' action to ensure compliance. Only a handful, such as the 1933 Tin Agreement and the 1937 Sugar Agreement, specified that such action should be legislative in form, although many of the agreements introduced a system of certificates of origin or required the detailed recording of transactions (the wheat agreements) in order to provide some check on the source of the commodity. (A summary of key features of the agreements is provided in the Appendix.) The 1962 Coffee Agreement was notable in requiring certificates of re-export in the case of coffee trade via an entrepôt. As a general rule export quotas were to be adjusted on an annual or a quarterly basis to meet changes in the patterns of demand. In some cases, such as the tin agreements, quotas were to be suspended when the price overshot the target range. In others, such as the 1975 Cocoa Agreement, quotas were to be varied according to the position of prices in an indicator range.

Views on the technical merits of export quotas as a mechanism, used on their own or in conjunction with other mechanisms, notably stock controls, have varied considerably. In 1958, for example, GATT's Haberler Report concluded that they were 'apt to introduce an undesirable rigidity into the world production and trade' since they made it 'difficult for a low-cost exporter to expand his output at the expense of the high-cost producer.' In addition, the Report pointed out that such arrangements were liable to break down unless they covered virtually all exporters or unless the importing countries in the agreement took effective measures to limit their imports from outside countries. Otherwise, it was concluded: 'outside suppliers are apt to make hay while the sun shines by expanding their output for sale at prices which are maintained by restrictions on the exports of the member countries.'(4) This view has been supported by subsequent commentators who have also pointed out that export quotas based primarily on historic production levels may ossify existing patterns of production, supporting inefficient producers at the expense of their more efficient counterparts.(5)

(3) Stock Policy

Of the thirty-nine international commodity agreements since 1931, almost half incorporated some form of stock policy and the majority of those referred to national stocks. The tin agreements since 1937, the 1934 Rubber Agreement and the 1953, 1958, 1968 and 1977 Sugar Agreements, for example, specified maximum required levels of national stocks; the 1953, 1958 and 1968 Sugar Agreements established, in addition, minimum required stock levels; the 1949, 1953 and 1956 Wheat Agreements, in contrast, required simply that 'adequate' stocks should be held by exporting member countries. The burden of national stock holding policy fell in general on the shoulders of the exporting member countries with little or no operational or financial participation by importing members. Recommended stock levels were specified in terms of a proportion of domestic production, ranging from $12\frac{1}{2}$ per cent to 25 per cent, or at a level related to permitted exports. In terms of policing, only the coffee agreements required that levels of nationally held stocks should be formally verified. (Waivers could be granted in specific cases where the holding of such stocks involved hardship.) Such national stocks, held either by governments or by private firms, were an addition to commercial and strategic stocks and their main purpose was to enable a greater degree of control over trade in the commodity in question.

In addition to recommended levels of national stocks, internationally administered stocks, held either internationally (the post-War tin agreements and cocoa agreements), nationally (the 1979 Rubber Agreement) or either nationally or internationally (the 1977 Sugar Agreement), were also a recurrent, if less common, feature of international commodity agreements. The aim of such stocks was to hold back supplies in times of excess supply, to store them and to release them when a shortage arose in order to moderate price instability. Their composition varied. The tin agreements, for example, specified preferred ratios of tin metal and cash contributions whereas the cocoa agreements were less flexible, permitting contributions only in cocoa beans (1972 and 1975) or in

78

cocoa beans and paste (1980). Contributions were required from exporting members almost exclusively although provision was made in the tin agreements of the 1970s for contributions from consuming members. The burden of financing, similarly, fell more commonly on exporting rather than importing countries, particularly before the 1970s. Exceptions included the 1980 Tin Agreement, the cocoa agreements (where the cost was met by a levy on cocoa traded) and the 1979 Rubber Agreement.

It was the perception by UNCTAD that existing facilities to finance international buffer stocks, such as those available from the IMF, were inadequate and that the cost of buffer stock activity was a major stumbling block in the implementation of international commodity agreements which prompted the inclusion of the Common Fund as a central element in the Integrated Programme. As outlined in Chapter 2, a major aim of the Fund was to finance internationally co-ordinated stocks in order to facilitate the negotiation and operation of international commodity agreements.(6) However, despite the international sanction conferred upon them as a control mechanism, which dated back to the 1930s, the usefulness of such stocks was far from universally accepted. The essential principle of buying in years of low prices and of selling in periods of higher prices was complicated in practice by the difficulty of establishing appropriate purchase and sales intervention points; these depended, in turn, on the magnitude of shifts in supply and demand. Further problems arose when technological change or substitute products led to an unforeseen decrease in demand. Another prerequisite of successful intervention was that the executive body administering the agreement should be given sufficient resources, financial and administrative, to carry out the pricing objectives. Even then, as the GATT Haberler Report stressed in 1958, considerable dangers existed of ill-judged or ill-timed policy in the operation of a buffer stock since:

'. . . if a buffer stock authority, because it misjudges the market or because it is forced to do so by legislation or political pressure, purchases stock even though the price is not really exceptionally low, the time will come when it is loaded up with a surplus stock without the finance or storage capacity to add further to it. The surplus stock will overhang the market and its eventual disposal may greatly reduce prices. The last state may be worse than the first.'(7)

As a recent UNCTAD study has clearly demonstrated, for any commodity there is a trade-off between the degree to which price fluctuations are reduced and the burden of financing the buffer-stock. This trade-off has often contributed to the difficulty of reaching agreement on revisions to the price range.(8)

79

There has also been an active debate on the suitability of commodities for buffer stock activity. Even such apparently obvious characteristics as whether the quality of the commodity deteriorates in storage have been fiercely disputed (for example, in the case of tea) and UNCTAD's list of ten commodities considered suitable for buffer-stocking (Chapter 2) has been far from universally accepted. It has also been emphasised that, although buffer stock activity might be suitable for several of UNCTAD's 'core' commodities, its effectiveness - in reducing period-to-period fluctuations in prices, suppliers' incomes and buyers' expenditures - might not be great.(9)

Both national and international regulatory stock policy have been influenced also by the existence of strategic stockpiles, the largest and most comprehensive of which has been that of the US (Chapter 3). The impact of US stockpile policy will be considered in more detail in Chapter 6 with reference to the case of tin. It should also be noted here that the operation of buffer stocks since the early 1970s has been complicated further by a dramatic increase in the volume of speculative finance in the international system. This, by increasing the likelihood of potentially destabilising movements of funds into and out of commodity markets, may have increased demands made on buffer stocks as market stabilisers.

(4) Production Controls

If agreement were reached on export quotas, the participating countries were faced with the problem of how to control domestic production. Production controls, that is limits on acreage or output, were an alternative to measures such as diversification which influenced investment decisions in the medium rather than the short-term. They were applied in the tea, tin, rubber and sugar agreements of the 1930s and were a legacy of voluntary restriction schemes in the 1920s. After the Second World War, in contrast, precise quantitative restrictions on domestic production or acreage were rarely specified within the agreements. Exceptions included the 1962 Coffee Agreement, which provided the International Coffee Organization with the authority to establish production quotas (although these provisions were not continued in its successors); and the 1972 and 1975 Cocoa Agreements, under which producing members made a general commitment to adjust the level of production with a view to maintaining a reasonable balance with consumption requirements.

Although the inclusion of explicit controls on national production in international commodity agreements was largely a pre-1945 phenomenon, the application of nationally administered and financed restrictions on output, in contrast, was more common. Key examples include controls on coffee in Brazil and the grains 'set-aside' programme in the US (Chapters 7 and 10).

(5) The Conferral of Preference

The granting of special terms to signatories is not generally cited as a form of control mechanism. However, such preferences formed an important aspect of several agreements and in their most clearly delineated form, the multi-lateral contract, were perhaps the most formal of all the control mechanisms used. They are included, therefore, in this survey.

The most common form of preference involved the limitation of imports from non-participants during a given period to a quantity not larger than that imported during a preceding period. In return, the governments of exporting countries undertook to take 'all practicable action' to ensure that the demands of participating importers were met. Under the terms of the coffee agreements, the International Coffee Council had authority to impose additional limitations on imports from non-member countries if necessary and transactions were recorded by means of certificates of origin and re-export. The cocoa agreements stipulated also that imports in excess of a given quantity should be deducted from the quantity that such a member would be permitted to import in the next quota year; non-compliance could involve the suspension of voting rights.(10)

The multi-lateral contract went further than these general commitments and conferred legal status on the obligations of each member. Since this mechanism was included only in the wheat agreements, these will form the basis for discussion. The first wheat agreement to be based on the multi-lateral contract procedure was that of 1949. The Agreement set out the guaranteed purchases of importing countries and the guaranteed sales of exporting countries within a specified price range for the four years covered by the Agreement. The International Wheat Council was required to keep a record of such transactions and was empowered to adjust the guaranteed quantities in certain circumstances, such as a default on exports or the withdrawal of a member. Disputes were to be settled by negotiation or by reference to the Council. Transactions outside the price range were permissible but did not count to the fulfilment of obligations.(11)

From 1959, the form of the multi-lateral contract agreement was modified slightly. The concept of guaranteed quantities for purchase by importers and for sale by exporters was abandoned in favour of undertakings by each importing member to purchase from exporting members in each crop-year not less than a specified percentage of its total commercial purchases in that year at prices within the set range. The obligation of exporters was to supply, in association with one another, wheat to satisfy the commercial requirements of importing countries at prices within the range set. If the maximum price level were reached, exporters had to supply wheat equal to the average volume of commercial purchases made from them by importing members over the preceding five crop-years. In this situation, the percentage obligations of importers no longer applied.(12)

Unlike other of the control mechanisms, the multi-lateral contract left the control of output to the discretion of individual members and the success of such agreements depended on the ability of those countries to exercise such control at the national level, particularly over stocks. The multi-lateral contract extended the bi-lateral contract common in wheat trade to participants covering a large proportion of total world trade. However, such an extension did not mean that multi-lateral contracts replaced bi-lateral trading arrangements; on the contrary, recent evidence suggests that the reverse was the case, at least since 1967 (Chapter 7). A perceived advantage of multi-lateral over bi-lateral contracts was that in the case of the former no production restrictions were required and new producers were still eligible to participate. (For this reason, UNCTAD's Integrated Programme favoured multi-lateral rather than bi-lateral commitments.)

(6) Measures relating to Consumption

Measures relating to consumption have also featured regularly in international commodity agreements. The early agreements couched such ideas in general terms: the 1933 Wheat Agreement, for example, aimed to 'adopt every possible measure to increase the consumption of wheat' and proposed the removal of (unspecified) measures 'which tend to lower the quality of breadstuffs and thereby decrease the human consumption of wheat'. Other of the agreements, such as the Rubber Agreement of 1934, specified the need both for research into new applications for rubber and for increased promotion; the Agreement provided for a cess to be levied on exports to finance these policies.(13)

In contrast, the post-War agreements contained more specific policy recommendations regarding the general aims of increasing the consumption of, and finding alternative uses for, the commodity in question (although they relied to a large extent on the initiative of the relevant commodity authority for their implementation). The 1956 Olive Oil Agreement and its successors, for example, aimed to increase the consumption of olive oil by a concerted publicity campaign financed by signatory countries and by improved quality control involving the standardisation of labelling and classification. The sugar agreements required the International Sugar Council to consider ways of promoting consumption, particularly in those countries where the level of consumption was low. The 1968 Sugar Agreement, more precisely, required members periodically to inform the Council of measures adopted in respect of customs duties on sugar, internal taxes, fiscal charges and quantitative or other

82

controls and established a Sugar Consumption Committee, composed of both exporting and importing members, to study the effects on sugar consumption of substitutes and taxation and to investigate means of promoting consumption. This committee was retained in subsequent sugar agreements.(14)

Measures on consumption included in the coffee agreements showed remarkable variation. The 1962 Coffee Agreement, for example, emphasised the need for 'a continuing programme' to promote the consumption of coffee and sanctioned the establishment of a Coffee Promotion Committee. In general, members were urged progressively to remove obstacles to trade in coffee.(15) The 1968 Coffee Agreement formalised the Promotion Committee and established a separate Diversification Fund, with a view to encouraging the production of alternative commodities. Participation in the Fund was compulsory for non-importers with export entitlements of over 100,000 sacks although voluntary participation was also permitted. Contributions were to be used for programmes approved by the Fund. In addition the International Coffee Council was sanctioned to promote studies on the opportunities for the expansion of coffee consumption.(16) Although the 1976 Coffee Agreement disposed of the Diversification Fund, it introduced the Promotion Fund, making more finance available via a compulsory levy on coffee exports. Importing members were also entitled to present proposals for coffee promotion.(17)

An interesting and unusual feature included in the 1972 Cocoa Agreement which should also be mentioned was the authority given to the Buffer Stock Manager to divert surplus cocoa to non-traditional uses when the quantity of cocoa held exceeded the maximum capacity of the buffer stock. The Agreement also authorised studies into the economics of cocoa production and consumption together with opportunities for its expansion.(18)

(7) Conclusions

Despite their variety of forms, each of the mechanisms used in international commodity agreements depended on domestic/national back-up measures. Some type of stock policy seems to have been required for the successful implementation of all of the agreements, and this helps to explain why stock provisions, national and international, were common features of the agreements. The difficulties faced by each type of control have been outlined above. A recurrent problem was the margin of error involved in forecasting future trends; this margin was greatest for agricultural crops owing to seasonal variations. Another difficulty was that, in order to be effective, agreements based on quotas required the participation of the major producers which could depend, in turn, on the ability to agree on a common forecast of future trends. Finally, the ability of the control mechanisms to operate effectively was dependent also on the power conferred on the operating body to police the agreement. In general, sanctions were couched in remedial rather than preventative terms with the withholding of future benefits arising from the agreement a common feature. The application of the mechanisms in practice is considered in Part III.

2. International (Raw Material) Cartels and Control Mechanisms
a. General

A cartel may be defined as a body of producers or traders in some class of business organised to reduce or defeat competition and to control production and/or distribution to their common advantage. (Such a cartel is called a trust when it consists of a combination of commercial and industrial companies with a central governing body of trustees which holds a majority or the whole of the stock of each of the combining firms, thus having a controlling vote in the conduct and operation of each.) In contrast to international commodity agreements, which have tended to be published, and, since the Second World War, specified in accordance with internationally accepted principles, cartels have usually been secret, if not a challenge or act of defiance (after the Italian cartello, a placard or challenge) to the principles of free trade. This has meant that it has often been difficult even to identify the existence of a cartel, still less to ascertain with any degree of certainty the terms of reference under which it operated. As a result, what follows relies of necessity on partial data based on survey, secondary and supporting statistical sources. It should also be noted that, despite the greater preponderance of industrial cartels,the discussion centres here on raw material cartels since the aim is to consider in what ways cartel action has differed from or posed a viable policy alternative to international commodity agreements.

b. Cartels before 1945

Between the Wars a League of Nations survey (published subsequently by the United Nations) identified twenty-two raw material cartels. (This compares with an unspecified but estimated far greater number of industrial cartels. It should be noted that the League's definition of a raw material cartel is broader than that used in this study.(19)) The cartels, whose main features are summarised in Table 4:2, covered petroleum (1928, 1929 and 1932), copper (1926 and 1935), lead (1931 and 1938), zinc (1928 and 1931), tin (1921 and 1931), wood pulp (1929, 1930 and 1935), rubber (1922 and 1934), aluminium (1926), mercury (1928), cement (1937), sulphur (1923), potash (1924) and phosphate rock (1933).

The aims of the inter-War cartels were very similar to those of the international commodity agreements negotiated in the same period: most aimed to stabilise prices within a given range in the context of falling levels; only a few were designed specifically to raise prices. Of the cartels with objectives which departed markedly from this mould, the potash cartel had as its main purpose the ending of price competition; the phosphate rock cartel aimed to increase US competition in Europe following the devaluation of the US dollar; and, in addition to their price stabilisation objectives, the 1926 Copper Cartel aimed to eliminate middlemen and the 1926 Aluminium Cartel to enable an exchange of patents.

The proliferation of cartels, like the international commodity agreements of the same period, was associated with the rapid expansion of commodity production during the First World War resulting both from increased demand and the desire of countries to compensate for the loss of previous sources of supply. The reconstruction boom that followed the War tended to stimulate further expansion and it was only when the boom slackened that surplus capacity in the raw material industries became a serious burden. An initial reaction to bridge the gap between output and demand was an attempt to secure additional outlets through expanded exports, a procedure often facilitated by tariff protection for many industries. The international price declines which ensued for many commodities then encouraged the negotiation of producer agreements to restore more stable marketing conditions.

The measures taken by raw material cartels were very similar to those adopted by international commodity agreements, namely, export quotas to allocate the markets available and/or production quotas to restrict output. Whereas international commodity agreements attempted to influence the price by volume, cartels in contrast usually adopted more specific pricing policies. The aluminium, mercury, tin and phosphate cartels, for example, provided for uniform export prices to be charged by members in all export markets. It was only occasionally, as for instance in the international zinc cartel, that export prices were not fixed and that restrictions on output provided the main mechanism. The pre- Second World War cartels were more precise than their international commodity agreement counterparts in the division of markets. National markets were usually reserved to national producers; export markets were divided up. Where market division provided the main control instrument, a common pricing policy was often not applied since the complete separation of markets permitted wider price differentials. The division of markets and the concomitant drastic reduction in competition was a feature of the potash, sulphur and phosphate cartels. The reservation of domestic markets to national producers was often aided by the imposition of protective tariffs.(20)

Table 4:2: International Raw Material Cartels in the Inter-War Period[a]

Product Covered	Date of Conclusion	Main Purpose	Main Activities	General Comments
Aluminium[a]	1926, renewed 1931	Exchange of patents and experience; reduction and stabilisation of prices.	Sales quotas for markets outside the US. Domestic market reservation. Prices fixed uniformly for all export markets. From 1931, restricted output.	Policy enhanced by rising level of demand.
Cement[a]	1937	Counteracting a sharp price decline.	Export quotas established. Fines and bonuses for under or over-production.	The cartel incorporated a network of bi-lateral agreements. It covered almost all export markets except for the US.
Chemical Wood Pulp[a] (Sulphite)	1930	Stabilisation of market.	Production restriction to 1935; then, export quotas.	–
Copper	1926	Stabilisation of prices; elimination of middlemen.	Prices fixed by two central offices; open market replaced by bargaining with each consumer; from 1929, restricted output.	Covered over 85 per cent of world production.
	1935	Stabilisation of prices.	Restricted output initially to 70 per cent of capacity; later, gradually relaxed the restriction.	–
Lead	1931	Raising and stabilisation of prices.	Restricted output.	Covered only about 50 per cent of output.
	1938	Raising and stabilisation of prices.	Restricted output.	–
Mechanical Wood Pulp[a]	1929	Stabilisation of market.	Restricted output.	–
	1935	Stabilisation of market.	Sharp export restriction to 50 per cent of capacity.	Prices remained low.
Mercury	1928, renewed 1939	Stabilisation of prices.	Established a common sales organisation and production quotas.	The pricing policy led reportedly to increased mercury production in the US and Mexico.
Crude Petroleum	1928	Division of the Indian market.	Division of the Indian market.	Although the three companies concerned, Standard Oil, Shell and Anglo-Persian, covered the bulk of world production, the cartel led to increased competition from outsiders.
	1929	Division of the European market.	Division of the European market.	

	Year	Objective	Methods	Comments
	1932	Maintenance of production at existing level.	Production and export quotas established for Romanian producers. A maximum output figure set for the US.	Included the same participants as the 1928 and 1929 cartels plus Romania. Romanian producers abandoned restrictions in 1933 when US producers exceeded the limit set.
Phosphate rock	1933	Increasing of US competition in Europe following the devaluation of the dollar.	Export quotas for European markets.	-
Potash	1924	Ending price competition.	A common export agency established in 1926. Some reservation of domestic markets and division of export markets.	The cartel, representing French interests, as part of Alsace-Lorraine, replaced a pre-First World War German government-controlled cartel.
Rubber[b]	1922	Raising and stabilisation of prices.	Restricted output and exports.	Expansion of output in Indonesia weakened the scheme.
Sulphur	1923	Counteracting a decline in prices.	Reservation of domestic markets to national producers; division of export markets. Sales prices fixed.	Cartel action weakened substantially by competition of sulphur made from pyrites.
Tin	1921	Disposal of surplus stocks.	Government purchases of stocks, releasing them in 1923.	Achieved its short-term objectives.
	1931	Counteracting a sharp price fall.	A buying pool established to hold stocks.	Introduced informally to support the 1931 Tin Agreement.
Zinc	1928	Raising and stabilisation of prices.	Restricted output from 1929.	Restriction stimulated expansion of output by outsiders.
	1931	Stabilising prices and liquidating stocks.	Restricted output and introduced a system of penalties and bonuses for under or over-production.	-

Note: a   For the League's definition of a (raw material) cartel, which is slightly different from that used in this study, see Note 19.

b   The 1934 Rubber Agreement accords to the definition of an international commodity agreement used in this study and is considered in Chapter 9.

Source: League of Nations, International Cartels (published subsequently by the United Nations, New York, 1947, II.D.2), Table 1.

Whereas international commodity agreements became common in the 1930s, international raw material cartels, with a few exceptions, such as the cartels for lead, cement and phosphate, had their origins in the 1920s. The measures taken, whilst alleviating immediate difficulties, did not affect the underlying problem of surplus capacity. Consequently a number of cartels failed to survive the Depression and, where they did, failed to prevent a severe fall in prices. Many were formed again after the Depression but abandoned in the late 1930s. Similarly, whereas international commodity agreements were applied to commodities in which developing countries led production, raw material cartels were concerned largely with commodities for which European producers had a greater participation rate. Examples included mercury, cement, potash and wood pulp; in another key cartel, copper, the US was the major producer. However, as outlined above, raw material cartels constituted only a small fraction of the total. One estimate, for example, suggests that as much as 42 per cent of total world trade between 1929 and 1937 was cartelised.(21)

c. Cartels since 1945

Post-Second World War cartels differed from their pre-War counterparts both in frequency and in objectives. Full data are not available but there appear to have been few major raw material cartels of importance during the 1940s and 1950s. In contrast, the 1960s marked the start of a flurry of cartel action (oil, copper and iron ore) which was carried forward and became intensified during the 1970s. By the mid-1970s, cartel action had become associated more with developing than developed countries and with attempts to push prices upward rather than with price stabilisation. This view, based largely on the casual observation of one cartel, OPEC, ignored the large number of industrial cartels which existed in developed countries and the fact that some raw material cartels, such as that for iron ore, were dominated by developed country exporters.(22)

The raw material cartel attracting most public attention was OPEC, associated as it was with sharp rises in oil prices during the 1970s. In addition to OPEC, other examples included the International Bauxite Association (IBA, 1974), the Uranium Cartel (1972), the International Association of Mercury Producers (ASSIMER, 1975), the Conseil Intergouvernemental des Pays Exportateurs de Cuivre (CIPEC, 1966) and the Association of Iron Ore Exporting Countries (AIEC, 1974). Mention should also be made of the cartel-styled action applied to coffee, rubber and tea which will be discussed in the individual chapters on these commodities.

Overall, a shift took place in the aims of post-War raw material cartels which mirrored the shift in the objectives of international commodity agreements. The main thrust was in favour of attempting to secure higher receipts from the exported raw material rather than focussing simply on price stabilisation measures. It reflected the perception of primary producers and exporting countries that their real incomes had been or were being eroded and that the international terms of trade were working in the favour of manufactured goods rather than raw materials. In contrast to pre-War cartels, it is interesting to note that those following the War seem to have been motivated at least as much, if not more, by developing rather than developed countries even though the production of the commodities in question was often led by developed country participants. However, exceptions to this rule were uranium, where North-American producers took the leading role, and mercury, where developing country producers accounted for a very small proportion of total output.(23)

A related change in emphasis of several of the post-War cartels, notably the IBA and OPEC, was the desire to secure more complete national control over the commodity in question. In addition to traditional control mechanisms, such as stock withdrawal and production restrictions, nationalisation measures and the increasing of royalties and levies on foreign producers were also used in pursuit of the cartels' broader objectives, particularly where the resource in question was non-renewable. In the case of OPEC, political objectives also provided a major and clearly articulated under-current. A further interesting feature was that the initiative for cartel action often came from the dominant producer or price leader, for example, Brazil in the case of coffee and Jamaica in the case of bauxite.

d. Conclusion

It is clear from even a brief appraisal such as this that cartels for raw materials called on a far wider range of mechanisms than their international commodity agreement counterparts. This should not disguise the fact, however, that in general the most commonly used techniques were the same - export and production controls and stock withdrawal - and that the overriding aims of the agreements were often comparable. It is worth pointing out that the dividing line between international commodity agreements and cartels was an extremely fine one, particularly before the Second World War, when consumers were infrequently represented in either. In their latter-day aims of raising export earnings, some international commodity agreements continued a close association with the objectives of cartel-styled action and, as illustrated in Part III, producer interests reverted to cartelisation when it appeared to them that the international agreement did not represent their interests to the full. The existence of an international commodity agreement, then, in no way precluded the existence, even contemporaneously, of a cartel for the same commodity.

Where cartels have shown the clearest differentiation from international commodity agreements has been in the scale of participation - on average, far less with little consumer participation - their lesser degree of international acceptability and the strength of common interest which spurred producers to attempt to challenge current economic conditions. It is also possible that the general lack of public disclosure of debates between participants provided cartels with an environment which worked in favour of their survival rather than their disintegration, in contrast to the greater degree of exposure experienced by international commodity organisations. However, although the general absence in cartels of large-scale back-up organisations with various administrative committees may have speeded the decision-making process, less opportunity was available, by the same token, for consultative discussion in the event of a breakdown.

Notes

1   On the general subject of fair labour standards see also U. Kullemann, 'Fair labour standards in International Commodity Agreements', Journal of World Trade Law, vol. 14, no. 6 (November:December 1980) and P. Alston, 'Commodity Agreements - As Though People Don't Matter', Journal of World Trade Law, vol. 15, no. 5 (September-October 1981).   G. Hansson, Social Clauses and International Trade (Croom Helm, London, 1983), also offers an interesting general account of social clauses in trade policy.

2   'International Cocoa Agreement, 1975' (HMSO, London, 1976, Cmnd. 6448), Article 1 and 'International Cocoa Agreement, 1980' (UNCTAD, Geneva, 1980, TD/Cocoa.6/7).

3   Pertot, International Economics of Control, p. 120.

4   GATT, Trends in International Trade, pp. 75-6.

5   See for example G.K. Helleiner, International Trade and Economic Development (Penguin, Middlesex, 1972), p. 57.

6   As early as 1937, the League of Nations Raw Materials Committee recommended the formation of a buffer stock with both consumer and producer participation as a possible method of 'correcting excessive movements in price, particularly in an upward direction . . .' However, such techniques were viewed as being essentially ancillary to regulation schemes, as in the case of the early tin agreements, in marked contrast to schemes propounded at the United Nations Conference on Food and Agriculture in 1943.   At the latter, for example, the UK delegation submitted a declaration of principle suggesting that a long-term balancing of supply and demand might be achieved, together with a reasonable return for the most efficient producers, by buffer stock action.   See League of Nations, Report of the Committee for the Study of the Problem of Raw Materials, pp. 56-62 and Ibid., 'Extract from General Statement issued to the Press by the Chairman of the United Kingdom Delegation to the United Nations Conference on Food and Agriculture', in ILO, Intergovernmental Commodity Agreements, pp. 155-56.

7   GATT, Trends in International Trade, pp. 71-2.

8   A. Maizels, Selected Issues in the Negotiation of International Commodity Agreements: an Economic Analysis (UNCTAD, Geneva, 1982, TD/B/C.1/244), p. 14.

9   D.L. McNicol, Commodity Agreements and Price Stabilization (Lexington Books, Lexington, Mass., 1978), pp. 64-5. The literature on buffer stocks is copious. See for examples M.K. Bennett, International Commodity Stockpiling as an Economic Stabilizer (Stanford University Press, Stanford, 1949), J. Colebrook, 'The Cost of Stocking Primary Commodities', Journal of World Trade Law, vol. 11, no. 4 (July:August 1977), W.C. Labys, Optimal Portfolio Analysis of Multicommodity Stocking Arrangements (University of West Virginia Press, Morgantown, 1976) and F.H. Weymar, 'The Supply of Storage Revisited', American Economic Review, vol. 56 (December 1976).   UNCTAD has also published a substantial volume of work on this subject.   See UNCTAD, A Common Fund for the Financing of Commodity Stocks: Suitability for Stocking of Individual Commodities: Country Contributions and Burden Sharing, and some Operating Principles (UNCTAD, Geneva, 1975, TD/B/C.1/1969).

10   See for examples 'International Coffee Agreement, 1962' (US, Department of State, Washington, 1962), Articles 44-5 and 'International Cocoa Agreement, 1975', Articles 55-6.

11   'International Wheat Agreement' (US, Department of State, Washington, 1949), Parts 2 and 3.

12   See Chapter 7 for a more detailed account.

13   'Final Act of the Conference of Wheat Exporting and Importing Countries' (25 August 1933) in ILO, Intergovernmental Commodity Agreements, Article 6 and 'Agreement for the Regulation of Production and Export of Rubber' (7 May 1934) in ILO, Intergovernmental Commodity Agreements, pp. 104-13, Article 19.

14   For a more detailed account see Chapters 8 and 13. For the 1968 Sugar Agreement, see 'International Sugar Agreement' (HMSO, London, 1969, Cmnd. 3887).

15   'International Coffee Agreement, 1962' (US, Department of State, Washington, 1962).

16   'International Coffee Agreement, 1968' (International Coffee Organization, London, 1968), Articles 46, 47, 52, 54 and 56.

17   'International Coffee Agreement, 1976' (HMSO, London, 1976, Cmnd. 6505), Articles 47 and 48.

18   'International Cocoa Agreement, 1972' in International Cocoa Conference 1972 (United Nations, New York, 1973, TD/COCOA 3/9), Articles 45, 51 and 57.

19   League of Nations, International Cartels (published subsequently by the United Nations, New York, 1947, II.D.2), pp. 1-7. The League's definition of a cartel ('voluntary agreements among independent enterprises in a single industry or closely-related industries with the purpose of exercising a monopolistic control of the market') was slightly different from that used in this study. The League included as a cartel the 1934 Rubber Agreement even though the Agreement was negotiated under government auspices and did not seek monopolistic powers.

20   League of Nations, International Cartels, p. 20 reported that so close was the association between cartels and tariffs that in 1927 it was proposed at the World Economic Conference that a comprehensive network of international cartels be set up to replace tariffs. The general attitude to this proposal, however, was that the undesirable effects of cartels - high prices, restricted output, exploitation of the consumer - and the difficulty of supervision gave rise to serious objections. See also W. Berge, Cartels: Challenge to a Free World (Public Affairs Press, Washington, 1944) and C. Edwards, Economic and Political Aspects of International Cartels (US Government Printing Office, Washington, 1944).

21   E. Hexner, 'International Cartels in the Postwar World', Southern Economic Journal (October 1943), p. 124, F.A. Fetter, The Masquerade of Monopoly (Harcourt Brace, New York, 1931) and W. Oualid, International Raw Materials (Paris, 1939).

22   See for example Szuprowicz, How to avoid Strategic Materials Shortages, p. 38. The OECD in 1974 identified several hundred manufacturing cartels in Germany, Japan, the Netherlands, Spain, the UK and the US. See OECD, Export Cartels (OECD, Paris, 1974).

23   In 1970, for example, Mexico was the only developing country producing a significant amount of world mercury. See Commodity Research Bureau, Commodity Yearbook 1981 (New York, 1981), p. 219. See also P.L. Eckbo, Opec and the Experience of Previous International Commodity Cartels (Massachusetts Institute of Technology, Cambridge, Mass., 1975), F. Kottke, The Promotion of Price Competition where Sellers are Few and H. Kronstein, The Law of International Cartels (Cornell University Press, Ithaca, 1973).

5: NATIONAL COUNTERPARTS AND ALTERNATIVES

> 'The contracting parties . . . commit themselves to reduce trade frictions, overcome protectionist pressures, avoid using exports subsidies inconsistent with . . . Gatt and promote the liberalisation and expansion of trade.'

(GATT Declaration, November 1982)

1. General

International commodity controls relied for their implementation on counterpart measures applied at the national and regional level. These included production quotas, export quotas and national stock policies - all of which have already been discussed in Chapter 4. In addition to these counterpart measures, additional alternative or, in some cases, countervailing measures have also been applied at the national and regional level. Those already considered include the introduction of trading preferences, farm support policies, regulated pricing systems and national strategic stockpiles (Chapter 3). There remains to consider finally the national and regional mechanisms alternative to those employed in international commodity agreements. This chapter, accordingly, offers a brief over-view of six instruments of trade policy - the tariff, the tariff quota, the state trading monopoly, the embargo, the import quota and the subsidy - which have had an important impact, direct and indirect, on primary commodity trade. For those already familiar with these instruments, it will add nothing new. For those, in contrast, who are not, it is hoped that it will demonstrate the other national and regional controls which have an important bearing on international trade in commodities.(1)

2. The Tariff

The inclusion of the tariff in this selective review requires little justification. The impact of the tariff was demonstrated forcibly in the Depression when the imposition by the US of the protective Hawley-Smoot Tariff in 1930 set in train retaliatory measures by many other countries and contributed to a fall in the quantum of world trade. As one source commented, 'country after country cracked down on imports, seeking to stimulate domestic production by protecting business against foreign competition'.(2) A basic tenet governing trade policy after the Second World War, in reaction, was that a general reduction in tariffs was desirable since, it was anticipated, it would lead to an increase in world trade to the benefit of producers of primary and manufactured goods alike. It was the failure of successive post-War tariff rounds to produce the expected result, especially with regard to agricultural products, which encouraged developing countries to seek the multi-faceted approach to trade issues via the Integrated Programme (Chapter 2).

What, then, are the distinctive qualities of the tariff as an instrument of trade policy?

The tariff is essentially a tax levied on the import or export of goods entering a country, in transit within a country or leaving a country. It has been characterised by a multiplicity of forms, the most common of which has been the ad valorem tariff levied as a percentage of the total value of the commodity. Less common has been the duty levied on individual units of a commodity, known as a specific tariff. Occasionally compound duties have been imposed consisting of a combination of a specific and an ad valorem tariff. Commodities have been defined in tariff schedules with varying degrees of detail subject to frequent revision, re-definition and adjustment. In addition to the different types of tariff, different tariff rates may be imposed depending on the country of origin of the commodity.

The tariff owes its prominent role in economic history to a variety of reasons. First, it has provided a relatively straightforward and simple device for collecting taxes. As Helleiner has suggested, where accounting skills are scarce, administrative competence imperfect and record keeping rare, it is difficult to raise revenue through income and property taxation. Therefore, the tariff has been considered one of 'the easiest and cheapest devices for collecting taxes in poor countries' since produce passing in or out of a country is normally funnelled through relatively few ports or border posts at which administrative control is feasible. This function was as important to the English Staple Act of 1663, which laid down that all goods, English or foreign, intended for the colonies, should be shipped from an English port in order to increase the yield of the customs, as it is at the present for most developing countries, where foreign trade taxes constitute the major source of government revenues.(3)

94

However, the revenue effect of the tariff is only part of the explanation for its longevity. Perhaps equally important has been the perception of its protective function. The reasons behind the quest for protection have varied over time: the English Plantation Duties Act of 1673, for example, which placed a substantial export duty on certain commodities shipped from one colony to another, was designed both to protect English shippers and the monopoly of the mother country over colonial trade. The use of the tariff in the continental system in France, on the other hand, was partly a response to the loss of colonial trade in war-time, partly a policy of economic warfare against the British and partly a plan to encourage the development of French industry.(4) In the international trade crisis of the 1870s, as in that of the 1930s, cries for protection by higher tariffs came both from agrarian and industrial interests as prices fell in the face of shrinking markets. Since the Second World War, selective protection by tariffs has been justified on the grounds of the need to nurture infant industries, especially in developing countries, where tariff protection is often accompanied by import quotas.(5)

If revenue and protective reasons appear to have provided the principal motivating forces behind the introduction of tariffs, a number of other effects have also governed the decision by policy-makers to use the tariff as an instrument of commercial policy. A notable example has been the desire to correct payments imbalances.(6) It has been a common practice, for example, to cut back on the import of goods deemed to be 'non-essential' while continuing to permit entry of capital goods and intermediate inputs to domestic industries free of any restrictions. The initial balance of payments effect of a tariff may be to alter the volume of imports or exports. However, the ultimate balance of payments effect depends on the total income effect: if income diverted from imports/exports is spent then, if the country is not in a condition of full employment, income and employment may be raised. Conversely, in the country whose exports are reduced by the tariff, the reverse effect would apply. This 'beggar-my-neighbour' attitude has been criticised as a means of exporting unemployment.

The theoretical literature on the subject of the tariff has devoted considerable space to assessing both the variety of factors motivating its imposition and ways of measuring its impact. These have included a consideration of the redistributive effect of duties in changing the level of internal prices, the terms of trade effect - whether or not the country imposing the tariff improves its terms of trade by acquiring imports more cheaply - and the cost of protection. No justice can be done here to the wide range of empirical work which has been conducted on the subject.(7) It is sufficient to note that, in contrast to international commodity agreements, the tariff represents a relatively flexible instrument of trade policy which can

95

assume many forms. In function, however, the differences between the two instruments are less pronounced. Both on occasion have attempted to raise revenue or earnings deriving from the commodity to which they were applied. Finally, both can also have important repercussions for the balance of payments of the country in which they are applied. It is these common functions which have led policy-makers to perceive international commodity agreements as alternative channels via which to pursue the same or similar goals.

3. The Tariff Quota

In addition to the tariff, which acts through the price mechanism, a related national control instrument is the tariff quota. This allows a specified amount of a commodity to be imported duty-free or at a lower rate of duty; imports in excess of that amount are subject to a higher tariff. The tariff quota thus combines the features of the tariff and the quota, which, as outlined in Chapter 4, reduces trade by means of quantitative controls. Tariff quotas, like tariffs, have been legal under GATT provided that they have been administered in a non-discriminatory fashion.

Examples of the use of tariff quotas include the EEC with its common external tariff. In order to avoid the danger of encouraging a first come, first served mentality, an upper limit was placed on what any one country could supply under a given tariff quota. These limits ('butoirs') added to an already complex administrative machinery: imports subject to tariff quotas had to be accompanied by an import licence. Tariff quotas were also favoured on an occasional basis by the US. An example was the imposition of tariff quotas at the beginning of the 1960s to prevent excessive quantities of cheaper foreign oil from entering the country. Overall, however, tariff quotas have occupied only a minor place in international commercial policy compared with the widespread use of tariffs.(8)

4. State Trading Monopolies and Embargoes

A state trading monopoly on either the export or the import of a commodity is perhaps the most clearly defined national control mechanism. Essentially a refinement of quantitative import control, under this method all trade is channelled via state-operated organisations which regulate the amount of the commodity to be purchased or sold. The devices used under this system are frequently bulk purchase agreements and bi-lateral trade agreements. Under the former, the importer agrees to purchase a certain quantity of a commodity from suppliers. Under the latter, an agreement is made with another government for purchases to be made for a specific period of time, which may or may not be extended.

Scammell has identified three levels of state trading: trade involving state agencies in mixed economies; trade between a fully collectivised state, buying and selling through state agencies, and private enterprises in a mixed economy; and trade between two fully collectivised states. The state agencies may buy for public or for government consumption.(9) Although a genus most commonly associated with Soviet bloc countries, state-trading monopolies have by no means been confined to centrally planned economies. During the Second World War, for example, the UK Government regulated the importation of staple commodities to a large degree through bulk purchase agreements negotiated by the Ministry of Food and various boards were appointed to regulate specific sectors of trade and industry. Similarly, long-term agreements have proved a common feature of international trade in wheat and have tended to be negotiated at the government level.

As an alternative to international commodity controls, state trading arrangements may provide a greater element of assurance both for the producer and for the consumer. At their most successful, they may enable long runs of production for a guaranteed market within an agreed price framework. However, by their nature, bi-lateral trading agreements may be susceptible to sudden disruption. Examples include the cancellation of US sugar contracts with Cuba in the early 1960s (Chapter 8) and the partial US embargo on exports of wheat to the USSR in 1980 (Chapter 7). The resulting embargoes on exports or imports, however temporary, may have far-reaching and sustained effects which, like tariffs, may apply to the whole of a country's trade, to individual articles or groups of articles or only to sales to or purchases from certain countries. The economic impact of an embargo depends on the conditions under which it is introduced so that no generalisations are possible. However, embargoes may in principle have a strong influence on international prices and as such constitute an extreme instrument of economic policy.(10)

5. Import Quotas

Whereas the tariff restricts imports/exports through the price mechanism, leaving quantities free to find their own level, the quota, as outlined in Chapter 4, restricts the volume of goods traded. As a result, import quotas have been described as 'the most restrictive selective measures used to limit trade'.(11) Import quotas on raw materials have been applied more commonly before 1945 than since, with the Depression witnessing their proliferation in a number of European countries. Subsequent examples, though less frequent, have proved an important factor in respect of a few leading commodities such as sugar and coffee (Chapters 8 and 10).

Like export quotas, import quotas require a bureaucracy to administer what may be an elaborate system of licensing, the conventional method by which individuals may import specific quantities or values of the commodity. The quotas have tended to be determined in proportion to the pattern of trade at a fixed base period during which such trade was free so that, in their allocative function, such controls have favoured old-established importers for whom the right to a quota will become a valuable asset.(12) The impact of import quotas has been the subject of great debate which is beyond the scope of this study. It is sufficient to note here that by offering protection to selected domestic producers, such quotas could have a distorting and potentially restraining effect not only on the domestic economy but also on foreign producers of the commodity in question. This distortion could be magnified when political rather than economic factors determined the allocation of the quota between foreign suppliers (see Chapter 8 for the case of sugar).(13)

6. Subsidies

It has been the subsidy to domestic production which has provided the most explicit example of the way in which national control measures can bear directly on international commodity trading conditions. Whereas the impact of the tariff and of quotas has tended to be indirect, subsidies have directly affected levels of production and production costs. Similarly, subsidies on exports or in the form of export credit provisions bear directly on the financing costs of such trade.

A subsidy, after the latin subsidium meaning aid, is an expense rather than an increase in government revenues. It consists of a grant or a contribution of money furnished by the State or a public corporation in addition to the market price of the commodity or product. Although they may assume different names - premia, subventions, concessions, incentives - all forms of subsidy imply a limitation of government consumption by an increase in expenditure. They may be granted to industries considered to be in unusual economic difficulties or deserving assistance on national, defence or other grounds, to attract new industries to certain areas, or to stimulate the export of a specific commodity or industrial product. Dumping is deemed to occur when goods are sold abroad at a price below that prevailing on the home market.

Examples of the conferral of subsidies are manifold although for the purposes of this discussion only those applying to raw materials are of direct interest. The agricultural sector of developed countries provides the clearest illustration: reference has already been made to the price supports and export subsidies applied under the EEC's Common Agricultural Policy and to the subsidy schemes governing certain farm sectors in the US. Further illustrations are provided in subsequent chapters. These include the bounty system, which facilitated the expansion of beet sugar production in Europe in the nineteenth century (Chapter 8) and the extensive use of subsidies in the wheat sector in North America (Chapter 7). Agricultural subsidies have been used either to reduce the cost of agricultural input, such as fertiliser, or to increase farm prices. The latter has been attempted either by the payment of a fixed sum per unit or by deficiency payments, under which the government makes up the difference between a guaranteed price and the market price. As Hallett has suggested in a recent study, the use of deficiency payments requires an adequate administrative framework and is limited ultimately by budgetary constraints.(14)

International attention has focussed on subsidies deemed to lead to dumping: anti-dumping legislation was introduced in Canada, for example, as early as 1904. As outlined in Chapter 2, an Anti-Dumping Code was incorporated in GATT under the Kennedy Round. This condemned dumping which caused or threatened to cause material injury to an established industry in the territory of a contracting party or which materially retarded the establishment of a domestic industry. In contrast, dumping which arose from a commodity stabilisation scheme in the exporting country was permissible if the parties concerned determined that the scheme did not unduly stimulate exports.(15)

7. Conclusion

International commodity agreements have been described as the direct opposites of instruments specifically influencing internal relative prices such as tariffs, premia, quotas and embargoes with bi-lateral and multi-lateral contracts considered to be an intermediate group of instruments affecting both internal and external relative prices.(16) It is the contention of this chapter that distinctions are in practice less finely drawn. Although each of the instruments approached policy from a different angle to that of international commodity agreements, their objectives were in several cases remarkably similar. For example, tariffs also aimed to raise revenue or earnings deriving from the commodity concerned, state trading monopolies to increase the security of supply at assured prices and import quotas to control the volume of the commodity traded. Furthermore, where the country imposing a tariff or a subsidy, for example, was a major producer/consumer, as in the case of North-American wheat production, the 'spill-over' effect on international trade and, in consequence, for international endeavours collectively to control such trade, could be large.

Notes

1   For examples of the detailed literature available on these subjects see H.G. Johnson (ed.), Trade Strategy for Rich and Poor Nations (Toronto University Press, Toronto, 1971), B. Balassa (ed.), Studies in Trade Liberalisation (Johns Hopkins University Press, Baltimore, 1967), W.M. Corden, The Theory of Protection (Oxford University Press, London, 1971), G. and V. Curzon, Hidden Barriers to International Trade (Trade Policy Research Centre, London, 1971) and J. Bhagwati, 'On the Equivalence of Tariffs and Quotas' in R.E. Baldwin (ed.), Trade, Growth and the Balance of Payments: Essays in Honour of Gottfried Haberler (North-Holland Publishing Co., Amsterdam, 1966).

2   P.B. Kenen and R. Lubitz, International Economics (Prentice-Hall, New Jersey, 1971) on the 1914-1939 period and R.H. Ferrell, American Diplomacy in the Great Depression (Yale University Press, New Haven, 1957).

3   Helleiner, International Trade and Economic Development, p. 112.

4   A. Milward and S.B. Saul, The Economic Development of Continental Europe (Allen & Unwin, London, 1973), p. 268 and J.H. Parry, Europe and a Wider World, 1415-1715 (Hutchinson, London, 1977), p. 124.

5   See for instance T. Kemp, Industrialization in Nineteenth Century Europe (Longman, London, 1976), pp. 28-9.

6   Pertot, International Economics of Control, pp. 90-1.

7   See for examples W.M. Scammell, International Trade and Payments (Macmillan, London, 1974) and B. Balassa, The Structure of Protection in Developing Countries (Johns Hopkins University Press, Baltimore, 1971).

8   See M. Rom, The Role of Tariff Quotas in Commercial Policy (Macmillan, London, 1979), G. Patterson, Discrimination in International Trade - the Policy Issues (Princeton University Press, Princeton, 1966) and Curzon, Hidden Barriers to International Trade.

9   Scammell, International Trade and Payments, pp. 235-36.

10   Pertot, International Economics of Control, pp. 129-30. If embargoes are the most public and explicit of government controls on trade, there are a number of other ways in which governments can discriminate in terms of trade more discreetly but perhaps equally pervasively. The first area is in terms of customs valuation practices. There is no common system for classifying goods for tariff valuation nor a uniform valuation base for assessing tariffs. An example of discrimination in this area is the American selling price system under which imports were valued at the selling price of similar products sold in the US rather than at the wholesale price. An example was the application of the selling price to imports of benzenoid chemicals, a system introduced in 1922, designed to provide the domestic industry with a high protective wall. Such practices may create uncertainty which may in turn adversely affect planning. Under the Kennedy Round, the US conditionally agreed to abolish the system, although this was opposed by Congress.

In addition to restrictive customs procedures, border adjustments for internal taxes may also provide a form of restrictive trade practice. An example is found in the case of Germany where in 1970 most foreign products entered with a tax of 11 per cent on the import plus duty value of the goods.

In his pioneering work on the subject Baldwin lists a number of other areas in which governments exercise control over both visible and invisible trade. These include discriminatory government procurement policies, such as Buy British and Made in Canada campaigns, the solicitation of bids for government contracts together with the timing and information on bidding requirements, and controls over foreign investment. The latter case may be considered to be important in the production of a number of commodities, such as oil, bauxite and copper. It is important to note that unlike international controls, such as national controls, particularly of a governmental nature, may be public or discreet, blanket or limited in scope, and independent or linked to other forms of control. As such, they present complex economic forces which defy precise quantification.

11 R.E. Baldwin, Non-Tariff Distortions of International Trade, p. 30.

12 See for example I.F. Pearce, International Trade, (Macmillan, London, 1970), Book I, pp. 250-52 and H. Heuser, Control of International Trade (George Routledge, London, 1939), Part I. French restrictions were imposed on flax, wood, wine, cattle, meat and sugar, for example, in 1931-32. By the end of 1936, practically all agricultural commodities were limited by quotas. Similar examples are provided by other countries such as Holland and Switzerland.

13 See, for example, M.F.G. Scott, W.M. Corden and I.M.D. Little, The Case Against General Import Restrictions (Trade Policy Research Centre, London, 1980) for the case against import controls.

14 Hallett, The Economics of Agricultural Policy, pp. 206-12. Literature on agricultural price and income support policies is, of course, abundant. See for example United Nations, Food and Agriculture Organization, An Enquiry into the Problems of Agricultural Price Stabilisation and Support Policies (United Nations, Food and Agriculture Organization, Rome, 1960), P. Streeten, 'The Case for Export Subsidies', Journal of Development Studies, vol. 5, no. 4 (1969), D.N. Balaam and M.J. Carey, Food Politics: The Regional Conflict (Croom Helm, London, 1981) and United Nations Food and Agriculture Organization, 'New Protectionism and Attempts at Liberalization in Agricultural Trade', Food and Agriculture Organization Commodity Review and Outlook 1979-80, no. 17.

15 R. de C. Grey, The Development of the Canadian Anti-Dumping System (Private Planning Association of Canada, Montreal, 1973), GATT, The Role of GATT in relation to Trade and Development, R. Dale, Anti-Dumping Law in a Liberal Trade Order (Macmillan, London, 1980), P. Lloyd, Anti-dumping Actions and the GATT System (Trade Policy Research Centre, London, 1977), J. Viner, Dumping: A Problem in International Trade (University of Chicago Press, Chicago, 1923) and C. Phegan, 'GATT Article XVI.3: Export Subsidies and 'Equitable Shares'', Journal of World Trade Law, vol. 16, no. 3 (May:June 1982).

16 Pertot, International Economics of Control, p. 146.

PART III : INTERNATIONAL CONTROL IN PRACTICE

Introduction

The previous sections have established the framework and the techniques of international commodity control. This section, conversely, will adopt a commodity-by-commodity approach. It makes no apology for doing so for just as international commodity controls for each commodity cannot fully be understood without reference to the international context and to the control mechanisms used, so too the international context and control mechanisms cannot fully be appreciated without reference to controls on a commodity-by-commodity basis. By combining both approaches the aim is to paint, albeit with a broad brush, a picture of international commodity control which is three-dimensional rather than one.

The discussion which follows considers first the cases of tin, wheat and sugar, the commodities which have been subject to the most frequent international commodity agreement action since the 1930s and which may be considered, therefore, of major importance to the history of international controls. It goes on to examine controls for rubber, the tropical beverages and olive oil, commodities for which international agreements have been regular but less frequent. Finally, it deals with examples of those commodities, such as crude petroleum, copper, mercury, bauxite, uranium and iron ore, for which cartelisation rather than formally negotiated international commodity agreements has been of major importance.

6: TIN

'The Tin Agreement can be regarded as a kind of pilot study for the development of world commodity policy. It is an exercise in international co-operation demonstrably effective in its application.'

(Harold W. Allen, Executive Chairman, International Tin Council, 1975)

1. General

As outlined in Chapter 1, tin is a relatively minor commodity in world trade in value terms. However, as the object of the most regular international commodity agreements since 1930 and of producer action in the 1920s and 1980s, as a commodity exported principally by developing countries and as a core commodity under UNCTAD's Integrated Programme, tin must occupy a central place in any history of international commodity control. As such, it is assigned more space in this analysis than if ranked purely on the basis of its importance in world trade.

The essential properties of tin are its appearance, a soft white-gray colour, its malleability, its low melting point, its corrosion resistance and its lack of tenacity. A metal known and highly valued from remote times, tin was in all probability used in the alloy bronze for an indefinite period before it was known in its separate condition. As a non-renewable metal with limited scrap reclamation value, tin has also become a commodity of strategic importance and for the US, in particular, tin has featured as an important element in the domestic government stockpile established in 1946. Only a few countries, Bolivia, Malaysia and Rwanda, currently depend on tin for a large proportion of their export earnings.(1)

Although for two thousand years the South-West of England was the world's principal source, the conspicuous feature of world tin production in the twentieth century has been its concentration in the hands of four countries: Malaysia, which has generally dominated about a third of the world total and which, as outlined below, has exercised an influential role in international policy on tin; Indonesia and Thailand, which between them have accounted for about a quarter; and Bolivia, which in 1930 accounted for about a quarter and more recently for only one-seventh. A fourth South-East Asian producer, Burma, has not operated on a large scale in global terms since the 1930s. Elsewhere, Nigeria played an important role in the 1920s but since the end of the 1960s has dwindled in terms of world tin production and Zaire emerged as a major producer in the 1930s but subsequently became less important. More recently, Brazil has entered the world arena as a major participant since the 1960s and Australia has re-entered since the 1960s with the emphasis on producing tin from low-grade deposits. In the UK, Cornish tin production showed signs of revival in the 1960s but subsequently met with difficulties owing to the low grades of deposits. China and the USSR, each major producers, are perforce excluded from the market shares owing to paucity of data. However the USSR, at least, has been an influential force in the world trade of tin in terms of periodic sales and purchases.(2)

About 80 per cent of non-communist world tin production comes from unconsolidated alluvial deposits and the rest from mines, chiefly in Bolivia. Compared with commercially viable deposits of copper, lead, zinc, nickel and bauxite, tin deposits are generally small. Alluvial ores are extracted by means of simple panning (for example, in Malaysia), the use of gravel pumps and by dredging (a mechanised and floating factory limited to South-East Asia). Of these, the dredge method is considered the more expensive but is expected to have a longer working life.

Production costs have also varied enormously from country to country, with Bolivian mines and Indonesian gravel enterprises generally experiencing the highest. They have been raised generally by the lower quality of ore exploited since the Second World War. An important factor affecting relative costs between countries has been government taxation, which in Bolivia, for example, appears to have provided a disincentive to new investment. A number of other influences, including the loss of Chinese workers after the abortive Communist coup in Indonesia in 1962, the aftermath of nationalisation in Bolivia and civil war in Zaire, meant that, with the exception of 1940 and 1941, a pre-Second World War production peak in 1937 was not matched until the early 1970s (Table 6:1).(3)

The marketing of tin is conducted in a variety of ways: by supply contracts between governments, by direct sales by agencies, by traders and merchants and by competitive bids. The price is

Table 6:1: World Production of Tin-in-Concentrates,
1921-25 to 1980 (metric tons)[a]

Year	Total
1921-1925[b]	124,765
1930	174,752
1935	131,064
1937	201,600
1940	226,568
1945	87,376
1950	164,897
1955	170,688
1960	138,684
1965	154,330
1970	185,900
1972	202,300
1975	180,800
1980	199,700

Notes: a   figures exclude China, the USSR and the Democratic
               Republic of Germany and refer to the tin metal
               content of tin-in-concentrates.

           b   average per year

Sources: derived from International Tin Council, Statistical
           Yearbook 1968 (International Tin Council, London, 1969),
           pp. 22-3, Ibid., Tin Statistics 1968-1978 (International Tin
           Council, London, n.d.), pp. 17 and 22 and World Bureau of
           Metal Statistics, World Metal Statistics (London, February
           1982), p. 96.

determined on one of three markets: the London Metal Exchange,
Penang and New York.
      Smelting operations are dominated by nine major companies,
four of which are controlled by the Patiño group. Before the Second
World War, Western European smelters handled one-third of non-
communist output and the US had no smelting facilities. Since then,
the share of smelting conducted in Western Europe has contracted
while, in contrast, smelting by the US and by developing (producer)
countries has increased.
      Only Australia, South Africa, the UK and Brazil of non-
centrally planned tin producing countries consume a large proportion

106

of their tin; most export the major part although tin traded goes to a relatively small number of industrialised countries, led by the US and including the UK, Germany, France and, more recently, Japan. The US share has fallen from about a half in the late 1920s to about a third in the late 1970s, and that of the UK from about a seventh to only a fifteenth. In contrast, the share taken by Japan has increased substantially from a negligible proportion in the 1920s to about a fifth in the late 1970s.

In its refined form, tin has a variety of uses. During the twentieth century, the manufacture of tinplate (steel - formerly iron - sheets coated with tin) has led consumption (40 to 45 per cent), with the tinplate used, owing to its resistance to oxidisation, for lining culinary and other articles, notably the tin can. Another major use is in combination with lead to form tin alloys known as solders (20 to 25 per cent). Solders are used for making joints in electrical and electronic products and, particularly before the Second World War, in plumbing. Finally, tin is employed with white metal alloys for composite use, in the formation of alloys such as bronze and to form pewter, and for a variety of lesser purposes such as in anti-friction metal, chemicals and collapsible tubes and foil.

The volume of tin consumption fell slightly between 1929 and 1979 in the face of a number of influences. First, the development of the electrolytic process in the 1930s and its introduction on a large scale during the Second World War nearly halved the amount of tin required to produce tinplate.(4) Secondly, restrictions imposed on the use of tin in the UK and the US during the Second World War encouraged the development of aluminium as a substitute for tin as canning material, foil and collapsible tubing. Since compared with other base metals tin is essentially an expensive material, the impact of substitution over the long term has been important even though the cost of tin is generally a small proportion of the total cost of the end-product. According to Robertson in his recent study, the competitive position of tin undoubtedly weakened in the post-War period. This helps to explain the sustained interest of producers in international controls on tin.(5)

International controls on tin have fallen into two phases: those introduced before the Second World War, which consisted essentially of agreements between producing countries, and those introduced during or after the Second World War, which involved the participation of consumers or consuming countries (in accordance with the principles outlined in the Havana Charter). The former were supported initially by cartel-styled action. The latter, in contrast, operated on average in a far more open and consultative fashion (although the operation of the 1980 Tin Agreement has led to criticism by consumers that producers were secretly manipulating the market). Each will be considered in turn.

2. Tin Controls to 1939

The first major attempt at governmental control on tin production was recorded in 1921 when, in a period of sluggish growth in consumption and falling prices, the governments of Indonesia and Malaysia agreed to withhold stocks in order to secure higher prices in what became known as the Bandoeng Pool. The arrangement succeeded in its short-term objective: by 1923 world tin prices had risen to £202.25 per ton from £165.375 on average in 1921 and the governments released the accumulated stocks from the pool. Between 1924 and 1926, tin prices remained high due to strong consumer demand.(6) This encouraged substantial new investment, particularly in Malaysia and Bolivia, which led to a production peak of 195,682 metric tons in 1929, rapid rises in stocks (from 15,106 metric tons at the end of 1926 to 25,361 metric tons in 1929) and downward pressure on prices throughout the period. The collapse of world demand for tin brought sharp declines in prices - to £100 a ton in May 1931, the lowest price for 30 years and less than half the lowest price of 1928.(7) (Figure 6:1 charts the general course of prices in this period.)

As early as June 1929, tin producers banded together to form the Tin Producers' Association in London with the objective of ensuring a reduction of supplies of tin coming on to the market and of forming a stockpile of tin concentrates to be financed by the newly formed Anglo-American Tin Corporation. Despite limited membership, consisting largely of British interests in Malaysia, Nigeria and Burma, and a decision to drop the stock withdrawal policy, the Association proceeded with a policy of the voluntary limitation of output in 1930, when Indonesian and major Bolivian producers joined the scheme. However, as Fox has pointed out in his detailed appraisal of the international tin agreements, the Association was not strong enough to cope with an accumulated excess of world production which would have required a reduction in production in all areas of about one-third in order to secure the desired recovery in prices. The failure of the Association to meet its objectives attracted interest in controls which were more international in nature and gamut.(8) Agreement backed by governments was precipitated by the Billiton Company in Indonesia and Patiño in Bolivia, both of which in May 1930 threatened to withdraw from the Tin Producers' Association, 'if it were not re-organised upon efficient lines', that is with binding agreements sanctioned by the governments of the countries concerned.(9)

From a government standpoint, plummetting levels of duties and royalties on the production and export of tin and declining levels of employment in the tin industry not only heightened public awareness of the problems but also encouraged attempts to secure their solution. A draft intergovernmental agreement to restrict tin

Figure 6:1: Tin Prices, 1920-1938
(annual average, £ sterling per ton of standard tin)

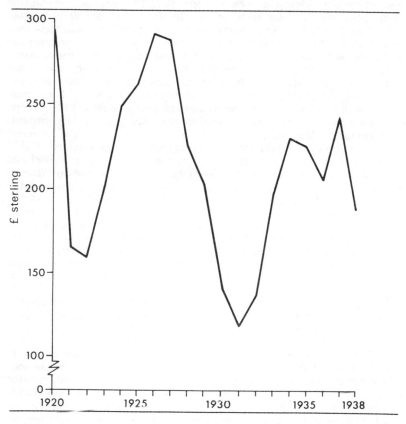

Source: Tin Producers' Association, Tin World Statistics 1939 (Tin Producers' Association, London, n.d.).

production was approved in principle by representatives from Malaysia, Nigeria, Bolivia and the Netherlands in November 1930 but the UK was concerned that the interests of consumers should be satisfactorily met. The agreement which resulted in February 1931, which aimed to secure 'a fair and reasonable equilibrium between production and consumption with the view of preventing rapid and severe oscillations of price'(10), appeared to allay UK fears, and it was signed by the governments of Malaysia, Bolivia, Indonesia and Nigeria, together accounting for over 85 per cent of world tin production during the boom year of 1929.(11)

The 1931 Tin Agreement allotted export quotas to the signatory countries on the basis of an agreed assessment of output in 1929. By this procedure, Malaysia was allocated 37.19 per cent of world exports, Bolivia 23.63 per cent, Indonesia 20.63 per cent and Nigeria 5.34 per cent.(12) The governments in question took on the responsibility for allotting the national quota among individual producers and for controlling export quotas so that they were distributed as uniformly as possible throughout the year (March to February). In addition, an International Tin Committee was established for the purpose of compiling statistics and for recommending when changes were needed to the quota.(13) (For a brief summary of the main provisions of this and subsequent tin agreements, see the Appendix, Table 1.)

Although the Agreement was introduced with the support of the major tin producing countries, it was not considered as a sufficient means in itself to secure the rise in prices from the depressed levels of 1931 that the producers hoped to achieve. As a result, a private international tin pool, reminiscent of the Bandoeng Pool of 1921, operated between 1931 and 1934, accumulating a total of about 21,000 tons of tin in the winter of 1931 alone. The pool received a degree of legitimisation since its chairman was also the chairman of the International Tin Committee. The size of the stock represented nearly half of the world's visible supply of tin in 1932 and was instrumental, together with restrained production levels, in providing upward pressure on tin prices.(14) By 1933, the price of tin averaged £195 per ton and the operation of the pool, together with continued restrictions on tin exports, brought the average price to £230 per ton in 1934, the highest average level since 1927 (Figure 6:1). During the same period world production of tin fell sharply.(15)

Given its success in the eyes of tin producers in raising rather than in stabilising tin prices, it is not surprising that a second agreement on tin was negotiated in 1933. However, agreement was not reached without some debate as to the appropriate level of national export quotas, particularly for new entrants such as Zaire. A new feature of the 1933 Agreement was its term of three years as opposed to two. An ancillary agreement in July 1934 provided for a buffer stock of 8,282 tons of metal, contributed by the signatory governments and held and administered by a Buffer Stock Committee under the International Tin Committee. The Committee was empowered to use the stock 'as an adjunct to the International Tin Control Scheme'.(16) The buffer stock, however, was established for an initial period of only a year and a half.

Operating conditions for the second Agreement were very different to those prevailing during the course of the first. The export quota was raised gradually from the initial level set in January 1934 (40 per cent of 1929 production) to 100 per cent in the first quarter of 1937, the start of the third Agreement. There were a variety of reasons for the International Tin Committee's endorsement of progressively higher levels of production. On the one hand, it was clear by 1935 that world demand for tin had recovered and was rising; on the other, short supplies from Bolivia in 1936, resulting from the loss of skilled labour during the Chaco War, allowed a redistribution of Bolivia's shortfall.(17)   Throughout the period tin prices operated within a relatively narrow range.(18)

In contrast to the first and second tin agreements, the third, negotiated in 1936 and signed in 1937, enjoyed little success in its objective of 'adjusting production to consumption, preventing rapid and severe oscillations of price, and maintaining reasonable stocks'(19) even though its provisions were based firmly on the preceding agreements. (A new feature was a Tin Research Scheme, designed to promote research on, and the development and consumption of, tin in January 1938.(20)) The reason for its relative lack of success was the different market conditions it faced, rather than a new and less serviceable formulation of the operating procedures.

The 1937 Agreement encompassed two distinct phases: controls before and after the outbreak of the Second World War. Although it is fair to examine the economic provisions of the Agreement with respect only to the former, the latter period is interesting in revealing the way in which a commodity institute could be used by the major powers in an effort to secure maximum available supplies in time of war.

The Agreement started auspiciously enough: in 1937, tin consumption was at its highest level since 1929 and the price of tin, which averaged £242.25 per ton, the highest for ten years (Figure 6:1).   However, the very buoyancy of demand encouraged the International Tin Committee to sanction production increases which were to prove over-expansionary in the light of subsequent developments. By the end of 1937, when the export quota had been at 110 per cent for three quarters, prices came under strong downward pressure in the face of a sharp rise in production, and in 1938 export quotas were severely pruned - to 35 per cent by the third quarter - as demand fell sharply. Although the rapidity of the fall in export quotas meant that some countries over-subscribed their allotment, a sufficient reduction of output was achieved, nevertheless, to bring about a halt in the slide of tin prices. By mid-1939, prices had recovered sufficiently for the newly formed buffer stock to sell rather than to purchase tin on the world market. With the outbreak of War, conditions changed markedly: the buffer stock was exhausted within a fortnight and the export quota was raised abruptly - to 60 per cent and subsequently to 120 per cent in the first quarter of 1940.(21) In effect existing international controls on tin were then replaced by stronger, more direct controls by the Allied Powers.

111

3. War-time Controls

The role of tin as a strategic commodity was clearly exhibited during the Second World War. At the onset, the price of tin rose rapidly in the face of rising demand to average £256.6 per ton in 1940 compared with £226.3 in 1939. In 1940, the US Government arranged with the International Tin Committee to buy all the tin available under the quota at current prices to be held for seven years subject to use in emergency circumstances. Any stock liquidation at the end of that period was to be conducted in an orderly fashion after consultation. Between June 1940 and April 1941, in what Fox reported as 'the biggest tin deal /yet/ negotiated in history', the US Metals Reserve bought 60,000 tons of tin and in November 1941 became the sole US buyer and distributor with the aim of building an initial reserve of 100,000 tons. The US rather than the International Tin Committee, became, thus, the principal agency in control of international stocks of tin although with the occupation of Malaysia and Indonesia in early 1942, the US was not able to reach the target level set. In 1942, for instance, world tin production fell to less than half of its 1941 level and output remained sluggish throughout the War.(22) In this context, the International Tin Committee in September 1942 abandoned what production controls remained.

Despite the dislocation of traditional patterns of trade and production by war, consideration of a replacement for the 1937 Agreement was initiated as early as December 1940. Between 1931 and 1940 the allocation of quota rights had become slightly distorted by the desire of the International Tin Committee to encourage outsiders to join the agreements. In addition, the major producers vied with each other for the quota they regarded as optimal. It was therefore only after considerable debate that an agreement was drawn up in 1942, in the names of the governments of Belgium, Bolivia, the UK and the Netherlands, to regulate exports of tin from Zaire, Bolivia, Malaysia, Indonesia and Nigeria. The Agreement, a largely academic exercise in terms of the regulation of production, trade and stocks, provided for a continuation of the International Tin Committee to collect and publish statistics and to set export quotas if it deemed them to be applicable.(23)

During the War, the Combined Raw Materials Board of the Allied Powers was concerned primarily with building up the strategic supplies of tin for the use of the US Government discussed above.(24) In view of the uncertain nature of tin supplies following the War, particularly in South-East Asia, the Combined Raw Materials Board established a specialised Combined Tin Committee 'to keep the tin metal position under review and to allocate supplies of tin metal to member and non-member countries'.(25) Members included the UK, the Netherlands, Belgium and the US. However, any country was entitled to claim an allocation of the right to buy (rather than a guarantee of supply). The functions of the Committee were limited to the allocation of tin metal available for export and excluded the largest source, the US strategic stockpile, and supplies of tin concentrates from Bolivia, Malaysia and Nigeria under direct contract with the UK or US Governments.(26)

With a rough balance between world production and limited commercial consumption of tin in 1947, the function of the Combined Tin Committee became less important; and when in 1949 the restrictions on the use of tin in the UK were lifted and the US stockpile was firmly established, the Committee recommended its own dissolution. The London metal market resumed active trading in the same year and interest then turned to the negotiation of a new international tin agreement.(27)

4. Controls on Tin between 1949 and 1960

In contrast to the 1931 Tin Agreement, negotiated spontaneously and relatively expeditiously in very depressed trading conditions, the first post-War agreement became effective only after five years of discussion, set in motion by the appeal of the International Tin Committee for a new agreement in 1946. An International Tin Study Group was established under the terms of the Havana Charter in 1947 with delegates and observers from twenty countries committed to negotiating an agreement within eight years; and a first draft was considered as early as October 1948 on the basis of proposals put forward by the Belgians. The draft was based on the assumption that a prevailing shortage of tin would in the near future be converted into a surplus and sought to allocate supplies within a formal price range to be set for five years (although adjustments to the price range were also contemplated). In a period of shortage, an international council was to be empowered to organise distribution between consumers and to sanction arrangements to guarantee US supplies. In December 1948, two further drafts were put forward for consideration, one modelled partly on the Belgian proposals and partly on the recently completed International Wheat Agreement, the other reflecting the thinking of the International Tin Study Group. At a Washington meeting, discussion centred on the division of votes between producers and consumers, the allocation of tin in periods of short supply and prices. It took two further working drafts - those of 1949 and 1950 - before a United Nations conference on tin was called in Geneva in October 1950 formally to discuss the subject.(28)

The 1950 conference coincided with particularly unstable conditions in world commodity markets associated with speculation regarding the Korean War. Strong US demand for tin, in particular, boosted the price from its average of £605.8 per ton in 1949 to over £1,000 in 1951.(29) It is not surprising that in these generally uncertain conditions, the conference could do little to induce agreement between producers and consumers. Points of dissent were the appropriate floor price for tin against which a buffer stock should operate, with producers favouring £720 per ton and the US, the major consumer, suggesting a lower floor of £680; and the size that the buffer stock should reach before export controls should be applied, the producers preferring a degree of flexibility in contrast to the US, which stated that a stock of 30,000 tons was desirable. It was only in 1953, when prices had fallen back to the lower levels which had preceded the 1950 Conference in the face of substantially reduced US demand, that producers and consumers found sufficient common ground to reach agreement. Even then, although the Agreement covered 90 per cent of world tin production, only 40 per cent of consumption was represented.(30) The US, the USSR and West Germany were all important absentees.(31)

Although a further three years were to elapse before the new agreement, dated 1954, became functional, its importance as a foundation for future tin agreements should not be overlooked; protracted negotiations may well have contributed to the survival of its essential principles in subsequent renewals. The Agreement established floor and ceiling prices for tin, set initially at £640 and £880 (Table 6:2), centred on the current price, and provided for the revision of the price range automatically if exchange rate movements so required. In addition, an International Tin Council (the Council) was established to replace the former International Tin Committee, empowered to determine export quotas for tin, if necessary, to keep the price within the target range; Malaysia, Bolivia and Indonesia were allocated between them four-fifths of the total quota. A buffer stock was also established of 25,000 tons of tin metal equivalent, three-quarters of which was to consist of metal and the remainder of cash. Producers were required to contribute to the buffer stock on a pro rata basis whereas consumers were entitled but not obligated to do so. For the purposes of administrative guidance the price range was divided into three ranges of equal size. The manager was permitted to sell when the price was in the upper of the three bands and to buy when it was in the lower. On the termination of the Agreement, the balance of the buffer stock was to be redistributed to the contributing countries. The Agreement specified also that national stocks held by producers should be limited to 25 per cent of their net tin exports in the preceding twelve month period.(32)

The technical aspects of the 1954 Tin Agreement thus borrowed heavily from the mechanisms of the pre-War agreements whilst providing more detailed terms of reference for their implementation. Increased sophistication in the 1954 Agreement also extended to its administrative provisions, a factor due at least in part to the greater number of participants compared with pre-War agreements, boosted notably by the inclusion of consumers. Considerable debate had been conducted during the draft stages on the composition and

114

Table 6:2: Price Ranges in the Tin Agreements, 1956 - 1972

Period of Operation								Unit	Floor Price	Ceiling Price
1	Jul	1956	-	22	Mar	1957		£/ton	640	880
22	Mar	1957	-	12	Jan	1962		"	730	880
12	Jan	1962	-	4	Dec	1963		"	790	965
4	Dec	1963	-	12	Nov	1964		"	850	1,000
12	Nov	1964	-	6	Jul	1966		"	1,000	1,200
6	Jul	1966	-	22	Nov	1967		"	1,100	1,400
22	Nov	1967	-	16	Jan	1968		"	1,283	1,633
16	Jan	1968	-	2	Jan	1970		£/metric ton	1,280	1,630
2	Jan	1970	-	21	Oct	1970		"	1,260	1,605
21	Oct	1970	-	4	Jul	1972		"	1,350	1,650

Source: International Tin Council, Tin Statistics 1968-1978 (International Tin Council, London, n.d.), p. 60.

voting procedure of the newly instituted International Tin Council. What emerged was a Council consisting of one delegate from each contracting Government's metropolitan territory and one for each dependent territory/territories participating separately under the Agreement. These delegates were required to select an independent chairman and two vice-chairmen, one from the delegates of producing countries and one from the delegates of consuming countries. The voting procedures specified in the Agreement were complex: for some decisions, such as the establishment of floor and ceiling prices and the assessment of members' export quotas, a simple majority vote of both producers and of consumers was sufficient; for others, such as committee membership, a two-thirds majority of both consumers and producers was required, calculated on the basis of a total of two thousand votes, divided equally between producers and consumers, and then sub-divided with each delegate receiving five initial votes and in addition a proportion as 'nearly as possible equal to the proportion which his country's tonnage' bore to world trade in tin as calculated for the purposes of the Agreement. The total votes of any consuming country were limited to one hundred and fifty if there were more than thirty consuming country delegates.(33)

In addition to its technical responsibilities, the 1954 Agreement conferred on the Council the role of arbitrator in the event of a breach. The Council was also empowered to deprive a country, judged to have committed such a breach, of its voting rights or 'of any other rights of which the country concerned can be deprived under the provisions of [this] Agreement in relation to the subject

115

matter of the dispute . . .'(34) Similarly, the Council was given the authority to introduce amendments to the Agreement and to suspend countries which did not ratify the amendments under certain conditions.(35)

The international tin market was subject to a number of destabilising influences between 1954 and 1957. On the one hand, output was stimulated by further US purchases of tin for its strategic stockpile in 1953 and 1954. When the stockpile reached the required level of about 350,000 tons in 1955, almost twice world output, purchases ceased and downward pressure was imposed on prices. On the other, the entry into force of the Agreement and the Suez Crisis in the second half of 1956 both exerted speculative upward pressure on tin prices which penetrated the upper limit of £880 per ton briefly at the end of the year. In 1957, a third influence, sales of surplus tin, imported formerly from China, by the USSR, also served to complicate operating conditions.(36)

The reaction of the Council to unstable conditions when the Agreement entered into force was to call on both traditional and new methods. In 1957, for example, when reduced demand and large USSR and Bolivian sales depressed prices, the Buffer Stock Manager entered the market as a buyer. However, prices reached the revised floor of £730 in October 1957 and, in view of the further surplus year forecast, the Council introduced export controls in December. In early 1958 the buffer stock was replenished, in a flexible move at the producers' request, by a Special Fund consisting of producer members' contributions of cash and commercial borrowings. Finally, when sales of USSR tin continued to depress prices, pushing them below the floor in September 1958, the Council first recommended that members should curb imports of tin from that source, a course followed by several major importers, and subsequently reached agreement with the USSR that it should export less to non-centrally planned economies. By May 1959, the price was pushed back to the middle sector of the target band. Nonetheless, it was only in September 1960, when the price appeared to have stabilised in that band, the buffer stock stood at 10,000 tons, consumption had been in excess of world production for over a year and sales of tin from the USSR had substantially diminished, that export controls were formally lifted.(37)

Between the coming into force of the 1954 Tin Agreement and the United Nations conference to discuss its successor in May 1960, international tin controls had been put severely to the test. Apart from falling below the target range in September 1958, an event unusual in the history of tin controls, tin prices had been subject to a number of unpredictable influences such as US stockpile activity and large USSR sales of tin which made the formulation of policy open to a wide margin of error, particularly since neither of these countries was a member of the Agreement. As an addition to the mechanisms specified in the Agreement it is interesting also that restrictions were introduced against USSR tin exports in a display of united national and international policy amongst participants.

A further remarkable feature of this period was the barter by the US Department of Agriculture of surplus agricultural supplies such as rice and tobacco for tin from producing countries. At the end of 1958, for example, Bolivia exchanged over 5,000 metric tons of tin, Zaire 7,000 metric tons, and Thailand nearly 2,000 metric tons. Trade was conducted via private contracts and exports of tin were reported to be sold at a margin below the prevailing world price. The advantage for the producer was two-fold: a net saving was made on the use of foreign exchange for the purchase of imports; and, under a ruling of December 1958, the Council pronounced that such barter deals would not count toward the fulfilment of the producer's export quota, provided that stock levels did not exceed a maximum specified. For the US, the strategic stockpile was supplemented at no additional capital cost with the deployment of excess supplies of agricultural products. Although such trade was sanctioned by the Council, it was not strictly controlled by it; the net effect was to boost trade, albeit on different terms, at a time when the Council was operating a policy of supply restraint. It was not until the mid-1960s, when sales were made from the US, that the implications of diverting such a large proportion of world tin supplies to a third party not even signatory to the Agreement were fully realised.(38)

5. Controls during the 1960s

The 1960 Tin Agreement was based firmly on the 1954 model. The producing members were the same while, on the consumer side, Japan and Mexico joined as signatories. Contributions to the buffer stock were reduced and specified in terms of 12,500 tons of tin metal and 7,500 tons equivalent in cash in the first instance.(39) Other changes reflected to a large extent shortcomings experienced in the previous Agreement. The Council was given authority for the first time to borrow for the purposes of the buffer stock on the security of tin warrants held by it, a move which sprang directly from the need for additional cash contributions to supplement the buffer stock in 1958. A further modification was the requirement that sales or purchases in the middle band of the range required a two-thirds 'distributed majority' (two-thirds majorities of both consumers and producers) of the Council rather than a 'distributed simple majority' (a simple majority of both consumers and producers) making action more difficult to institute. The introduction of export quotas, in contrast, was made more flexible: a control period could be introduced for two to five months as opposed to only three; and 'special exports' (exports not counted as exports for the purposes of a control period) were permitted if they were destined to form part of a strategic government stockpile and were unlikely to be used for any commercial or industrial purposes during the currency of the Agreement. (The latter reflected the authorisation of the special barter purchases of the US in 1958.) Finally, the 1960 Agreement specified more precisely the shares of production and votes of each signatory and laid down detailed rules for any future re-determination of such percentages in several annexes. The votes of consuming countries, for example, were based on their average consumption level of tin for the preceding three years. In a similar way, the permitted stockholdings of each producing country were also listed formally in an annex to the Agreement.(40)

The serious shortage of tin which emerged during the 1960 Tin Agreement was attributable to three main influences: the fact that export controls were lifted only in September 1960, the halting of supplementary supplies from the USSR and rising levels of consumption. These combined to exert strong upward pressure on prices and the buffer stock was sold out by mid-1961. In June of that year, the price of tin penetrated the ceiling set.(41)

Pressure from producers led in January 1962 to a rise in the price range from £730 to £880 to £790 to £965.(42) This range remained in operation for almost two years (Table 6:2) during which a shortage of tin continued despite large sales from the US strategic stockpile (Table 6:3).

Prices were volatile, ranging from £845 per ton to £1,035, attributable at least in part to speculation regarding the US sales. In November 1963, the price again penetrated the ceiling and the Council raised the target range further - to £850 to £1,000 - in the following month. Continued uncertainty regarding strategic disposals by the US together with supply shortages did little to stabilise conditions: by mid-1964 the price of tin was once again well above the ceiling, by October it had reached £1,584 per ton, and in November, the Council raised the target range to £1,000 to £1,200 per ton. However, as Fox has pointed out, even the new ceiling was well below the current market price and the Council had no tin in the buffer stock with which to enforce it.(43) The target range had thus been shifted upwards by over a third since the signing of the 1960 Agreement (Table 6:2).

The United Nations Tin Conference of 1965 focussed, not surprisingly, on measures which could be taken to alleviate the shortage of tin. The 1960 Tin Agreement had provided that in the event of a tin shortage an assessment should be made of the conditions of supply and demand 'With a view to ensuring the maximum development of production in the producing countries . . . to assuring to consuming countries the equitable distribution of the available supplies of tin metal, at a price . . . not . . . higher than the ceiling price . . .'(44) In practice, it had become clear that this provision was an inadequate method of narrowing the gap between

Table 6:3: Government Stockpile Disposals of Tin, 1956-1974 (metric tons)

Year	US[a]	Total[b]
1956	-	-
1957	-	-
1958	-	-
1959	-	3,557
1960	-	1,538
1961	-	4,333
1962	1,422	4,900
1963	10,797	11,904
1964	31,647	32,733
1965	22,081	23,204
1966	16,537	17,097
1967	6,245	6,245
1968	3,551	3,551
1969	2,081	2,081
1970	3,087	3,087
1971	1,764	1,764
1972	367	367
1973	20,269	20,269
1974	23,508	23,508
Total 1956 to 1970	143,356	160,138

Note: a   General Services Administration Sales

b   Other participants were Canada, with sales of 2,751 metric tons between 1961 and 1963, Italy, with sales of 5,073 between 1960 and 1966, the UK with sales of 4,996 between 1959 and 1960 and the US Texas City smelter, with sales of 3,962 between 1961 and 1962.

Source: International Tin Council, Trade in Tin 1960-1974 (International Tin Council, London, n.d.), p.9.

supply and demand. Producers suggested that incentives should be offered in the form of tax concessions to encourage the exploitation of lower grade deposits. Consumers, on the other hand, criticised the rigidities inherent in the operation of the buffer stock which meant that it was ineffective in defending the targeted price range.(45)

Despite the new spirit of UNCTAD I in which it was drafted, and the inclusion of the aim of increasing export earnings from tin, especially for developing countries, the mechanisms employed in the

119

1965 Tin Agreement remained the same as those in the other post-War tin agreements. Despite recent experience, the buffer stock was set at only 20,000 tons, although the Council was given a freer hand in deciding what proportions of the contributions should be in cash or in tin metal and to review disposals of government non-commercial stocks of tin. Quota provisions were left essentially unchanged.(46)

Despite the fact that the 1965 Agreement broke little if any new ground, its negotiation was not without incident. Malaysia, for example, issued a statement in December 1965 to the effect that a tin agreement would be 'unlikely to be effective in arresting any immediate trend in world tin price in view of the strong demand for tin' and that Malaysian support for it would be withheld. Although Malaysia eventually joined the Agreement, a question mark remained as to the strength of the support of this major producing country. The US, the main consumer, continued to remain outside although, overall, participation of consumers increased in the course of the Agreement.(47)

During the first two years of the 1965 Agreement, a number of factors exerted downward pressure on prices. On the one hand, sales from the US strategic stockpile, which had commenced in 1962 and peaked in 1964, continued to represent over 10 per cent of total sales in 1965 and 1966 (Table 6:3). On the other hand, and more importantly, the high prices prevailing between 1963 and 1964 stimulated increased production and, with sluggish rates of consumption growth, output exceeded demand in 1967 for the first time since 1958.(48) Despite the trend in prices the Council permitted a rise in the price range in July 1966. When in January 1967 the price fell to the top of the lower band, the buffer stock began buying and some stability was preserved throughout the first half of the year. Pricing was then complicated by the devaluation of sterling by one-seventh in November 1967. Although the price range was moved upward by a similar amount (one-sixth), market prices failed to follow, moving up by only about a tenth. Speculators, who had reportedly bought tin on the basis of the expected devaluation, then offloaded their supplies and exerted further downward pressure on prices despite supportive buffer stock action. In the face of a number of contradictory factors and with the price of tin near to the floor, the Council agreed to introduce export control provisions in September 1968, with production limited initially by about 4 per cent. However, even this delayed action was ill-timed: consumption strengthened at the end of 1968 and throughout 1969, partly reflecting an increase in US demand, and in December 1969 the price rose above the ceiling. In this context, the Council ended the export control period and in a reversal of policy encouraged producers instead to increase their export volume.(49) By the end of 1970, when prices had risen to an average of £1,554 per ton compared with £1,451 in 1969, the Council also agreed to a further increase in the price range - to £1,350 to £1,650 per ton (Figure 6:2).(50)

120

Figure 6:2: Tin Prices, 1960-1980
(annual average, £ sterling per metric ton of standard tin)

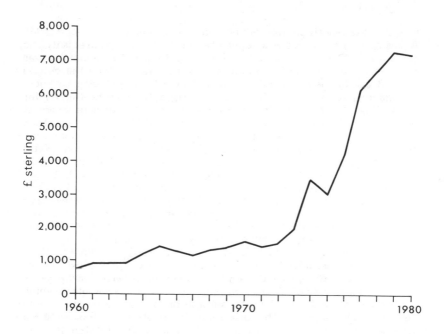

Sources: International Tin Council, Trade in Tin 1960-1974
(International Tin Council, London, n.d.), Ibid., Tin
Statistics 1968-1978 (International Tin Council, London,
n.d.) and Ibid., Monthly Statistical Bulletin (International
Tin Council, London, various issues).

Although special factors such as sales from the US strategic
stockpiles and the devaluation of sterling were important influences
on the operation of 1965 Tin Agreement, errors in judgement also
provide a key explanation for its lack of success in meeting the
pricing objectives set. The ill-timed raising of the price range in
1966 and introduction of an export control period in 1968, for

121

example, did little to advance the aims of the Agreement. In contrast, technical factors such as the size of the buffer stock, played a less incisive role although, as on other occasions, the mechanisms were better able to defend the floor rather than the ceiling price.

6. Controls since 1970

Despite the shortcomings which had been manifest in the 1965 Agreement, a successor was negotiated in 1970 based on precisely the same lines. Modifications were slight: the Buffer Stock Manager was empowered to offer tin for sale at the market rather than the ceiling price if the latter exceeded the former in order to enhance his room for manoeuvre; similarly, he was authorised to operate the buffer stock when the price of tin was in the upper or the lower sectors of the range in order to increase the flexibility of buffer stock operations. The Agreement also conferred on the Council the discretion to specify the market price used - the London Metal Exchange price or the Penang price, cash or forward - according to circumstance.(51) Other new developments included the undertaking by the Netherlands, a consumer, to make voluntary contributions - of about £0.6 million - to the buffer stock, the first such undertaking in the history of international tin controls, and the acceptance by the IMF that the Agreement met the conditions it required to approve buffer stock financing for balance of payments reasons.(52)

The operation of the 1970 Agreement, which became effective in 1971, coincided initially with a period of short supplies. However, in 1972 output soared to the highest level for nearly thirty years almost eroding the deficit between production and consumption which had existed since 1969. Despite substantial purchases of tin by the Buffer Stock Manager, the price of tin, quoted for buffer stock purposes in Malaysian dollars after the pound was floated in July 1972, showed considerable weakness and the Council found it necessary to introduce a period of export control from January 1973 designed to keep exports from rising further. The market turned round abruptly, however, toward the end of 1973 and the combination of considerable international uncertainty, the OPEC oil price hike and increased US demand pushed the price of tin to £2,025 per (metric) ton in August from an average of £1,506 in 1972 (Figure 6:2). In September, when it had become clear that a major price explosion was underway, the Council abandoned export controls and raised the price range in line with market prices (M $635 - M $760), which represented an 8.9 per cent increase in the floor and a 5.8 per cent increase in the ceiling.(53)

Into this complex of supply and demand considerations came the announcement by the US in April 1973 of proposed sales of 210,000 tons of tin from the strategic stockpile. This followed five years of very small sales and reflected a reduced stockpile objective of only 40,500 tons following the ending of the Vietnam War. In an atmosphere of general uncertainty, prices rose sharply and by the end of the year stood at levels nearly fifty per cent higher than those prevailing at the onset, despite substantial US sales (Figure 6:2). Prices continued at high levels during 1974 despite a fall in consumption and further disposals from the US stockpile.

The 1973 to 1974 boom in tin prices, though less acute than that which had prevailed during the Korean War, owing largely to sales from the US stockpile, was in several respects more damaging for the tin market. On the one hand, the International Tin Agreement, which had been in operation since 1956 and had achieved international acceptability as a pro forma for international commodity control, proved conspicuously ineffective in defending the ceiling price owing partly to the size of the buffer stock but perhaps more importantly to the unusual conditions of uncertainty prevailing in the international exchange markets. On the other, the US was reported to have displayed a distinct lack of consultation with the Council in disposing of its excess tin supplies. This was illustrated in 1973, for example, when the Council itself drew attention to the problems caused by the release of US tin and sought 'the co-operation of the US Government to the extent that the US, in any disposal programme, should give due consideration to the provisions of the International Tin Agreement by not selling tin at times when the market conditions /are/ such that the Buffer Stock Manager may buy tin or when export control /is/ in force to protect the floor price . . .' The Council also expressed regret that the US was not a member of the Council.(54)

By May 1975, when the fifth post-War Tin Agreement was negotiated, market conditions had changed dramatically again: in the face of a pronounced US recession, tin consumption fell well below output; and despite large purchases by the buffer stock and the introduction of export controls (designed to reduce exports by 18 per cent), prices remained far below their 1974 peak. International political conditions also shifted markedly: as outlined in Part I, the US, for example, conducted a review of its commodity policy which resulted in its consideration of participation in international commodity agreements on a case-by-case basis; and in 1974, it will be recalled, the General Assembly of the United Nations adopted the Declaration on the Establishment of a New International Economic Order which was to lead to UNCTAD's Integrated Programme. One result was that the 1975 Tin Agreement included the US amongst its signatories; the USSR also joined as a consuming country.

The distinguishing factor between the 1975 Tin Agreement and the other post-War tin agreements was the greater detail of its provisions. Changes, however, were largely administrative in nature. For example, the Agreement provided that the Council should draw up in its Rules of Procedure a method of appointing an Acting Chief

Executive Officer, responsible for the administration and operation of the Agreement in the event of temporary absences of the Executive Chairman or pending the appointment of a new Executive Chairman.(55) Similarly, the budget for the administrative account of the Agreement was specified in greater detail.(56) A more interesting departure was an article instructing the Council amongst other things to 'keep itself informed of new uses of tin and the development of substitute products which replace tin in its traditional uses', 'encourage closer relationships with and wider participation in organizations devoted to research into the efficient exploration for and production, processing and use of tin' and 'make a study of alternative means to supplement or replace existing methods of financing the buffer stock'.(57)

It is not surprising that the passage of time and the accession of new signatories to the agreements should bring with it an increased refinement of their terms and administrative provisions. It is interesting that despite their shortcomings in the past, the economic provisions - the buffer stock, national stocks and export quotas -were retained intact. The course of the 1975 Agreement was to change this situation.

When it was negotiated, it appeared to the drafters of the 1975 Agreement that prices had reached their peak. However, although prices on average in 1975 were lower than in 1974, the trend was upward during 1976 and price increases accelerated and became pronounced in 1977, to a sterling peak of £6,953 per metric ton in November 1977. Thereafter, prices fell to mid-1977 levels of about £6,000 per metric ton before resuming a strong upward movement from mid-1978 to a new peak in March 1980. (See Figure 6:2 for the general movement in prices.) Between early 1977 and July 1980 the tin price was thus persistently above the ceiling.

The explanation for these sharp movements in prices lies in a number of factors: in 1976 and 1977, on average, the production of tin metal lagged behind consumption, generating weak supply conditions. (Until June 1976, export controls acted as an official restraint on output.) Additional pressure came from speculation following a further scaling down of US strategic stockpile requirements. Although the legislation concerned was eventually blocked, it drew vigorous complaints from the Bolivian Government who at one point complained to the Organisation of American States that the US was committing an act of economic aggression.(58)

Action by the Council to bring prices back down to the target range was ineffective: the buffer stock ran out in January 1977 and although a total of 13,000 metric tons of tin metal was pledged by consumers to the buffer stock in 1978, including 5,000 from the US, to bring it to a capacity of 33,000 metric tons, faith in its ability to keep prices on the desired path was seriously called in question. A

US Treasury official, for example, commented in 1976 that the operation of the buffer stock had had no appreciable effect on US prices of tin.(59) Nor was the criticism of the size of the buffer stock limited to consumer countries: as early as 1975, Harold Allen, Executive Chairman of the International Tin Council, expressed the view that a much larger buffer stock would be advantageous in providing the Council with greater resources for 'cushioning the reactions of the market'.(60)

From mid-1980, however, the Council faced new conditions of sluggish demand associated with the world recession. It was in these changing conditions that meetings were held to discuss renewal of the 1975 Agreement and discussions broke new ground in questioning the fundamental principles on which the post-War Tin Agreements were based.(61) Producers such as Malaysia argued that a large buffer stock tended to dampen market prices; the US, obversely, argued that adequate buffer stock provisions made resort to export quotas, with their damaging implications for future supplies and prices, unnecessary.(62) This questioning of fundamentals was to characterise the following two years.

Despite much soul-seeking, the objectives and control mechanisms written into the 1980 Tin Agreement coincided broadly with those of the 1975. However, minor changes were made to other parts of the Agreement: the seat of the Council, for example, was to be 'in the territory of a Member' and not necessarily in London as specified in 1975; and the Council was empowered to establish operational rules for the buffer stock including financial measures to be applied to members which failed to meet their obligations.(63) In addition, specific provision was made for subsidiary bodies to continue to assist the Council in its functions. These were to include an Economic and Price Review Panel, an Administrative Committee, a Buffer Stock Finance Committee, a Committee on Costs and Prices, a Committee on Development, a Credentials Committee and a Statistical Committee.(64) Perhaps of more consequence was the increase in the size of the buffer stock - from 20,000 metric tons to 30,000 -together with the addition of a 'stock of 20,000 metric tons to be financed from borrowing, using as security stock warrants, and, if necessary, government undertakings'.(65) A new article was also added stating that when UNCTAD's Common Fund became active the Council should negotiate for 'mutually acceptable terms and modalities for an association agreement . . . in order to seek to take full advantage of the facilities of the Fund'.(66)

Unlike the previous agreements, the Sixth post-War Agreement made compulsory the financing of the buffer stock by producers and consumers on an equal basis. A further major difference was that contributions could be called up in cash only and not merely in tin metal or in a combination of cash and metal. The contributions were to be drawn from all members according to their respective shares of production or consumption and the amounts of the contribution were to be determined on the basis of the floor price in effect when the contribution were called. If not all countries who negotiated the Agreement joined, the financial obligations of the remainder were limited to a maximum of 125 per cent of their contributions as laid out in the Agreement. Clearer specifications were also given with respect to the introduction of an export control period and a new article was introduced on consultation, under which the Council would consider at the request of any member factors directly affecting supply and demand.(67)

The 1980 Agreement, in sum, borrowed heavily from its antecedents in terms of structure. However, in terms of participation, it represented a fragile compromise between the different parties and emerged only after some fourteen weeks of intensive bargaining. Even then, the US, the world's largest consumer, and Bolivia, the third largest producer, rejected on the one hand the perceived inadequacy of the buffer stock provisions and, on the other, the price range, which was regarded as likely to cause 'irreparable damage to the extractive tin industry'.

The lack of faith in the ability of the newly drafted agreement to achieve its pricing objectives was also reflected in the transformation of the tin market by a support buying campaign by an unidentified group believed to represent producer interests, from July 1981. The campaign, which was reported to have cost between $500 and $600 million, helped to push prices to new record levels only to collapse again in March 1982, when they fell from over £9,000 per metric ton to £7,035. This followed the imposition by the London Metal Exchange of a limit of £120 per metric ton on the premium for tin sold cash for delivery the following day, essentially a fine on traders who did not meet delivery contracts. A further factor which depressed tin prices was the decision by the US to sell tin from the strategic stockpile to non-US nationals as well as to domestic buyers. Subsequent sales were severely criticised by Malaysia as 'an act . . . not becoming in a nation . . . many, many times richer than Malaysia'.

Producers adopted a dual reaction to the collapse in prices. Malaysia, it was reported, approached Indonesia and Thailand in March 1982 with a view to forming a producers' association to press for a 'fair, stable and remunerative price reflecting the cost of production and the depletable nature of tin as an economic resource'. Such an association, it was envisaged, would have financial resources and economic controls such as a buffer stock. Other producers, including Indonesia, however, were reported to favour a continued close association with the Tin Agreement which had come into being despite the absence of the US and Bolivia. Lack of confidence in the

Agreement which materialised kept interest alive, nevertheless, in uni-lateral producer action. In the early 1980s, the Agreement was thus subject to as great a challenge as it had been at any other time in the course of its history.(68)

7. Conclusion

A consideration of international controls on tin since the 1920s reveals a number of recurrent themes. First, controls were initiated by producers, often in times of low or falling prices. Secondly, buffer stocks and export controls were the common mechanisms for both cartels and international commodity agreements with the focus on short-term pricing rather than any other of the objectives specified. Thirdly, interest in controls was stimulated and their negotiation was complicated by a number of special factors. These included the sensitivity of tin to changes in industrial demand, the role of tin as a strategic commodity and the association of tin with speculative flows of capital.

The recurrence of these themes is both a measure of the scale of the problems faced and an indication of the inability of the agreements to bring about solutions to the problems. For, despite their broad scope and broadening compass, the agreements concentrated in practice on short-term pricing objectives and made little attempt to deal with the structural problems outlined in the first part of this chapter despite their importance for long-term price movements. Similarly, the 1975 and 1980 Tin Agreements, which included as an objective the increasing of the role played by developing countries in the marketing of tin, were not endowed with supporting mechanisms to secure this objective. Despite their increasing complexity, then, the post-War tin agreements were thus essentially little different from their pre-War counterparts.

The efficacy of the agreements in pursuit of the pricing objectives on which they concentrated was far from unambiguous. The 1931 and 1933 Agreements enjoyed perhaps the clearest degree of success in this regard, although in the case of the latter this was probably due to special circumstances of short supplies rather than to operation of the Agreement. The 1937 Tin Agreement, in contrast, proved to be over-expansionary in the light of subsequent developments whereas the action taken by its post-War successor, in contrast, led to short supplies in the early 1960s. The operational problems faced by the Council were epitomised in the case of the 1965 Tin Agreement. An ill-timed rise in the price range in 1966 was followed by the equally ill-timed introduction of export controls in 1968; this did little to prevent prices from breaching the ceiling in 1969. Overall, the agreements may be judged to have succeeded more in defending the floor than the ceiling price. (The notable example of the undershooting of the floor level was in 1958; the ceiling, in contrast, was exceeded on a number of occasions such as in 1963, 1964, 1965, 1966, 1974 and in 1977 to 1980 - although inflation may also have played its part in the process since the price range was always adjusted upward rather than down.)

It is possible to point to technical factors, such as the limited size of the buffer stock and the great ability of the mechanisms used to defend the floor rather than the ceiling price, as the main explanation for the shortcomings of the agreements in meeting their pricing objectives.   To do so, however, would be to ignore the decisive role played by national policies, notably those of the US, the USSR and Malaysia.   Much empirical work has been conducted on the impact of the US strategic stockpile policy.   An assessment by Smith and Schink in 1976, for example, concluded that the Agreement endured partly because the US stockpile policy deprived it of effective power on pricing decisions.(69)   Elsewhere, Smith argued that the impact of the Agreement's buffer stock had only a minor impact on prices between 1956 and 1973 compared with the major influence of US stockpile sales.(70)   It may be argued, further, that the US stockpile provided an element of uncertainty in the international tin market, the negative impact of which defies precise enumeration.   This uncertainty was enhanced by the failure of the US to participate in the agreements on a regular basis.

Although US policy offers the most outstanding example of the impact of national policies on tin, the USSR provides a second vivid illustration.   The unusually large sales of tin in the late 1950s depressed prices at a time when the Buffer Stock Manager was attempting to support them by purchase operations.   The subsequent application of export controls to attempt to raise prices contributed in turn to the problem of future supply shortages.

Finally, the lack of commitment by Malaysia, the leading producer, to the terms of the tin agreements in the 1960s and in the early 1980s did little to enhance their credibility as effective instruments of trade policy.   When this lack of commitment was coupled with a uni-lateral support buying campaign, as suspected in 1981, and by attempts to formalise a tin cartel in 1982, the viability of the Agreement became a serious cause for concern.   As in the case of other international commodity agreements, the tin agreements survived as long as participants were bound by a common set of interests and as long as the action of non-participants did not fundamentally undermine their provisions.   At the beginning of the 1980s neither of these pre-conditions appeared fully to be met.

Notes

1   See Chapter 1 for various measures of instability relating to tin prices.

2   See W. Fox, The Working of a Commodity Agreement: Tin (Mining Journal Books, London, 1974), International Tin Study Group, Statistical Yearbook 1949 (International Tin Study Group, London, 1950), International Tin Council, Tin Statistics 1968-1978 (International Tin Council, London, n.d.) and W. Robertson, Tin: Its Production and Marketing (Croom Helm, London, 1982), pp. 52-4. The long professional association of Fox with the International Tin Council makes his detailed study of the working of the agreements of particular interest and it will be quoted extensively in this chapter. There is a large literature on tin at the national level. See for examples L. St. Clare Grondona, Australia in the 1960s (Anthony Blond, London, 1962), D.B. Barton, A History of Tin Mining and Smelting in Cornwall (D.B. Barton, Truro, 1967), D.J. Fox, Tin and the Bolivian Economy (Latin American Publications Fund, London, 1970) and Y.Y. Hoong, The Development of the Tin Mining Industry of Malaya (University of Malaya Press, Kuala Lumpur, 1969).

3   Robertson, Tin: Its Production and Marketing, pp. 1, 59-60, 64-5 and 68. There has been much disagreement between producers and consumers regarding production costs. See, for example, International Tin Council, Tin Production and Investments (International Tin Council, London, 1979), H. Hughes and S. Singh, 'Economic rent: incidence in selected metals and minerals', Resources Policy, vol. 4, no. 2 (1978) and M. Gillis et. al., Taxation and Mining: Non-Fuel Minerals in Bolivia and Other Countries (Ballinger, Cambridge, Mass., 1978).

4   Robertson, Tin: Its Production and Marketing, pp. 3-5 and 25-7. Tin consumption declined by 1.6 per cent. According to some authorities, the electrolytic process may have helped tin's competitive position. See Ibid., p. 86.

5   Ibid., p. 85.

6   Consumption of primary tin metal rose from 136,144 metric tons in 1924 to 148,336 metric tons in 1926; stocks fell from 19,254 metric tons at the end of 1923 to 15,106 metric tons at the end of 1926. See International Tin Council, Statistical Yearbook 1968 (International Tin Council, London, 1968), p. 27 and International Tin Study Group, Statistical Yearbook 1949 (International Tin Study Group, London, 1950), p. 30. Tin prices were quoted in £ sterling per long ton to 1970 and then in metric tons.

7   Tin Producers' Association, Tin World Statistics 1939 (London, n.d.), pp. 26-7 and Fox, The Working of a Commodity Agreement, p. 118. The average price in the year was £118 per ton. Stocks increased to 49,869 metric tons in 1931.

8   Fox, The Working of a Commodity Agreement, p. 123.

9   Comment by Houwert of the Billiton Co, quoted in Fox, The Working of a Commodity Agreement, pp. 126-27.

10 'Agreement on the International Tin Control Scheme' (28 February 1931), in ILO, Intergovernmental Commodity Agreements, pp. 73-5, Article 1.

11 Thailand also entered into the Agreement in the course of 1931 and remained party to subsequent agreements before the War.

12 'Agreement on the International Tin Control Scheme' (28 February 1931), Article 11.

13 Ibid., Articles 13-24.

14 Fox, The Working of a Commodity Agreement, pp. 151-54.

15   Tin Producers' Association, Tin World Statistics 1939, p. 26.

16   'Agreement for the International Tin Control Scheme' (27 October 1933) and 'Agreement for the Tin Buffer Stock Scheme' (10 July 1934), Article 1, in ILO, Intergovernmental Commodity Agreements, pp. 75-9 and 80-1.

17   Fox, The Working of a Commodity Agreement, pp. 161-62.

18   Ibid., pp. 167-69.

19   'Agreement on the International Tin Control Scheme' (5 January 1937), in ILO, Intergovernmental Commodity Agreements, pp. 81-6, Article 1.

20   'Agreement on the Tin Buffer Stock Scheme' (20 June 1938) and 'Agreement on a Tin Research Scheme' (25 January 1938), both in ILO, Intergovernmental Commodity Agreement, pp. 80-94.

21   Fox, The Working of a Commodity Agreement, pp. 173-84. For the statistics covering the period see International Tin Study Group, Statistical Yearbook 1949 and Tin Producers' Association, Tin World Statistics 1939.

22   International Tin Council, Statistical Yearbook 1968, pp. 22-3. Production fell from 242,824 metric tons in 1941 to 116,840 in 1942. A good source on the US stockpile is International Tin Study Group, Statistical Yearbook 1949, pp. 62-3. For the account of the building up of the US stockpile see Fox, The Working of a Commodity Agreement, pp. 85-86.

23   'Agreement for the International Control of the Production and Export of Tin' (9 September 1942), in ILO, Intergovernmental Commodity Agreements, pp. 95-103, Articles 4, 7 and 10-12.

24   See K.E. Knorr, Tin Under Control (Stanford University Press, Stanford, 1945).

25   Fox, The Working of a Commodity Agreement, p. 203.

26   See International Tin Study Group, Statistical Year Book 1949 for the allocations.

27   In 1947, for example, world tin consumption totalled 122,834 metric tons compared with the pre-War peak of 192,024 in 1937. See International Tin Council, Statistical Yearbook 1968, p. 27.

28   Fox, The Working of a Commodity Agreement, pp. 214-18.

29   International Tin Study Group, Statistical Bulletin (International Tin Study Group, London, February 1957).

30   'International Tin Agreement, 1953' (United Nations, New York, 1954, II.D.4). Membership was open in principle to 'any Government, whether represented at the 1953 session of the United Nations Tin Conference or not . . .' (Article XXII).

31   Fox, The Working of a Commodity Agreement, pp. 258-59, reported that the German tinplate industry was obsessed with the fear that tin prices might be manipulated to a high level.

32   'International Tin Agreement, 1953', Articles IV, VI, VIII, IX, XII and Annex A.

33   Ibid., Article IV.

34   Ibid., Article XVII (7).

35   Ibid., Article XVIII.

36   The average price per ton of tin metal for 1956, 1957 and 1958 was £788, £755 and £735 respectively.   See International Tin Council, Trade in Tin 1960-1974 (International Tin Council, London, n.d.), p. 11.

37   Export controls were lifted gradually with the export quota being raised from a low point of 20,000 tons in the first quarter of 1959 to 36,000 tons in the first quarter of 1960 before being abandoned at the end of the third quarter.

38   T. Geer, 'The Post-War Tin Agreements: A Case of Success in Price Stabilization of Primary Commodities', Schweizerische Zeitschaft für Volkwirtschaft und Statistic, no. 2 (1970) provides a useful analytical account.

39   'Second International Tin Agreement' (HMSO, London, 1961, Cmnd. 1332), Article VIII.

40   Ibid., Articles VII-IX and XVI and Annexes A, B, C and D. See also United Nations, United Nations Tin Conference 1960: Summary of Proceedings (United Nations, New York, n.d., 61.II.D.2) for an account of the conference.

41   International Tin Council, Trade in Tin 1960-1974 (International Tin Council, London, n.d.), p. 11.

42   Fox, The Working of a Commodity Agreement, p. 316.

43   Ibid., p. 321.

44   'Second International Tin Agreement', Article XIII.

45   United Nations, United Nations Tin Conference, 1965: Summary of Proceedings (United Nations, New York, 1965, 65.II.D.2), pp. 14-15.   Greater incentives for investment were proposed by the Nigerian representative, Mr Adebo, for example, and by Mr Sethaput of Thailand. For comments on the operation of the buffer stock see Ibid., pp. 15-16. See also P.P. Courtenay, 'International Tin Restriction and its Effects on the Malayan Tin Industry', Geography, vol. 46 (1961) for a regional assessment.

46   'Third International Tin Agreement' (United Nations, New York, 1965, II.D.2), Articles VI and X.

47   For the quotation, see Fox, The Working of a Commodity Agreement, p. 357. The US participated in the United Nations Tin Conference. The Agreement restricted accession in a way in which its predecessors had not. Membership was restricted to governments represented at the 1965 United Nations Tin Conference, participants in the Second International Tin Agreement and members of the United Nations or its specialised agencies (Article XXV). Poland and Hungary joined, for example, in 1969 and Yugoslavia in 1970.

48   For the statistics covering this period, see for example International Tin Council, Statistical Yearbook 1968, pp. 27-33.

49   International Tin Council, Trade in Tin 1960-1974, p. 10.

50   Ibid. and International Tin Council, Tin Statistics 1968-1978 (International Tin Council, London, n.d.).

51   'Fourth International Tin Agreement' (HMSO, London, 1970, Cmnd. 4493), Article 25.

52   See Part I.

53   International Tin Council, Trade in Tin 1960-1974 and for the price statistics, see UNCTAD, Monthly Commodity Price Bulletin: Supplement: Monthly and Annual Price Series 1960-1980 (UNCTAD, Geneva, 1981, TD/B/C. 1/CPB/1.1/Add.1).   See also G. Blau, 'Some Implications of Tin Price Stabilisation', Malayan Economic Review, vol. 17, no. 1 (April 1972).

54 International Tin Council, 'The International Implications of the United States Disposal of Stockpiled Tin' (International Tin Council, London, n.d.), pp. 27-8. In the second half of 1973 alone, for example, the US sold 18,000 metric tons from the stockpile.

55 International Tin Council, Annual Report 1975-1976 (International Tin Council, London, 1976), pp. 20-1 and 'The Fifth International Tin Agreement' (International Tin Council, London, 1976), Article 10(g).

56 'The Fifth International Tin Agreement', Article 19 and, for comparison, 'Third International Tin Agreement', Article V.

57 'The Fifth International Tin Agreement', Article 9 and S.H. Burger 'The Fifth International Tin Agreement', Law and Policy in International Business, vol. 9, no. 2 (1977).

58 International Tin Council, Annual Report 1978-1979 (International Tin Council, London, 1979), pp. 22-3 reported a scaling down of the US stockpile in October 1976 from 40,500 to 32,499 tons. See also G. Goodwin and J. Mayall (eds.), A New International Commodity Regime.

59 US, Department of the Treasury, Department of the Treasury News (Washington, 9 June 1976), p. 5.

60 H.W. Allen, 'The International Tin Agreement: Why It Works', speech given to New York University's First International Metals Commodities Conference, 15 December 1975, published in Tin International (London, December 1975).

61 See IMF, 'IMF Survey' (February 8 1982) for tin market conditions between 1977 and 1982.

62 Financial Times, 30 June 1981.

63 'Sixth International Tin Agreement' (UNCTAD, Geneva, 1981, TD/TIN.6/14), Articles 3 and 7.

64 Ibid., Article 9.

65 Ibid., Article 21. An export control period could be declared by the Council either by a two-thirds distributed majority when at least 70 per cent of the maximum volume of the buffer stock was held in tin metal or by a simple distributed majority when at least 80 per cent of the maximum volume of the buffer stock was held in tin metal.

66 Ibid., Article 25.

67 Ibid., Articles 22 and 32. See also S.H. Burger, 'The Fifth International Tin Agreement'.

68 Financial Times, 7 January 1982, Ibid., 8 January 1982 and Ibid., 3 February 1982 and Wall Street Journal, 24 February 1982. Agreement on the form to be taken by a producers' association, however, was the major point of disagreement. See also Financial Times, 19 November 1982, Ibid., 4 December 1982 and Ibid., 11 February 1983.

69 G.W. Smith and G.R. Schink, 'International Tin Agreement: A Reassessment', Economic Journal, vol. 86 (1976), pp. 715-28.

70 G.W. Smith, 'US Commodity Policy and the Tin Agreement' in D.B. Denoon (ed.), The New International Economic Order (Macmillan, London, 1979), Chapter 6. Smith recommended that the US should contribute to the buffer stock, heavily if necessary, and coordinate tin disposal policy as a 'symbol' of willingness to cooperate in 'reasonable agreements' run along 'economically sound' principles.

7: WHEAT

'As a start to the programme of international food security, we call for an early conclusion of the International Grains Arrangement, and increases in emergency food supplies.'

(Brandt Report, 1980)

1. General

Wheat ranks as a leading primary commodity with exports totalling $442 million in 1938 and $20.8 billion in 1980.(1) As a commodity produced principally by developed countries, it was not included in UNCTAD's list of 'core' commodities in 1976 but this did not prevent UNCTAD adding cereals to the list of commodities suitable for buffer stock arrangements under the Integrated Programme; and in 1970 and in 1978 to 1979 wheat negotiations were held under UNCTAD's auspices.(2)   Like tin, wheat has been the object of regular international commodity agreements since the 1930s and the more recent agreements have also given coverage, albeit of a limited nature, to coarse grains and rice. However, such coverage has been peripheral to the workings of the agreements and in this chapter, accordingly, the discussion will centre largely on wheat.(3)
An essential aspect of wheat, the most important of all cereal grasses, is its value as a foodstuff and as the chief raw material for bread production.(4) A second characteristic is the multiplicity of types of wheat that have been cultivated. The International Wheat Council distinguishes between the genetically different 'triticum durum' and 'triticum vulgare'. Durum wheat, which is characterised by its hard flinty kernels, is pre-eminently suitable for pasta manufacture and for this purpose it is milled into semolina. Triticum

vulgare, usually called 'bread wheat', may itself be broken down into 'hard' and 'soft' varieties according, broadly, to their gluten content. The latter is an important factor in the strength of the flour: hard (or stronger) types are used to produce a close grained bread with a long shelf life. Within these broad categories there are numerous subdivisions. Grading plays a very important role in the wheat trade and prices vary accordingly.(5)

Despite its renewability, wheat has been seen as a commodity of political and even strategic importance. At the national level, it featured as a political weapon in respect of the US grain embargo on some grain sales to the USSR and at the forefront of several national development plans (for example, in India and the Sudan). Internationally wheat, with other cereals, became a central plank of the United Nations world development plan in 1970 in a drive to 'bridge the protein gap' and in the International Food Reserve established in the US under the Carter Administration(6).

It is the high proportion of the grain which may be used for human consumption which has made wheat rank above coarse grains in national food production programmes. Food and feed usages together account for most wheat consumption, a relatively minor proportion going to beverage manufacture, industrial uses and seed production.(7) The feed use of wheat, generally lower in developing countries, varies from year to year according to the size of the crop. In 1975/76, for example, a poor wheat crop and a lower than average coarse grain harvest led to supplies of grain for livestock feeding being considerably reduced in the USSR, despite an unprecedented volume of grain imports and a drawdown of stocks.(8)

A notable feature of world wheat production has been the divergent trends in acreage and yields. In developed countries, for instance, there has been a general expansion of production, particularly in the EEC, due largely to increases in wheat yields. Such increases in yields reflect technological advance, with improved varieties of wheat, the greater use of fertilisers and mechanisation major contributory factors. Production in developing countries has also expanded, notably through a steady increase in acreage, although yields have also risen. Despite these broad developments, however, there have been wide year-to-year fluctuations in wheat crops, due largely to unpredictable weather conditions.(8) Prices are set largely on the basis of North-American output.

An important aspect of trade in wheat compared with other commodities under consideration is the comparatively low proportion of production entering world trade - about 22 per cent, for example, in 1980. Although this is a higher proportion than for other grains, the world market is thus essentially a residual market. Before the Second World War, developing countries as a whole were net exporters of cereals; since the War, only Argentina has featured as an important exporter on a regular basis. World trade in wheat both before and after the Second World War has been dominated by the industrialised countries, particularly Canada, the US, Australia and those of the EEC. After a period of virtual stagnation of world trade in wheat, along with other grains, in the first half of the century, rapid growth took place during the 1950s and 1960s - from 21.4 million metric tons in 1954 to 49.3 million in 1963/64, 58.2 million in 1973/74 and 94 million in 1980/81.(9) This reflected the stimulus to production given by post-War food shortages, higher prices, the support of national policies (notably in North America and the EEC) and the growing use of wheat as a principal food. The USSR, formerly a major net exporter, mainly to the Comecon bloc, has been an importer on the world market for more than a decade.

World trade in wheat is concentrated in the hands of a few major companies. A recent study, for example, has estimated that five companies handle between them 90 per cent of the EEC's trade in wheat and corn, 90 per cent of Canada's barley exports and 89 per cent of Argentina's wheat exports. Two of the biggest handle each about 25 per cent of US grain exports. The companies, Cargill and Continental of the US, André of Switzerland, Louis Dreyfus Company of Paris and Bunge of Argentina, are well established, privately owned and multi-national, with interests in shipping, insurance, banking and market intelligence.(10) Their control over stocks has generated considerable interest, particularly in the mid-1970s when it was reported that the USSR was able to purchase large quantities of grain through the grain companies without the US authorities being aware of what was happening.(11)

A second notable element in the world wheat trade is the important role played by the futures market. Wheat constitutes the biggest and most important of all commodity markets with the Chicago market the largest and most active. In London, in contrast, the market is smaller and more specialised owing to the existence of the EEC grain price system which, reportedly, reduces the incentive to speculate in wheat and to hedge.(12)

Whereas in the 1930s Europe took nearly three-quarters of world imports of wheat, and Europe and North America were the major consumers, post-War wheat consumption has followed a different trend with developing and centrally planned countries playing an important role in increasing overall demand, particularly during the 1970s. Population changes, changes in per capita calorific intake and the promotion of convenience foods, such as bread, appear to have been the main factors affecting demand.(13) The general rising trend in the consumption of wheat has led to some substitution from rice and other foodstuffs in developing countries. The possibilities of substitution among wheat and other coarse grains, with the exception of maize, as well as competition between coarse grains and lower quality wheats as feed, have ensured that there has been some similarity in movement between prices of wheat and coarse grains.(14)

2. Controls on Wheat to 1939

In view of the leading role played by wheat and wheat products in
world trade, it is not surprising that controls on wheat have well
established historical roots. At the international level, for example,
the Corn Laws in Great Britain first restricted then facilitated the
expansion of the international grain trade, allowing for the growth of
trade with Canada and the US. At the national level, import duties
on wheat flourished from the late nineteenth century when the
competition of new and abundant supplies from North America
became a serious cause for concern in countries such as Germany,
France and Italy. However, in the form of international commodity
control which has been defined in Chapter 1, the question of
cooperation between countries on wheat matters was not raised until
the International Economic Conference in Geneva in 1927 in the
context of general discussions on the condition of world agriculture.
In contrast to other commodities, wheat producers faced relatively
favourable market conditions, with prices at acceptable levels to
producers, so that there appears to have been no strong impetus for
formal controls on trade in wheat.(15)

Between 1927 and 1931, the situation changed markedly. Under
the influence of abundant supplies and reduced import purchasing
power, the price of wheat fell by a substantial 65 per cent between
1929 and 1931 and in these circumstances a series of meetings -
sixteen, for example, in 1930 and 1931 alone - were held between
producing countries to discuss the world wheat situation. The
meetings culminated in an International Wheat Conference held in
London in May 1931, which was attended by eleven wheat exporting
countries. The objective of the Conference was to obtain agreement
on restricting world exports of wheat. However, the failure of the
US to accept the proposal and disagreement on the part of the USSR
regarding the size of its proposed export quota meant that no
agreement was reached apart from a general acceptance of the
principle that each country should reduce its wheat acreage where
possible. In addition, a committee was established to serve the wheat
exporting countries and, in particular, to investigate alternative uses
of wheat.(16)

The lack of success of the wheat exporting countries in securing
an international wheat marketing strategy did not prevent, and
indeed probably encouraged, the introduction of a variety of national
control measures. In Canada, for example, the problem of wheat
surpluses came to a head earlier than elsewhere owing to a record
1928 crop. The initial reaction of the farmers' cooperative marketing
associations (the 'pools') was to deal with the problem themselves.
However, their policy of allowing producers an advance payment of a
dollar a bushel led to extreme difficulty in 1930 when the price of
wheat fell to Canadian $ 56 cents. At this stage the Federal

Government intervened to guarantee the pools' borrowings and in 1931 itself agreed to purchase all the wheat offered at a fixed price. However, as Lamartine Yates has pointed out, this policy did little to raise the world price and may well have contributed to the loss of markets by Canada to Argentina.(17)

Another important example of national control measures invoked is offered by the US where the efforts of the Federal Farm Board in providing guaranteed prices and withholding supplies from the market mirrored the action of the Canadian Government. However, the circumstances under which it operated were far less auspicious with bumper crops in 1931 and 1932 substantially boosting the cost of the measures. Accordingly, the scheme was abandoned in 1933, when Roosevelt came into office, in favour of a policy of reducing wheat acreage, administered by the Agricultural Adjustment Administration. Reductions were encouraged by a system of subsidies on permitted production levels for the home market financed by a tax on flour based on historic average production levels. In practice, however, four years of short crops meant that the acreage reduction was not enforced.

Australia provides a third example of national controls on wheat which were adopted in this period. In this case, subsidies were granted to assist farmers following the bumper crop of 1930 which induced a large fall in prices. The cost of the scheme, which was not tied to restricted output, was considerable. One estimate has concluded that between 1931/32 and 1935/36 the subsidies amounted to £14 million of expenditure, financed partly through a tax on flour milling but mainly from general revenues. (A fixed price scheme was introduced by the Federal Government in 1935 but disallowed by the courts.)

A further example is provided by Argentina where assistance also first took the form of a guaranteed price for wheat with no restriction on output. In 1933, however, the Government went further and depreciated the currency by 20 per cent and itself bought three-quarters of the crop. The price set, although low by comparative international standards, was sufficient to provide some return to Argentinian producers whose costs were the lowest in the world.(18)

The question of international controls on wheat was raised again by Premier Bennett of Canada at the 1933 Monetary and Economic Conference held in London. As a result, a conference on wheat was convened in August 1933; this led to the first multi-lateral agreement on wheat. As in the case of the pre-War tin agreements, the first wheat agreement was drafted to cope with what was considered to be a large and persistent world surplus (Figure 7:1). Its aim was to raise wheat prices from the low levels currently prevailing to that 'remunerative to the farmers and fair to the consumers of breadstuffs'.(19)

137

The technical aspects of the 1933 Wheat Agreement were relatively straightforward: exports of wheat in the crop-year 1934/35 (August-July) were to be limited in the case of the major exporting countries to 85 per cent of average production between 1931 and 1933 inclusive, after deducting 'normal domestic requirements'(20). Minor exporters, Bulgaria, Hungary, Romania and Yugoslavia, agreed that their combined exports during the same period should not exceed 50 million bushels whereas the USSR agreed to limit exports for 1933/34 to an unspecified level to be negotiated with other wheat exporting countries; export levels in the following crop-year were also to be negotiated. Although export restraint was the main control mechanism introduced, the Agreement also provided that an extension of the area of wheat sown should not be encouraged and that 'every possible measure' should be taken to increase consumption of wheat and to lower tariffs imposed on wheat trade. Following the example set by the 1931 Tin Agreement, a Wheat Advisory Committee was established in London on a temporary basis to exercise a general watchdog function.(21) (For a brief summary of the key features of this and subsequent wheat agreements, see the Appendix, Table 2.)

The 1933 Wheat Agreement attracted a relatively high degree of participation perhaps because it covered only a short, two-year time span. However, despite its modest compass, the Agreement had broken down within a year. A catalyst to the disintegration of the Agreement was a bumper crop in Argentina which led to the Argentinians exceeding their quota and dumping wheat on to the world market. As a result the price of wheat fell rather than rose as the Agreement had anticipated. The Argentinians, subject to some criticism, complained in their turn that North-American producers had also failed to restrain their production, an assertion not supported by the statistics available.(22) Whatever the burden of responsibility, the Agreement became inoperative, having achieved little success in meeting its immediate objectives. However, the Committee was preserved to monitor developments in the world wheat market and between 1935 and 1938, when over-burdening wheat surpluses were reduced under the influence of a succession of severe droughts (Figure 7:1), it kept alive the idea of a new agreement. It was assisted in this function by the support of Henry Wallace, a former US Secretary of Agriculture, in his new capacity as Vice-President of the US.

In 1938, when a bumper crop materialised, meetings were held in London to discuss US proposals for 'an international granary plan'. The aim of this scheme was to stabilise the amount of wheat offered to the world market by producing countries. When the meeting failed to secure a new agreement, the US adopted national measures to subsidise exports. However, talks continued throughout the autumn and winter of 1938 and by the time that war was declared in 1939, a

Figure 7:1: Stocks of Wheat in the Four Major Exporting Countries,
1922-1959 (millions of metric tons)

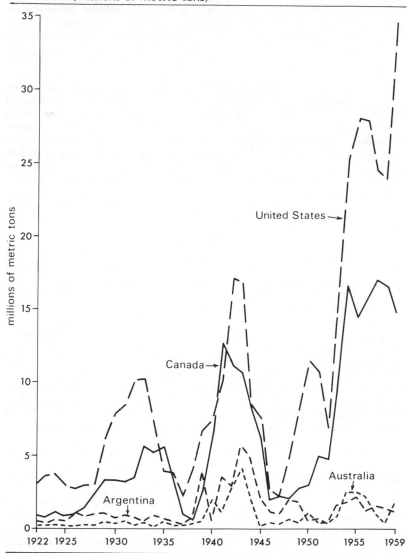

Source: International Wheat Council, <u>Review of the World Wheat
            Situation</u> (International Wheat Council, London, April
            1960), quoted with permission.

draft wheat agreement had been brought near to the point of adoption by Argentina, Australia, Canada and the US. The draft called for wheat export quotas and a world minimum price to be established for a selected reference wheat. In broad outline, therefore, it built on the abortive Wheat Agreement of 1933.(23)

3. War-time Controls

During the War, complete governmental control of wheat production and marketing was established in the UK, Australia and later in Canada and the US. In contrast to the supply position of other commodities, world wheat stocks remained high, with abundant harvests counter-balancing production cuts attributable to war-time disruption (Figure 7:1). The surplus position highlighted the continuation of problems in the international marketing of wheat and in July 1941 the governments of Argentina, Australia, Canada, the US and the UK met in Washington to resume the wheat discussions interrupted by the outbreak of war. The conclusion of the meeting and its successor in September, both of which were held in secret, was that a draft wheat agreement should be prepared to meet the problems of post-War wheat surpluses and, more precisely, 'to prevent a wheat war from breaking out with its serious economic and political consequences'.(24) In April 1942, accordingly, countries which had attended the two 1941 wheat meetings, initialled a memorandum which provided for a draft wheat agreement to come into effect on the cessation of hostilities and pending the conclusion of an international wheat conference. The draft was never implemented but remains worthy of a brief examination because it served as a basis for further years of discussion at wheat conferences in 1945 and 1946 and because it reflected a transitional phase between pre-War and post-War wheat control philosophy.

The 1942 draft exceeded the 1933 Agreement in its degree of complexity. It addressed the problem of anticipated wheat surpluses by two types of control mechanisms: export controls in the form of quotas, as in the 1933 Wheat Agreement; and national controls on output and stock holdings by each producing country participant. In addition, an International Wheat Council was to be established with the authority to set maximum and minimum prices for wheat, to administer a relief pool 'for intergovernmental relief in war-stricken countries and other necessitous areas of the world'(25) and to take decisions on a wide variety of subjects, including arrangements with international shipping factors to facilitate the exportation of wheat and cooperation 'with bodies engaged in the task of improving human nutrition'. An Executive Committee was authorised to administer the provisions of the Agreement which was given a life of four years (a marked extension of the two-year period written into the 1933 Wheat Agreement) and open to accession by any government.(26) In sum, the 1942 Draft Wheat Agreement aimed to provide a fairly detailed modus operandi for dealing with potentially large wheat surpluses.

Although the 1942 Draft Wheat Agreement was never formally implemented, an International Wheat Council came into being in August 1942, with its seat in Washington, and this superseded the Wheat Advisory Committee. By the end of the War, membership of the Council had risen to include twenty-eight countries and with the increase in participation came a greater divergence of opinion regarding the future pattern of post-War wheat controls. In accordance with the 1942 Draft, an international wheat conference was convened in 1947 in London to discuss a new international wheat agreement. A draft agreement, based firmly on the 1942 model, was presented for discussion but was abandoned in favour of an entirely new concept incorporating multi-lateral purchase and sales contracts as the control mechanism. Production controls were omitted and export quotas were to be enforceable only at minimum and maximum price levels. The 1947 Conference failed to bear fruit owing to differences of opinion regarding the appropriate level of prices. However, the new principle was to form the foundation of subsequent international wheat agreements.(27)

4. Controls to 1959

In contrast to the situation envisaged in the 1942 Draft Agreement, wheat supplies after the War were far from in massive surplus. Indeed, there was a general concern in 1945/46 that world food supplies had fallen to a critically low level (Figure 7:1) owing to reduced European production - as a result both of military operations and unfavourable weather conditions - and also to crop failures in India and South Africa. The war-time machinery which had been established to organise and to distribute available supplies - the Cereals Committee of the Combined Food Board - attempted to apportion grain supplies to the areas of greatest need. As a result, bread rationing was introduced in the UK in July 1946 whereas bread had been unrationed during the war years.(28) Estimated production figures suggest that output was erratic between 1946 and 1948 and in these circumstances of unpredictable supply, the inability of a 1947 Wheat Conference to secure agreement on pricing provisions was not surprising.(29)

It was only in 1948, at a special session of the International Wheat Council in Washington, that agreement was reached on the terms of a new international wheat agreement to subsist for a five-year span. Its objective was 'to assure supplies of wheat to importing countries and to assure markets to exporting countries at equitable and stable prices'.(30) Maximum and minimum prices were established (on the basis of Number 1 Northern Manitoba in store at Fort William/Fort Arthur), based roughly on prices then prevailing and with the minimum price reducing by (Canadian) 10 cents per bushel each year since it was expected that the supply position would grow progressively easier throughout the duration of the Agreement. Three of the major exporting countries, Australia, Canada and the US, committed themselves to exporting a total of 500 million bushels (13.6 million tons) per year at not more than the maximum prices. Thirty-three importing countries in their turn undertook to purchase 500 million bushels (with individual purchase levels guaranteed) at prices not less than the minimum specified. The Council was given the responsibility for recording those transactions of wheat which were part of the guaranteed quantities. The Agreement specified further minimum carry-over stock levels to be maintained by the exporting countries. In the event of the free market price falling below the lowest price prescribed in the Agreement, both exporters, in the first instance, and importers, subsequently, were required to build reserves up to 10 per cent of their respective guaranteed quantities for each crop-year to be sold or used when the price rose above the minimum level. No mechanism was introduced for controlling output since it was not anticipated that stocks would become burdensome within the five year span covered by the Agreement.(31)

Despite the broad measure of agreement reached on its provisions, the 1948 Wheat Agreement did not come into effect owing to the failure of the US to ratify by the required date of 1 July 1948. As a result the UK and several other members withdrew their support. Between the shelving of the 1948 Agreement and the implementation of its successor in mid-1949 the position of the importing countries was strengthened by an improvement in the international supply of wheat. Consequently, the maximum guaranteed price was shaded down to Canadian $1.80 from Canadian $2.00 throughout the course of the Agreement. The 1949 Wheat Agreement did not differ essentially from that negotiated in 1948, although it covered four compared with five years. France and Uruguay added their names to the list of wheat exporters guaranteeing sales, slightly raising the quantity guaranteed and the list of importing countries was extended to thirty-seven from thirty-three. The stock provisions were drafted generally to require each exporting country simply to maintain stocks at a level 'adequate' to ensure that they fulfilled their guaranteed sales under the Agreement(32) and an adjustment procedure was provided in the case of a short crop or the necessity to safeguard a country's balance of payments position or monetary reserves. In certain circumstances, the International Wheat Council was authorised to relieve a country of a part or all of its obligations under the guaranteed quantity provisions of the Agreement and to re-distribute the available quantities amongst willing participants.(33)

The 1949 Wheat Agreement represented a new phase in the history of international wheat controls and proved to be the model for a series of consecutive agreements. Despite the fact that it excluded two major exporting countries, Argentina and the USSR, the former on the grounds that the maximum prices conceded were too low and the latter on the grounds that its export quota was insufficient, it embraced over half of world trade in wheat. There was a substantial inducement for full participation on the part of wheat importing countries since the Agreement operated during a period when, generally, wheat was in short supply and the open market price exceeded the maximum specified in the Agreement. Some indication of the relative success of the Agreement is given by the growth in the total amount of wheat trade guaranteed. According to the International Wheat Council, at the inception of the Agreement guaranteed quantities amounted to 12.4 million metric tons. Even by the end of the first crop-year covered by the Agreement (1949/50), this quantity had risen to 14.3 million metric tons and by 1952/53, guaranteed quantities amounted to 15.8 million metric tons. Transactions under the terms of the 1949 Wheat Agreement increased from 51 per cent of world trade in 1949/50 to 60 per cent in 1952/53.(34)

Judged in terms of its own objectives, namely 'to assure supplies of wheat to importing countries and markets for wheat to exporting countries at equitable and stable prices'(35), the 1949 Wheat Agreement may be considered to have been reasonably successful in its stabilisation function although this applied only to trade covered by the Agreement and rapid movements in prices took place on the free world market. At the end of 1950, for example, at the onset of the Korean War, these rose rapidly to well above the levels prescribed in the Agreement and the US and Canada were held in some suspicion by the consumers on the International Wheat Council for having withheld stocks in order to manipulate an increase in the price range. The huge losses incurred on Wheat Agreement sales of US wheat were met by the US Treasury and it has been suggested that if US wheat prices in this period had been determined largely by the Agreement's pricing arrangements, the world would have witnessed the development of 'a truly critical world wheat shortage'.(36) The conclusion of a United Nations study on the prospects for commodity trade in 1953, which cited the 1949 Wheat Agreement as an example of a successful multi-lateral type of agreement in which 'stability had a value in itself', must therefore be viewed with considerable caution.(37)

The last year of the 1949 Agreement coincided with a narrowing of the spread between free market prices and those which had been negotiated under the Agreement as more abundant supplies emerged gradually from the war-damaged wheat-producing areas of Europe and from an exceptionally large crop in Canada. Carry-over stocks almost doubled at the end of 1952/53 compared with the same period in the preceding year (Figure 7:1).(38) Negotiations for a renewal of the Agreement, which took place in Washington in April 1953, devoted considerable time, in consequence, to the question of the appropriate price range. Agreement was reached eventually on a higher price range of Canadian $1.55 to $2.05 per bushel, that is, below the average price prevailing at the time of negotiation. Despite this, the UK, the major wheat importer, withdrew from the Agreement in protest at what it considered to be the excessively high level set. The only other refinement worthy of mention was the inclusion of Rules of Procedure for the International Wheat Council (regarding elections, the conduct of proceedings, voting), the Executive Committee and the Advisory Committee on Price Equivalents (whose task was to consider the price equivalent of any description of wheat of an exporting country).(39)

Under the 1953 Wheat Agreement, the supply position was transformed from one of comparative scarcity to one of surplus, a situation more familiar to the pre-War pattern. A rise in consumption failed to match strong levels of production and world wheat stocks in the five main exporting countries rose to 43.9 million metric tons at the end of 1955/56 compared with 26.9 million metric tons at the end of 1952/53 (Figure 7:1). Despite the healthy supply position, there was no dramatic fall in world prices owing to continued price support operations in Canada and the US. However, a downward trend was to continue unabated until the early 1970s. Although the 1953 Agreement operated within a price range which was similar to that prevailing on the world market, its impact was reduced by the much lower level of quantities guaranteed under the Agreement and a fall in the volume of recorded transactions. On average, only 26 per cent of world trade in wheat was covered by the Agreement (Table 7:1).

In practice, the balance of power in international wheat transactions continued to be located in North America and in national price supports rather than in the International Wheat Council and international controls. The problem of mounting wheat surpluses located largely in North America fell outside the terms of reference of the Agreement since the wheat produced did not enter world trade. The problem, however, did not escape international attention entirely: in 1954, the United Nations Food and Agriculture Organization adopted Principles on Surplus Disposal and later, in 1957, it established a Group on Grains to provide a consultative forum for the whole of the grains sector.(40)

The Agreement was renewed again in 1956 with few changes apart from a reduction in the price range to Canadian $1.50 to $2.00 from Canadian $1.55 to $2.05 per bushel. Signatories included the return of Argentina and the addition of Sweden as exporting members; the UK remained outside the Agreement.

Table 7:1: Guaranteed Quantities and Transactions Recorded under
the 1953 Wheat Agreement

Crop-year	Millions of metric tons		Transactions as percentage of:	
	Guaranteed Quantities	Transactions Recorded	Guaranteed Quantities	Transactions Recorded
1953/54	10.6	6.1	58	25
1954/55	10.7	7.9	74	28
1955/56	10.7	6.9	64	24
Annual average	10.7	7.0	65	26

Source: International   Wheat   Council,   'International   Wheat
           Agreement: A   Historical   and   Critical   Background'
           (International   Wheat   Council   Report   EX/74/74   2/2,
           London, October 1974).

The trends identified in the 1953 Wheat Agreement became
more pronounced and consequently a greater cause for concern under
its successor: stock levels remained very high (Figure 7:1); and
transactions under the terms of the Agreement fell to 16 per cent of
world trade compared with 26 per cent under the 1953
Agreement.(41) As in the case of the earlier agreements, the relative
stability of wheat prices represented a deliberate policy response on
the part of the North-American authorities to encourage stock
withdrawals and, in the case of the US Government, to take on the
burden of financing the requisite stocks. Between 1949 and 1959,
Canada and the US together held between 80 and 90 per cent of the
total stocks of the five major exporting countries.(42)
The conclusion to be drawn from the operation of the first
three post-War wheat agreements was that the relatively stable
behaviour of wheat prices during the 1950s was not wholly nor even
principally attributable to the workings of the Agreement itself. As
the International Wheat Council commented in 1953, the direct
effect of the Agreement on world markets was limited(43) and it was
national rather than international controls which were the most
important influence. The former brought their own unfortunate side
effects. As a United Nations Food and Agriculture Organization
study concluded in 1959:

'guarantees ... will continue, together with technological
advance to stimulate, year after year, an output larger than can
be absorbed by normal effective demand'.(44)

145

At the end of the 1950s, as an illustration of this phenomenon, stocks of wheat stood at almost three times the 1950 level, with output boosted also by higher yields.(45)

5. Controls between 1959 and 1970/71

It was not surprising that after a decade in which little modification had been made to the Agreement changes should eventually be felt to be necessary. A major difference between the 1959 Agreement and its predecessors was its wider scope.   The objectives of the Agreement, for example, were broadened to include the expansion of the international trade in wheat and wheat-flour, the freest possible flow of this trade and the encouragement of increased consumption(46).   Although the enlargement of the aims was in no way unusual amongst international commodity agreements in this period, it took on a special significance in bringing the wheat agreements more into line with those for other commodities and away from the standard wheat trading contract. In this respect, also, the concessions made in the 1959 Agreement to the requests by importing countries for changes in the contract system are also worthy of note. They help to explain, at least in part, why the UK found it possible to adhere.   A further factor was probably the reduction in the price range to Canadian $1.50 to $1.90 from $1.50 to $2.00.(47)

The technical changes made to the multi-lateral contract system sprang from the importers' concern that the existing system of guaranteed quantities was unduly restrictive since it did not allow for varying levels of import requirements. The latter was abandoned and replaced by undertakings by each importing member to purchase from exporting members not less than a specified minimum proportion of its total commercial purchases that year at prices within the prescribed range. The obligation of exporting members, correspondingly, was to supply wheat, in association with one another, to satisfy the commercial requirements of the importing countries, also at prices within the range. If the maximum price level were reached, the exporting member was obliged instead to supply wheat equal in volume to the average level of commercial purchases made by importing members during the preceding five crop-years. In these conditions, importers were no longer bound by their percentage obligations and were free to obtain their supplies from other countries outside of the Agreement.(48) An increasing flexibility regarding the volume of total transactions between participants was thus balanced by the requirement that the obligation to trade applied throughout the price range and not just at the minimum or maximum levels. To facilitate the formulation of future price ranges and to assist the International Wheat Council in its work, an annual review of the world wheat situation was commissioned from the Council.

With the participation of the UK and the modifications to the technical aspects of the Agreement, more trade came under its auspices: in its three year term, about 36 per cent of world trade was covered by the Agreement, a proportion higher than that prevailing between 1956 and 1959 in a period when non-commercial transactions were expanding. During the life of the Agreement, the percentage obligations of importing countries were more than fulfilled and prices remained on average within the range, although there was a fairly pronounced rise in the last year to within Canadian 2.75 cents of the upper limit. However, as in previous years, the relative stability of prices reflected the voluntary stock withdrawal by North-American interests rather than the positive stabilising influence of the Agreement itself.(49)

Despite the continuance of large and over-burdening surpluses, the 1962 Wheat Agreement introduced no new measures apart from raising the price range by Canadian 12.5 cents at both the top and the bottom to Canadian $1.625 to $2.025. Indeed, in appraising the operation of the 1959 Wheat Agreement, the International Wheat Council acknowledged that if the major exporting countries continued to operate voluntary buffer stocks and to incur the financial cost of operating such policies, it was unnecessary to make formal provision for stock-holding or the control of exports through quotas.(50) The Agreement thus survived in the 1959 mould and, with the addition of the USSR as a participant, it covered virtually the whole of world commercial trade in wheat - although this amounted to only one-third of total world trade in wheat owing to the large volume of special transactions.

A number of factors served to increase the demand for wheat in the year 1963/64 and to bring the first major upturn in prices since the early 1950s. On the one hand, the USSR entered the market to make purchases on a large scale to compensate for short domestic crops. On the other, poor European crops coupled with production restraint in some of the major European producing countries led to a fall in production. In these circumstances of slack supply and strong demand, stocks were run down by one-fifth bringing them to the lowest level since 1952. Remarkably, in view of the market conditions, prices remained within the prescribed range, a factor ascribed by the International Wheat Council to the success of the Agreement in dealing with unusual stresses in an orderly fashion.(51) Whilst there can be little doubt that the International Wheat Agreement provided a framework for dealing with rapidly changing market conditions, the existence of the North-American stocks also helped by acting as a shock absorber. The supply shortage was solved in part in 1964/65 by a rise in output.

The operation of the 1962 Wheat Agreement coincided with negotiations under GATT regarding the possibility of a more comprehensive agreement for grains.(52) The 1962 Agreement was extended, as a temporary measure, for one year in 1965 and by a further year in 1966. By May 1967, the GATT cereals negotiations were concluded with the adoption of a 'Memorandum of Agreement' on the terms of reference for the discussion of a (new) world grains arrangement. As a result, a conference on grains was convened in Rome in the summer of 1967; this led to agreement on the text of an International Grains Arrangement. In contrast to other wheat agreements, the 1967 Grains Arrangement was drawn up by a relatively limited and closed group of contracting parties within the GATT Cereals Group.(53) It consisted of two separate instruments, the Wheat Trade Convention and the Food Aid Convention, linked by a common preamble and open to separate ratification.(54) Despite the broad compass of its title, only the Food Aid Convention covered grains other than wheat; the Wheat Trade Convention, in contrast, constituted a continuation of the economic and administrative provisions of the 1962 Wheat Agreement. The USSR and Brazil, which had both signed the 1962 Wheat Agreement, withdrew from its successor.

The Food Aid Convention merits examination since it broke entirely new ground within the concept of an international commodity agreement. The object of the Convention, simply stated, was 'to carry out a food aid programme with the help of contributions for the benefit of developing countries'.(55) The Convention was open to the Governments of Argentina, Australia, Canada, Denmark, Finland, Japan, Norway, Sweden, Switzerland, the UK, the US and the EEC on condition that they sign the Wheat Trade Convention. It provided that the signatories should contribute annually to developing countries 4.5 million metric tons of grain 'suitable for human consumption and of an acceptable type and quality' or the cash equivalent thereof. In 1967/68 this was equivalent to 1.5 per cent of wheat production. Countries party to the Convention were also permitted to specify a recipient country or countries. The scheme was to be administered by a Food Aid Committee which was given the responsibility for monitoring food aid contributions and for organising an 'exchange of views', if necessary, to deal with emergency conditions. Although the Food Aid Committee was to be separate from the International Wheat Council, the Convention provided that it could use the services of the Council in the fulfilment of its administrative duties.(56)

The Food Aid Convention, which added a new dimension to international wheat controls, seems to have met with very little opposition. The aim was to secure a minimum supply of aid no matter what world market conditions prevailed and to involve developed countries which had not hitherto given assistance in this form. In this, as in other aspects of international commodity control, the role of the US was of paramount importance: the US agreed to contribute 42 per cent of the total under the Convention whereas the

EEC contributed 23 per cent and Canada 11 per cent. Although the quantities in question were comparatively small, the Food Aid Convention marked an important launching pad for what was to be a discreet but steady form of (largely bi-lateral) aid.(57)

The Wheat Trade Convention, obversely, built on the pattern laid down in the 1962 and 1959 Wheat Agreements with the multi-lateral contract retained as the control mechanism, although several refinements were made to its terms of operation. The exporters and importers were permitted to enter purchases from other importing members against their obligations under the Convention. In addition, in contrast to the earlier agreements, the 1967 Grains Arrangement based the price schedule on fourteen types of wheats for which price differentials were specified. Overall, the price range represented an increase of US 20 cents over the previous Agreement, with No. 1 Manitoba Wheat being replaced by US Hard Red Winter No. 2 (ordinary) fob Gulf ports as the basic reference wheat on the grounds that the latter was traded more regularly throughout the year than the former.(58) A Prices Review Committee was also established consisting of the EEC, five other importing countries and five exporting countries, chosen annually. The function of the Committee was to monitor market prices for wheat with a view to computing appropriate minima and maxima for the Agreement.(59) Finally, guidelines were included for concessional transactions: members undertook to conduct any such transactions 'in such a way as to avoid harmful interference with normal patterns of production and international commercial trade'; members engaging in such transactions agreed to consult with exporting members who might be affected by them.(60)

Even before the 1967 Grains Arrangement became operative, conditions in the wheat market had been far from stable. In 1965/66, for example, the volume of world wheat imports surged markedly, reflecting increased demand from both the USSR and India. This provided scope for a substantial drawing down of stocks although strong crops in 1966/67 and in 1967/68, together with weak world demand, meant that they were rapidly re-built: by 1968/69, against all expectation, stocks held by major exporters had risen to 55.7 million metric tons, a level which almost matched the peak year of 1960/61.(61)

1968/69, the first crop-year to be covered by the Arrangement, thus provided an inauspicious start; abundant supplies and contracting demand combined to exert strong downward pressure on prices so that, by September 1969, prices for most of the grades of wheat mentioned in the Arrangement had fallen below the minima. Despite this dramatic turnaround in supply conditions, the International Wheat Council invoked no formal action. Instead, informal discussions were conducted between the major exporting countries which led to corrective action by Australia, Canada and the US to reduce supplies entering the world market. This served to arrest the downward trend although prices remained below the minima in 1969/70.

The period 1968/69 to 1970/71 was critical in the history of international wheat controls. It demonstrated that, despite detailed drafting, the Arrangement achieved few of its objectives. One major problem was the time taken to negotiate the Arrangement which meant that its pricing provisions were out of date almost as soon as it was implemented. Another cause for concern was the fact that national control measures, enacted by three of the major producers, again deflected the locus of control from the centre - the International Wheat Council - to the periphery. Thirdly, the property of wheat as an agricultural crop subject to variations in yield, posed major obstacles for the successful implementation of the Arrangement.

6. Controls since 1971/72

Despite the difficulties which had been encountered during the life of the 1967 Grains Arrangement, a wheat conference was held under the auspices of the United Nations at the beginning of 1971 to negotiate a successor. Opinion was divided between those who favoured a return to the more flexible pricing arrangements of the early 1960s, those who proposed alternative control methods such as export quotas and those who felt that an improved 1967 Grains Arrangement could provide an effective instrument. In the event, the 1971 Conference foundered in respect of technical control measures with the choice of a reference wheat and the pricing system major articles of dispute. As a result, the 1971 Wheat Agreement did not include economic provisions, apart from those relating to food aid(62), but was simply assigned the function of providing a framework 'for the negotiation of provisions relating to the prices of wheat and to the rights and obligations of members in respect of international trade in wheat'.(63) A negotiating conference was to be convened if thought appropriate.

Under the 1971 Wheat Agreement, an Advisory Sub-Committee on Market Conditions was introduced to review market conditions and to advise on the 'appropriate time' for introducing pricing and other economic provisions.(64) Conditions prevailing in the early 1970s, however, were hardly auspicious for economic provisions to be negotiated. The USSR, for example, changed its role from an exporter to an importer of wheat on a large scale in 1972/73 after a crop shortfall and, with record volumes of wheat traded, stock levels were almost halved to a twenty-one year low point and prices rose by almost 50 per cent.(65) Prices continued on their upward course in 1973/74, despite a slight decrease in consumption requirements and a record wheat crop, due in part to factors which defy precise enumeration, such as the uncertain international financial and monetary situation and oil price movements. Against this background, the toothless 1971 Wheat Agreement was simply extended in its existing form for a further year from July 1974.

This did not mean, however, that the subject of wheat had disappeared entirely from the international agenda. On the contrary, developments proceeded in two different directions. The United Nations convened a World Food Conference in November 1974 to discuss what it viewed as the crisis of a world food shortage, emanating from the coincidence of poor crops in 1972. The conference ascribed the rapid rises in wheat prices to a chain reaction stemming from a 'bout of currency devaluations and revaluations', 'the attempts of importers to lay in large stocks', 'a switch of speculation from traditional types of securities to commodities' and 'the sharp rise in oil prices'.(66) It drew attention to the widening gap in self-sufficiency in cereals between the developed and developing countries, the former, with superior technology, increasing their output and exportable surpluses, the latter unable to increase production sufficiently to meet demand. It pointed out that between 1971 and 1973 developed countries, with only 30 per cent of the world's total population, had accounted for about 60 per cent of its food production and that the developing countries' share in agricultural trade had declined steadily from 40 per cent in the 1960s to about 30 per cent by the early 1970s. The Conference recommended that food production should be stepped up substantially in developing countries. In addition, it suggested that a world food policy should be elaborated in order to expand food aid, to establish substantial emergency food reserves, 'either at central points or close to known or suspected centres of disaster', and to promote 'more flexible trading arrangements and production policies'.(67)

The other new influence on international trade in wheat was the mushrooming of bi-lateral trading arrangements, with the negotiation of an agreement between the USSR and the US in 1975, a notable example. This agreement provided for the sale of at least 6 million metric tons of US wheat and maize annually to the USSR over a five-year period at the price prevailing at the time of purchase/sale and in accordance with usual commercial terms. In addition, the governments of each country agreed to consult in advance of purchases/sales in excess of 8 million metric tons of wheat or corn in any one year.(68) Other examples included a three year agreement between Canada and China in 1979 for the sale of 6 to 9 million metric tons of grain, a four year agreement between the US and China in 1980 concerning the sale of 6 to 8 million metric tons per year and the USSR's five year agreement with Canada in 1981 in respect of 25 million metric tons of grain. Egypt, Japan and Brazil were also regular participants on the purchasing front.(69)

151

The proliferation of bi-lateral wheat agreements was not without its administrative problems and political risks. This was amply demonstrated in January 1980 when the US imposed a partial embargo on the sale of grain to the USSR in retaliation for the USSR invasion of Afghanistan. The embargo, lifted only in April 1981 by the new Reagan Administration, blocked USSR purchases of some 17 million metric tons of grain in addition to the annual 8 million metric tons which had been permitted without further authorisation under the five year agreement. Although the impact of the embargo is difficult to quantify, it appears on balance that the USSR was able to secure adequate supplies from alternative sources such as Argentina or by purchasing US grain from third parties. Its political impact, however, is less easy to dismiss and the attractiveness of the embargo as an economic and political weapon remained sufficient for President Reagan to suggest that a series of sanctions, including a grain embargo, might be imposed on the USSR if the situation in Poland worsened in 1982.(70) Although on the face of it these reactions to the unstable conditions prevailing in the international wheat market in the 1970s were very different, in practice they had one important feature in common. Each addressed the problem of instability and the concomitant need to further international cooperation via a route which by-passed the machinery established, namely the International Wheat Council. The World Food Conference of 1974 went so far as to state explicitly that in its view past efforts to stabilise prices had not been successful on account of the difficulty of reconciling conflicting national interests, especially between developed countries.(71) Overall, it was national rather than international controls which continued to dominate trade in wheat (Chapter 3).(72)

Nonetheless, attempts were made to revive the economic provisions of the Wheat Agreement at preparatory meetings held under the tutelage of the International Wheat Council. The feasibility of establishing an international buffer stock for food grains was a key focal point. Views on the role that such a buffer stock should play varied considerably. The US, for example, was reported to favour a nationally held but internationally financed and coordinated buffer stock, although in 1977 it announced its own plans for a national grain reserve, consisting of 30 to 35 million metric tons of food and feed grains. This was designed to meet several objectives, including the provision of a hedge against future shortages ('at the least cost to the taxpayer and the most benefit to the farmer'), the underscoring of President Carter's commitment to fight against world hunger and the aim of ensuring that domestic grain supplies were sufficient to meet food aid commitments.(73) Elsewhere, there was little agreement on the appropriate size, cost and trigger mechanism of an international buffer stock. One estimate suggested that such a stock would need to be at least 60 to

70 million metric tons in order to dampen fluctuations in world prices of wheat. Others pointed to the difficulty of running an internationally coordinated buffer stock when private stocks played such an important part in the international grain trade.(74)

Failure to agree on the format of a new agreement was not limited to the question of the buffer stock. The question of the appropriate price range remained an extremely contentious issue. Large movements in international wheat prices, which swung from a peak of almost US $230 per metric ton in December/January 1974/75 to less than half that level in the summer of 1977, before moving upward again, in no way assisted the debate or suggested an easy solution.(75) A further complication was the desire of the EEC that coarse grains used for animal feeds should be included as a central element in any future agreement and the insistence by the US in the early stages that its agreement to controls on feed-grain prices should be matched by EEC concessions on wheat tariffs under the GATT Tokyo Round.(76)

1978 was the first year of three in which extensive discussions to negotiate a new agreement failed to bear fruit. Consequently, the 1971 Wheat Agreement was extended several times: for one year to June 1979, for two years to June 1981 and for a further two years to June 1983. The only major change was the negotiation in March 1980 of a new Food Convention allowing for food aid commitments by donors of 7.6 million metric tons of grain compared with 4.2 million tons in 1971. This amounted to 1.7 per cent of world wheat production in 1980/81, a slight increase from the 1967 and 1971 proportions.(77) It is perhaps ironic that the Food Aid Convention, considered in the first instance only a useful embellishment to the Wheat Agreements, represented one of its major achievements. Between 1972/73 and 1981/82, for example, 'special' exports of wheat, which included both non-commercial credits and gifts, averaged 7.5 per cent of total trade in wheat and covered 54 million metric tons of wheat or wheat equivalent (Table 7:2).

Despite the hiatus in the economic provisions of the Agreement and the increase in bi-lateral trading relations, the importance of the role that the wheat agreements could play continued to be recognised. In 1980, for example, Williams, Executive Director of the United Nations World Food Council, stated that a new agreement remained 'the centre-piece of world food security'. In its absence he recommended that a separate world food reserve should be created, that food aid within the Agreement be expanded further and that the IMF should create special facilities to help developing countries to pay for food imports.(78) The final point was met at least in part by the introduction in 1981 of an IMF food financing facility to help members encountering unforeseen balance of payments difficulties arising from excess cereal import costs. This facility, outlined in Chapter 2, was intended mainly for developing countries.(79)

153

Table 7:2: Commercial and Special Exports of Wheat and Wheat Flour, 1972/73-1981/82 (millions of metric tons wheat equivalent)

Crop Year	Total Trade	Commercial	Special	of which: non-commercial credits	Gift
1972/73	63.30	57.20	6.10	2.50	3.60
1973/74	55.48	51.67	3.81	1.04	2.77
1974/75	59.61	54.14	5.47	2.28	3.19
1975/76	64.51	59.45	5.06	2.52	2.54
1976/77	58.21	50.98	7.23	3.95	3.28
1977/78	66.51	60.72	5.79	3.27	2.52
1978/79	64.36	59.28	5.08	3.04	2.04
1979/80	83.06	78.42	4.64	2.82	1.82
1980/81	87.83	82.71	5.12	2.30	2.82
1981/82[a]	95.62	89.54	6.08	3.27	2.81

Note: a   preliminary

Source: The figures are based on those published annually in the International Wheat Council's 'Record of Operations'. They exclude trade between countries which are not members of the Agreement (which is thought to have been negligible) and also certain exports by the USSR and countries of Eastern Europe. The latter have usually amounted to 2 to 3 million metric tons in recent years. For these reasons, the figures of 'total trade' shown above differ from the global estimates published in the International Wheat Council's World Wheat Statistics.

There remains to mention, finally, the shift in attitudes to, and relations within, the international wheat trade in the early 1980s. On the one hand, the failure to secure a new international wheat agreement and prevailing depressed market conditions prompted Canadian officials in December 1981 to propose a conference of major exporters to discuss 'an orderly marketing programme'. On the other, a clash took place between the stance of US policy towards mounting surpluses in 1981 and 1982, which consisted essentially of stepping up a set-aside programme and boosting exports to developing countries, and that of the export subsidies of the EEC under the CAP. Failure of these two groups to resolve the issue at the GATT Ministerial Summit in 1982 and, notably, the EEC's reluctance to abandon export subsidies, brought by the beginning of 1983 the serious threat that the US would subsidise the sale of 120 million metric tons of stored grain and butter. In these circumstances, the brief of the International Wheat Council to negotiate a new international agreement was made even more difficult than it had been in the turbulent conditions of the 1970s.(80)

7. Conclusion

The case of wheat reveals the predominance of national and regional over international control measures. In general, the wheat agreements with economic provisions survived best when relatively simple in aim and format, such as those of the 1950s, and when their aims coincided with those of North-American, and notably of US, producers. The initiative for the first international controls on wheat in the 1930s, for example, came from North America; and the US was instrumental in blocking the 1948 Draft. North-American producers, similarly, were responsible for maintaining the pricing provisions of the agreements during the 1950s by taking on the burden of stock withdrawal. And the role of the US was also of critical importance from the 1970s, since by negotiating bi-lateral agreements, imposing a grain embargo and threatening to subsidise the sale of surplus grain, it did little to advance the negotiation of a new international wheat agreement with economic provisions.

From the early 1970s, the EEC also emerged as a voice of importance in international wheat negotiations. The introduction of cereals as the first product group under the CAP led both to an expansion of EEC production of and to an increase in export subsidies on grain. Export subsidies and the import levies charged by the EEC to bring the world market price to the EEC threshold level not only protected EEC producers but also discouraged sales to the EEC from outside sources. These policies, together with the evolution of the EEC as an important negotiator in its own right, added to rather than detracted from existing pressures on the international wheat agreements.

In addition to the stronger influence of national and regional rather than international controls, the wheat agreements faced other problems of a more operational nature. Key amongst them was the difficulty of forecasting accurately even the direction of price movements. An example of failure in this regard was the 1967 Wheat Arrangement whose pricing provisions were out of date even before the Agreement entered into force. The difficulty faced by forecasters was not limited to the drafters of the international wheat agreement: as late as 1970, for example, a United Nations Food and Agriculture Organization study on the stabilisation of trade in grains concluded, mistakenly, that the medium-term outlook for exportable supplies of cereals was 'ample relative to foreseeable import demand'.(81) In circumstances of rapid movements in prices the most that an international wheat agreement could hope to offer was an arrangement of sufficient flexibility to adapt to changing market conditions. In this context, the multi-lateral contract probably did not provide the most flexible of control mechanisms.

The Agreements were handicapped also by the general increase in instability in international trading and financial conditions in the 1970s. The large import demands of the USSR in 1972, for example, and the magnitude of rises in wheat prices between 1972/73 and 1973/74, were serious obstacles to the negotiation of pricing provisions. Similarly, depressed world trading conditions in the early 1980s and the greater attraction of bi-lateral and tri-lateral trading arrangements provided little encouragement for international discussions on wheat. On the plus side, however, the Food Aid Convention may be adjudged a positive achievement of the Wheat Agreement, even though it was considered inadequate by the World Food Conference, which proposed more far-reaching measures to secure world food supplies. The food aid programme not only set up the machinery for, but also acted as the channel of, a steady stream of 'special' exports of wheat. It may well be that, in a period of future grain shortages, the value of such machinery will prove itself even more fully.

1   For comparison, maize exports (fob) in 1980 were $11.9 billion, rice exports were $5.0 billion and total cereal exports, $40.2 billion. See United Nations, Food and Agriculture Organization, Trade Yearbook 1980 (United Nations, New York, 1981).

2   The Rome conference of 1967, in contrast, was convened by the International Wheat Council 'in cooperation with UNCTAD'.

3   Each of the Food Aid Conventions (1967, 1971 and 1980) covered coarse grains in addition to wheat. The only Wheat Trade Convention to refer to grains was that of 1967 and even then members' obligations to respect the price ranges and to supply each other with specific quantities related only to wheat. The 1971 Convention reverted entirely to wheat although the International Wheat Council was briefed to monitor developments in other grains which had a bearing on the world wheat situation.

4   Wheat is now important as a major source of nutrition both in temperate and tropical countries. In the case of the latter, this is a comparatively recent development of the last two or three decades with bread displacing some consumption of traditional local foods, notably in urban areas.

5   The 'gluten content' matters as much as its quality; both gluten content and gluten quality are broadly related to 'protein content'; wheat specifications are often in terms of the latter. Examples of hard bread wheats are Nos. 1, 2 and 3 Canadian Western Red Spring, United States Dark Northern Spring and Australian Prime Hard. Softer varieties, such as United States Soft Red Winter and most French, British and Argentine wheats, are used as fillers to combine with harder varieties or to produce a more open-textured loaf. They are also used extensively for the manufacture of noodles in Japan and China and for biscuits. Although wheat is used as animal feed, most farmers aim to produce wheat of millable quality and would grow barley or maize more specifically for feed purposes.

6   The literature on each of these subjects is copious. For illustrative accounts see C. Luttrell in Federal Reserve Bank of St Louis Review (September 1980), B. Sidhu, Land Reform, Welfare and Economic Growth (Bombay, 1976), Ford Foundation Agricultural Production Team, Report on Indian Food Crises and Steps to Meet It (Government of India, New Delhi, April 1959), E.A.G. Robinson and M. Kidron (eds.), Economic Development in South Asia (Macmillan, London, 1970), United Nations, Food and Agriculture Organization, A Strategy for Plenty: the Indicative World Plan for Agricultural Development (United Nations, Food and Agriculture Organization, Rome, 1970) and W.W. Cochrane, 'International Commodity Management as a Policy Problem for the United States: The Grains Case' in Denoon (ed.), The New International Economic Order: a US Response, Chapter 5.

7   See, for example, International Wheat Council, Trends and Problems in the World Grain Economy 1950-1970 (International Wheat Council, London, 1966), Appendix X. In 1980, for example, the International Wheat Council estimated in an unpublished account that, of 450 million metric tons of wheat consumed, 290 million went directly for human food, 80 million to feed animals (two-thirds in the USSR), 40 million for seed and 40 million for other uses.

8   International Wheat Council, Review of the World Wheat Situation 1979/80 (International Wheat Council, London, 1980). The crop-year refers to July to June.

9   Ibid. and International Wheat Council, World Wheat Statistics 1970 (International Wheat Council, London, 1971).

10 D. Morgan, Merchants of Grain (Weidenfeld & Nicolson, London, 1979) and E. Caves, 'Organisation, Scale and Performance of the Grain Trade', Food Research Institute

<u>Studies</u>, vol. XVI, no. 3 (1977-78). A distinctive feature in the US was also the substantial number of cooperative organisations; these received over a third of grain sold and were exempt from anti-trust provisions. Official marketing agencies in North America also played an important role in terms of wheat exports.

11   A.E. Peck, 'Implications of Private Storage of Grains for Buffer Stock Schemes to Stabilise Prices', <u>Food Research Institute Studies</u>, vol. XVI, no. 3 (1977-78), F. Vannerson, 'An Econometric Analysis of the Postwar United States Wheat Market', unpublished PhD thesis, Princeton University, Princeton, 1969 and P. Helmberger and R. Weaver, 'Welfare Implications of Commodity Storage under Uncertainty', <u>American Journal of Agricultural Economics</u>, vol. 59, (November 1977).

12   E. de Keyser (ed.), <u>Guide to World Commodity Markets</u> (Kogan Page, New York, 1977). Wheat futures are also traded in London, Minneapolis and Kansas City.

13   International Wheat Council, <u>Review of the World Wheat Situation 1979-80</u>, Section VIII.

14   International Wheat Council, <u>Trends and Problems in the World Grain Economy</u>, pp. 15-16 and I.M.T. Stewart, <u>Information on the Cereals Market</u> (Hutchinson, London, 1970), pp. 54 and 356.

15   London Corn Trade Association, <u>Grain Trade Lectures</u> (Northern Publishing Company Ltd, Liverpool, 1946/47), pp. 11-13 and League of Nations, <u>The World Economic Conference, Geneva, 1927</u>.

16   International Wheat Council, 'International Wheat Agreements: A Historical and Critical Background' (International Wheat Council, Report EX/74/74, 2/2, London, October 1974), pp. 2-3, quoted with permission.

17   P. Lamartine Yates, <u>Commodity Control: A Study of Primary Products</u> (Jonathan Cape, London, 1943), pp. 35-6.

18   Ibid., pp. 34-7.

19   'Final Act of the Conference of Wheat Exporting and Importing Countries', (25 August 1933), Preamble, in ILO, <u>Intergovernmental Commodity Agreements</u>, pp. 1-6.

20   Ibid., Articles 1 and 2.

21   Ibid., Articles 3-7, sets out the constitution of the Wheat Advisory Committee.

22   International Wheat Council, 'International Wheat Agreements', pp. 4-5.

23   The statistics covering this period are not available in a very convenient form. The International Wheat Council produced its own estimates of wheat production, trade and stocks in March 1947 based on a large number of national and international sources; and International Wheat Council, <u>International Wheat Prices</u> (International Wheat Council, London, 1961) and Ibid., <u>Tables and Charts of Wheat Prices</u> (International Wheat Council, London, May 1958) provide coverage of wheat prices. Stock levels peaked at 1,186.4 million bushels in 1934 and declined to 567.0 million bushels in 1937. Production peaked earlier at 5,566.8 million bushels in 1933 but rose again to the bumper crop of 6,741.6 million bushels in 1938. For information on the 1938 Draft, see International Wheat Council, 'International Wheat Agreements', p. 5.

24   'Memorandum of Agreement concerning Draft Wheat Convention' (22 April 1942) in ILO, <u>Intergovernmental Commodity Agreements</u>, pp. 10-25, League of Nations, <u>Food, Famine and Relief 1940-1946</u> (League of Nations, Geneva, 1946), which gives a useful country by country account, and J.S. Davis, 'New International Wheat Agreements', <u>Wheat Studies of the Food Research Institute</u> (November 1942), pp. 26-7.

25   'Memorandum of Agreement concerning Draft Wheat Convention', Articles 2-7.

26   Ibid., Articles 7, 8, 12 and 14.

27   D.A. MacGibbon, The Canadian Grain Trade 1931-1951 (University of Toronto Press, Toronto, 1952), pp. 147-48 reported that minimum prices were the main bone of contention.   Minimum prices of US $1.20 per bushel for 1949/50 and US $1.10 for 1950/51 were carried by the conference in the face of UK opposition.   The UK had signed an agreement with Canada in 1946 which agreed a minimum price of US $1 for 1949/50.   See also A.C.B. Madden, 'International Wheat Agreements', International Journal of Agrarian Affairs, vol. I, no. 3 (September 1949).

28   Great Britain, Ministry of Food, Second Review of the World Food Shortage July 1946 (HMSO, London, 1946, Cmd. 6879), pp. 1-9.

29   Production figures for this period are extremely tentative since they often excluded the output of some producers, such as China, and USSR output was estimated.   The International Wheat Council has provided the following estimated data from its own sources:

Wheat Production (millions of metric tons)

1945	130
1946	152
1947	150
1948	165
1949	160

30   'International Wheat Agreement, Washington, 6 March 1948', International Journal of Agrarian Affairs, vol. I, no. 3 (September 1949), Article I.

31   Ibid., Articles II, III, VI and IX.

32   'International Wheat Agreement' (US, Department of State, Washington, 1949), Articles III, VI and VII.

33   Ibid., Article X.

34   International Wheat Council, 'International Wheat Agreements', Table 1.

35   'International Wheat Agreement' (1949), Article I.

36   Several detailed accounts of developments in this period are available.   See, for example, H.C. Farnsworth, 'International Wheat Agreements and Problems, 1949-56', The Quarterly Journal of Economics, vol. LXX, no. 2 (May 1956), p. 226 and F.H. Golay, 'The International Wheat Agreement of 1949', The Quarterly Journal of Economics, vol. LXIV, no. 3 (August 1950).

37   United Nations, Commodity Trade and Development (United Nations, New York, 1953, E/2519, II.B.1), pp. 42-3 although this did point out that such multi-lateral contracts could be empty shells if the price range were too wide and the period covered too short.

38   For a detailed breakdown of production and trade data in this period see International Wheat Council, The World Wheat Situation (International Wheat Council, London, 1954).

39   'Agreement Revising and Renewing the International Wheat Agreement' (Washington, 1953), Article VI and Part III, Rules of Procedure.

40   United Nations, Food and Agriculture Organization, The Stabilization of International Trade in Grains: An Assessment of Problems and possible Solutions (United Nations, Rome, 1970). The UK was an active member of the Food and Agriculture Organization's Group on Grains. The stock data refer to Argentina, Australia, Canada, France and the US.

41   'International Wheat Agreement, 1956' (International Wheat Council copy, no date or place reference), Articles VI and VII, and International Wheat Council, 'International Wheat Agreements', pp. 12-13.

42   International Wheat Council, 'International Wheat Agreements', pp. 13-14. H.C. Farnsworth, 'Imbalance in the World Wheat Economy', p. 4 points out that this pattern of stocking existed also in 1932, 1942 and 1951.

43   International Wheat Council, Annual Report of the Council for the Crop-Year 1953/54 (International Wheat Council, London, 1954), p. 7.

44   United Nations, Food and Agriculture Organization, Report of the Fourth Session of the FAO Group on Grains to the Committee on Commodity Problems (United Nations, Food and Agriculture Organization, Rome, 1959), p. 10.

45   It could be argued, conversely, that such cooperation would not have been feasible without the apparatus of the Agreement.

46   'International Wheat Agreement and Rules of Procedure' (HMSO, London, 1960, Cmnd. 1074), Article 1.

47   Ibid., Article 6.

48   Ibid., Articles 3-14.

49   For a useful account see United Nations, Food and Agriculture Organization, The Stabilization of International Trade in Grains.

50   'International Wheat Agreement, 1962' (HMSO, London, 1962, Cmnd. 1709) and International Wheat Council, 'International Wheat Agreements', p. 17.

51   International Wheat Council, International Wheat Agreements, p. 18.

52   See Chapter 2.

53   Members of the GATT Cereals Group included, for example, Argentina, Australia, Canada, Denmark, the EEC, Finland, Japan, Norway, Sweden, Switzerland, the UK and the US. The USSR was not a contracting party to GATT. See United Nations, Food and Agriculture Organization, The Stabilization of International Trade in Grains, p. 28.

54   'International Grains Arrangement 1967' (International Wheat Council, London, 1968). However, the Food Aid Convention came into force only if the parallel Wheat Trade Convention entered into force.

55   Ibid., 'Food Aid Convention', Article I.

56   Ibid., Articles II, III, IV and VI.

57   Ibid., Article II.

58   'International Grains Arrangement, 1967, Wheat Trade Convention', Article 6. The price range was quoted in US as opposed to Canadian dollars.

59   Ibid., Articles 31 and 32.

60   Ibid., Articles 4 and 24.

61   International Wheat Council, International Wheat Agreements, p. 21.

62   'International Wheat Agreement 1971 incorporating the Wheat Trade Convention and the Food Aid Convention' (HMSO, London, 1971, Cmnd. 4643), 'Food Aid Convention, 1971', Article II.   Denmark, Norway and the UK, who were parties to the 1967 Convention, did not join the 1971 Convention at its onset.   The main reasons were that these countries, which were not traditional exporters of grain, felt that they could make more effective aid contributions in other ways.   Denmark and the UK rejoined the 1971 Convention in 1973 as a result of their accession to the EEC.   Norway rejoined the 1980 Convention.

63   Ibid., 'International Wheat Agreement, 1971', Article 1.

64   'International Wheat Agreement, 1971', Article 16.   The Committee was a committee of technical experts rather than a negotiating body.

65   For the statistics covering the period, see International Wheat Council, Review of the World Wheat Situation 1975/76 (International Wheat Council, London, 1976).

66   United Nations, Food and Agriculture Organization, Things to Come: the World Food Crisis - the Way Out (United Nations, Food and Agriculture Organization, Rome, 1974), pages not numbered.

67   Ibid., 'Food Aid' section.

68   International Wheat Council, Review of the World Wheat Situation 1975/76, pp. 84-5.

69   The International Wheat Council publication, Review of the World Wheat Situation, provides annually a list of bi-lateral agreements in operation.

70   A detailed study of this period has yet to be written.   For anecdotal evidence see Guardian, 6 February 1981, which suggested also that the USSR evaded US restrictions by making use of CMEA nations as third party importers.

71   United Nations, Food and Agriculture Organization, 'Things to Come', 'Stabilization' section.

72   See also Chapter 5.

73   A full and interesting account of the US Food and Agriculture Act of 1977 which covered the stocks is available in International Wheat Council, Review of the World Wheat Situation 1976/77 (International Wheat Council, London 1977), Part V.   The Act also provided that the Secretary of Agriculture had authority to promote acreage diversion or 'set-aside' programmes.   Farmers who failed to participate would not be eligible for loans, purchases or payments in the wheat programme or in any US commodity programme.   It should be noted that the US was not alone in its national food reserve policy.   The International Wheat Council reported in 1980 ('Wheat Market Report Part Two Prospects for Wheat in the 1980s', London, 1980), p. 4, that more stocks were held by importing countries at the end of the 1970s than at the beginning and that India, in particular, had established a 'substantial food grain reserve'.

74   For the 70 million metric ton estimate see W.W. Cochrane, 'International Commodity Management as a Policy Problem of the United States', p. 177.   The storage costs of grain in the US in 1976 were estimated at $8 to $9 per metric ton.   See also Peck, 'Implications of Private Storage of Grains for Buffer Stock Schemes to Stabilise Prices', and Helmberger and Weaver, 'Welfare Implications of Commodity Storage under Uncertainty'.

75   The price refers to Canada No. 1 fob Thunder Bay. See, for example, International
      Wheat Council, Review of the World Wheat Situation, 1975/76 (International Wheat
      Council, London, 1976), p. 48 and Review of the World Wheat Situation 1978/79
      (International Wheat Council, London, 1979), p. 58.

76   Brown, The Political and Social Economy of Commodity Control, pp. 8-11.

77   Full details are provided in International Wheat Council, Annual Report 1979/80
      (International Wheat Council, London, 1981), Part II. Another new feature was that
      rice could be used to fulfil obligations. Transactions were to be carried out in a way
      consistent with the United Nations, Food and Agriculture Organization's Principles of
      Surplus Disposal.

78   See Financial Times, 16 July 1980.

79   The International Wheat Council also pointed to the potential threat to world food
      security caused by other factors such as transportation bottlenecks. See International
      Wheat Council, Problems in Grain Handling and Transportation (International Wheat
      Council, London, 1980). The main obstacles were caused by severe winter weather,
      labour disputes and shortcomings in internal transportation. The Council pointed also
      to the need for an improved distribution of stocks world-wide.

80   These events received extensive press coverage. See, for example, Financial Times,
      26 November 1982, Ibid., 10 December 1982 and Ibid., 12 January 1983. In the US,
      farm income fell dramatically in 1981 and 1982 in the face of weak export markets,
      high interest rates and rising production costs. The US Administration aimed to boost
      exports to developing countries by an agricultural export credit programme introduced
      in October 1982.

81   United Nations, Food and Agriculture Organization, The Stabilization of International
      Trade in Grains, p. 11. Admittedly, the study started with the caveat 'Barring major
      crop disasters'.

8: SUGAR

> 'But however much the EEC huffs and puffs, there is little
> doubt that the encouragement of beet growing in the
> Community has disrupted the world sugar market and caused
> considerable economic distress to many developing countries.'

(John Edwards, Commodities Editor, Financial Times, 17 August
1982)

1. General

There are several reasons why sugar merits a prominent place in a
discussion of international commodity controls. First, sugar has been
the object of fairly regular international commodity agreements
since 1937 and of cartelisation in the 1930s.(1)   Secondly,
international discussions on sugar have well established historical
roots dating back at least to the nineteenth century. And, thirdly,
sugar stands out both as a commodity with high price instability in
the period covered by this study and as a core commodity under
UNCTAD's Integrated Programme.(2)   The complexity of production
and trading patterns for sugar mean that the introductory parts of
this chapter (Sections 1 to 4) are slightly longer than those for other
commodities considered and include a more detailed account of
national policies.

2. Production

Sugar is produced from two main sources, the sugar beet and the
sugar cane; in its completely refined form, white crystal, however, it
is indistinguishable and both sources require a complex technical

transformation process.(3) (Minor sources of sugar, such as maize and maple, and lower quality sugar, such as muscovado, are of little importance in the world sugar trades and will not therefore be considered in this chapter.) The producers of cane, are limited by climatic reasons to tropical and sub-tropical zones; the beet producers, on the other hand, are located in temperate climates. Since some understanding of the evolution of these separate strands of the sugar industry is essential to an appreciation of producers' attitudes toward international sugar controls, a very brief account of each will be attempted below by way of introduction.(4)

Cane sugar production is reported to date back to 400 BC in New Guinea and its neighbouring islands in the South Pacific. In the course of its more than two thousand year history, it spread to many other parts of the world and, with the conquest of the Americas, Florida, Louisiana, South Carolina, the Caribbean islands and North-East Brazil were all opened up to cane cultivation. By 1800, the Americas had become the world's leading source of supply. The expansion of the lands under sugar cane, requiring as it did a cheap and large labour force, was closely associated with the growth of the African slave trade. As a result, the sugar plantation evolved not only as an economic but also as a social unit.(5)

Cane production entered an important new phase in the nineteenth century with the gradual abolition of slavery in the main producing areas and the influence of technical change. Most notable was the development of the centrifuge which enabled the production of a higher quality sugar on a large scale. This, together with increasing mechanisation and improved transport facilities, often led to the envelopment of subsistence lands surrounding the plantation and tended to increase local dependency on sugar as a major source of income; as a result, sugar has attracted a relatively high degree of dependency as a source of export earnings in tropical countries. The pattern of cane sugar production established in the nineteenth century continued into the twentieth. However, output also expanded in areas outside of the Americas, although the latter remained the leading source of supply.(6)

In contrast to cane, beet sugar production was developed only relatively recently as the result of experiments by scientists such as Markgraf (1709-1782), Achard (1753-1821) and von Koppy (widely known as the 'father' of Silesian beet). Its growth was nurtured by the adoption of the bounty system in France, Germany, Austria/Hungary, the USSR, Belgium and the Netherlands. Although the bounty given varied in form from country to country, the underlying principle was identical in that an increase in domestic sugar production was sought by paying a drawback duty on sugar exported (tied, in the case of Germany, to the success of the producer in obtaining specified yields).(7) The results of this system were twofold: on the one hand, the production of sugar from the beet root, which assumed commercial proportions from the 1830s, rose sharply from 1,742,000 metric tons in 1880/81, about half of world sugar production, to 6,090,000 metric tons in 1900/01, a peak of 63.1 per cent of the world total. On the other, it has been estimated that the bounties paid by European countries between 1850 and 1904 led to some 60 to 65 million metric tons of sugar being placed on the world market at less than cost prices. The combination of these factors led to a decline in the international price of sugar from 25s 6d per cwt in 1872 to 7s 3d in 1902. The Brussels Convention, which brought an end to the bounty system by international agreement in 1902, represented the first major effort to regulate the international sugar market (see Section 5a below).(8)

From the 1890s, with the protected growth of the US beet industry, the pattern of beet production was also complete. However, the reliance of beet producers on sugar production for a source of income was considerably less than that of cane producers. Unlike cane, beet became an important element in a four crop rotation cycle owing to its nitrogen restorative qualities. Similarly, the residue of the beet, the pulp, could be used as animal fodder so that in beet areas sugar production could be combined with livestock rearing. In these respects there was thus an important distinction between the producers of beet and of cane; the latter had proportionately more to gain or to lose from the introduction of international commodity controls on sugar.

3. Sugar Trade and National Sugar Policies

World trade in sugar may be divided into two main groups: free market trade and trade outside the free market, the latter defined by the International Sugar Council to include internal movements between overseas territories and their mother countries (with the exception of those between the UK and her dependencies), exports of foreign countries to the US, and the exports of Czechoslovakia, Hungary and Poland to the USSR. Exports outside the free market account for a large proportion of the total - equivalent to 38.9 per cent of total world exports between 1954 and 1962 for example, although this share has since declined. Since international policy on sugar has been dominated by the existence of a complex network of preferential arrangements and national or regional policies, notably those of the US, the UK and the EEC, it is appropriate to preface any consideration of international controls with a brief analysis of the most influential national control measures. In this context, the discussion must start with the US, the largest single market for sugar and an important producer of both beet and cane in its own right.(9)

165

a. The US

In essence, the history of sugar production and consumption in the US is that of protection being afforded to the mainland industry and of preferences being extended to several suppliers of cane sugar. In 1902, for example, a Reciprocity Treaty extended a 20 per cent tariff preference to Cuban sugar producers and a 25 per cent preference to sugar from the Philippines. Under these concessionary arrangements production in the protected areas flourished. In 1934, however, changing world market conditions and the failure of the Chadbourne (cartel) Agreement (discussed below) induced the US to attempt to organise supplies of sugar to the US market in a more orderly fashion under the Jones-Costigan Act. An assessment was made each year of the sugar required, together with a calculation of the price which should be paid. Quotas were then calculated for each sugar producer, domestic or foreign, who supplied the US market with domestic producers being compensated for any lost production by the Government. A 1937 revision to the 1934 Jones-Costigan Act, induced by a Supreme Court ruling that a tax on the 'processors' of agricultural commodities was illegal, repeated the principles established in the 1934 Act. It remained in force until 1948 although the quota scheme was waived from 1942 owing to war-time conditions. The 1948 Act which replaced it formed the basis of US sugar policy until 1974.(10)

The 1948 Sugar Act aimed 'to regulate commerce . . .; to protect the welfare of consumers of sugars and of those engaged in domestic sugar-producing industry . . .; to promote the export trade of the US'.(11) It was based on a commitment to achieve self-sufficiency and stability in sugar supplies to the US market and introduced penalties for producers failing to fulfil their production quotas (Cuba was allocated a minimum quota until 1960). Most of the quotas allotted to domestic offshore or foreign areas could be filled only with raw sugar which was to be further refined or improved on the mainland. This offered a high degree of protection to domestic refiners.(12)

There has been little agreement on the impact of the 1948 Sugar Act. Whereas opponents have pointed to the cost of operating the programme, which maintained prices at levels higher on average than those prevailing on the free market, advocates have stressed its value in allowing the survival of the domestic industry in the period of low world prices between 1960 and 1962.(13) The failure to renew the Act in 1975 reflected a disenchantment with the rigidities inherent in the 1948 Sugar Act and as a result the US sugar market was transformed from conditions of strict regulation to a relatively free market. The transition was far from painless. In 1977, for example, when low prices were deemed to threaten the survival of the domestic industry, President Carter, under pressure to introduce import controls, found it necessary to draw up a programme of income support. At the same time, however, he expressed an interest in the negotiation of a new, more effective international sugar agreement. As a result, US support was secured for the Sugar Agreement of the same year.(14)

Mention should also be made of the importance of political factors in determining US sugar policy. This was illustrated most vividly by the dramatic reduction of Cuba's import quota by 700,000 short tons in July 1960. This followed the 1959 Cuban Agrarian Reform Law which introduced a policy of redistribution of land holdings and the collectivisation of large estates to form co-operatives without compensation. Cuban exports to the US fell from 2,393,633 short tons in 1960 to zero in 1961 and Cuba lost at a stroke half of its sugar market. Cuba's reaction was to expropriate all foreign-owned sugar mills and refineries and to negotiate with the USSR an increase in Cuban sales. The US, which had lost a third of its supplies, made good the shortfall from other sources such as Peru and Mexico.(15)

b. The UK

The (UK) Commonwealth Sugar Agreement of 1951 was but the most formalised of a long series of preferences granted by the UK: in 1651, for example, colonial sugar was given preferential tariff treatment which was maintained at varying rates until 1874 and re-introduced in 1919; in 1932, an additional preference was granted to colonial sugar in the form of a reduction in the general duty; and during the Second World War, the UK Government bought in bulk all the exportable surpluses of the Commonwealth at prices higher than those which had prevailed before the War but largely below the prevailing world price.

The Commonwealth Sugar Agreement, however, was broader in compass than its antecedents. It set export quotas for the countries on whose behalf it was signed, initially Australia, the British West Indies, Fiji, Mauritius and South Africa. Trade in sugar between the UK and these countries was based on a 'negotiated price quota' - the maximum annual quantity of exports to which a UK negotiated price applied, the latter assessed each year. The initial quota was fixed at 2,413,112 metric tons in 1951, that is, 17.1 per cent of world exports.(16) The Agreement price was higher than the world price in sixteen of the twenty-one years between 1951 and 1971; however, the situation was reversed from 1972 and the Agreement ended in 1974 when successor arrangements were negotiated with the EEC.(17)

167

c. The EEC

For the EEC, the CAP and the Lomé Conventions were the most important influences on sugar production and trade. These have already been considered in general in Chapter 3. In the case of the former, production quotas were allocated to each member which, in turn, allocated quotas among constituent producers. In the event of surplus production, producers were eligible to receive 'export refunds' to cover the difference between the EEC and world prices. Price guarantees were also provided for a basic quantity of sugar produced in each area. In the case of the latter, Lomé I guaranteed in the first instance an annual purchase of 1.4 million metric tons of sugar from ACP producers (including those of the British Commonwealth) at the price paid to EEC beet-sugar producers. This figure represented an attempt to reconcile the competing colonial and former colonial claims of UK and French producers.

EEC sugar policy has been criticised on a number of counts. First, it is reported to have encouraged an expansion of output in excess of EEC requirements and export subsidies came to represent a substantial burden on the Community Budget.   Secondly, ACP producers claimed that the Lomé Conventions did little to increase trade and were more than offset by the adverse influence of the EEC in dumping sugar on the world market to dispose of its excess supplies. Most important of all for the purpose of this discussion, the existence of the CAP and of Lomé did little to encourage EEC participation in an international sugar agreement; instead the EEC not only remained an important outsider from both the 1968 and the 1977 Sugar Agreements but also attracted severe criticism from participants. In 1980, for example, Australia complained to GATT about the level of EEC export subsidies on sugar and the EEC agreed to discuss the 'possibility of limiting the subsidies'.(18) US criticism of EEC sugar policy in 1982 is also considered below.

Even a brief analysis such as this highlights the importance of preferential arrangements between countries or trading areas in the conduct of the world sugar trade. Despite its changing contours in the 1970s - the non-renewal of the US Sugar Act, the end of the Commonwealth Sugar Agreement and the conclusion of Lomé - the free world market remained essentially a residual one. As one writer observed in 1977, net exports to the free world market were comparable to:

> '. . . the tail of the dog - a large tail, it is true, but still only a tail. And the task of regulating the fluctuations of the free market that international sugar agreements set themselves is rather like trying to restrain a dog from wagging its tail'.(19)

4. Consumption

North America and Europe have provided together the most important markets for world sugar although official figures reveal wide variations in consumption patterns. (Even these may not be taken as encompassing a full picture since non-centrifugal sugar consumption remains important locally in many cane-producing countries.) The main factors which appear to influence per capita sugar consumption are population growth, income and price although per capita sugar consumption is estimated to reach a saturation point at about 45 to 50 kilos. Sugar consumption has also been affected by the growth of alternative sources of sweetener - such as high fructose Corn Syrup in the 1970s - and artificial (non-calorific) sweeteners, such as saccharine during the 1960s.(20)

5. Controls on Sugar to 1939
a. The Brussels Convention and the World Economic Conference of 1927

It was the desire to end strong downward pressure on the international price of sugar, stemming from the over-expansion of beet production fostered by the bounty system, which led to the Brussels Convention of 1902. The Convention prohibited the payment of bounties on exported sugar and permitted the UK and the Netherlands to grant preferential tariff arrangements for their colonial sugar imports. The Convention, signed initially between the Governments of Austria, Belgium, the UK, France, Germany, Italy, the Netherlands, Norway, Spain, Switzerland and Peru, represented a compromise between beet producers and their principal markets. It heralded the advent of more favourable trading conditions for the producers of cane sugar.(21)

Between 1902 and 1927 there was a lull in international discussions on sugar. In contrast, developments in the international sugar market moved rapidly largely due to the dislocation of traditional supply patterns during the First World War. During this period the disruption of European beet production resulted in an unsustained increase in demand for cane sugar, which was met by an expansion of production; in Cuba, in particular, there was a rapid expansion of cane acreage. With the resumption of beet production in Europe after the First World War, sugar prices fell from their annual peak of £58 per ton in 1920 to only £15.25 per ton in 1922. Although there was some recovery between 1923 and 1924, prices fell in 1925 to below £14 per ton, inducing Cuba to embark on a national programme of sugar controls to restrict output and to limit new plantings of cane.(22) In the face of continuing low prices, a Cuban delegate at the World Economic Conference of 1927 proposed that the 'dumping' of sugar on to the world market should be prohibited and that producers should instead coordinate their marketing by establishing a cartel. The reaction of the Economic Consultative Committee, to which this proposal was referred, was lukewarm: the Committee consulted with world sugar experts, Prinsen, F.O. Licht and Mikusch, only to conclude that the sugar industry should resolve its own problems without international interference or intervention.(23)

b. The Chadbourne Agreement

In 1930, it became clear to Cuba that uni-lateral action in attempting to boost international sugar prices by restraining output had failed to achieve the desired result. One factor which acted against the Cuban initiative was the expansion of production in Java where the discovery of a new variety of cane in 1924 brought a steep rise in yields. As prices continued to fall during 1930, Cuba took the lead in calling a meeting in New York of representatives of producers supplying the US market. This meeting, later known as the Chadbourne Agreement, divided the import potential of the US between the sugar exporting countries attending the meeting.(24) By 1931 60 per cent of world sugar exporters were represented in the Agreement.
The Chadbourne Agreement was essentially a reaction by producers to the specific problems of excessive stocks and low prices which existed in 1930 and 1931. In this respect it mirrored the concerted action of the tin producers in the International Tin Pool of 1931. Producers were committed to reducing the volume of sugar manufactured. The burden of sacrifice, however, fell on those producers adhering to the terms of the Agreement: whereas the Chadbourne Group's output fell from 12.5 million tons in 1929/30 to 6.4 million in 1934/35, world production fell only slightly as countries outside the Agreement, such as those in the British Empire, Japan, Taiwan and the USSR, increased their output.(25) In the words of one observer, the Chadbourne Agreement fell between two poles: 'While not a commercial treaty among national governments, neither was it a strictly private cartel among private producers'.(26) Accordingly, when the Agreement was ended in 1935, all parties to it favoured a new agreement which was far more wide-reaching in dimension.

c. International Controls to 1939

As in the cases of tin and rubber, the first international sugar agreement, negotiated in 1937, arose from the failure of cartel-styled action to achieve the goal set. Much of the impetus for international controls came from Cuba, the leading world sugar exporter, which had introduced a wide range of national control

170

measures in 1930 to re-inforce its commitment to restriction. These included a four-tiered production quota system, consisting of quotas for home consumption, quotas for export to the free world market, quotas destined to form a sugar stock and quotas for export to the US. In addition, labour legislation in 1934 guaranteed the tenant cane supplier (colono) security of tenure provided that he produced a specified amount of subsistence crops in addition to cane.(27) However, the net effect of the Chadbourne Agreement for Cuba, where production fell dramatically and only reached the 1929 level again in 1946, was to reduce the guaranteed market for Cuban sugar in the US and to increase Cuba's dependence on the vagaries of the free world market. This effect was re-inforced by the tightening of the US system of preferences, and by UK policy, which from 1924 had heavily subsidised the development of a domestic beet sugar industry.(28)

Despite an attempt by Cuba to bring the subject of international sugar controls to the attention of the World Economic Conference of 1933, it was not until 1937 that an international sugar conference was convened to discuss the subject. Objections to international controls came from a variety of sources: India, for example, as an infant sugar producer, wanted no curbs on future output, a view shared by Brazil, anxious to increase its world market share; the UK, in contrast, favoured a continuation of the existing Chadbourne modus operandi. The 1937 International Sugar Conference thus represented a distinct new departure which brought together for the first time the major producers and importers of sugar. Its brief was to organise the free world market for sugar by attempting to obtain from sugar-importing countries the commitment to import at least the same quantity of sugar as they had done in the recent past.

The 1937 Sugar Agreement which resulted from the Conference encompassed all of the major sugar producers and resembled its peers for tin and rubber in terms of its principal objectives.(29) It emphasised the need to maintain 'an orderly relationship between the supply and demand for sugar in the world market', to assure 'an adequate supply of sugar . . . at a reasonable price . . .'(30) and to secure prices which allowed a 'reasonable profit' to 'efficient producers'.(31) No attempt was made, however, to define what constituted a reasonable level of profit or an efficient producer. The Agreement allocated export quotas for sugar traded on the world market and importers made various commitments to maintain the level of their imports. (The US, for example, agreed to at least maintain its import requirements at the 1937 level; and the UK undertook to limit domestic production and exports from the Empire to a specified level.) Producers also agreed to regulate their stocks so that they did not exceed 25 per cent of annual production levels. An International Sugar Council was established with both consumer

171

and producer interests represented to administer the Agreement and collect background statistics.(32) (For a brief summary of this and subsequent sugar agreements, see the Appendix, Table 3.)

In the words of Ramsay Macdonald, the purpose of the 1937 International Sugar Conference was 'to draw up rules which [will] apply to each group of countries to deal with the particular part they [are] playing as producers, exporters and importers in the activities of the complete sugar industry'.(33) However, the Agreement which emerged left existing bi-lateral commitments largely untouched and only applied to the free world market.

It is difficult to judge its strengths and weaknesses since operations were suspended in 1939 with the onset of war. However, in the short-term export quotas were based on an over-optimistic estimate of consumption requirements. Prices fell back during the course of 1938, for example, in the face of reduced demand, especially in the US and, in response, the International Sugar Council found it necessary to reduce export quotas by 5 per cent in April 1938. The situation was relieved, however, by the precautionary stock-piling which preceded the Second World War. In 1939, in the wake of this increase in demand, the price of sugar moved up sharply to average £7.33 per ton compared with £5.42 in 1938.(34)

6. <u>War-time Controls</u>

In common with many other commodities, sugar during the Second World War was characterised by short rather than abundant supply positions. World production declined from an annual average of 25,593,000 metric tons between 1935/36 and 1939/40 to 23,072,000 metric tons between 1940/41 and 1944/45. Declining beet production, particularly in Europe, accounted for much of this fall, although Javan cane was also a major casualty. Other regions, in contrast, experienced only minor declines and some, such as Central America, even managed to expand output. By 1940 and 1942 respectively, the UK and the US, the world's two major sugar importers, were forced to ration sugar supplies. In the US, sugar was the first commodity to be rationed and the last to be released from rationing.

The importance attached to sugar during the Second World War was demonstrated by the formation of the Combined Food Board Sugar Committee in 1942 as one of the first offspring of the Combined Food Board, whose task (as outlined in Chapter 2) was to coordinate and to monitor Allied food supplies. The main aim of the Sugar Committee was to allocate available supplies. A further development was the extension of the 1937 Sugar Agreement for a period of two years by the Allied Powers in 1942. However, with the absence of Germany, Hungary, Poland, France and China, the protocol was no more than a paper continuation of an agreement whose economic provisions had already long been suspended. As such its importance was limited to indicating the intention of the Allied Powers to continue international sugar controls at some future date.(35)

7. Controls between 1945 and 1962

With the removal of war-time controls, international sugar prices (quoted only in US cents between 1940 and 1955) fell dramatically from US 4.96 cents in December 1947 to US 3.96 cents in January 1948. They remained within half a cent of that level, in the face of buoyant supply conditions, until the Korean commodity price boom in 1950 to 1951. During that period world sugar prices moved sharply, rising to over US 7.00 cents (Figure 8:1), before falling back to average only US 3.41 cents in 1953. It was these rapid movements which re-awakened international interest in commodity controls for sugar and a conference was called by the United Nations under the terms of the Havana Charter to investigate the feasibility of drawing up an international commodity agreement for sugar. The result was the 1953 Sugar Agreement, signed initially by sixteen exporting and seven importing countries, and accounting for about 84 per cent of net exports to and 54 per cent of net imports from the free world market.(36)

In concert with other post-War international commodity agreements, the 1953 Sugar Agreement had a broad array of aims: in addition to the well rehearsed objective of balancing supply and demand and encouraging equitable and stable prices, it aimed to increase the consumption of sugar, and, in anticipation of the agreements of the 1960s, to 'maintain the purchasing power in world markets of countries ... whose economies /are/ largely dependent upon the production or export of sugar by providing adequate returns to producers and making it possible to maintain fair standards of labour conditions and wages'.(37) To fulfil these objectives the Agreement extracted general commitments from its signatories to notify the International Sugar Council of grants or subsidies maintained on the production or export of sugar; to 'reduce disproportionate burdens on sugar', such as those resulting from fiscal policy; and to maintain fair labour standards. Export quotas were established for exporting countries for their shipments of sugar to the free world market to operate within a prescribed price range of US 3.25 cents to US 4.35 cents. Exporters also agreed to regulate their stocks so that they would not exceed 20 per cent of annual production levels. The Council was empowered to adjust the export quotas according to market needs and to re-distribute any shortfalls among exporting countries. Importers for their part undertook to limit their imports from non-participating exporters to a figure not exceeding the levels during any one year between 1951 and 1953. Unlike the

Figure 8:1: Raw Sugar Prices, 1950-1952
(US cents per pound, fas, Cuba)

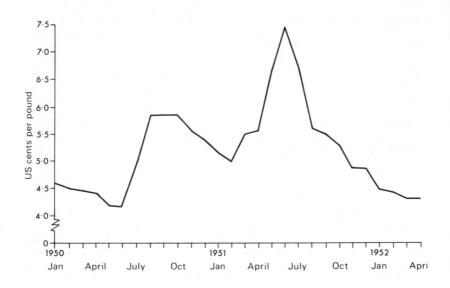

Source: International Sugar Council, <u>The World Sugar Economy</u>
<u>Structure and Policies</u> (International Sugar Council,
London, 1963), vol. II, p. 343.

1937 Sugar Agreement, that of 1953 made no explicit attempt to
restrict increases in production, but conferred on participants the
need to adopt appropriate measures to meet the Agreement's
objectives.(38)

The 1953 Sugar Agreement kept prices just within the specified price range in 1954 and just below the lower limit in 1955 despite the introduction of export quotas. Even this limited degree of success was attributable in part to the disciplined action of Cuba in restraining domestic output by a complex series of production quotas. Prices remained on target until the end of 1956 when the situation changed rapidly as crop failures in some European countries and speculation associated with the Suez crisis sent prices soaring to almost US 6.5 cents per pound in April 1957. In this context, the International Sugar Council responded by relaxing all export quotas. It was only in 1958, with the lagged effect of new sources of supply induced by the period of high prices, that prices retreated back down to the target range. Despite these shortcomings, the Agreement was re-negotiated in December 1958.(39)

The 1958 Sugar Agreement was modelled closely on its predecessor: the mechanisms remained a sugar export quota and a prescribed price range - the floor was kept the same at US 3.25 cents and the ceiling was brought down slightly from US 4.35 cents to US 3.75 cents in line with current prices - but despite this, there was a general raising of individual export quotas which varied from country to country. Cuba, for example, was granted a 7.3 per cent rise in its export quota, whereas Brazil, whose sugar output was expanding rapidly, and who had failed to accede in 1953 owing to the level of the quota provisionally established, was accorded a three-fold increase.(40) With the accession of Brazil and Peru the 1958 Sugar Agreement covered 90 per cent of the free market's suppliers.

The Agreement set off to an inauspicious start: sugar prices remained below US 3.25 cents for most of 1959 and in the face of fairly abundant supplies, there was a strong increase in stocks. Far more dramatic and damaging for the credibility of the Agreement, however, was the reduction by the US of Cuba's preferential sugar quota in July 1960. As discussed earlier, Cuba lost at a stroke half of its export market for sugar and the US a third of its supplies. With the USSR taking an increased volume of Cuban sugar exports from 1961 to compensate, and the US increasing its purchases from alternative sources and encouraging an expansion of domestic beet production, there was a dramatic shift in the pattern of world trade in sugar. Although additional sales to the US and to the USSR were not covered by the export quotas written into the 1958 Sugar Agreement, their existence and the fact that the sugar price remained below the floor throughout 1961 and most of 1962 did nothing to enhance the Agreement as a mechanism for stabilising and ordering the world sugar market. It was hardly surprising in these circumstances that the conference held in the autumn of 1961 to fix export quotas for 1962 ended in complete deadlock with Cuba, on the one hand, demanding that its new contracts with the CMEA bloc should be added to its basic export quota and other countries pointing out that such a quota, of the order of 7.3 million metric tons, would both exceed the combined quotas of every other country and would also be more than Cuba could reasonably hope to export. The economic provisions of the Agreement were therefore allowed to lapse and with its expiry in December 1963, no new agreement was negotiated to replace it.(41)

8. Controls between 1962 and 1972

Developments in the international sugar market between 1963 and 1966 did nothing to increase the prospects for a workable new international sugar agreement. Whereas the free world price for sugar fell from an average of US 8.34 cents per pound in 1963 to US 1.81 cents in 1966, the subsidised domestic US price for sugar in New York remained well above it (in the region of US 6 to 7 cents) and additional sugar beet acreage was sanctioned despite world stocks of almost 19 million metric tons, well above normal requirements. A similar distortion was exhibited in the USSR's long-term contract with Cuba which specified the price of US 6 cents per pound despite the much lower prevailing world price. Uncertainty was increased by the fact that the USSR occasionally re-sold a portion of these purchases on the free world market.(42) It was the divergence between the free world price and preferential price arrangements which proved a stumbling block at the 1965 international sugar conference, the first to be held under UNCTAD's auspices.(43) By 1968 producers were reported to be anxious to bring some order to the international sugar market in the face of strong competition from Cuba whose sugar was often sold below the cost of production. More interest was therefore displayed in initiatives made jointly by the International Sugar Council, the United Nations Food and Agriculture Organization and UNCTAD to draft a new international agreement and, as a result, agreement was reached with a new organisation, the International Sugar Organisation, replacing the International Sugar Council.(44)

The 1968 Sugar Agreement, reflecting the new mood of the international trade negotiating community, aimed to increase the export earnings of 'developing exporting countries', to secure prices which were remunerative to producers but not so remunerative as to encourage excessive production in developed countries, and 'to provide for adequate participation in, and growing access to, the markets of the developed countries for sugar from the developing countries'. A close watch was also to be kept on the use of sugar substitutes.(45)

The control mechanisms bore a close resemblance to those contained in the previous Agreement although there was a considerable refinement in their operating procedures. The Agreement committed exporting members to offering importing members supplies of sugar based on 'traditional trading patterns' and within the limits imposed by the export quotas when the price of sugar was above US 3.25 cents per pound. If the price rose above US 4.75 cents exporters were required to offer for sale half of the sugar held as minimum stocks; if the price rose further to above US 5.00 cents, the remainder of the minimum stock was to be available for purchase by importing members. When the price exceeded US 6.50 cents importers were entitled to purchase varying proportions of their traditional supply commitments from exporters at a price near to the ceiling price. Similarly, detailed provisions were made for the establishment and adjustment of quota levels according to the prevailing price. When the price was at or below US 3.50 cents, quotas were to be reduced to minimum specified levels; when the price rose above US 5.25 cents, all quotas were to be inoperative.(46) Elaborate arrangements were also included for the initial allocation of individual quotas and for action to be taken regarding unused quotas.(47) The total basic quotas allotted covered 34.6 per cent of world exports in 1968 compared with 31.5 per cent in 1958. Importers' commitments were similar to those of the preceding Agreement: they agreed not to import from non-members a quantity of sugar greater than the average imported between 1966 to 1968 and to prohibit such imports if the prevailing price fell below US 3.25 cents.(48)

To implement the detailed provisions of the 1968 Sugar Agreement, the International Sugar Organisation was given the authority to delegate to an Executive Committee, called the International Sugar Council. In addition, a Sugar Consumption Committee was established to review ways of encouraging increased consumption of sugar and to study such matters as the effects on sugar consumption of substitute sweeteners. Developing countries were given slightly preferential treatment under the terms of the Agreement in a number of respects: landlocked countries, Bolivia, Paraguay and Uganda, were exempted from meeting supply commitments; a hardship fund was established of up to 150,000 metric tons each quota year as additional authorised exports for developing countries who had, for some special reason, exceeded their quota; and developing countries were required to hold lower levels of minimum stocks. In addition, it was claimed later that developing countries had been favoured by substantially larger quota allocations.(49)

The 1968 Sugar Agreement, which operated between 1969 and 1973, coincided with an upturn in world sugar prices, a trend which continued until 1974 when prices stood at a peak over fifteen times greater than the price prevailing in 1968.(50) The main reason for the rise in prices was the growth of consumption requirements between 1969 and 1973, itself partly due to the low prices prevailing when the Agreement began which had encouraged a shift away from artificial sweeteners. Between 1971 and 1972 a negative differential between production and consumption opened up which led to a large drawing down of stocks (Figure 8:2). When the ceiling was penetrated in December 1971, the commitment of exporters to supply minimum quantities of sugar at that price came into effect and all export quotas were rendered inoperative. However, the enforcement of the supply commitments proved difficult, on account of the large numbers of producers concerned, and controversial, owing to the large number of developing countries amongst them. In addition, the stock provisions proved inadequate to stem the rapid rise in prices.

The 1968 Sugar Agreement was criticised on a number of other counts: according to F.O. Licht, the sugar broker, quotas were distributed 'not in accordance with the supply capabilities of the exporters but rather in recognition of negotiating strength and tactics'. Moreover, it noted that the management of the quota system could not be accomplished with sufficient degree of flexibility: a 15 per cent reduction in the quota was often insufficient to prevent the erosion of world prices whereas the suspension of quotas was pointless if no sugar was available for shipment.(51) Viewed against its primary objective of increasing stability within the international sugar market, the Agreement thus enjoyed very limited success. However, as in the case of its predecessors, the 1968 Sugar Agreement covered a limited and volatile proportion of the total world sugar market: the vulnerability of the world market was increased in periods of rapidly changing conditions since the demands made on it were proportionately greater.

9. Controls after 1972

Perhaps predictably, there was little enthusiasm for negotiating a new agreement in 1973 based on the lines of the 1968 Sugar Agreement. Instead, the economic clauses were dropped and the agreement which resulted merely carried forward the administrative apparatus of the 1968 Sugar Agreement, whilst encharging the International Sugar Organisation to seek a new agreement with full economic provisions. The 1973 Sugar Agreement was extended twice, in 1975 and in 1976.(52)

The mid-1970s were an important time of transition and re-structuring for the world sugar trade and it is only in this context that the renewal of economic sugar controls in 1977 may be fully understood. On the one hand, there was a strong increase in production in exporting countries such as Brazil, some Central American countries, South Africa and India as producers sought to benefit from the high prices prevailing during the early 1970s. These additional supplies came on stream just as world demand for sugar was turning down and contributed to the dramatic fall in world sugar prices from the peak annual average of US 29.7 cents in 1974 to only

Figure 8:2: Sugar Consumption and Stocks as a Percentage of Consumption, 1964/65-1976/77

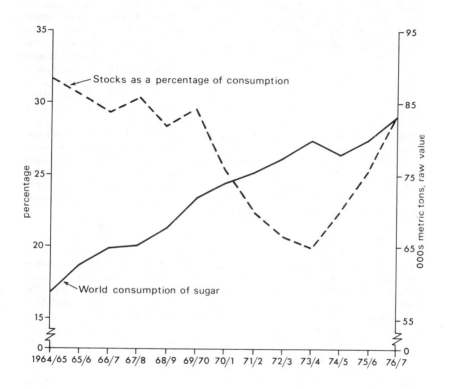

Source: derived from F.O. Licht, International Sugar Report: Problems and Prospects of a New International Sugar Agreement (F.O. Licht, Ratzeberg, Germany, 1977).

US 8.2 cents in 1977, a price estimated to be below the cost of production of even the most economic and efficient producers.(53) Secondly, as outlined above, the pattern of international trade in sugar also changed, with special arrangements such as the US Sugar Act and the Commonwealth Sugar Agreement expiring and the EEC countries introducing their own special arrangements vis à vis ACP countries. The net effect of these changes seems to have been to encourage producers to seek an international sugar agreement with economic provisions. The negotiations received a boost from President Carter's refusal to raise import duties or to impose quotas on sugar imports in response to the lobbying of domestic sugar beet producers and to propose instead that an effective international sugar agreement should be negotiated.(54)

The main objectives of the 1977 Sugar Agreement, which emerged after lengthy discussions, were identical to those of the 1968 Sugar Agreement although, as a new departure, administrators were required to take account of the effect of inflation or deflation, variations in exchange rates and the influence on sugar prices of changes in the world economic situation or monetary system.(55)

The same mechanisms were used, although the floor and ceiling prices, set initially at US 11 and 21 cents per pound respectively, provided a considerably wider range than that of the previous Agreement.(56) In addition, exporting countries were required to hold special stocks of uncommitted sugar (either within their territory or in the territory of any other country) to an aggregate total of 2.5 million metric tons apportioned on a pro rata basis according to their individual export tonnages. Such special stocks had to be verified by 'certificates of existence issued by the Government of the Member'. A special Stock Financing Fund was to be established to assist members to meet their commitments under the stock holding provisions and these stocks were to be released in a graduated fashion when the price of sugar rose above 19 cents per pound.(57) The commitments of importers remained similar to those specified in 1968: namely the agreement to limit imports from non-members to a quantity based on a previous period, in this case, 1973 to 1976. However, in 1977, a more detailed commitment was made to import only 75 per cent of that quantity if the price prevailing exceeded US 11 cents per pound and only 55 per cent if the price fell below US 11 cents.(58) The 1977 Sugar Agreement also continued the principle of according developing countries slightly preferential terms and made the first reference of any international commodity agreement to taking 'full advantage of any financial arrangement available' under UNCTAD's proposed Common Fund.(59)

A cloud hung over the 1977 Sugar Agreement even before it became operative owing to the failure of the EEC to adhere to its terms. Subsequent experience also fell far short of expectations. From prices below the floor in 1978, the price rose gradually to the middle of the range by November 1979 as purchases were increased from the USSR and China. During 1980, however, with a short crop in Cuba, the reserve stocks were used up and the price of sugar breached the ceiling. In this situation all export quota restrictions were lifted. By the autumn of 1981, in contrast, the price of sugar fell back to below the floor level, calling seriously into question the ability of the Agreement to exercise a moderating influence on price movements.(60)

In November 1981, agreement was reached to extend the sugar pact for a further two years without renegotiation, this despite its obvious shortcomings and at a time when the international price of sugar remained below the minimum specified in the 1977 Sugar Agreement. The sources of dispute were not limited to the specifications of the Agreement itself. On the contrary, the focus of discussion moved outside the framework of the Agreement to the bitter controversy between the US and the EEC regarding EEC export subsidies on farm products, estimated in April 1982 to amount to $2.2 billion to the US market alone. The US claimed that in the case of sugar, as in the case of cereals, such subsidies constituted an attempt to expand markets beyond traditional shares. Accordingly, the American trade representative at GATT, following similar action by Brazil and Australia in 1978, opened cases for arbitration against the alleged dumping of sugar. In May 1982 the US went further and announced a decision to set import quotas for overseas suppliers of sugar.(61)

It was not only the US which strongly criticised the stance of EEC sugar policy. The failure of the 1977 Agreement to fulfil its pricing objectives was blamed by many on the rapid expansion of sugar exports from the EEC during the 1970s; these rose from an average of 881,000 metric tons in the five years before 1977 to 5.3 million metric tons in 1981. A report by the National Corn Development Foundation in January 1983 went so far as to suggest that without subsidised sugar exports from the EEC, the price of sugar would have been more than US 21 cents per pound. In November 1982 the question of farm policy also formed a central element in the GATT Ministerial Summit (Chapter 2). The failure of the Summit to resolve differences, notably between the US and the EEC, and the low price of sugar prevailing, led to calls from major sugar producers for EEC participation in a new international agreement as a matter of urgency. The EEC in its turn was reported to have responded by proposing a new type of agreement with controls differentiated according to the scale of producers' exports of sugar.(62) Common ground between all interested parties was the realisation that the 1977 Sugar Agreement had not been able to fulfil its pricing objectives and that substantial revisions to the Agreement were needed both in terms of its mechanisms and of participation if it were to be more successful in the future.

10. Conclusion

Writing in 1977, Hagelberg of the Institute for Sugar Industry, Berlin stated:

> 'The modest success of the Brussels Convention fore-shadowed the limitations of subsequent international sugar agreements. They could formalise convergent views, smooth over differences, codify a set of rules that governments had come to recognise to be in their mutual interest, and establish a balance of rights and obligations. But they could not alter fundamental economic conditions and trends'.(63)

As in the case of other international commodity agreements, the sugar agreements lasted only as long as they reflected the mutuality of interests between the respective signatories, a set of common aims and interests which was not undermined by market developments. Of the post-War agreements, only those of 1953 and 1977 can be said to have completed their span: the economic provisions of the 1958 Sugar Agreement became inoperative in 1962, in the wake of the Cuban crisis, and the only operative provisions of the 1968 Sugar Agreement in the last two years of its life were the supply commitments under which exporting members were obliged to sell sugar at less than the prevailing market price.

All of the sugar agreements covered only the 'free', that is, the residual world market. The distortions caused by income supports and export subsidies together with the preferential trading arrangements which allocated a large proportion of the sugar markets of the major world importers until the mid-1970s worked against the aims of the international agreements by increasing the volatility of the free world market. In addition, in periods of rapid or unstable price movements, such as after 1969 and in the late 1970s, the credibility of the agreements was seriously undermined since the price band appeared to be too narrow to be effective. One commentator went so far as to suggest that price instability was probably increased as a result of the agreements since they provided too great a focus on the surpluses and shortages which appeared. The agreements appeared to have worked best, predictably, in periods such as 1954 to 1961 when no extreme price movements took place.(64)

A serious shortcoming of the agreements was their limited membership. In 1953 and 1958, for example, although 84 per cent and 95 per cent of net exports to the free market were covered respectively, the membership of importers, at 54 and 65 per cent of net imports from the free market, was not such that control could reliably be exercised.(65) The absence of the EEC and the US from the 1968 Agreement and the absence of the EEC from the 1977

Agreement undoubtedly weakened the potential for increasing the stability of the free world market. As outlined above, the problem was exacerbated by the fact that failure to participate did not represent passivity in respect of sugar matters. On the contrary, both the US and the EEC pursued actively policies which often ran counter to action taken under the terms of the agreements. A UK House of Lords Select Committee on the EEC commented in the following way in 1980:

> 'The Community's policy towards other exporters to the world sugar market appears to be one of selfishness and cynicism, which acts against the European Community's long-term interests'.(66)

The Committee recommended as an alternative that the EEC should reduce production levels in order that it could join the 1977 Sugar Agreement. The same theme has been repeated on a number of occasions since then.

Critics have pointed to further areas of weakness in the agreements such as inadequate stock data and the lack of attention paid to sugar substitutes. However, the magnitude of the problems faced should not be under-estimated. The very low price elasticity of demand for sugar, for example, tended to amplify price variability in the face of fluctuating production levels which resulted from unpredictable climatic factors. The number of countries producing sugar, both north and south of the Equator, also added substantially to the problem of securing an agreement which was at once representative and comprehensive enough in its coverage of the world market to ensure a high degree of success. Finally, neither shocks induced by political factors, such as the Korean War and the Cuban crisis, nor the rapid price movements in the mid-1970s could realistically have been anticipated by the terms of the agreements.

As in the case of the tin and wheat agreements, the conclusion resulting most clearly from an examination of the sugar agreements is that they did not and perhaps could not call the tune in ordering movements within the international market. National commodity policies regarding sugar, and notably those of the US and the EEC countries, were a decisive factor in respect of price movements. Subsidiary aims such as increasing world sugar consumption and increasing the export earnings of developing countries appear in practice to have been only secondary policy goals.

Notes

1   See Chapter 4.

2   See Chapters 1 and 2.

3   For the technical aspects of sugar production see V.P. Timoshenko and B. Swerling, The World's Sugar: Progress and Policy (Stanford University Press, Stanford, 1957), pp. 3-5 and G.L. Spencer and R. Meade, Cane-Sugar Handbook (New York, 1945).

4   It is impossible to do justice in the space available to a subject of such vastness and which has generated such a substantial literature. What follows is the bare bones of the background to the literature on world sugar production and those wishing for more detail should refer to one of the many specialised accounts available. See, for examples, N. Deerr, The History of Sugar (Chapman and Hill Ltd, London, 1950), L. Strong, The Story of Sugar (Weidenfeld and Nicolson, London, 1954), R.H. Cottrell, Beet-Sugar Economics (The Caxton Printers Ltd, Caldwell, Idaho, 1952), Timoshenko and Swerling, The World's Sugar: Progress and Policy, R.P. Humpbert, The Growing of Sugar Cane (Elsevier Publishing Co, London, 1968), S. Harris and I. Smith, World Sugar Markets in a State of Flux (Trade Policy Research Centre, London, 1973) and T. Turner, The Marketing of Sugar (Irwin Inc, Homewood, Illinois, 1955). In addition, the development of sugar production and policy on a national and even local basis has also led to copious publications. On the major producers, see as examples, the Coleção Canavieira published by Brazil's Instituto do Açucar e do Alcool, H. Thomas, Cuba or the Pursuit of Freedom (Eyre and Spottiswoode, London, 1971), British Sugar Corporation, Home Grown Sugar: Rise and Development of an Industry (London, 1961) and R. Bohall, 'The Sugar Industry's Structure, Pricing and Performance' (US, Department of Agriculture Report, Washington, 1977).

5   The association of sugar with slavery has led in its turn to a large volume of writing. For examples of illuminating studies on this subject see R.B. Toplin (ed.), Slavery and Race Relations in Latin America (Greenwood Press, Westport, Connecticut, 1974), Thomas, Cuba or the Pursuit of Freedom and J.C. Sitterson, Sugar Country: The Cane Sugar Industry in the South, 1753-1950 (University of Kentucky Press, Lexington, 1953).

6   See Chapter 1. Countries with a high degree of dependency in 1977, for example, included Reunion, Fiji and Mauritius, where sugar accounted for over 70 per cent of export receipts, and Cuba, where it accounted for about half. See UNCTAD, Handbook of International Trade and Development Statistics, Table 4.1.

7   International Sugar Council, The World Sugar Economy Structure and Policies (International Sugar Council, London, 1963), vol. II, pp. 24-5.

8   Ibid., pp. 24 and 32.

9   International Sugar Council, The World Sugar Economy, vol. II, pp. 163-64. Of the exports outside the world market, those between the US offshore areas and mainland and foreign exports to the US market on preferential terms were by far the most important, accounting for 29.3 per cent of the total in 1954. Apart from the US, the UK and the EEC, France, Portugal and the USSR also provided important preferential trading links.

10   Ibid., pp. 166-68, offers a concise description.

11   Ibid., p. 168.

12   Ibid., pp. 168-83.

13   US Beet Sugar Association, 'What is the US Sugar Program?' (Washington, March 1966), p. 20 and Bohall, 'The Sugar Industry's Structure, Pricing, and Performance' (US Department of Agriculture, Washington, 1977).

14   T.W. Tsadik, 'The International Sugar Market: Self Sufficiency or Free Trade', Journal of World Trade Law, vol. 16, no. 3 (1982) offers a useful account of this period. Under the 1977 scheme, processors could obtain loans from the Commodity Credit Corporation if market prices were low.

15   International Sugar Council, The World Sugar Economy, vol. II, pp. 177-80 and Thomas, Cuba or the Pursuit of Freedom.

16   International Sugar Council, The World Sugar Economy, vol. II, Part III provides a helpful account of this period. In 1951, world exports totalled 14,128,939 metric tons (raw value).

17   Great Britain, Parliamentary Report, World Economic Interdependence and Trade in Commodities (HMSO, London, 1975, Cmnd. 6061), p. 70.

18   Tsadik, 'The International Sugar Market', pp. 147-50 and UK, World Economic Interdependence and Trade in Commodities, p. 70. Tsadik, p. 148, for example, estimated the net cost from the Community Budget as 8 million European units of account in 1974 for net exports of 1 million metric tons rising to 475 million in 1979 for exports of 3.6 million metric tons.

19   G.B. Hagelberg, 'International Sugar Agreements, 1864-1977' in F.O. Licht, International Sugar Report: Problems and Prospects of a New International Sugar Agreement (F.O. Licht, Ratzeberg, Germany, 1977).

20   Ibid., pp. 123-24. In industrialised countries it is consumption in manufactured sugar-containing products that is the more important way of raising total sugar consumption. The rate of consumption appears to slow down considerably after the level of 30 to 35 kg has been passed. In the industrialised countries, therefore, future increases in consumption may depend largely but not exclusively on population growth. In contrast, consumption in developing countries has ample scope for advancement.

21   On the Convention and bounty system, see Deerr, The History of Sugar, pp. 501-08.

22   For the prices in this period, see International Sugar Council, The World Sugar Economy, vol. II, p. 342.

23   See League of Nations, Report of the Proceedings of the World Economic Conference (League of Nations, Geneva, 1927, C.356.M.129), vol. I, pp. 237-38; and Ibid., Sugar: Memoranda prepared for the Economic Committee by Dr. H.C. Prinsen Geerligs, Messrs F.O. Licht and Dr. Gustav Mikusch (League of Nations, Geneva, 1929, C.148.M.127). In contrast, the Conference reached the general conclusion that international commodity agreements between parties interested in the same commodity were both desirable and might assist in the more methodical organisation of production.

24   For the text of the Chadbourne Agreement see International Sugar Journal, vol. XXXIII (August 1931), pp. 391-401.

25   Lamartine Yates, Commodity Control, pp. 58-9.

26   B. Swerling, International Control of Sugar, 1918-1941 (Stanford University Press, Stanford, 1949), p. 45.

27   L.E. Aguilar, Cuba 1933 (Cornell University Press, Ithaca, 1972), pp. 56-7, Thomas, Cuba or the Pursuit of Freedom, pp. 509 and 708 and United Nations, A Study of Trade between Latin America and Europe (United Nations, Geneva, 1953), Appendix II, p. 70.

28 See United Nations, A Study of Trade between Latin America and Europe, p. 68, Timoshenko and Swerling, The World's Sugar: Progress and Policy and Great Britain, Ministry of Agriculture and Fisheries, Report on the Beet Sugar Industry at Home and Abroad (HMSO, London, 1931) for a few examples of the extensive literature on this subject. For a fuller bibliography see F. Gordon-Ashworth, 'International and National Commodity Control, 1930 to 1945: Sugar and the Brazilian Case', unpublished PhD thesis, University of Southampton, 1978.

29 For both the report of the 1937 Conference and the terms of the resultant Agreement, see League of Nations, International Sugar Conference held in London from 5 April to 6 May 1937. I: Text of the Agreement; II: Proceedings and Documents of the Conference (League of Nations, Geneva, 1937 C.289.M.190.II. B.8).

30 'Agreement concerning the Regulation of Production and Marketing of Sugar' (6 May 1937) in ILO, Intergovernmental Commodity Agreements, pp. 26-43, Preamble and Article 2.

31 Ibid., Article 2.

32 Ibid., Articles 8-9, 11, 19, 26 and 29-37.

33 League of Nations, International Sugar Conference held in London from 5 April to 6 May 1937, p. 27.

34 Rowe, Primary Commodities in International Trade, pp. 147-48; for a good statistical coverage of this period see International Sugar Council, The World Sugar Economy, vol. II.

35 International Sugar Council, The World Sugar Economy, vol. II, pp. 44-60. For sugar rationing see Timoshenko and Swerling, The World's Sugar: Progress and Policy, pp. 176-77, E. Roll, The Combined Food Board: A Study in Wartime International Planning, pp. 122-27 and 184-85 and G. Walworth, Feeding the Nation in Peace and War (Allen & Unwin, London, 1940), Chapter XXI. For the extension to the Agreement see 'Protocol to enforce and to prolong after August 31, 1942, the International Agreement regarding the Regulation of Production and Marketing of Sugar' in ILO, Intergovernmental Commodity Agreements, pp. 45-6.

36 International Sugar Council, The World Sugar Economy, vol. II, p. 343 and 'International Agreement for the Regulation of the Production and Marketing of Sugar' (HMSO, London, 1956, Cmd. 9004).

37 'International Agreement for the Regulation of the Production and Marketing of Sugar', Article 1.

38 Ibid., Articles 3-8, 13 and 20. Export quotas were to be reduced automatically by at least 5 per cent when the world price for sugar had fallen below the lower limit for fifteen consecutive market days (Article 21). Cuts were limited to 20 per cent of the permitted export tonnages set out in the Agreement (Article 23). When the price exceeded the ceiling, all export quotas were to be dismantled.

39 B. Swerling, 'The International Sugar Agreement of 1953', The American Economic Review, vol. XLIV, no. 5 (December 1954), p. 844; see also International Sugar Council, The World Sugar Economy, vol. I, pp. 124-27 for Cuban sugar policies and vol. II, p. 343 for prices.

40 'International Sugar Agreement of 1958' (US, Department of State, Washington, 1958), Articles 14-22 and 'International Agreement for the Regulation of the Production and Marketing of Sugar', Article 14.

41 See Rowe, Primary Commodities in International Trade, pp. 176-77, for a useful account of this period.

42   For the prices see UNCTAD, Commodity Survey 1968 (UNCTAD, Geneva, 1969, E.69.II.D.5) p. 35; for stock levels, see United Nations, Food and Agriculture Organization, 'The World Sugar Economy in Figures', pp. 114-17. See also Nappi, Commodity Market Controls, p. 52 and pp. 70-1 and A.D. Law, International Commodity Agreements (Lexington Books, Lexington, Mass., 1975), p. 50.

43   Nappi, Commodity Market Controls, pp. 71-2.

44   Brown, The Political and Social Economy of Commodity Control, pp. 22-3.

45   'International Sugar Agreement' (HMSO, London, 1969, Cmnd. 3887), Article 1.

46   Ibid., Articles 30, 48 and 53.

47   Ibid., Articles 47-9.

48   Ibid., Articles 28 and 48. Basic quotas covered 5,390,000 metric tons in 1953 and 7,689,000 metric tons in 1968.

49   Ibid., Articles 3, 6, 30, 34-9, 44, 53 and 55.

50   The average price on the free world market in 1968 was US 1.9 cents and in 1974, US 29.7 cents. See L. Myers, 'Analyzing Sugar Price Trends', Commodity Year Book 1977 (Commodity Research Bureau, New York, 1977).

51   H. Ahlfeld, 'The International Sugar Agreement of 1977: Problems of Regulating the Free World Market' in F.O. Licht, International Sugar Report (F.O. Licht, Ratzeburg, Germany, n.d.), pp. 13-14.

52   'Text of the International Sugar Agreement, 1973' (mimeo, UNCTAD, Geneva, 1973, TD/SUGAR.8/4).

53   International Sugar Organisation, Annual Report for the Year 1977 (International Sugar Organisation, London, 1978), pp. 8-21 and F.O. Licht, International Sugar Report: Problems and Prospects of a New International Sugar Agreement.

54   See for example Nappi, Commodity Market Controls, pp. 74-6.

55   'International Sugar Agreement, 1977' in United Nations, United Nations Sugar Conference 1977 (United Nations, New York, 1978, TD/SUGAR.9/12), Article 1.

56   Ibid., Articles 34-62.

57   Ibid., Articles 46-7.

58   Ibid., Article 57.

59   Ibid., Article 55.

60   Guardian, 27 April 1981 and Globe and Mail, 3 November 1979.

61   Guardian, 22 November 1982, The Economist, 17 April 1982 and Guardian, 10 May 1982.

62   Australia and other major exporting nations were reported to have made 'an urgent plea' for the EEC to 'offset the results of its past policies' at a special meeting at the GATT Summit. The EEC proposals were for an enlarged stock provision of 5 to 6 million metric tons held by the ten largest sugar exporters, a second tier of producers subject to export quotas and a special stocks arrangement; and a third tier of producers who would be permitted to export freely below an established ceiling. See Financial Times, 26 November 1982, Ibid., 13 January 1983, Ibid., 20 January 1983 and Guardian, 22 November 1982.

187

63 F.O. Licht, International Sugar Report: Problems and Prospects of a New International Sugar Agreement, p. 6.

64 P. Hallwood, Stabilization of International Commodity Markets (Jai Press, Connooticut, 1979), pp. 77-81.

65 F.O. Licht, International Sugar Report: Problems and Prospects of a New International Sugar Agreement, p. 8.

66 Great Britain, House of Lords, Select Committee on the European Community (HMSO, London, 19 March 1980), p. xxv.

9: RUBBER

'Rubber is in great demand all over the world; more and more of it is needed.'

(United Nations Food and Agriculture Organization, 1977)

1. General

Rubber affords an interesting fourth example of international commodity control in practice since it has faced peculiar problems of competition from within the industry itself with the development of synthetic rubber. However, synthetic rubber represents a negligible proportion of world trade in rubber and it is natural rubber for which international agreements (in the 1930s and in the late 1970s) and cartels (in the 1920s) have operated and which is a core commodity under UNCTAD's Integrated Programme. Reference in this chapter will be made largely, therefore, to natural as opposed to synthetic rubber except where the latter offers explanatory background to developments in the former.

The essential properties of natural rubber are its elasticity, its waterproofness, its solid tenaciousness, its high adaptability, its high abrasion and tear resistance, its low hysteresis (loss of energy through internal heat), its high resistance to oxidisation and its substantial resistance to the action of oil and heat. Rubber is a renewable material with limited scrap value and, like tin, was included in the US strategic stockpile. Unlike other raw materials produced largely by developing countries, rubber has not generated a high degree of dependency in terms of being a dominant source of export earnings. Demand for rubber is considered to be quite insensitive to price changes in the short-term although sensitive to changes in economic activity. The supply of rubber, similarly, is also insensitive to price movements in the short-term and rubber prices tend to fluctuate widely in the face of even small changes in economic activity.(1)

Rubber is the milky resinous juice - latex - of certain tropical trees which coagulates on exposure to air. Rubber trees are grown in tropical climates and require not only a high temperature but also plenty of humidity, a minimum period of five to six years before coming into bearing and a further six years thereafter before full production. After planting, a tree has an economic life of about thirty years although this is reduced by over-tapping. Natural rubber is differentiated by the quality of its processing but the processes applied to it are basically the same: the latex is washed, dried, pressed and often smoked and made into sheets of various types. Native rubber often has to be re-milled to remove impurities. In the mid-1960s, new processes were introduced which permitted the production of granual (block) instead of sheet rubber; this permitted rigorous technical specification and a saving in transport, handling and storage costs. By the mid-1970s a third of world rubber exports was in block rubber form.(2)

Rubber was reported to have been discovered by Columbus in Haiti in the 1490s. It was only in the first half of the eighteenth century, however, that research was carried out into a means of preventing the coagulation of latex and not until 1839 that Goodyear, in collaboration with Hayward, discovered the process of vulcanisation in the US. This involved mixing crude rubber and sulphur and heating them to obtain a stronger, more elastic material better able to withstand heat and cold. The growth of the rubber industry was further ensured by the invention by Dunlop of the pneumatic tyre in 1888 and the consequent development of the tyre industry in the UK and the US.(3)

This growth of the rubber manufacturing industry at the end of the nineteenth century generated increased demand for the large-scale production of natural rubber, prepared hitherto entirely from wild sources. In response, rubber cultivation on a plantation basis in the Far East was pioneered by the British, followed by the Dutch and later by the French: from 5,000 acres in 1900, plantation rubber increased to 1,000,000 acres in 1910 and to 8,500,000 acres in 1936. Other new areas opened up before the Second World War included Liberia, Nigeria, Zaire and parts of French Africa and a dramatic increase in yields was aided by improved production methods such as bud grafting. In contrast, attempts to establish rubber plantations in Brazil in 1910 and between 1927 and 1940 progressed at a far more modest pace due both to labour problems and to the difficult nature of the terrain.(4)

It will be apparent from the necessarily brief description of the development of the world plantation rubber industry that colonial forces were extremely influential in shaping its evolution. In 1938, for example, over half of world rubber exports came from the British Empire and rubber constituted one of the UK's most important colonial products. The importance of rubber for the Netherlands was also great whereas, in contrast, South American, Central American and African producers between them produced only 23.4 per cent of the total.(5) Of total production in Malaysia, two-thirds derived from plantations and the remainder from smallholdings; the equivalent proportions for Indonesia were 55 per cent and 45 per cent respectively. These two countries maintained a dominant position in world natural rubber production after the Second World War although the share of Malaysia rose slightly (from 39.5 per cent in 1938 to over 40 per cent in 1979) and, in contrast, that of Indonesia fell (from 35 to 23.4 per cent). The share of plantation rubber fell both in Malaysia and in Indonesia in the same period. In 1979, it constituted only 37.6 per cent of total natural rubber produced and natural rubber in its turn represented less than a third of total world rubber as a result of the post-War growth of synthetic rubber production.(6)

Some explanation is needed for what amounted to a major transformation of the world rubber market in the twentieth century with the development of synthetic rubber on a commercial basis. Synthetic rubber had been produced, albeit in a different form, by the Germans after 1915 and in the US and the USSR in the 1920s and 1930s. However, production costs far exceeded those for natural rubber and it was not until the Second World War that insecure Far Eastern supplies stimulated the large-scale development of synthetic rubber in the US under government tutelage. A Rubber Reserve Company was set up in 1940 with the dual purpose of building up stocks of natural rubber and of developing the synthetic rubber industry. In 1942, following a US Government report, this programme was expanded and led to the discovery of a range of monomers suitable for the commercial production of a variety of general and special purpose synthetic rubbers, plastics and fibres. After the War, the synthetic rubber plants were sold to private sector interests and during the course of the 1950s new rubbers were developed and synthetic rubber industries were built up in Europe, Japan and the USSR. In contrast to the natural rubber industry, the synthetic rubber industry was thus industrial in nature and located in developed market and centrally planned countries near to the manufacturing side of the rubber industry.

The competitive relationship between natural and synthetic rubber has been the object of extensive enquiry. At least until the mid-1960s synthetic rubber had the major advantage of being produced under technical conditions which permitted a stable and unified presentation to the market. However, with the development of block rubber this advantage was reduced and the 1973 oil crisis acted in the opposite direction by adding significantly to the cost of synthetic rubber production despite its proximity to the locus of demand. Growing concern for environmental protection also led to a new dimension in the world rubber economy with a shift in favour of renewable and natural as opposed to non-renewable and energy-intensive synthetic products. Although the main kinds of natural and synthetic rubber are in principle close substitutes for each other, the competitive relation between them is thus by no means clear cut.(7)

The established primary markets for rubber are Kuala Lumpur and Singapore whereas London, New York and Tokyo/Kobe represent the major terminal markets. For the locational reasons outlined above, only a negligible proportion of synthetic rubber enters world trade and predictably, given its end usage, the major industrialised countries have led the consumption both of natural and synthetic rubber. In 1947, for example, the US consumed 50.5 per cent of the world total consumption of natural rubber and 70.6 per cent of synthetic rubber. By 1979, however, the US share of consumption was only 18.9 per cent of natural rubber and 27.0 per cent of synthetic rubber respectively; this was partly due to the expansion of the share of natural rubber consumption of Japan (from 1.6 per cent of the total in 1947 to 9.2 per cent in 1979) and of synthetic rubber consumption by Western Europe (from 3.7 per cent of the total in 1947 to 21.5 per cent in 1979). A further factor influencing US demand for rubber was the halting of acquisitions for the Government stockpile and the commencement of disposals from the stockpile from 1959.(8)

Rubber has a wide variety of uses but since 1895 its principal use has been in the manufacture of pneumatic tyres. For this reason the large tyre manufacturers such as Dunlop and Goodyear were among the first important recruits to commercial rubber cultivation, with substantial estate holdings of their own, and the consumption of rubber has been closely associated with demand for motor vehicles. In 1978, for example, over 60 per cent of rubber in the US and Japan and almost 45 per cent in the UK was used to make tyres and related products. The shift in international rubber consumption patterns since the Second World War is explained at least in part by the shift in the world motor industry away from the domination by the US towards new growth areas such as Japan.(9) In addition to tyre manufacture, other uses of rubber include products such as mats, carpet backing and shoe soles.

2. Controls to 1945

As a commodity of (increasing) importance in world trade in the first half of the twentieth century, it is not surprising that rubber, like tea (Chapter 12), was early subject to commodity control. A good example was the attempt by Brazil to institute a national scheme to protect its natural non-plantation rubber from competition in the years before the First World War. The pressure for protection came from the producers who applied to the Federal Government in 1910 when the price of rubber started to fall rapidly after boom conditions. In 1911, the Federal Government entrusted the Banco do Brasil with the task of accumulating a large stock of rubber and withholding it from the market. However, the plan was still-born owing to an influx of rubber from the Far East. In 1912 a more detailed scheme, the Defesa da Borracha, established experimental stations and exempted from import duties tools and materials used in the rubber industry in an attempt to improve the international competitiveness of Brazilian rubber. However, as McFadyean has pointed out, although the plan was sound in its intent, it amounted to a case of shutting the stable door after the steed had been stolen. With plantation rubber coming on stream at a lower price, incentives offered to improve the quality and scale of Brazilian rubber production, though large, were inadequate. By 1913 most of the enterprises started under the auspices of the scheme had ceased operations.(10)

The rubber boom of 1909 to 1910 acted also as a catalyst to the introduction of national controls in Malaysia by encouraging a substantial increase in the area planted in rubber. The involuntary building up of stocks during the First World War owing to the shortage of shipping was such that in 1917 a voluntary scheme was established by the plantation companies to restrict output to three-quarters of capacity. A government committee was appointed to consider a compulsory restriction scheme but, with the ending of the War, even the voluntary scheme was ended. Interest was renewed in the idea of controls on rubber in the Far East, however, when in the late autumn of 1920 the post-War boom in rubber prices came to an abrupt end. In 1920, accordingly, the (British) Rubber Growers' Association agreed on a voluntary scheme to restrict output by 25 per cent in Malaysia and Sri Lanka. Although supported in their action by a large proportion of the members of the Dutch Rubber Growers' Association (Internationale Vereeniging voor de Rubber-cultuur) several factors worked against the success of the scheme. First, it was introduced when demand in the US, the main market, was severely depressed. Secondly, the output of small-scale rubber producers continued to rise which worked directly against the restrictive action of plantation producers. In 1921, as the situation deteriorated, the British Government appointed a committee of inquiry under Sir James Stevenson to investigate various courses of action. The Stevenson Plan to emerge was approved with no apparent difficulty and used the device, common to subsequent commodity arrangements, of export quotas based on historical production levels and assessed on a quarterly basis according to the prices ruling in the preceding quarter.(11)

Opinions vary regarding the degree of success of the Stevenson Plan in meeting its objective of securing higher prices in the rubber sector. Prices for rubber remained relatively stable during the 1920s apart from a slight boom in 1925 and it could be argued that the Plan at the least prevented prices from falling further. However, even within the British Empire the scheme was partial in its coverage, applying to only about 70 per cent of the total rubber acreage, and small-scale planters and producers in non-British areas were unrestricted in their output despite attempts to secure their support. The existence of the scheme was also reported to have encouraged increased production of reclaimed rubber. In 1928 rubber producers in both Malaysia and Sri Lanka called for the abolition of export restrictions citing loss of export markets to Indonesia as their reason. Although the British Government bowed to this pressure, the validity of the grounds for doing so was questionable. The share of the world market accounted for by British colonies increased gradually throughout the course of the 1920s -from 51.6 per cent in 1924 to 63.1 per cent in 1930. In contrast, the share of Indonesia fell - from 34.7 per cent in 1924 to 29.4 per cent in 1930 - despite unhampered production.(12)

Perhaps the most important long-term result of the Stevenson Plan was the stimulus it gave to new rubber production by presenting a veneer of stability to the international rubber market. New planting was also encouraged by the slight boom in rubber prices in 1925; and the Netherlands in 1928 pursued an active policy of encouraging new acreage in Borneo and Sumatra. This combination of factors, together with the ending of export restrictions in the British colonies in 1928 and the downturn in US demand from 1929, brought a sharp 72 per cent fall in world rubber prices between 1929 and 1931. Although the depth of the price decline was not anticipated, there was a sufficient degree of anxiety within the rubber industry in the major producing countries to bring about the formation of a British-Dutch Liaison Committee in January 1930, empowered to examine the rubber situation and to report back to their respective trade associations. Initial measures, such as the observance of a 'tapping holiday' of one month's duration, were soon recognised as insufficient to deal with the magnitude of the problem. In July 1930, accordingly, the Committee reported that a more comprehensive and mandatory scheme was needed to regulate the output of rubber and to discourage further extensions of the area planted. However, official responses were discouraging: the British Government was not prepared to initiate such a scheme; the Dutch went further and voiced strong objections to mandatory intervention, stating that the control of native rubber production would be very difficult to administer.

By 1931, however, the further fall in the price of rubber turned the tide of official opinion and the Dutch Government invited the

British Government to the negotiating table. Despite a series of meetings, the conclusion in 1932 was that it was impossible to frame and operate an international scheme which would guarantee the effective regulation of the production or export of rubber, this despite strong lobbies from small and large scale producers for some assistance.(13) By 1933, discussions shifted to the aegis of the rubber growers themselves. It was thus the Rubber Growers' Association which drafted a control scheme on which agreement was reached by all of the governments concerned in April 1934.

The objective of the 1934 Rubber Agreement reflected the same preoccupations as the preceding years of discussion: the need to regulate exports to the world's rubber markets, to reduce stocks to 'normal' levels and to stabilise prices at levels which were 'reasonably remunerative to efficient producers'. The methodology prescribed was a combination of export quotas based on approximate export statistics for the preceding few years, the prohibition of new planting and the reduction of stocks to one-fifth of annual production totals. An International Rubber Regulation Committee was set up to administer the Agreement, based in London with delegates from each of the territories to which the Agreement applied. The UK was given authority to convoke the first meeting and voting arrangements were weighted in accordance with rubber production giving British colonial interests a dominant role. An interesting feature was that the Agreement provided that three representatives of rubber manufacturers should advise the Rubber Committee.(14) (A brief summary of the key provisions of this and the 1979 Rubber Agreement is provided in the Appendix, Table 4.)

In terms of coverage, the 1934 Rubber Agreement embraced all but 3.4 per cent of world rubber produced and, despite the complication of regulating a large number of smallholders, permissible and actual exports showed a remarkable degree of correlation (Table 9:1). The Agreement coincided with an upward phase in the business cycle to 1937 which enabled stocks to be reduced sharply between 1934 and 1937 without the imposition of dramatically low quota percentages. In 1938, in contrast, when, with the accession of India and Thailand, the Agreement theoretically covered all of world production, prices fell by 40 per cent in the wake of a downturn in demand and quotas were clawed back to only 50 per cent of estimated export potential. However, with an increase in strategic stockpiling in 1939, stocks were reduced to very low levels and, when war broke out, prices rose steeply. Although the Agreement was retained as a vehicle of stock-building by the Allied Powers, it was rendered void from December 1941 with the interruption of supplies from the Far East.(15)

In broad terms, the 1934 Rubber Agreement may be deemed to have succeeded in its objective of regulating exports of rubber to the world market by stock control although it is debatable whether the

195

Table 9:1 : International Rubber Controls, 1934-1940 (metric tons)

Year	Permissible Exports	Actual Exports
1934 (Jun to Dec)	506,911	494,838
1935	782,188	793,195
1936	813,461	810,501
1937	1,110,393	1,105,774
1938	769,046	791,657
1939	893,205	901,722
1940	1,303,188	1,306,311
1941 (Jan to Nov)	1,496,950	1,350,152

Source: derived from A. McFadyean, The History of Rubber
Regulation 1934-1943 (Allen & Unwin, London, 1944),
p. 154.

prices were 'fair and remunerative'. In its own account, for example, the International Rubber Regulation Committee claimed in 1944 that the scheme had worked efficiently in providing large supplies of rubber at a price which yielded no excessive profits.(16) The average price of rubber throughout the pre-War period of regulation was 7.35d per pound, close to that prevailing when regulation was introduced in 1934.   Although the Committee devoted considerable time to assessing what the cost of production was for an efficient producer, it also admitted that such assessments (which produced a price of 8d to 10d per pound in July 1937) were only estimated and then from estate rather than from small-holding sources.(17)

Notwithstanding its· broad success in meeting its targets, the 1934 Agreement met with considerable criticism.   This was exemplified by a debate in the leader of the Straits Times in 1937 attacking the export quota control mechanism on the grounds that it gave preferential treatment in the matter of assessment to European as opposed to domestic producers.(18) Domestic producers claimed that, by introducing the controls in 1934 at a time when they were expanding their rubber acreage faster than the estates, the Agreement artificially checked their development and acted towards the preservation of the status quo.   Statistical problems, such as skeletal accounting systems, and administrative problems, such as poor representation on the Rubber Committee and the lack of a common voice, may also have weakened the position of the smallholders by leading to an under-assessment of their individual quota allocations.(19)

During the Second World War, Sri Lanka and India were the only major natural rubber producers to escape Japanese occupation. However, by mid-1941, even India became a net importer of rubber as the growth of its manufacturing industry exceeded domestic output. From a situation of restraint, rubber producers thus faced strong incentives to increase output. Planters in Sri Lanka, for instance, were induced to increase dramatically their tapping (to 'slaughter' tap since it shortened the productive life of the tree) in return for an undertaking by the government to pay the cost of re-planting of up to £45 an acre; and from March 1942, the entire rubber output of Sri Lanka was purchased by the UK Ministry of Supply with the Rubber Commissioner of Sri Lanka the sole exporter. By 1943, as a result, rubber production in Sri Lanka reached nearly double the pre-War level although production declined thereafter to 1949.(20)

3. Controls since 1945

With the formal ending of the 1934 Agreement in 1944, a Rubber Study Group was formed with British, Dutch, US and eventual French participation for the purposes of consultation and the continuing collection of statistical data on rubber.(21) It was not until 1952, however, that this group established a sub-committee to consider the negotiation of a replacement international agreement and this failed to bear fruit. Not least of the problems with which the Committee had to contend was a post-War marketing environment which had altered radically from its pre-War counterpart. A UK Commission, reporting in 1952 on production in Sri Lanka in the wake of a fall in world prices for rubber and rising production costs noted, for example, that Sri Lanka was at a disadvantage to Malaysia and Indonesia since the trees were older and had been heavily tapped during the War. The Commission proposed that some 200,000 acres of 'uneconomic' rubber land should be turned over to other crops or reafforested. In addition to variations in production costs, synthetic rubber also provided strong competition to natural rubber and by 1959 established its lead over natural rubber in terms of output.(22)

The absence of attempts to secure coordinated international controls on the world rubber trade between 1944 and 1976 is perhaps equally as interesting and worthy of attention as their existence in the pre-War period. Whilst the changing pattern of world rubber production provides part of the explanation, the changing pattern of ownership, on the other hand, also offers some clue to the lack of coordinated approach. The most notable example in this respect was the gradual achievement of independence by the major rubber producing countries and with it the dispersion of policy on rubber production to an increased number of national authorities. In several cases, these authorities adopted new forms of policies within a broader framework of national economic planning. An example of this is provided by the case of Malaysia which during the mid-1950s saw increased utilisation of unoccupied land as a way of improving rural growth. As a consequence, new planting was no longer discouraged (although re-planting was preferred where possible). Between 1956 and 1975, four five-year plans in Malaysia encouraged a substantial increase in rubber production (from 678,100 metric tons in 1956 to over 1,599,862 metric tons in 1979) with smallholders major contributors to this growth; by 1969, for example, the output from smallholdings almost equalled that of the estates for the first time and by 1973, it had taken the lead.(23)

One consequence of the fourfold increase in world natural rubber output between 1946 and the mid-1970s and of the rapid (eight-fold) expansion of synthetic rubber production was downward pressure on prices from the Korean War peak in 1951 to 1973 despite a fairly steady increase in demand. This is demonstrated in Figure 9.1. However, it was the volatility of prices between 1972 and 1976, together with the perception of UNCTAD that natural rubber was a commodity suitable for inclusion within the Integrated Programme, rather than the decline in rubber prices between 1950 and 1973 which provided the stimulus for the negotiation of an international agreement on rubber. In November 1976, in a first step, a producer agreement, the International Natural Rubber Agreement on Price Stabilization, was entered into by Indonesia, Malaysia, Singapore, Sri Lanka and Thailand under the auspices of the Association of Natural Rubber Producing Countries. The Agreement, set for a five year period, aimed to achieve a balanced growth of supply in relation to demand and to stabilise prices within an unspecified range taking into account the relative cost of synthetic vis à vis natural rubber. The control mechanisms introduced were an international buffer stock and the possibility of nationally held stocks.(24) Although initiated by producers, the 1976 Agreement provided for accession by any 'net producer or net consumer' country and in January 1977 meetings were held by UNCTAD to discuss bringing the scheme under the Integrated Programme. Proposals calling for a buffer stock of 400,000 metric tons and restrictions on the production of synthetic rubber met with little support from consumer countries, particularly and understandably those with large synthetic rubber industries. In November 1978, an UNCTAD meeting discussed instead a US proposal for a 700,000 metric ton buffer stock. Agreement was eventually reached on a stock of 550,000 metric tons and the results were formalised in the International Natural Rubber Agreement of 1979.

The main objective of the 1979 Agreement, the stabilisation of conditions in the international natural rubber trade by avoiding excessive price fluctuations, was very similar to that of the rubber agreements of the 1930s and the producers' Agreement of 1976. However, the main control mechanism, a nationally held buffer stock, to be held either in the territory of exporting or importing members,

Figure 9:1 : Natural Rubber Prices, 1950-1976
(annual average, $ per metric ton, New York)

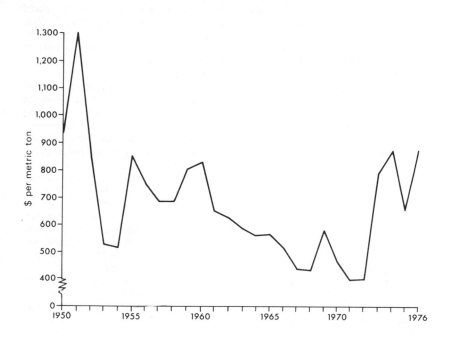

Source: International   Rubber   Study   Group,   World   Rubber
           Statistics Handbook 1946-70 (International Rubber Study
           Group, London, 1974) and Ibid., Rubber Statistical Bulletin
           (International Rubber Study Group, London, 1981).

encumbered by detailed terms of reference spanning some fifteen
articles (Articles 27 to 41), was a new phenomenon and reflected the
awakening of interest in national controls as a formal component of
an internationally administered agreement.   The buffer stock was
governed by a price range consisting of seven indicative prices fixed
initially in the range of 150 to 270 Malaysian cents per kilo, a range
below what was considered to be the prevailing very high market
price of about 300 Malaysian cents. An International Natural Rubber
Organization was established to administer the provisions and to
supervise the operation of the Agreement.   Interestingly, the

Agreement specified that the headquarters of this organisation should 'at all times' be located in the territory of a member. As in other international commodity organisations, votes were to be divided equally between importing and exporting member countries, who were also to share the commitment to finance the buffer stock. Unlike its pre-War antecedents, the 1979 Rubber Agreement thus contained no precisely specified production or export quotas although it committed its signatories, rather vaguely, to consultation on domestic natural rubber policies directly affecting supply and demand.(25)

The 1979 Rubber Agreement, the first to be negotiated under the Integrated Programme, faced considerable difficulties from its inception. The price range, considered at the time to be conservative and in need of later upward adjustment, had to be revised down by 1 per cent in May 1982 in the face of substantially reduced demand and a price fall which continued despite buffer stock purchases of 100,000 metric tons. Secondly, support was slow to materialise. By April 1982, for example, consumer participants were still 1 per cent short of the 80 per cent target required for the Agreement and Thailand, of the producers, had also failed to ratify.(26) Further uncertainty was generated in the summer of 1981 by large scale buying operations which some commentators felt could reflect an attempt by Malaysia to raise prices in the run-up to a general election in April 1982. In May 1982, following the cut in the buffer stock price range, Malaysia added to this uncertainty by declaring that it was re-examining its involvement in the Agreement. And, in October 1982, it was reported that Malaysia, Indonesia and Thailand had gone one step further in agreeing to a producer-administered stock withdrawal scheme.(27)

4. Conclusion

The case of rubber reveals some interesting features of international commodity control agreements. First, controls were applied exclusively to rubber deriving from agricultural and developing country sources as opposed to industrial and developed country sources. The explanation for this must lie in the greater preoccupation of, first, colonial and, then, newly independent governments to minimise the adverse effects of low or unstable rubber prices and their concern to maximise export receipts from rubber production. In addition, the nature of natural rubber as an agricultural product with a long gestation period, rendering suppliers insensitive to price change in the short-term, and a strong dependence for demand on the world automobile industry, which could cause rubber prices to fluctuate widely, provided further inducements for international control measures. Synthetic rubber producers, in contrast, were more concerned with ensuring a secure supply of rubber of a uniform quality at a cost which did not compare unfavourably with that of natural rubber rather than with goals relating to price or earnings stability or maximisation. Their comparative lack of interest in international controls was heightened by the large degree of integration between raw material producers and industrial manufacturers, often the same entity.

A second point of interest is that pre-War controls exceeded their limited post-War counterpart in terms of coverage, their terms of reference and the control mechanisms employed. Their comprehensive coverage was facilitated by the limited number of (colonial) participant signatories and this also contributed to their relative success in meeting the targets set. The 1979 Agreement, in contrast, experienced more limited support and relied in major part on a buffer stock as the control mechanism. The Agreement was handicapped from its inception by the unexpected depth of the fall in demand for rubber associated with the depressed world automobile industry. However, the complexity of the terms governing the operation of the buffer stock was also criticised since, it was claimed, these led to its use in the wrong place at the wrong time. The general disillusionment with the Agreement as a vehicle for achieving the targets set was reflected by moves by producers to consider uni-lateral action to support rubber prices by means of production cuts in 1981 and 1982.

Notes

1   In 1977, for example, no country depended on rubber for over half of the value of their export earnings. For the price elasticities see E.R. Grilli, B.B. Agostini and M.J.'t Hooft-Welvaars, The World Rubber Economy: Structure, Changes and Policies (IBRD, Johns Hopkins University Press, Baltimore, 1980), pp. 35-6.

2   P.T. Bauer, The Rubber Industry: A Study in Competition and Monopoly (Longmans, Green & Co, London, 1948) and Grilli, Agostini and Hooft-Welvaars, The World Rubber Economy, pp. 28-9.

3   A. McFadyean, The History of Rubber Regulation 1934-1943 (Allen & Unwin, London, 1944), pp. 1-5. The first car fitted with pneumatic tyres was put on the road in 1895.

4   P.W. Allen, Natural Rubber and the Synthetics (Crosby Lockwood, London, 1972) and McFadyean, The History of Rubber Regulation, pp. 8-13.

5   League of Nations, The Network of World Trade and see Chapter 1.

6   International Rubber Study Group, Rubber Statistical Bulletin (International Rubber Study Group, London, 1949) and Ibid., Rubber Statistical Bulletin (International Rubber Study Group, London, March 1981), Table 5.

7   Bauer, The Rubber Industry, pp. 288-90, P.W. Allen, P.O. Thomas and B.C. Sekhar, The Techno-Economic Potential of Natural Rubber in Major End-Uses (Malaysian Rubber Research and Development Board, Kuala Lumpur, 1973) and J.G. Anderson, 'The Rubber Manufacturers' Choice: Natural or Synthetic Rubber?', Plastics and Rubber International (July/August 1977). Grilli, Agostini and Hooft-Welvaars, The World Rubber Economy, Chapter 3 also offers an interesting assessment of market interaction between natural and synthetic rubbers and a detailed analysis of the many kinds of synthetic rubber available in Appendix A. A further factor affecting the demand for natural rubber was the introduction in the early 1960s of radial tyres, which have a higher natural rubber content than cross-ply tyres.

8   An interesting survey of trade in rubber is contained in United Nations, The Maritime Transportation of Natural Rubber (United Nations, New York, 1970, TD/B/C.4/60 Rev. 1). For the statistics covering 1946 to 1979 see International Rubber Study Group, World Rubber Statistics Handbook 1946-1974 (International Rubber Study Group, London, 1974), Tables 10 and 17 and Ibid., Rubber Statistical Bulletin (March 1981). In 1947, the US consumed 58.9 per cent of natural and synthetic rubber. For details of US and UK government stock disposals, see International Rubber Study Group, World Rubber Statistics Handbook, Table 7.

9   International Rubber Study Group, Rubber Statistical Bulletin (March 1981), Tables 38 and 39. In the US, synthetic rubber accounted for 70 per cent of rubber consumed as tyre and tyre-products whereas the proportion was only 58.4 per cent in the UK and 62.3 per cent in Japan. Because of its properties of physical resistance, natural rubber has been preferred for the manufacture of products requiring high strength and low heat generation such as plane and giant lorry tyres. Developments in the world auto industry are covered by a large literature. See for examples G. Maxcy, The Multinational Motor Industry (Croom Helm, London, 1981), G. Bloomfield, The World Automotive Industry (David & Charles, Newton Abbott, 1978), L.J. White, The Automobile Industry since 1945 (Harvard University Press, Cambridge, Mass., 1971) and K. Bhaskar, The Future of the World Motor Industry (Kogan Page, London, 1980).

10 McFadyean, The History of Rubber Regulation, pp. 24-5 and E. de Sousa, A Crise da Borracha (Rio de Janeiro, 1913).

11 J. Stevenson, Rubber Situation in the British Colonies and Protectorates, 1922' (HMSO, London, 1922, Cmd. 1678) and W.L.S. Churchill, The Economist, 26 September

1925. Winston Churchill, for example, stated that the plan was approved since 'the Cabinet felt that the scheme was so excellent that it required no discussion, or that it was so complicated that discussion was impossible'.

12   League of Nations, The Statistical Yearbook of the League of Nations 1933/34 (League of Nations, Geneva, 1934, II.A.6), p. 106, Ormsby Gore, 'Report on Malaya, Ceylon and Java during the Year 1928' (HMSO, London, 1928, Cmd. 3235) and C. Whittlesey, Governmental Control of Crude Rubber: The Stevenson Plan (University of Princeton Press, Princeton, 1931).

13   Communiqué of the British and Dutch Governments of 19 March 1932 quoted in McFadyean, The History of Rubber Regulation, p. 40.

14   'Agreement for the Regulation of Production and Export of Rubber', (7 May 1934), in ILO, Intergovernmental Commodity Agreements, pp. 104-113. See, for example, Preamble and Articles 4, 5, 11, 15 and 18.

15   For the amendments and revisions to the 1934 Rubber Agreement see ILO, Intergovernmental Commodity Agreements, pp. 113-31. These were dated 27 June 1935, 22 May 1936 and 5 February 1937. An extension to the 1934 Rubber Agreement was provided in 'Annex II Revised Text of the Agreement of 7 May 1934' in Ibid., pp. 118-31. See also Lamartine Yates, Commodity Control, p. 122.

16   McFadyean, The History of Rubber Regulation, p. 155.

17   Bauer, The Rubber Industry, and McFadyean, The History of Rubber Regulation, pp. 112-13.

18   Bauer, The Rubber Industry, pp. 141-42. Subsequently, the leader was refuted and then re-stated a few months later.

19   See also G.C. Allen and A.G. Donnithorne, Western Enterprise in Indonesia and Malaya (Allen & Unwin, London, 1957), pp. 125-27. According to this source discrimination against smallholders was greatest in Malaysia.

20   Commonwealth Economic Committee, A Review of Commonwealth Agriculture, p. 103.

21   Bauer, The Rubber Industry, p. 308.

22   Commonwealth Economic Committee, A Review of Commonwealth Agriculture, pp. 103-4.

23   On Malaysian policy in this period, see for example C. Gunnarsson, Malaysian Rubber Production: Patterns of Growth 1900-1975 (Ekonomisk-Historiska Institutionen, Lund University, 1979) and F. Chan, 'A Preliminary Study of the Supply Responses of Malayan Rubber Estates between 1948 and 1959', Malayan Economic Review, vol. 7 (1962). New planting had been prohibited until 1947 and was severely restricted thereafter. Part of the increased output in the 1960s and 1970s was also attributable to productivity growth associated with replanting with higher yielding varieties.

24   For details of the 1976 Agreement, see U. Wassermann, 'Jakarta Natural Rubber Agreement 1976', Journal of World Trade Law, vol. 11, no.3 (May:June 1977).

25   United Nations, 'Elements of an International Agreement on Rubber' (UNCTAD, Geneva, 1976, TD/B/IPC/Rubber L.2), U. Wassermann, 'Commodities in UNCTAD: Rubber', Journal of World Trade Law, vol. 11, no. 3 (May:June 1977), Brown, The Political and Social Economy of Commodity Control, pp. 192-96 and 'International Natural Rubber Agreement, 1979' (United Nations, New York, 1980, TD/Rubber/15/Rev. 1), Articles 1, 3-5, 15, 27-41 and 45.

26   Financial Times, 26 November 1981 and Ibid., 7 April 1982.

27   Financial Times, 6 April 1982, Ibid., 11 May 1982 and Guardian, 1 November 1982. In
      January 1983, however, Malaysia was reported to have requested that UNCTAD should
      investigate the possibility of adding export quotas to the 1979 Agreement's
      mechanisms. See Financial Times, 20 January 1983.

10: COFFEE

'The principal innovation in the coffee industry in the twentieth century has been the series of measures taken by the Brazilian government, unilaterally and in co-operation with other nations, to regulate production, exports and world prices for coffee.'

(Poppino, Brazil, 1968)

1. General

Coffee has increased in importance from a middle ranking commodity in world trade in 1938 to a leading item after the Second World War. The importance of coffee for developing countries in particular is great since they are the exclusive producers and a large number of countries depend on coffee or on coffee and one other commodity such as cocoa, cotton and bananas for a large proportion of their export receipts. A core commodity under UNCTAD's Integrated Programme, for which national and international controls have both been introduced, coffee thus affords a useful fifth example from which to view the operation of international commodity control in practice.(1)

The essential properties of coffee, a genus of the species Coffea, are its flavour, which varies from bitter to mild, its aroma and its stimulatory caffeine content; its value as a foodstuff is negligible. Although storable, the quality of stockpiled coffee deteriorates rapidly after three years and eventually becomes unusable. In most areas where agriculture is devoted largely to coffee both the short-term and the long-term elasticity of supply tend to be low. The income elasticity of demand for coffee declines with increasing incomes since coffee consumption is subject to saturation points. In the US at least, the price elasticity of demand is higher at higher price levels with strong consumer resistance developing when the price rises above a certain level. This is an important factor to be taken into account when seeking to frame a pricing policy for international control measures.(2)

Coffee, attributed as native to Abyssinia, is widely cultivated throughout the tropics. However, commercial coffee production, which dates back to the nineteenth century, has been dominated by one country, Brazil, and Brazil has occupied a central place in the history of coffee controls both at the national and at the international level. In the crop-year 1906/07, for example, Brazil produced 84.5 per cent of the world coffee total, the remainder being produced largely in other South American countries. (For the details of crop-years, see Table 10:1.) Although the domination by Brazil of world coffee production declined throughout the course of the twentieth century - from less than 60 per cent in 1930/31 to only 48 per cent in 1937/38 and to about 33 per cent at the beginning of the 1980s - this reflected a deliberate policy of stock withdrawal and production restraint on the part of Brazil, which is considered in more detail below.(3) In contrast, producers in new areas such as East Africa (notably the Ivory Coast, Ethiopia and Uganda) pursued a deliberate policy of expanding output. As a result the relative simplicity of the world coffee sector, concentrated in Central and South America, was complicated by an influx of newcomers. The coffee tree first comes to harvest only three to four years after planting and full yields are reached after five years; yields normally begin to decline after fifteen years. However, the tree continues to yield for at least fifty years so that with high fixed costs it has often been worth the producer's while to harvest the crop provided the price was higher than variable costs. Yields vary also according to climate and weather, and even when the weather is favourable, good and bad crops tend to alternate. The world coffee market has been characterised by short periods of supply shortage with very high prices followed often by extensive periods of over-supply and low prices.

There are two main types of coffee cultivated: most common, and preferred by consumers owing to a milder flavour, is the arabica grown in a large number of countries; the robusta, in contrast, is grown in fewer countries, such as Brazil, Dahomey, Togo, Gabon and Congo. Capital and labour intensive, coffee is grown both on smallholdings and on plantations. A great variety of processing methods are used for coffee preparation. However, the technical aspects of the conversion of beans into beverage is relatively simple: the green beans are roasted and ground and hot water is then used to extract the soluble parts. The resulting beverage is then consumed directly or resolidified by evaporating the water, yielding soluble coffee. However, only a small proportion of world coffee is traded in processed form.(4)

Table 10:1 : World Coffee Production 1980/81 (000 sacks)[c]

Country	1980/81
Brazil[b]	31,000
Colombia[a]	12,400
Indonesia[b]	5,581
Ivory Coast[a]	4,883
Mexico[a]	4,100
Ethiopia[a]	3,333
El Salvador[a]	2,680
Guatemala[a]	2,530
Uganda[a]	2,334
India[a]	2,250
Costa Rica[a]	2,038
World Total	92,942

Notes: a   crop-year beginning in October
        b   crop-year beginning in April/July
        c   sacks of 60 kilos of green coffee

Source: International Coffee Organization, Quarterly Statistical Bulletin, no. 16 (1980), p. 8.

The world's largest individual consumer of coffee is the US although its share has fallen from over half the world total in the early 1950s to about a third in 1980. The EEC is also an important market. There are wide variations in per capita consumption levels, the highest being in Scandinavian countries, where an average is around 12 kilos per annum, compared with levels of 5 kilos per annum in the US and the EEC.(5) Although total demand has increased steadily since 1945, per capita consumption has slowed considerably in several countries, including the US, due partly to changes in consumer preference toward soft drinks and fruit juices and partly to the growing share of coffee that is processed into soluble coffee since soluble coffee requires fewer green beans to yield the same number of cups as roasted coffee. Until the early 1950s, virtually all coffee was consumed as ground roasted coffee; since then, soluble coffee has increased its share and in the UK and Japan it now accounts for over three-quarters of total coffee consumption.(6) In addition to encouraging the standardisation and concentration of coffee marketing, this has paved the way for an increase in the share of robustas from Africa and Asia, which are inferior in flavour but have a higher yield of soluble coffee per pound of green beans.(7)

207

2. Controls to 1939

The first major attempt at controlling the world coffee market took place in 1906. It took the form of uni-lateral action by Brazil with a view to arresting the process which had brought the price of coffee from 6$175 Brazilian reis (for ten kilos of Rio coffee) in 1904 to 4$603 in 1906 and 3$660 in 1907. These price falls were attributable to the over-planting of coffee bushes in the last decade of the nineteenth century although it was the mammoth coffee crop of 1906 which acted as the immediate catalyst to the introduction of a more organised system of coffee marketing.(8) An agreement, signed at Taubaté in the state of São Paulo between the presidents of the three major coffee-producing states, São Paulo, Minas Gerais and Rio de Janeiro, authorised São Paulo to purchase excess coffee supplies, to store them until the market (New York) price for coffee improved and then to release them gradually. The scheme, which pledged producers to a policy of attempting to increase coffee prices by withholding supplies, became known as valorisation after the Portuguese verb valorizar, meaning to value highly. The policy of valorisation was to continue in different guises until 1937.(9)

It was Brazil's dominant position in world coffee production which encouraged planters to believe that controlled marketing could offer a solution to the problems of overproduction; a law of 1902 to reduce the planting of new coffee bushes seems largely to have been evaded or ignored. Taubaté was also an attempt to restore the element of control within Brazil to the producer rather than to the exporter and isolated voices calling for the destruction of at least part of the large coffee stock were ignored in favour of the loan negotiated by São Paulo, financed by a tax on each sack of coffee exported, to enable the immediate withdrawal and storage of stocks.(10) The São Paulo loan was arranged in 1908 and total purchases of coffee in that year alone amounted to over eight million sacks (of 60 kilos). The resulting increase in the coffee price in 1909, enhanced by a series of short crops, contributed directly to the advance of the coffee frontier into new areas, such as the state of Paraná.(11)

Superficially successful repetitions of the 1906/7 valorisation in 1917/18 and 1921/22 were followed by the same pattern: intermittent periods of high prices which served only to encourage the expansion of production. The Institute for the Permanent Defence of National Production (Instituto pela Defesa Permanente da Produção Nacional), established in 1921, and the São Paulo Coffee Defence Institute (Instituto pela Defesa do Café), which replaced it in 1924, appear to have continued the same tactics, namely, the negotiation of loans with foreign bankers(12) for the purpose of the regulation of the flow of coffee on to the market at an even rate in an attempt to stabilise prices.(13) By 1925, these activities had contributed to a substantial rise in the price of coffee at the same time as encouraging a further expansion of coffee planting.(14) The impact of the latter was felt only in 1929 and 1930 when the price of coffee fell dramatically (by 60 per cent between 1929 and 1931) in the face of increased supplies and reduced demand. This led to serious balance of payments difficulties for Brazil and to urgent calls from the Brazilian coffee sector for some form of relief.(15)

The response of the new revolutionary government of Getúlio Vargas between 1930 and 1937 represented a continuation of, rather than a change from, the policy of valorisation despite its general strategy of attempting to broaden Brazil's economic base.(16) A temporising coffee loan negotiated in 1930 was succeeded by an embryonic National Coffee Council (Conselho Nacional do Café), financed by producers by a further tax on each sack of coffee exported, and encharged with destroying excess stocks, banning new coffee planting, establishing production quotas and administering local coffee institutes.(17) It is interesting that coffee destruction and restricted planting, the hallmarks of the National Council, were accepted internationally as a reasonable solution to the problem of excess supplies despite their failure in the past.(18) An editorial in the trade journal Wileman's Economic Review in 1934, for example, described Brazilian coffee policy as 'decidedly good'. Quoting Longfellow, the editor advised:

'Look not mournfully into the past - it comes not back again - wisely improve the present - it is thine; go forth to meet the shadowy future without fear, and with a manly heart'.(19)

Brazil's interpretation of meeting the shadowy future was to burn 77 million sacks of surplus coffee between 1931 and 1943. Of this total, 30 million were destroyed in two years alone, 1933 and 1937.(20)

Until 1937, Brazil thus attempted to exert a positive influence on world coffee prices almost single-handed. As a result, a history of controls to this date is essentially a history of national controls introduced by Brazil. However, the burden of these actions, financial, political and economic, was considerable and between 1931 and 1937 Brazil made repeated efforts to induce the other Latin American coffee-exporting countries to agree to an international export restriction scheme. When the last of the conferences on this subject broke down in 1937, Brazil decided to cut its losses and to re-enter the world market as a competitor to regain its former market share. Between 1937 and 1939, as a result, Brazilian exports of coffee rose from 12,123,000 sacks to 17,113,000 sacks. However, with the outbreak of war in 1939, the accessible world market changed substantially in size and complexion, making any attempt to establish a firm gain subject to considerable uncertainty.(21)

3. War-time Controls

The outbreak of war brought with it a willingness on the part of the producers of 'mild' coffee, increasingly cut off from their European markets, to engage in a dialogue on an international coffee marketing policy. Consequently, at the initiative of the US, and in a move limited to the American continents, an Inter-American Coffee Agreement was negotiated in 1940. The text of the Agreement was brief and lacked the broad compass of a full international commodity agreement. It established an Inter-American Coffee Board with the responsibility of setting import quotas for coffee entering the US market. The US, in its turn, undertook to limit coffee from non-participants to 355,000 sacks.(22) If a world shortage arose, producers were entitled to transfer to the 'free' world market part of their US quota allotment, although, in the context of 1940, the only readily accessible alternative markets were those of the other Allied Powers.(23) The Inter-American Agreement, in sum, was essentially an arrangement to allocate the US market between competing suppliers in the Western hemisphere and it contained no pricing provisions.

In contrast to many other commodities, the Second World War saw a continuation of excess supplies of coffee with the disappearance of the European market and a trebling of output in Africa, even though the problem of surplus was alleviated by two consecutive years of frosts in São Paulo in 1941 and 1942. However, at the beginning of the War, US importers, whose stocks were low, bought heavily, exerting upward pressure on prices. This induced the US authorities to peg the price of coffee at the end of 1941. By 1943, even the limited allocative function of the 1940 Agreement became redundant as coffee supplies came under the control of the Combined Food Board's Committee on Cocoa, Coffee and Spices.(24)

4. Controls to 1976

The coffee industry to emerge from the Second World War was in an even less dynamic condition than that which had entered it in 1939. Planting and crop care had been neglected and the pegged price provided little inducement to increased production even though stock levels declined. Accordingly, with the ending of price control in the US in 1946, the price of coffee rose sharply from an annual average of US 41 cents per kilo to US 111.3 cents in 1950 in the wake of the recovery of demand. Prices stabilised around that level until the autumn of 1953 when exaggerated reports of a frost in Brazil pushed the price of coffee to an annual average of US 173.5 cents in 1954.(25)

The reaction to higher coffee prices was fairly predictable: on the one hand, producers increased dramatically their planting levels,

210

Figure 10:1 : Coffee Prices, 1950 - 1980 (annual average,
US cents per kilo, spot Brazilian)

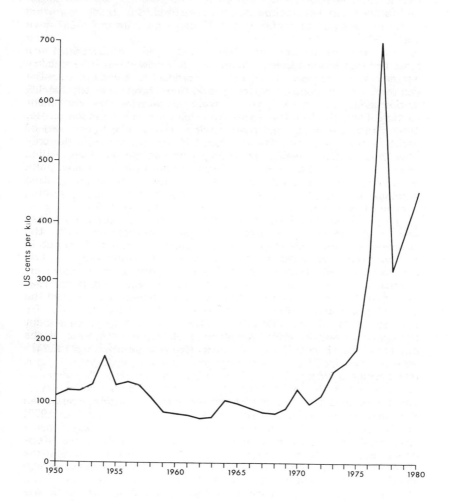

Source: IBRD, <u>Commodity Trade and Price Trends</u> (Johns Hopkins
            University Press, Baltimore, 1981).

particularly in Africa, so that output doubled between 1950 and 1959. Consumers, on the other hand, reduced their per capita consumption levels: in the period of high prices between 1950 and 1954, for example, US demand for coffee fell by 23 per cent. Expanded output and falling consumption growth were reflected in a steady downward trend in the price of coffee to US 75 cents per kilo in 1962 (Figure 10:1).(26)

It was the decline in coffee prices which encouraged Latin American coffee-producing countries to renew their dialogue on coffee marketing policy. In 1957, producers signed a pact of commitment to control coffee marketing through a withholding arrangement and in 1958, with fifteen signatories, the agreement became formalised as the Latin American Coffee Agreement. By 1959, France, Portugal and their African colonies had also acceded and they were joined in 1960 by the UK and her African colonies. This brought the coverage to ninety per cent of world exportable production and by 1961 the stock withheld equalled about one and a half times the annual volume of world imports. As in the case of previous periods of stock withdrawal, Brazil, the major producer, bore much of the financial burden, accumulating stocks of more than 40 million sacks, equivalent to 37.7 per cent of Brazil's average annual exportable production between 1957/58 and 1960/61. However, Colombia also made a major contribution, withholding over 4 million sacks or about 14 per cent of its exportable production in the same period (Table 10:2). The retentions were financed by 'sacrifice quotas' imposed on growers, a tax in kind, and, in the case of Brazil, by profits accruing through the operation of a multiple exchange rate system.(27)

It was the Cuban missile crisis, however, and the perception by the US that Latin America was an area of strategic interest, which provided the impetus for a fully fledged international coffee agreement. Having refused categorically to participate in any international agreement on coffee as late as 1956, the US announced its reversal of this policy and its willingness to join a long-term agreement on coffee to stabilise prices at the prevailing level at the first meeting of the Inter-American Economic and Social Council of the Organization of American States (OAS) in August 1961. Discussions on a draft prepared by the International Coffee Study Group of the United Nations ended in failure but provided the starting-point for negotiations which culminated in the first post-War international coffee agreement in 1962.(28)

The 1962 Coffee Agreement, the first international agreement for coffee, aimed to achieve a balance between the supply of and the demand for coffee, to alleviate hardship caused by surpluses, to assist in increasing the purchasing power of coffee exporting countries and to encourage the consumption of coffee 'by every possible means'. Unusually among international commodity agreements, it permitted

212

Table 10:2 : Retentions of Coffee in Individual Countries,
1957/58 - 1960/61 (000s sacks)

Country	Retentions 1957/58 - 1960/61	Percentage of Exportable Output
Brazil[a]	42,100	37.75
Colombia	4,100	14.25
Costa Rica	331	9.5
El Salvador	443	8.0
Guatemala	450	9.0
Mexico	379	9.0
French African producers	1,045	8.7
British East Africa	270	5.0
Other	962	-
Total	50,080	-

Note: a 1.6 million bags of Brazil's retentions probably
         represented unrecorded exports.

Source: United Nations, Coffee Study Group, The World Coffee
         Problem: Present Status of the Industry and Future
         Prospects (United Nations, Washington, 1961).

two or more contracting parties which were net exporters to join the
Agreement as a group provided that they had shown a 'common or coordinated economic policy in relation to coffee and 'a co-ordinated
monetary and financial policy'.(29) The Agreement established the
International Coffee Organization and an executive International
Coffee Council on which voting powers were evenly distributed
between producing and consuming countries in proportion to their
volume of imports and exports after an initial allocation of five
votes.(30)

In terms of economic provisions, the Agreement provided
quarterly export quotas, set initially at a total of 46 million sacks (33
million for Latin American and 13 million for African and Asian
producers). This control mechanism was advocated most forcefully
by Brazil and Colombia, anxious to preserve their market shares, but
led to considerable controversy with African producers, who wanted
to increase their coffee output. For supervisory purposes, every
export of coffee had to be accompanied by a certificate of origin
although, where countries were defined as having a low per capita
consumption level, exports were not charged to the quotas. A World

Coffee Promotion Committee was established to sponsor increased coffee consumption. The Agreement could also require importers to limit their imports from non-members to a quantity not in excess of the average annual imports from such sources for the previous three years. In contrast to other agreements, the 1962 Coffee Agreement specified no complex pricing formulae: 1962 prices were regarded as the lowest threshold acceptable but no provision was made for updating or amending this benchmark.(31) (A brief account of the key features of the coffee agreements is provided in the Appendix, Table 5.)

At first glance, the 1962 Coffee Agreement offered a fairly flexible framework for regulating the world coffee market. However, in practice, this proved not to be the case. The short-term response was a pronounced rise in prices to a peak of US 108 cents per kilo in March 1964, due partly to a crop shortfall in Brazil and partly to the imposition of export restrictions. In the medium-term, the commitment of the 1962 Coffee Agreement to sustain prices above the 1962 level enhanced the familiar pattern of over-production. In 1966, by which time stock levels exceeded annual output by a large margin, the International Coffee Council introduced indicator price ranges for the four main groups of coffee and provided for the re-allocation of the global quota in order to meet the demands of new and small producers who were threatening to withdraw from the Agreement if they did not receive a larger share. A diversification fund was also established to encourage reduced coffee plantings.(32)

By the time that the 1962 Coffee Agreement was re-negotiated in 1967, it was clear that although the price objective had been broadly met - the price of coffee was on balance above the 1962 level in the 1963 to 1967 period - this had only been at a considerable cost in terms of stock withdrawal. As in previous periods, Brazil had borne the main burden and the export certificate system had proved inadequate in policing export volumes owing to frequent infringements and the inadequate powers of the Council to enforce it.(33) Despite its shortcomings, however, the 1962 Coffee Agreement was replaced by another which closely resembled it. An addition was a Diversification Fund, designed to limit coffee production in order to bring supply back into reasonable balance with demand. Contributions to the Fund were compulsory for non-importers with export quotas of over 100,000 sacks and were to be made in proportion to the level of exports over that level. The Fund was to be deployed in 'any programmes or projects approved by the Fund'.(34)

The 1968 Coffee Agreement, like its predecessor, contained no detailed pricing mechanisms. However, whereas the 1962 Coffee Agreement had seen a small range in the price of coffee, its successor experienced large price fluctuations ranging from an annual average of US 82.5 cents per kilo (1968) to US 120.4 cents (1970). In 1969, the price fell below the 1962 floor owing to the liquidation of inventories in the US, following a threatened dock strike, and a cut-rate selling campaign by Brazil. A US proposal to halt the decline by cutting export quotas, however, failed to achieve sufficient support. In 1970, this trend was reversed and prices rose steeply on the news of a severe frost in Brazil. From surplus supplies in the late 1960s, climatic conditions (frosts, droughts and excessive rainfall in Brazil in 1970 to 1972), brought coffee demand and supply into virtual equilibrium in the early 1970s. This permitted a substantial drawing down of stocks to less than half of their peak 1966 level and a rise in prices to almost twice the 1962 level in 1972.(35)

Critics of the 1968 Coffee Agreement cite its unimpressive price performance as the major reason for its failure to be renewed in 1972. Law goes so far as to suggest that price instability with the 1962 and 1968 Agreements was 50 per cent greater than it would have been without and that for the bulk of the 1962 to 1972 period the price of coffee was appreciably higher than would otherwise have been the case.(36) Whether this view is accepted or not, the higher prices prevailing in the early 1970s, together with what was perceived to be the unfair undercutting by Brazil of the North-American soluble coffee market, led to a fading of support for renewal and the withdrawal of the US from negotiations. Thus, although the 1968 Coffee Agreement was extended nominally until 1975, it was devoid of economic provisions. The locus of control shifted instead in the last four months of its operation to a producer arrangement, the Geneva Agreement, formed by Brazil, Colombia, the Ivory Coast and Portugal (acting for Angola). This aimed to sustain coffee prices by supporting Brazil's policies of limiting sales from its national stockpile. The Agreement attracted a high degree of support - some 90 per cent of world coffee exports were represented by twenty-one countries - and was complemented by a parallel arrangement established by the Central American producers (known as Otras Suaves) and by an export quota agreement among the members of the Inter-African Coffee Organization.(37)

5. Controls since 1976

The International Coffee Agreement of 1976, negotiated in 1975, thus arose from a very different background to that prevailing when its predecessors were being drafted. On the one hand, the support of both the major consumer, the US, and the major producers, Brazil, Colombia and the Ivory Coast, had paled considerably; on the other, supply conditions had been transformed from those of surplus in 1962 and 1968 to those of shortage in 1975 in the face of severe weather conditions in Brazil. This was reflected in a virtual doubling in the price of coffee between 1975 and 1976.(38) Nevertheless, despite these notable changes in circumstances, an agreement was concluded which was based firmly on that of 1968 and continued to use the export quota as the main control mechanism. An article in the 1968 Coffee Agreement which prohibited discriminatory treatment in favour of processed coffee was toned down, however, following disputes on this subject between the US and Brazil, the Diversification Fund was dropped and the Promotion Fund given greater financial backing by a compulsory levy on coffee exports.(39)

The 1976 Agreement broke new ground in providing formally for the introduction of indicator price ranges. However, in practice, uncertainty in the international coffee market made the negotiation of such ranges between producers and consumers impossible until 1980, thus rendering the economic provisions of the Agreement inoperative. Low production levels in Brazil and increased demand, generated in part by uncertainty regarding future supplies from Brazil and from Angola, due to the Angolan Civil War, served to push coffee prices to a peak in April 1977, about three times above the 1975 level. A subsequent fall in prices in the face of declining consumption encouraged producers to negotiate with consumers in the course of 1978, but, despite several meetings, no agreement was reached. This failure and the threat in 1979 of a Brazilian frost contributed to a short-lived price rise and again deflected producer interest from an agreement with consumer participation. Instead, eight Latin American producers, including Brazil and Colombia, joined forces as the Bogotá Group, with a view to attempting to prevent prices from falling by intervening on the London and New York markets.

Predictably, these moves were strongly resented by importers; the US, in particular, announced a refusal to participate in any of the conferences on the Agreement if the Bogotá Group continued to operate. In 1980, when a break occurred in relations between the producers and consumers, producers formalised their cartel arrangement in a company, Pancafé, with an initial capital of US $500 million. Despite its activities of stock withdrawal, however, Pancafé was unable to resist a continuing slide in prices in the face of reduced consumer demand. As prices continued to fall in 1980, producers conceded defeat and expressed their willingness to negotiate with consumers on the understanding that Pancafé would be disbanded once agreement had been reached.(40)

After a plenary meeting in London in September 1980, the economic provisions of the 1976 Coffee Agreement were activated for the first time. In a compromise move to satisfy the demands both of Brazil, whose output had fallen, and African producers, whose production levels had expanded, it was agreed that quotas should be based on historical production levels in one of two periods (1968 to 1972 or 1976/77 to 1977/78). The trigger price for the introduction or suspension of export quota restrictions was based on a wide band of US 115 to 155 cents per pound.

216

The newly specified Agreement was given wide support from countries covering all but one per cent of world coffee production and 90 per cent of consumption.(41) In November 1981, Beltrão, the Executive Director of the International Coffee Organization, was able to report that Agreement had succeeded in holding prices within target, a trend which was to continue on balance in 1982, in what was described as 'a successful salvage operation'. However, this degree of success was not without its negative aspects, since producers had withheld some 12 million sacks of coffee only at a considerable cost - estimated to be $ 1 billion, that is, 12 to 15 per cent of the coffee revenues of exporters in the first year of controls alone. Although negotiations were successfully concluded for a replacement agreement based on the same lines to operate from October 1983, it was stressed by Beltrão that producers should consider structural adjustments in order to avoid over-production in the future and to ensure that they were producing the (higher) quality of coffee demanded by the market. A further course suggested was a more dynamic effort in the field of marketing and promotion.(42)

6. Conclusion

A distinct pattern emerges in a consideration of international coffee controls which is similar to that identified by Beltrão and reflects the characteristic of short periods of shortages and high prices followed by extensive periods of over-supply and low prices highlighted at the beginning of this chapter. It may be summarised as a strong interest in controls when prices were turning down with the response of stock withdrawal owing much to the role played by major producers, notably Brazil, in sustaining the financial burden involved. Rises in the price cycle tended to lead to a weakening of interest in stock withdrawal and production restraint and encouraged a further expansion in coffee planting. In 1906, as in 1981, the problems giving rise to the introduction of controls were essentially structural in nature, and these were aggravated after the Second World War by the increasing complexity of the world coffee market in terms of the number of participants. Additional factors which complicated world trade in coffee, such as the perception by the US that coffee was a commodity of strategic interest and the emergence of strong competing products, such as soft drinks, were of minor importance in comparison, particularly in the North American market.

Unlike other post-War agreements, the coffee agreements attempted to address structural questions in a positive way. The Diversification Fund, introduced in the term of the 1962 Coffee Agreement and continued during the life of its successor, was one manifestation of this. However, the resources of the Fund were small compared with funds devoted to stock withdrawal and inadequate in respect of the magnitude of resources needed to effect

217

a substantial diversification away from coffee production. In any case, as critics have pointed out, loans tended to be allocated to projects located in or near to coffee-growing areas, where land was marginal and high-cost; they were designed also to encourage the production of alternative agricultural crops, such as tea, bananas and oil palm, which could be subject also to similar problems of over-supply and price instability. It should be noted, furthermore, that attempts at diversification by turning the land over to cattle grazing in São Paulo ran counter to one of the other aims of the agreements, namely the maintenance of employment, since grazing required minimal labour compared with coffee production.(43)

Another example of an endeavour to solve structural problems was the Coffee Promotion Fund. However, the room for manoeuvre of the Fund was limited, similarly, by the scale of its resources and its objective was questionable from the point of view of the Agreement's general aim of increasing the export earnings of developing countries since alternative products included the other tropical beverages in which they specialised. It has been suggested, in addition, that in its administration a large proportion of the Fund's resources was directed to the North-American market where saturation points in coffee consumption had already been reached.(44)

The shift from valorisation (cartel) to war-time agreement to post-War producer agreements, to international commodity agreement and back to cartel again in the 1980s indicates the long-standing nature of controls on coffee. It is not sufficient, therefore, to cite the technical deficiencies of the international agreements - the abuse of the export quota system and the inability of the mechanisms to defend the price ceilings - as the reason for their lack of conspicuous success in meeting policy objectives. Their shortcomings stemmed in major part from the difficulties inherent in attempting to resolve long-term structural problems with policy instruments which were short-term in horizon and directed largely at pricing objectives. The case of coffee reveals also that even when one producer dominated production, as in the case of Brazil, it could not hope necessarily to control prices, even if output were strictly regulated.

Notes

1   See Chapter 1 and UNCTAD, Handbook of International Trade and Development Statistics, Table 4:3 (A). UNCTAD reports six countries, Burundi, Uganda, Ethiopia, Rwanda, El Salvador and Colombia, as dependent for more than 50 per cent of their export earnings on coffee in 1977. Rangarajan, Commodity Conflict, p. 82, cites coffee as the commodity which has generated the highest degree of dependency with twenty-four countries depending on coffee exports 'to a significant extent' in the early 1970s.

2   Coffee supplies are relatively price inelastic in the short run with price response lowest in smallholder areas and a stronger response on the estates. See Singh, de Vries, Hulley and Yeung, Coffee, Tea and Cocoa, pp. 31-7 and de Vries, 'Structure and Prospects of the World Coffee Economy' (IBRD Working Paper 208, Washington, 1975).

3   See F. Gordon-Ashworth, 'Agricultural Commodity Control under Vargas in Brazil, 1930-1945' Journal of Latin American Studies, vol. 12, part 1 (May 1980), pp. 90-4.

4   There are several good general books dealing with the production and marketing of coffee. In addition to Singh, de Vries, Hulley and Yeung, see for example V.D. Wickizer, Coffee, Tea and Cocoa (Stanford University Press, Stanford, 1951), J.W.F. Rowe, The World's Coffee (HMSO, London, 1963), B. Fisher, The International Coffee Agreement: A Study in Coffee Diplomacy (Praeger Publishers, New York, 1972) and the publications of the United Nations, such as United Nations, Food and Agriculture Organization, World Coffee Survey (United Nations, Rome, 1968). In addition to international coverage, coffee production in Brazil has also generated a substantial literature. For examples see A. Taunay's pioneering História do Café no Brasil (Departamento Nacional do Café, Rio de Janeiro, 1939) and A.D. Netto, 'Foundations for the Analysis of Brazilian Coffee Problems' in C.M. Peláez (ed.), Essays on Coffee and Economic Development (Rio de Janeiro, 1973).

5   International Coffee Organization, Quarterly Statistical Bulletin on Coffee, vol. 4, no. 4 (October-December 1980), pp. 43 and 70. World imports in 1980 totalled 59,489,000 sacks and average per capita consumption was 4.22 kilos.

6   See for example, Singh, de Vries, Hulley and Young, Coffee, Tea and Cocoa, Chapter 2.

7   International Coffee Organization, 'Statement by the Executive Director' (February 1982, London), p. 5. It was reported that there were less than two hundred companies engaged in the roasting and processing of coffee in the US, of which four held three-quarters of the market.

8   A. Chapman, 'Trade of Brazil for the Year 1907' In Great Britain, House of Commons, Accounts and Papers, vol. CIX (London, 1908, Cd. 3727-137), p. 2.

9   An abundance of writing has taken place on the theme of Brazilian coffee policies in this period. See T. Halsay Holloway, 'The Brazilian Coffee Industry and the First Valorization Scheme of 1906-7', unpublished MA thesis, University of Wisconsin, 1971, C.M. Peláez, (ed.), Essays on Coffee and Economic Development and V.D. Wickizer, The World Coffee Economy with Special Reference to Control Schemes (Stanford University Press, Stanford, 1943).

10   Brazil, Ministry of Agriculture, Industry and Commerce, O Brasil Actual (Ministry of Agriculture, Industry and Commerce, Rio de Janeiro, 1930), p. 37. In 1906/07 Brazil produced 20,409,000 sacks (of 60 kilos) of coffee. See also J.F. Normano, Brazil: A Study of Economic Types (Chapel Hill, 1965), pp. 43-4.

11   J.M. Bello, História da República, 1889-1954 (4th ed., São Paulo, 1959), p. 200 and A.E. Taunay, História do Café no Brasil, pp. 358-70. The state of São Paulo introduced

token measures to prevent new planting of coffee bushes in 1910 but their impact was neutralised by the new plantings in Paraná. The declining value of Brazilian paper also served to raise export earnings in gold.

12   Taunay, História do Café no Brasil, pp. 370-74, Bello, História da República, p. 260, Great Britain, Department of Overseas Trade, E. Hambloch, Report on the Economic and Financial Conditions in Brazil September, 1925 (HMSO, London, 1925), p. 15 and Ibid., Report on the Economic and Financial Conditions in Brazil, October 1926 (HMSO, London, 1927), pp. 12-13.

13   A scheme was initiated by the Federal Government in 1923 but taken over by the provincial government owing to political differences. See also Rowe, Primary Commodities in International Trade, pp. 124-25.

14   Brazil, Ministry of Foreign Affairs, Brasil 1933 (Ministry of Foreign Affairs, Rio de Janeiro, 1934), p. 78. Sterling prices for coffee in 1923/24 averaged £3 13s 0d (per sack) and £5 14s 0d in 1924/25.

15   Brazil, Ministry of Foreign Affairs, Brasil 1933, pp. 65-80. Within Brazil, the growth in coffee output was most pronounced in Paraná and Espírito Santo where output increased by 568 per cent and 223 per cent respectively between 1909/10 and 1931/32. In São Paulo output increased by a more modest 47 per cent.

16   On Vargas' aims see G. Vargas, A Nova Política do Brasil (José Olympio, Rio de Janeiro, 1938-1947), vol. I, pp. 69-74 and on his agricultural policy, Gordon-Ashworth, 'Agricultural Commodity Control under Vargas in Brazil, 1930-1945'.

17   Great Britain, Department of Overseas Trade, J. Garnett Lomax, Economic Conditions in Brazil December, 1930 (HMSO, London, 1931), pp. 27-32 and Ibid., Economic Conditions in Brazil December, 1931 (HMSO, London, 1932), pp. 16-18. For the report of Sir Otto Niemeyer, the Rothschilds' emissary, see E. Carone, A Segunda República, 1930-1937 (Difusão Europeia do Livro, São Paulo, 1973), pp. 103-16. For the funding loan see Great Britain, Department of Overseas Trade, E. Murray Harvey and J. Garnett Lomax, Economic Conditions in Brazil December, 1932 (HMSO, London, 1933), pp. 16-17.

18   F. Gordon-Ashworth, 'International and National Commodity Control, 1930 to 1945: Sugar and the Brazilian Case', Chapter Four.

19   Wileman's Economic Review (New York), 8 January 1934, pp. 3-4.

20   Brazil, Ministry of Foreign Affairs, Brasil 1943 (Ministry of Foreign Affairs, Rio de Janeiro, 1943), p. 261. In 1933, 13,687,012 sacks were destroyed and in 1937, 17,194,428 sacks.

21   C.M. Peláez, 'Análise económico do Programa brasileiro de Sustentação do Café', 1906-1945: Teoria, Política e Medição', Revista Brasileira de Economia, vol. 25 (1971) and Brazil, Ministry of Foreign Affairs, Brasil 1940-42 (Ministry of Foreign Affairs, Rio de Janeiro, 1942), p. 124.

22   'Inter-American Coffee Agreement' (28 November 1940) in ILO, Intergovernmental Commodity Agreements, pp. 59-66. Brazil was granted a US quota of 9,300,000 sacks of coffee. Colombia, the other major Latin American producer, was granted a quota of 3,150,000 sacks. If the quota allocated were exceeded, the US established that the quota set for the next year would be lowered according to the degree of the infringement. Coffee exporters in total commanded two-thirds of the votes on the Board.

23   Ibid., Article 5 and for a contemporary account see P. Daniels, 'The Inter-American Coffee Agreement', Law and Contemporary Problems, vol. VII (Autumn 1941), pp. 708-21.

24   Lamartine Yates, Commodity Control, pp. 78-9, Rowe, Primary Commodities in International Trade, pp. 177-78,who reports that the price, fixed at a maximum of US 13.4 cents per pound became less attractive to producing countries as the years went on and their general price levels rose, and Roll, The Combined Food Board, pp. 82, 238 and 240-45. For the working of the Committee, see also International Labour Office, Food Control in Great Britain (International Labour Office, Montreal, 1943) and League of Nations, Food Rationing and Supply 1943/44 (League of Nations, Geneva, 1944).

25   International Coffee Organization, Annual Coffee Statistics, no. 18 (1954), p. 67 and IBRD, Commodity Trade and Price Trends (1980), pp. 36-7. The prices refer to Brazilian Santos 4 in New York.

26   International Coffee Organization, Annual Coffee Statistics (1969), pp. A 100 - A 103 and United Nations, Coffee Study Group, The World Coffee Problem: Present Status of the Industry and Future Prospects (United Nations, Washington, April 1961).

27   D.J. Ford, 'Commodity Market Modelling and the Simulation of Market Intervention: the case of Coffee' in F.G. Adams and S.A. Klein (eds.), Stabilizing World Commodity Markets, Analysis, Practice and Policy (D.C. Heath & Co., Lexington, Mass., 1978) and United Nations, Coffee Study Group, The World Coffee Problem, pp. 9-12 and p. 27. Exporters in Brazil surrendered foreign exchange for cruzeiros at differential rates of exchange; the difference between the export and import rates, known as the ágio, accrued to the government. The use of exchange profits to finance coffee retentions was not offset by the curtailment of expenditures elsewhere; as a result, the scheme was reported to have added markedly to inflationary pressure in Brazil in the four years to 1961.

28   See Dell, A Latin American Common Market, pp. 33, 123-35 and 183-86 on the Alliance for Progress, negotiated between the US and Latin American countries at the August 1961 meeting. See also Fisher, The International Coffee Agreements and Rowe, The World's Coffee.

29   'International Coffee Agreement, 1962' (US, Department of State, Washington, 1962), Articles 1 and 5.

30   Ibid., Articles 7-24.

31   Ibid., Articles 27, 28, 36, 40, 44 and 45 and Fisher, The International Coffee Agreements, pp. 54-5.

32   International Coffee Organization, International Coffee Council, Resolution ICC-155 (6 September 1966) in Pan American Coffee Bureau, Annual Coffee Statistics (New York, 1966), Appendix E and Law, International Commodity Agreements, pp. 44-5.

33   The International Coffee Organization, in contrast, claimed that the agreements 'helped prices to remain relatively stable throughout the years 1963 to 1972 and production and consumption became more evenly balanced'. (International Coffee Organization, 'International Coffee Organization', London, March 1982), p. 3. The only powers available to the Council were the suspension of voting rights and a reduction of the quota.

34   'International Coffee Agreement, 1968' (International Coffee Organization, London, 1968), Articles 54 and 27. The only new feature of interest was the chapter which prohibited discrimination of treatment in favour of processed coffee (Chapter IX). According to Brown, The Political and Social Economy of Commodity Control, pp. 32-3, the Diversification Fund was not without its critics among consumers who saw the financing of the Fund as 'a form of wealth transfer over which they would have no control'.

35   The prices used for comparison are the International Coffee Organization's composite price.

36   Law, International Commodity Agreements, p. 46.

37   Brown, The Political and Social Economy of Commodity Control, pp. 24-35 offers a useful insight. See also Rangarajan, Commodity Conflict, pp. 123-34.

38   International Coffee Organization, Quarterly Statistical Bulletin, (October-December 1980), p. 83.

39   'International Coffee Agreement 1976' (HMSO, London, 1976, Cmnd. 6505).

40   M. Venkataratnam, 'The Coffee Agreement', Planters' Chronicle (November 1980), pp. 469-72. In its period of operation, Pancafé witnessed coffee prices falling to their lowest level for five years.

41   See International Coffee Organization, 'Quotas' (International Coffee Organization, London, October 1981) for details of how the quotas were allocated.

42   International Coffee Organization, 'Statement by the Executive Director' (International Coffee Organization, London, November 1981), p. 6.

43   Brown, The Political and Social Economy of Commodity Control, pp. 32-3, for example, reported that total contributions to the Fund, which lasted until October 1973, were US $ 111 million, of which $ 73 million had been used to finance 31 projects in 21 of the 30 participating producer countries. See also Haslemere Declaration, Coffee: The Rules of Neo-Colonialism: A Study of International Coffee Trade and the International Coffee Agreement (Haslemere Declaration, London, n.d.), pp. 13-14.

44   Haslemere Declaration, Coffee: The Rules of Neo-Colonialism, estimated that 59 per cent of the Fund's resources were deployed in North America. See also L. de Silva, 'Cocoa, Coffee and Tea: Producer Co-operation for Structural Change', Marga, vol. 6, no. 3 (January 1982).

11: COCOA

> 'Monseigneur was about to take his chocolate. Monseigneur could swallow a great many things with ease, and was by some few sullen minds supposed to be rather rapidly swallowing France; but his morning's chocolate could not so much as get into the throat of Monseigneur, without the aid of four strong men besides the cook'.

Charles Dickens, A Tale of Two Cities

1. General

Cocoa is a middle-ranking commodity in world trade and, like the other beverages which are considered in this study, it is produced predominantly by developing countries. A core commodity under UNCTAD's Integrated Programme, cocoa is a renewable resource produced only in tropical and sub-tropical climates with adequate rainfall; like coffee and tea, its essential characteristic is its distinctive flavour. Unlike the former, cocoa also has value as a nutrient. Cocoa was the object of cartel action in the 1930s but of international commodity agreements only from 1972.

The early leading producers of cocoa were Brazil, Ecuador and Trinidad and Tobago, but after the First World War Latin American producers were overtaken by the emergence of Ghana, Nigeria and the Ivory Coast. Ghana retained its position as the leading cocoa producer until relatively recently when its rank was usurped by the Ivory Coast, and by Brazil (which had mounted a vigorous production programme) (Table 11:1). Production has been subject to a high degree of concentration with six countries, Ghana, Nigeria, the Ivory Coast, Cameroon, Ecuador and Brazil, accounting for three-quarters of world output since the 1930s.

223

Table 11:1 : World Production of Raw Cocoa, 1900/01, 1937/38 and 1980/81 (000s metric tons)

	1900/01	1937/38	1980/81[a]
Ecuador	23	19	81
Brazil	18	140	354
São Tomé and Principé	17	11	8
Trinidad and Tobago	12	16	2
Venezuela	9	20	14
Dominican Republic	7	24	32
Cameroon[b]	1	29	120
Ghana	1	244	258
Ivory Coast	-	51	412
Nigeria	-	100	155
Total	115	736	1671

Notes: a   estimate

   b   German Cameroon until 1916 which split into French (East) Cameroon and British (West) Cameroon. French Cameroon became an independent republic in 1960 and was joined in 1961 by West Cameroon.

Source: Gill & Duffus, Cocoa Statistics (Gill & Duffus, London, April 1981), pp. 2-7 and Ibid., Cocoa Statistics (Gill & Duffus, London, May 1982), p. 3.

   For the first four decades of the twentieth century cocoa production rose steadily. However, it fell sharply during the Second World War and recovered only slowly in the post-War years because the low prices of the 1930 to 1946 period led to the abandonment and neglect of many cocoa-producing areas.   From the mid 1950s, however, acreage was expanded briskly, in response both to higher prices and to improvements in pest and disease control, and production levels continued to rise until the mid 1970s. As a result, the volume of cocoa production since the Second World War has increased by $2\frac{1}{2}$ times - in contrast to the more modest growth of tea production.[1]

   Cocoa is grown on a variety of scales: Brazil, for instance, has produced cocoa traditionally on a plantation basis whereas other of the main suppliers, Nigeria and Ghana, have relied on the small-holding form of cocoa production. (Cocoa is recommended for cultivation on a small scale by the United Nations Food and Agriculture Organization.) For most of the period covered in this study, there has been a three to five year gestation period and full bearing is reached only after ten years. More recently, however, the development of quickly maturing hybrids has meant that this is no longer necessarily the case.(2)

The processing of cocoa is relatively simple: the beans on reaching the manufacturer are cleared of waste material and roasted. They are then separated from their husk and ground first into cocoa liquor and then into cocoa cake and powder or cocoa butter. Over two-thirds of processing takes place in the consuming countries and London, Paris and New York constitute the major cocoa markets. A recent UNCTAD report has drawn attention to the relatively small number of parties involved in the cocoa trade: in the UK, for example, three-quarters of cocoa trade is reported to be conducted by only four companies. The companies in question exercise substantial control over cocoa production both directly, through investment, and indirectly through marketing facilities. UNCTAD has estimated, for example, that only twelve companies account for 80 per cent of the production of cocoa and cocoa products.(3)

The industrialised countries are the major importers and consumers of cocoa: in 1979, the US alone accounted for 17.1 per cent of total world imports and only 1.1 per cent went to countries outside the major industrialised countries and the USSR. Similarly, Western industrialised countries account for over 46 per cent of world cocoa grindings.(4) Demand for cocoa has been strongly associated with movements in per capita income although the price elasticity of demand is relatively low. The main uses of cocoa and its products are in the manufacture of chocolate and chocolate drinks (see the chapter head for an example of the ritual which has surrounded chocolate consumption) although it is also used in the preparation of some cosmetics, pharmaceuticals and soaps. Locally produced items include cooking fat, candle fat, bread and biscuits and its range is thus far broader than, for example, that of tea. As a beverage it is regarded as an alternative to tea and coffee, especially for children.(5)

The total quantity of cocoa consumed compared with tea and coffee is very small: 1.5 kilos per head in the US, for example, in 1979 compared with about 5 kilos for coffee.(6) In the US, the main competitors to chocolate are sugar candy, chewing gum and soft drinks; in Japan, in contrast, lower per capita consumption has been attributed to different social usage and climatic factors together with the absence of a satisfactory distribution network. Consumption has also been affected, although only to a limited extent, by the introduction of cocoa substitutes based on the shorea species, the carob and on natural oils, such as coconut and palm oil.(7)

2. Controls to 1939

Although the problems faced by cocoa producers in the 1920s and 1930s were similar in nature to those facing other primary commodity producers - namely, an over-expansion of production followed by a dramatic fall in prices from the late 1920s to the mid 1930s - in contrast to other commodities considered in this study, no formal international commodity agreement was reached on cocoa. Instead, the burden of controls resided largely at the corporate and national levels, with limited early endeavours by producers to bring a greater stability to cocoa prices. An example was the Accra Pool of 1925, which consisted of shippers and dealers. The Pool, which aimed to regulate supplies, disintegrated in 1928 as cocoa prices fell at a quickening pace from their peak of US 17.2 cents per pound in March 1927 to an eventual trough of US 3.6 cents in January 1933.(8)
 The focus of consultative interest then turned to the need to promote higher levels of cocoa consumption and in 1931 an International Office of Chocolate and Cocoa Manufacturers was established to serve as a centre for data collection and dissemination. In 1932, this organisation convened a conference to consider a concerted publicity campaign with a view to increasing consumption levels. However, no agreement was reached and these and subsequent discussions at the World Monetary and Economic Conference in 1933 on a Trinidadian proposal for a world cocoa buffer stock ended in stalemate.(9) Subsequent efforts to improve conditions in the world cocoa market during the 1930s took place instead at the national level. Trinidad and Brazil, for example, advanced subsidies or loans directly to the estates. In West Africa, where the control of cocoa trade was concentrated increasingly in the hands of five large companies - the United African Company, Cadbury & Fry's, CFAO, Union Trading Co and G.B. Ollivant - discussions were conducted by exporter interests in 1937 in the context of a dramatic fall in prices.(10) The agreement which followed between the five major companies and a sixth, Lyons, allotted a share of the crop to be purchased to each company according to the volume of past purchases. A subsidiary aim of the agreement also was reported to have been that of breaking the power of the marketing system based on middlemen.(11)
 The scheme, introduced in October 1937, brought a swift reaction from producer interests. In Ghana, African producers refused to market the cocoa crop and, between October 1937 and April 1938, held up production and exercised a total boycott on goods imported by the European firms. The situation was serious enough for a (UK) Commission of Inquiry to be appointed. The Commission was very critically disposed towards the companies, viewing their action as an attempt to impose a buyers' monopoly. It recommended in 1938 that a compulsory marketing scheme should be established

under government supervision. This was never formally implemented, however, owing to opposition both from exporters and from some of the producer interests.(12)

3. Controls between 1939 and 1971

During the Second World War, most cocoa was marketed by the UK under the auspices of the Combined Food Board. In 1944, a British parliamentary report suggested that the war-time controls should be continued after the War prior to the negotiation of a fully fledged international commodity agreement. In the event, however, UK control of marketing was retained until 1947 and full discussions on a possible international agreement were not initiated until the 1960s, when the impact of the brisk expansion of output in the 1950s began to be manifest in terms of declining prices.(13)

A United Nations conference met in October 1963 to discuss a draft agreement. However, this broke down on the question of the appropriate pricing mechanism and the impetus for controls reverted instead to producer interests alone. In 1964, for example, five major producers introduced an export quota system with an indicative price of US 23.75 cents per pound - slightly above the level prevailing. In 1966, when cocoa prices strengthened as a result of rising demand, interest was diverted from further co-ordinated controls at either the producer or producer/consumer level. Conferences held to discuss an international agreement in 1966 and 1967 foundered as a result on questions such as the appropriate price range and the treatment of shipping costs and it was only in 1972, with a break discernible in the rising price trend, that UNCTAD's preparatory work on an international agreement was brought to fruition.(14)

4. Controls after 1971

The 1972 Cocoa Agreement reflected both the desire of producers to improve their current operating conditions ('To alleviate serious economic difficulties' and 'To prevent excessive fluctuations in the price of cocoa') and the broader aims encompassed in current UNCTAD philosophy ('To make arrangements which will help stabilize and increase the export earnings from cocoa of producing countries thereby helping to provide such countries with resources for accelerated economic growth and social development').(15) An International Cocoa Organization was created in London with a council and an executive committee and members undertook to accept as binding all decisions of the Council under the provisions of the Agreement.

The economic provisions of the Agreement consisted of a buffer stock of a maximum size of 250,000 metric tons (15.8 per cent of production in 1971/72), empowered to make purchases in periods of export regulation which were determined in turn by the prevailing price level and based on production levels in the preceding three crop-years for which data were available. There were two particular points of interest in the form taken by the buffer stock; on the one hand, it was financed on the basis of existing trading patterns (an export/import levy of one US cent per pound) avoiding the difficulty of negotiating the size of subscriptions. Secondly, the proceeds of sales from the buffer stock were to be meted out, similarly, in proportion to the scale of the individual producers' contributions.(16) (For a summary of the key features of the cocoa agreements, see the Appendix, Table 6.)

The price range specified in the Agreement was US 23 to 32 cents per pound.(17) Even by the end of the second negotiating conference, however, in October 1972, the New York spot price had risen sharply to US 38.1 cents per pound from US 25.8 cents at the beginning of the year. By May 1973, when the Agreement was timetabled to enter into force, the price had risen to an average of US 61.6 cents under the influence of fast-growing demand, the devaluation of the US dollar and the modest expansion of production. The situation was to deteriorate further as far as consumer interests were concerned: the price of cocoa in New York peaked only in May 1974 at US 116.8 cents - almost four times higher than the upper limit of the target range.(18) The ability of the 1972 Cocoa Agreement to deal with what amounted to unusually volatile international conditions proved to be severely circumscribed. The buffer stock was redundant when the market price was far above the ceiling level and, as in other international commodity agreements, an asymmetry existed between the mechanisms provided to defend the floor price on the one hand and those to defend the ceiling on the other.

Given its track record, it may seem surprising that a second Cocoa Agreement was negotiated in 1975, entering into force in 1976. The main explanation seems to be that the conference to negotiate the new agreement was held in a downward phase in the price cycle which served to revive producer interest. The acceptance of a price range of US 39 to 55 cents per pound, well below the record levels which had been experienced in the early 1970s, suggests that producers expected this downward trend to continue. The control mechanisms remained essentially the same - a buffer stock and export quotas - although some details were slightly modified. For example, a wider range of prices was specified, with a reduced number of 'trigger points' for the operation of export controls, and changes were made in the terms on which producers could sell cocoa to the buffer stock.(19)

The conditions in which the 1975 Cocoa Agreement operated were hardly more promising than those which had governed the first. Unexpectedly, New York spot prices reached a new record of over US

228

250 cents in 1977 as, with short crops in Brazil, Ghana, Nigeria and Cameroon, production fell to the lowest level for ten years. As the International Cocoa Council itself commented wryly in 1977, 'The mechanisms have not yet been tested . . . because the market price has yet to fall within the range'.(20) This situation was not to alter within the life of the Agreement although, with a recovery in production levels, prices fell back slightly during 1977/78.

Negotiations to secure a new agreement which took place during 1979 ended in failure as ten major producing countries engaged instead in discussions aimed at formulating a producer stabilisation scheme, including the establishment of a buffer stock. The initiative for the discussions came from Brazil and the Ivory Coast, the latter of which was reported to have stockpiled cocoa beans in an attempt to exert upward pressure on falling world prices from the end of 1979.(21) In March 1980, with the disintegration of support, the 1975 Cocoa Agreement was abrogated and the International Cocoa Organization put into dissolution.(22) Full details of the withholding of supplies by producers during 1980 are not available. However, one estimate has suggested that by October 1980 the Ivory Coast had spent $95 million in stock withdrawals in the face of a very large crop and its determination to develop the country's export earnings from a large investment programme in cocoa.(23) Despite this policy, a downward trend in prices continued with only minor interruptions between 1979 and November 1980, when a new international agreement was negotiated.

The 1980 Cocoa Agreement retained many of the details of its antecedent, including the maximum capacity of the buffer stock (250,000 metric tons) and the financing levy. The major change introduced concerned the price structure with the fixed range of prices within the agreement being replaced by a system allowing 'semi-automatic adjustments'. A basic range was set at US 100 to 160 cents per pound with a more complex indicator price system established to assess buffer stock intervention points. 10,000 metric tons of cocoa paste (liquor) was also permitted within the terms of buffer stock purchasing arrangements.(24) Unlike the 1975 Agreement, no production or export quotas were included in that of 1980. Instead, members were authorised to develop their own programmes 'to adjust production'.

Even the more diluted provisions of the 1980 Agreement were seriously threatened at an early stage: the US, the major consumer on the one hand, and the Ivory Coast, a leading producer on the other, failed to accede, the former because it considered the price range to be too high ('out of touch with market conditions'), and the latter because it considered the price range to be too low. In consequence, the deadline for ratification of 13 May 1981 passed with insufficient signatories and it was only in August 1981, following further United Nations discussions, that sufficient support was obtained, including that of the EEC. Even then, the Ivory Coast and the US remained conspicuous by their absence.(25)

Economic conditions also contributed to the problems facing the Agreement at the start of its operating life. This coincided with the ending of a brief but sharp upturn in cocoa prices so that after four successive seasons of surplus, stock levels at the end of 1981/82 stood at their highest level for fourteen years. In these circumstances, buffer stock purchases of over 100,000 metric tons were insufficient to maintain the floor price. This situation continued in the following year, despite substantial rises in prices in the face of short crops. The credibility of the Agreement was further undermined in the same period by the inability of signatories to agree on how best to use a $75 million loan secured to bolster the resources of the International Cocoa Organization.(26) The interplay of these unfavourable factors suggested strongly that the 1980 Cocoa Agreement was even less likely to succeed in meeting its objectives than its predecessors.

5. Conclusion

It is difficult to reach anything but a pessimistic conclusion in considering cocoa as an example of international commodity control in practice for in the case of cocoa the difficulties inherent in operating an agreement for an agricultural commodity are frankly exposed. The over-expansion of production which took place in the 1920s, for example, was repeated in the 1960s and in the late 1970s. In a situation where over-production prevailed, producer and producer/consumer responses alike were equally inadequate in dealing with structural problems associated with the long gestation period of the traditional type of cocoa produced. Stock withdrawal, a major mechanism used by each, was effected only at a substantial cost and with limited results.

The international agreements also faced the additional pressures of the dramatic price movements of the 1970s, which were not simply related to demand and supply conditions, the destabilising influence of variable levels of support from both producer and consumer interests and a transformed pattern of supply in which Brazil and the Ivory Coast, in particular, encouraged the expansion of national cocoa output as part of their general economic strategy. In these circumstances and given the limitations of the control mechanisms prescribed, the agreements could offer little in the way of permanent solution. Their most perceptible achievement was in pressing for international consultation and in constructing a framework within which divergent groups could be brought together to consider mutual areas of interest.

Notes

1   See Chapter 12.

2   T.A. Kofi, World Trade in Cocoa (Third World Forum, Occasional Paper no. 10, Switzerland, 1977), United Nations, Food and Agriculture Organization, Cocoa (United Nations, Food and Agriculture Organization, Rome, 1977) and G.A.R. Wood, Cocoa (Longman, London, 1975).

3   UNCTAD, Marketing and Distribution System for Cocoa (UNCTAD, Geneva, 1975, TD/B/C.1/164), pp. 69-72, J.R. Behrman, 'Monopolistic Cocoa Pricing', American Journal of Agricultural Economics, vol. 50, no. 3 (August 1968) and United Nations, Food and Agriculture Organization, Processing of Raw Cocoa for the Market (United Nations, Food and Agriculture Organization, Rome, 1963).

4   Gill & Duffus, Cocoa Marketing Report, no. 296 (July 1981), pp. 14-15 and 18, and F.H. Weymar, The Dynamics of the World Cocoa Market (Massachusetts Institute of Technology, Cambridge, Mass., 1968).

5   The price elasticity of demand for cocoa has been estimated at between -0.20 and -0.47 and the range of estimates of the income elasticities of world demand as 0.25 to 0.57. See Singh, de Vries, Hulley and Yeung, Coffee, Tea and Cocoa, p. 95 and Behrman, 'Monopolistic Cocoa Pricing', p. 706.

6   Gill & Duffus, Cocoa Market Report, no. 296, p. 18 and International Coffee Organization, Quarterly Statistical Bulletin on Coffee October - December 1980, p. 70. The US cocoa consumption level compared with the high average of 3.6 kilos per capita in Switzerland and the low average of 0.5 kilos in the USSR.

7   International Cocoa Organization, 'Study of Cocoa Production and Consumption Capacity' (International Cocoa Organization, London, various issues and dates). See Ibid., 1976, ICC/5/8 Add. 1 for the US, 1978, ICC/5/8 Add. 5 for Japan and 1977, ICC 5/8 Add. 2 for the UK. See also Singh, de Vries, Hulley and Yeung, Coffee, Tea and Cocoa, pp. 95-6. There has also been a trend toward reducing the cocoa content of chocolate products.

8   For the Accra Pool see Kofi, World Trade in Cocoa, pp. 37-8. See also Gill & Duffus, Cocoa Statistics (Gill & Duffus, London, December 1979), pp. 9 and 40.

9   Hexner, International Cartels, p. 186, Kofi, World Trade in Cocoa and League of Nations, Report of the Economic Commission, Annex II.

10   Kofi, World Trade in Cocoa, p. 39, V.D. Wickizer, Coffee, Tea and Cocoa and A. Leeds, 'Economic Cycles in Brazil: The Persistence of Total Culture Patterns - Cacao and Other Cases', unpublished Ph.D thesis, University of Columbia, 1967. Prices fell from a peak of US 12.1 cents in January 1937 to US 5.6 cents in December.

11   C. Gunnarsson, 'The Gold Coast Cocoa Industry, 1900-1939: Production, Prices and Structural Change' (mimeo, Lund, 1978), pp. 119-29.

12   Ibid., pp. 138-61 and Hexner, International Cartels, pp. 184-86.

13   United Nations, Food and Agriculture Organization, Report of the Preparatory Commission on World Food Proposals (London, 1947, Cmd. 703), Roll, Combined Food Board and 'British Plan is Countered by Witkin with Program Based on Free Trade', Journal of Commerce (1 November 1944).

14   For prices in this period see Gill & Duffus, Cocoa Statistics (1979). The average annual price (New York spot) rose from US 23.4 cents per pound in 1964 to US 45.7 cents in 1969 before declining to US 26.8 cents in 1971. See also United Nations,

231

'Report of Working Party I on Prices and Quotas' (United Nations, New York, March 1966, TD/COCOA.1/WP 1/2), Law, International Commodity Agreements, p. 66 and Rowe, Commodity Control Schemes, p. 214.

15   International Cocoa Organization, 'International Cocoa Agreement 1972' in United Nations, International Cocoa Conference 1972 (United Nations, New York, 1973, TD/COCOA.3/9), Articles 1 and 5-12.

16   Ibid., Articles 30-43.

17   Ibid., Articles 28 and 29. The price was to be determined by reference to a daily price, the average taken daily of the quotations for cocoa beans of the nearest three active future trading months on the New York Cocoa Exchange at noon and on the London Cocoa Terminal Market at closing time. The London prices were to be converted to US cents per pound by the current six months forward rate of exchange and an indicator price (the average of the daily prices over a period of 15 consecutive market days or, for the operation of export quotas, over a period of 22 consecutive market days).

18   Gill & Duffus, Cocoa Statistics (Gill & Duffus, London, April 1981), p. 49. The rise was less pronounced, however, compared with the indicator price. For 1974 as a whole, for example, the indicator price averaged US 70.74 cents per pound compared with the New York spot price average of US 98.00 cents. See Gill & Duffus, Cocoa Statistics (Gill & Duffus, London, May 1982), p. 23.

19   United Nations, United Nations Cocoa Conference 1975 (United Nations, New York, 1976, TD/COCOA 4/10) contains the account of the conference. For the Agreement see 'International Cocoa Agreement, 1975' (HMSO, London, 1976, Cmnd. 6448), Articles 29, 34 and 37-41.

20   International Cocoa Organization, 'International Cocoa Organization' (International Cocoa Organization, London, 1977), p. 10 and Gill & Duffus, Cocoa Statistics (1981), p. 49.

21   See, for instance, Guardian, 27 May 1980, which reported that Brazil and the Ivory Coast had agreed to contribute $42 million worth of cocoa each to finance a buffer stock. Brazil planned to import Ivorian cocoa for processing and storage.

22   U. Wassermann, 'Breakdown of International Cocoa Agreement', Journal of World Trade Law, vol. 14, no. 4 (July:August 1980), p. 360.

23   Third World Quarterly, vol. II, no. 4 (October 1980), p. 663 and Gill & Duffus, Cocoa Market Report, no. 292 (September 1980), p. 2.

24   United Nations, 'International Cocoa Agreement, 1980' (UNCTAD, Geneva, 1980, TD/COCOA 6/7), Articles 26, 27 and 30. If cocoa purchases for the buffer stock exceeded 100,000 metric tons in any 12 month period, the intervention price was to be revised downward by US 4 cents per pound (Article 27).

25   Gill & Duffus, Cocoa Market Report, no. 296 (July 1981), p. 1.

26   Guardian, 4 October 1982, reported that producers and consumers failed to reach agreement on further measures to support cocoa prices under the auspices of the International Cocoa Organization despite the US $75 million replenishment to the exhausted Buffer Stock Fund secured from Brazilian bankers in June. Leading producers Brazil, Ghana and Nigeria all favoured higher prices, not least for domestic reasons. At 1 October 1982, world stocks were reported to stand at 688,000 metric tons, the highest level since 1965.

12: TEA

'When tempers get heated and things are fogged, adjourn for tea. It is a priceless prescription.'

(Lord Curzon, British Foreign Secretary, 1922)

1. General

Like tin, tea is a minor commodity in world trade: the value of exports totalled $202 million in 1938 and rose only hesitantly thereafter. However, it is extremely important to developing countries who dominate its production and trade and as such was included as a core commodity under UNCTAD's Integrated Programme. Tea was the object of cartelisation in the 1920s, of regular international commodity agreements between 1933 and 1955 and of an informal arrangement under UNCTAD in 1969. Like coffee, it is characterised by its flavour, and by its stimulatory caffeine content; its value as a foodstuff is negligible and it has no scrap value.(1) Tea does not conjure the same degree of dependency as coffee, although it is an important commodity in the export of several countries, notably Sri Lanka, Kenya and India.

There are three major types of tea plant: the China, the Assam and the Cambodian. The three types are distinguishable by the heights to which they grow in their wild state and their yields. The Assams, for example, are considered to be the best yielders. The tea plant thrives on soil of nearly any texture but requires a moist climate. According to existing records, tea was first cultivated and the leaf prepared for infusion as a beverage in China and the first consignment of tea was brought to Europe by the Dutch in 1610 who exchanged dry sage for it with the Chinese. Thereafter, the Dutch

233

became importers of tea which was introduced to England in about 1645.(2)

The history of tea production may be judged to have had two distinct phases: the first started in 1610 and lasted until the nineteenth century in the form of the China tea trade. The second phase began in 1825 in Java and in India in 1833 with the European development of large-scale tea production. Sri Lanka entered the second phase in 1875 and Sumatra in 1910 and subsequently these early producers were joined by new entrants in East Africa, such as Kenya and Rwanda. Whereas in the period between the Wars world production and exports was almost wholly shared between India, Sri Lanka and Indonesia, after the Second World War the share of African tea producers rose - from 5.4 per cent of world exports in 1955 to 21.9 per cent in 1979; the share of India, Sri Lanka and Indonesia fell, in contrast, from 81.8 per cent in 1955 to 55.5 per cent in 1979.(3)

An important feature of tea production and marketing has been the degree of integration between the agricultural, industrial and marketing sides of the business. The crop comprises the young leaves and unopened leaf buds of the tea plant. The plucked leaves are withered - the moisture content is lost - rolled, sifted, fermented, fired (when bacteria are destroyed), dried, sorted, graded and packed on the tea estate itself. No further processing is applied although different teas may be blended. The degree of integration is heightened by the direct participation of leading tea brokers in the production process, although this has fallen considerably since the Second World War, especially in countries such as Sri Lanka which have embarked on nationalisation schemes. However, the tea market remains very concentrated with most blenders, packers, dealers and exporters belonging to the Tea Buyers' Association in the UK. The four largest houses supplying tea to the market are Brooke Bond, Typhoo, CTS and Lyons. In the UK the degree of control exercised by these companies led in 1970 to a government investigation. This concluded that Brooke Bond, with 43 per cent of UK sales of tea, should not consider a price increase in the foreseeable future and that a price reduction should be considered if the price of tea imports fell.(4)

Particularly in India, tea exports are subject to what are considered by producers to be onerous levels of taxation. However, as a result of tariff reductions and suspensions in the Kennedy Round, imports of bulk tea to developed countries are duty free except in Japan and Portugal, although in some cases, such as Germany in 1970, internal taxes are imposed.(5) The multiplicity of grades and varieties of teas traded have made it unsuitable for futures trading.

The UK has traditionally provided the major market for world tea exports, taking three-quarters, for example, in 1935, although this proportion fell to only a quarter in 1979, with North America providing a major alternative market. In addition, developing

234

countries in Asia, notably India, made a strong contribution; India's share of total imports alone, for example, increased from 7.7 per cent of the total in 1947 to 24.3 per cent in 1979.(6) This has had an important influence on negotiating international controls for tea since the market has grown more complex both in terms of the numbers of producers and consumers. In addition, although variations in yield can to some extent be neutralised by finer or coarser plucking, the level of tea consumption has been adversely affected by the introduction of tea bags and of soluble instant tea, which have reduced the quantity of tea needed per cup and raised the demand for plain, usually cheaper teas, and by competition from other beverages, such as coffee and soft drinks.(7)

2. Controls to 1955

The first concerted attempt to control tea output took place in the years following the First World War which had disrupted shipping patterns and left producers with excessively large stocks.   The impetus for the controls came from the British tea planters in India and Sri Lanka and did not include Indonesian producers, whose production levels expanded rapidly during the 1920s.   A short-lived scheme to restrict production may have assisted in restoring prices to more remunerative levels during 1921, although bad weather in India and a general recovery of demand were also important contributory factors.   By 1927, however, rising levels of production and less buoyant consumption growth led to a long-term downward trend in the price of tea.   The onset of the Depression exacerbated this situation and from their peak of 19.79d per pound in 1924, the average annual price of tea sold at the London auction fell to a trough of 9.45d in 1932 (Figure 12:1).(8)

It was the severity of the price fall which encouraged producer associations to seek some form of coordinated response to conditions in the international tea market, following the failure of a voluntary scheme in 1930.   The Dutch authorities took the lead in suggesting such an approach - British colonial tea producers were already assisted by the devaluation of sterling in September 1931 and the restoration of a preferential duty in April 1932 - and the 1933 Tea Agreement which resulted was a cross between a producer arrangement and an international commodity agreement. It specified as a condition for operation the need for the approval and continued approval of each of the governments of the producing countries and the latter administered the Tea Agreement by means of an International Tea Committee based in London.   The Agreement allocated export quotas to producers in Sri Lanka, India and Indonesia, based on the maximum export of tea from each producing country in any of the years 1929 to 1931.   An initial aggregate quota was set at 85 per cent of this level for 1933/34 and prohibitions were

Figure 12:1: Tea Prices, 1922-1938
(annual average, London, pence per pound)

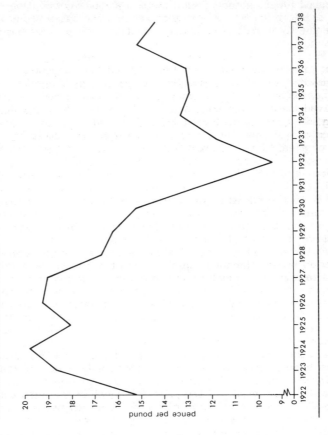

Source: International   Tea   Committee,   Annual   Bulletin   of
Statistics   (International   Tea   Committee,   London,   June
1948).

236

introduced for plantings on new land; total new planting was limited to 1½ per cent of the total planted acreage.(9) (For a brief account of the key features of the tea agreements, see the Appendix, Table 7.)

In comparison with other agreements negotiated during this period, the objectives of the 1933 Tea Agreement were comparatively modest: it contained no pricing provisions and aimed more generally to achieve a better balance between the supply of tea and its demand. Considered in these terms, the Agreement was distinguished neither with great success nor with great failure. The average annual price of all teas sold in London between 1934 and 1936, of about 13d per pound, rose to over 15d at the beginning of 1937 and then dropped to 14.38d in 1938 (Figure 12:1), after which the prospect of war exercised a strong upward influence. In the same period, the export quota was adjusted within an 82½ per cent (1935/36) to 92½ per cent (1938/39) range. However, the restraint of the three major producers did not prevent increased production by minor competitors whose market shares rose from 12.5 per cent of the total in 1933 to 17.8 per cent in 1938.(10)

A revised version of the 1933 Tea Agreement was signed in 1938 and included the same principal participants. Within the terms of this revision new plantings of tea were permitted where bushes needed replacing or when the land had been lying fallow in accordance with usual farming practice. The new Agreement, like its predecessor, was administered by government representatives of the major tea-producing countries who continued to advise on quotas even during the War. In 1942, for example, when tea prices rose steeply, the total tea production quota was raised to 95 per cent of average production between 1929 and 1931 and later to 110 per cent. Overall, during the period covered by the Agreement, prices rose gradually whilst the locus of control shifted from the tea companies to the Combined Food Board for most tea entering the market, namely that from British colonial sources.(11)

The 1938 Tea Agreement was extended in 1943 for five years to March 1948. Members included the major British producers (except for those in countries such as Malaysia which was occupied by the Japanese) together with the newer African producers in Kenya, Uganda and Tanzania. The export quota system was retained until 1947/48 although permitted exports were set at 125 per cent. As the International Tea Committee readily admitted, this constituted unlimited production. Full details of production levels for the war-time period are incomplete for obvious reasons. However, output fell well below demand in each of the years for which data are available from 1941/42 and at the end of the War prices stood almost fifty per cent higher than in 1939.(12)

In 1948, an Interim Producers' Agreement replaced the International Tea Agreement for a two year period to 31 March 1950 in anticipation of the negotiation of a fully-fledged agreement under the auspices of the still-born International Trade Organization. Only India, Pakistan, Sri Lanka and Indonesia acceded although the export quota was assessed on the same basis as under the previous schemes. New plantings of tea were limited to 2 per cent of permissible acreage and replacement plantings to 5 per cent. The Agreement was followed in 1950 by another between India, Pakistan, Sri Lanka and Indonesia, with export quotas set at the same level as in 1948. Both the Interim Agreement and its successor faced unusually volatile conditions in the international tea market. On the one hand, prices were swept upward in the train of the Korean War commodity price boom in 1950; on the other, bulk buying and rationing, which had characterised the tea market in the UK since the early 1940s, were replaced by a reversal to pre-War trading practices. Short supplies in 1952 and 1953 pushed prices to record levels in 1953 and 1954, almost twice the 1951 annual average. In these circumstances the agreements were ill-equipped to bring about the balance between supply and demand which had been their goal; instead, with high prices and more favourable market conditions prevailing, producers lost interest in preserving the machinery for regulation. In consequence, no agreement was reached on renewal although the International Tea Committee, which had remained in existence after 1948, was again retained as a centre for the collection and publication of statistical and other information relating to tea.(13)

Given the closed market conditions within which they operated, their limited membership and their circumscribed terms of reference, only the 1933 Tea Agreement provided any test for the operation of international controls on tea in practice. From 1938, the agreements acted essentially as monitoring devices and exercised little real power over market conditions. Despite restrained planting, for example, output rose gradually even among the participants.(14) When a return to free market conditions took place in 1950, the Agreement was shown to be unable to deter producers from expanding their tea acreage in the face of what were deemed to be strong demand conditions. This was particularly the case for the East African producers whose participation in the 1943 extension of the 1938 Tea Agreement had in any case been contingent upon generous quota allocations.

3. Controls since 1955

The 1955 to 1968 period was characterised by a steady expansion in tea production and exports; in contrast, the importance of the UK market declined, as outlined above, although this was partly offset by rising consumption levels in India and the US. Overall, however, tea prices fell from a high point of US 71 cents per pound in 1955 to only US 44.1 cents per pound in 1969 in the face of a secular decline in demand. As in the 1930s, it was the fall in the price of tea to what was regarded as crisis levels that promoted renewed interest in international controls. The result was ad hoc consultations under the auspices of the United Nations Food and Agriculture Organization in 1965 and in 1967. These brought little agreement among exporting countries except on the need to stimulate tea consumption. In 1969, a third meeting was held in the face of a steep price decline. This resulted in an informal and non-binding understanding between producers to limit exports of tea for the 1970 season by 90 million pounds, a reduction of 14 per cent from the 1969 level. In addition, it was agreed that exporting countries should 'match the increment in import demand ... estimated at about 13-15 million pounds per annum so as to maintain the improved price level'. No details, however, were given on how this matching was to be effected although the major producers recognised formally the needs of the newer (African) producers to expand their production as part of diversification programmes. A more formal agreement was reported to have been thwarted by disagreement between traditional and new producers on respective shares of a static market.(15)

Although the essential nature of the problems facing tea exporters in 1969 were the same as those which had prevailed in 1933 - declining prices in the face of over-production and reduced demand - a coordinated attempt to secure their solution was hampered by the larger number of producers and the different interests that they represented. Most notable was the lack of compatibility at the negotiating table between traditional producers such as India and Sri Lanka, whose exports of tea had declined, in volume in the case of the former and in value in the case of the latter, and those of new producers, such as those in East Africa, whose exports of tea had shown a spectacular increase both in value and in volume terms during the 1960s. Although the problems were slightly eased by a recovery in tea prices in 1970, little progress was made in addressing formal quota and pricing provisions for tea exporters. The question of the international regulation of tea thus remained a drawing board item at the United Nations Food and Agriculture Organization with the Intergovernmental Group on Tea rejecting buffer stocks as a control mechanism in 1970 on the grounds that tea exhibited little price instability, particularly when compared with other beverages. Meeting in June 1974, the same group supported a recommendation by its Sub-Group of Exporters that a working party should be established to assess the feasibility of an international commodity agreement for tea. However, these and subsequent discussions appear to have foundered on the lack of consensus between the different producer groups. It was only in 1978, after a period of considerable instability in the tea market, reflecting rising costs (for fuel, fertiliser, packaging and transport) and short crops, particularly in Sri Lanka, that new discussions were started in earnest under the auspices of UNCTAD and the Integrated Programme.(16)

Much of the discussion on tea after 1978 centred on the question of tea's suitability for storage and the desirability of a buffer stock as a control mechanism. Whereas many in the tea industry attested to the deterioration of tea's flavour if stored unless turned over frequently, others pointed to the contrary example of tea stranded in a ship in the Suez Canal for seven years following the Yom Kippur War which showed no serious deterioration. A report prepared jointly by the United Nations Food and Agriculture Organization and UNCTAD in 1979 concluded that a buffer stock designed to maintain tea prices within $\pm$ 10 and $\pm$ 20 per cent of given references prices during the 1980 to 1984 period might reduce the instability of tea prices by 60 per cent and 35 per cent respectively compared with the period 1960 to 1977.[17] However viewed, the issues were far from clear cut and consumer reaction to an UNCTAD package, which included buffer stocks, export quotas, product promotion and the removal of barriers to trade, was mixed. According to Brown, most consumers, including the UK, favoured export quotas with production control.[18]

In May 1982, producers called for the regulation of supply through an export quota system supported, where necessary, by a buffer stock. Once again, the consumers came out in favour of an agreement based primarily on export quotas rather than on a buffer stock. Disagreement between producers and consumers was also reported on the question of the appropriate price range for the operation of such an agreement. In October 1982, similarly, talks on a scheme proposed jointly by UNCTAD and the United Nations Food and Agriculture Organization foundered on the question of an acceptable system of export controls. In sum, the debate moved forward little from the areas of dissent expressed in 1978 although with the sharp decline in tea prices from their peak in 1977 and resultant large losses for tea producers in India, Sri Lanka and Kenya, the producer group displayed more cohesion than, for example, in the 1969 negotiations.[19] After more than a decade of discussion and research, the international tea trade was thus subject in 1982 to no more formal controls than it had been since the lapsing of the previous international tea agreement in 1955.

4. Conclusion

The case of tea demonstrates further the problems faced by international commodity negotiators. Controls to 1955, although limited in membership and circumscribed in terms of reference, exercised a monitoring function over tea acreage in countries they covered. After 1955 the international tea market became far more complex with new producers expanding their tea production in the 1960s and 1970s owing to the attraction of increasing their export receipts despite declining prices. This exacerbated the problems of traditional producers even though their total volume of production increased only modestly (the case of India) or declined (Sri Lanka).(20)   The divergence of interests between old and new producers made more difficult the negotiation of an agreement in which export quotas were expected to play a central role.   And the UNCTAD proposals for a buffer stock as an additional control mechanism added to rather than detracted from the complexity of the debate by providing a new element on which both producers and consumers took firm views. It is difficult to see how in any case an agreement based largely on short-term quantitative provisions, which required the support of many participants, could substantially have improved what were fundamentally structural problems.

This analysis would be incomplete without mentioning, finally, the establishment of a sub-group on tea promotion within the United Nations Food and Agriculture Organization's Inter-Governmental Group on Tea in 1972 and the formation of an International Tea Promotion Assocation in Rotterdam in 1979.   The latter, an exclusively producer country body, was established as a result of an inter-governmental agreement negotiated under the auspices of the UNCTAD/GATT International Trade Centre.   As in the case of other tropical beverages, however, the appropriateness of even these limited moves was questionable since part at least of the competing market also consisted of developing country primary commodity products.   However, the moves reflected a concerned awareness of at least one of the structural problems facing the international tea industry, namely declining per capita consumption levels, and in this context some action was probably better than none.

Notes

1   United Nations, Supplement 1980: Handbook of International Trade and Development Statistics, Table 4.3 and Singh, de Vries, Hulley and Yeung, Coffee, Tea and Cocoa, pp. 59-61.

2   C.R. Harler, The Culture and Marketing of Tea (Oxford University Press, London, 1964), p. 225.

3   International Tea Committee, Annual Bulletin of Statistics (International Tea Committee, London, June 1964), p. 8 and International Tea Committee, Annual Bulletin of Statistics (International Tea Committee, London, 1980), pp. 16-17. Singh, de Vries, Hulley and Yeung, Coffee, Tea and Cocoa, p. 20 noted that between 1955 and 1973, the growth of world tea production averaged 3.3 per cent per year, ranging from 1.3 per cent per annum in Sri Lanka to 10 per cent in East Africa; world exports of tea grew more slowly, at less than 2 per cent per year.

4   Great Britain, National Board for Prices and Incomes, 'Tea Prices' (HMSO, London, 1970, Cmnd. 4456).

5   L. Ali, 'The Regulation of Trade in Tea', Journal of World Trade Law, vol. 4 (July:August 1970), pp. 578-79.

6   International Tea Committee, Annual Bulletin of Statistics, (International Tea Committee, London, June 1948), p. 25 and Ibid., Annual Bulletin of Statistics (1980), p. 72.

7   Ali, 'The Regulation of Trade in Tea', pp. 578-79 and G. Sarkar, The World Tea Economy (Oxford University Press, London, 1972).

8   See for example A.J.H. Latham, The Depression and the Developing World, 1914-1939 (Croom Helm, London, 1981), p. 109, Rowe, Primary Commodities in International Trade, pp. 148-49 and International Tea Committee, Annual Bulletin of Statistics (1948), pp. 48-50.

9   'The International Tea Agreement, 1933-1938' (9 February 1933) in ILO, Intergovernmental Commodity Agreements, pp. 47-51.

10   International Tea Committee, Annual Bulletin of Statistics (June 1948), p. 50 and League of Nations, Statistical Yearbook of the League of Nations 1941/2 (League of Nations, Geneva, 1942 II.8), p. 113.

11   'The International Tea Agreement 1938-43' (25 August 1938) in ILO, Intergovernmental Commodity Agreements, pp. 52-8. See also International Tea Committee, Annual Bulletin of Statistics (June 1948), pp. 50 and 59.

12   International Tea Committee, Annual Bulletin of Statistics (June 1964), pp. 4, 7, 31 and 51.

13   International Tea Committee, Annual Bulletin of Statistics (June 1948), p. 4, Ibid., Annual Bulletin of Statistics (June 1964), pp. 4, 7, 31, 44 and 51 , Ibid., Annual Bulletin of Statistics 1974 (International Tea Committee, London, 1974), p. 5 and Ali, 'The Regulation of Trade in Tea'.

14   Among the three major producers, for example, India, Sri Lanka and Indonesia, output rose from 770,499,000 pounds in 1933 to 941,757,000 pounds in 1941. See International Tea Committee, Annual Bulletin of Statistics (June 1948), p. 7. The area planted rose only modestly - from 1,856,473 acres at the end of 1933 to 1,922,638 acres at the end of 1940. (The 1941 figure is not available.) (Ibid., p. 6). By 1955, production had risen further to 1,207,859,000 pounds whereas acreage had fallen back to 1,631,986 acres. See International Tea Committee, Annual Bulletin of Statistics (June 1964), pp. 6-7.

242

15   A good assessment of developments in this period is found in Singh, de Vries, Hulley and Yeung, <u>Coffee, Tea and Cocoa</u>, Chapter 3. The report of the 1969 meeting is available in mimeo from UNCTAD entitled 'Report of the Meeting of Tea Exporting Countries' (Mauritius, 1969). See also Rangarajan, <u>Commodity Conflict</u>, p. 41.

16   Ali, 'The Regulation of Tea', pp. 578-89, for example, estimated that between 1957 and 1967 instability (the average deviation from a linear trend unit value) for tea was 1.6 per cent, compared with 12 per cent for coffee and 13.9 per cent for cocoa. See also Chapter 1, which suggests that the price volatility of tea prices increased markedly, both in nominal and real terms, in the 1973 to 1981 period, H. Roy, 'Some Observations on a new international Tea Agreement', <u>Economic Affairs</u>, vol. 17 (1972) and M. Singh, 'The Economics of an International Tea Agreement: A Study of Some Aspects of Stabilization of Commodity Prices', <u>Indian Economic Journal</u>, vol. 4 (1970).

17   UNCTAD, 'Prospective Supply/Demand Balance for Tea and the Implications for an International Buffer Stock Arrangement and for an Export Quota Scheme, for the Period 1980-84' (mimeo, UNCTAD, Geneva, November 1979, TD/B/IPC/TEA/AC/0), p. 2.

18   Brown, <u>The Political and Social Economy of Commodity Control</u>, p. 198.

19   <u>Financial Times</u>, 19 October 1982.

20   China, a traditional producer, has also contributed to this problem by expanding its exports of black tea in recent years in order to obtain foreign exchange.

13: OLIVE OIL

'El campo andaluz, primado
por el sol canicular,
de loma en loma rayado
de olivar y de olivar!'

('Los Olivos', Antonio Machado)

1. General

Olive oil is a minor item in world trade: it accounts for only about an eighth of the value of exports of edible vegetable oils in contrast to the greater importance of palm oil and soyabean oil, both of which account for about a quarter. Similarly, there is no country dependent on olive oil or even on vegetable oils as a group for a large proportion of its export earnings. Despite this, however, olive oil production is very important to the regions where it is produced where alternative land use in dry, rocky and often steep areas is often difficult to find. It is perhaps these latter factors which help to explain why olive oil alone of the vegetable oil commodities has been subject to international commodity agreement action (although vegetable oils as a group were included as a core commodity under UNCTAD's Integrated Programme) and the object of EEC production aids.

Olive oil is produced from the fruit of the olive tree, a genus of about thirty species of trees or shrubs mostly African and Asian in origin. The quality and purity of the oil varies according both to the country of growth and to the processes adopted for its extraction. Virgin olive oil, flowing from the fleshy pericarp of the olive, is of the finest quality. Fine or salad oil is obtained by crushing the entire fruit at a gentle heat. By allowing the fruit to ferment previous to pressing it, a lower quality of oil is obtained.

244

The production of olive oil is located principally in Mediterranean countries which, together with the US, have been the major consumers.(1) In addition to its long productive life of up to a hundred years, a problem with regulating olive oil production has been the extreme variability of yields with abundant crops tending to be followed by one or two bad or below average harvests. Wide fluctuations in supplies and prices have also contributed to the substitution of other soft oils for olive oil even though the latter retains a preference owing to its distinctive flavour, a fact which allows it to maintain prices significantly higher than those of other vegetable oils. Because of its high price, olive oil is not generally used as a component in manufactured fat products such as margarine. Likewise, edible olive oil is not used to any large extent in non-food products. As a result of these special characteristics, controls on the olive oil market have taken a different form to those for other commodities.

2. Olive Oil Controls

Moves to introduce internationally coordinated stabilisation measures for the olive oil market took place following a report by the United Nations Food and Agriculture Organization in 1955. The Working Party recommended that there should be a standardisation of the labelling and classification of olive oil, a promotion campaign to increase consumption levels and an Olive Oil Council to advise participating countries on domestic policies. These recommendations were incorporated in a draft international commodity agreement which had as a general objective the reduction of fluctuations of supplies to the market.(2)

The draft agreement was adopted with little alteration in 1956. The Agreement was open to all countries producing or consuming olive oil and did not provide control mechanisms designed to stabilise prices, incomes or production, although the Olive Oil Council was required to examine supplies and requirements with a view to making recommendations with respect to stabilisation measures, if it deemed them to be appropriate. The main focus of the Agreement was on the improvement of statistical services, advertising and the standardisation of labelling and international contracts for olive oil transactions. (The key features of the olive oil agreements are summarised in the Appendix, Table 8.)(3)

In contrast to other international commodity agreements, the 1956 Olive Oil Agreement was a mild affair which attracted little comment or criticism. Little disagreement existed on the potential advantages of a more coordinated approach to the international olive oil trade especially since the Agreement specified no precise economic measures to be taken. This was to remain the case throughout the life of the 1956 Agreement and its successors in 1963 (amended and extended in 1969 and 1973) and in 1979. A slight broadening of the economic powers was included in the 1963 Agreement which commissioned the Olive Oil Council to 'facilitate direct negotiations between exporting and importing concerns of participating countries' on the basis of their statistical information on supply and demand. Subsequent extensions and amendments did not include full economic provisions.(4)

In March 1979, a new Olive Oil Agreement was negotiated in Geneva under the auspices of UNCTAD to replace the 1963 Olive Oil Agreement. The Agreement, which entered into force in 1980, bore a close resemblance to its predecessor: in the context of a structural surplus in world olive oil production, it aimed to promote increased consumption by the continued operation of the Publicity Fund. The Agreement aimed also to improve production and processing methods, so that by reducing costs, olive oil might become more competitive with alternative products. A special fund of $ 100,000 was allocated for this purpose. A possible future link was seen also with UNCTAD's Common Fund. As with previous olive oil agreements, the agreement attracted a considerable measure of support covering 95 per cent of world olive oil production.(5)

3. Conclusion

Judged strictly against their stated aims - the reduction of fluctuations in olive oil supplies and the standardisation of the quality of and contractual arrangements concerning olive oil trade - the olive oil agreements may be viewed as having broadly succeeded. Their full coverage of olive oil production and their explicit guidelines on issues such as labelling and packaging undoubtedly fulfilled the goals specified in 1956. However, the broader problem of the tendency of olive oil production to surplus, which had been recognised by the United Nations in 1955 and formed one of the underlying reasons for the first olive oil agreement, was as serious in 1979 as it had been in 1955. A recognition of the problem and a desire to remedy the situation thus formed a more urgent aspect of the 1979 Agreement.

Perhaps the clearest conclusion to emerge from the case of olive oil is that international commodity agreements may provide a useful service in the areas of quality control, publicity and the maintenance of a statistical service. Although less spectacular than, for example, market intervention via buffer stock operations, it may be argued that these services could be equally valuable. Their less controversial nature may help to explain why the agreements survived with no serious challenge.

Notes

1   Spain was the leading producer, for example, both before and after the Second World War and Italy, Greece, Turkey and Portugal were also important producers of olive oil in this period.

2   United Nations, Food and Agriculture Organization, The Stabilization of the Olive Oil Market (United Nations, Food and Agriculture Organization, Rome, 1955), which also contained the draft 1956 Agreement.

3   See, for example, 'International Agreement on Olive Oil' (modified by the Protocol of 3rd April 1958) (HMSO, London, 1960, Cmnd. 1954).

4   'International Olive Oil Agreement 1963' (HMSO, London, 1963, Cmnd. 2155), Article 19(4), 'Protocol for the further extension of the International Olive Oil Agreement 1963' (HMSO, London, 1970, Cmnd. 4432), United Nations, United Nations Conference on Olive Oil, 1973 (United Nations, New York, 1973, TD/OLIVE OIL 5/6 Rev. 1) and Ibid., United Nations Conference on Olive Oil, 1978 (United Nations, New York, 1978, TD/OLIVE OIL 6/10).

5   See U. Wassermann, 'UNCTAD: International Olive Oil Agreement 1979', Journal of World Trade Law, vol. 13, no. 5 (September:October 1979). For the agreement, see United Nations, 'International Olive Oil Agreement 1979' (UNCTAD, Geneva, 1979, TD/OLIVE OIL 7/7).

14: CARTELS

> To each a share in the market,
> And let supplies be divided,
> And as reduction of the price
> Cannot by now be avoided,
> Let us arise and all declare:
> "A new measure is decided,
> Lest we lose these markets we seek,
> And feel disturbed or derided."

(Dr. Mana Said al Otaiba, Oil Minister, The United Arab Emirates, 1983)

1. Introduction

Chapter 4 attempted to provide a broad over-view of the frequency, aims and mechanics of raw material cartels since the 1920s. It concluded that the dividing line between international commodity agreements and cartels was an extremely fine one, particularly before the Second World War, when consumers were infrequently represented, and that producer interests have on occasion regarded cartel action as a realistic alternative or addition to international commodity agreement action.

The purpose of this chapter is to explore further whether raw material cartels have differed markedly in practice from international commodity agreements. Several examples have already been examined with reference to tin, coffee, cocoa and rubber, commodities which were subject also to formal international commodity agreements. In this chapter, accordingly, the discussion is restricted to commodities for which there have been no

248

international commodity agreements in the past. These commodities may be divided into two groups: those, such as crude petroleum, copper and mercury, for which cartel action was important both before and after the Second World War; and those, such as bauxite, uranium and iron ore, for which cartel action was largely a phenomenon of the 1970s. Of these, copper, iron ore and bauxite were considered to be suitable candidates for international commodity agreements under UNCTAD's Integrated Programme. The volume of data available has made it necessary to exclude quite ruthlessly anything which is only of marginal interest and to allocate the space available to a brief consideration of those cartels which appear to offer the most interesting examples.

2. Crude Petroleum
a. General

As a leading world export since the 1920s and the commodity most commonly associated with cartel action, crude petroleum, literally rock-oil, offers the obvious point of departure for any consideration of raw material cartels. The commercial production of petroleum dates back to the middle of the nineteenth century in Romania and the US. Output was stimulated during and after the First World War by the increasing use of the internal combustion engine for transportation and thereafter other countries gradually entered the field. It was only in 1948 that the US lost its position as the world's first-ranking exporter; and from the early 1970s the US became a major importer. Since the Second World War, production in the Middle East has grown in importance together with new sources of supply such as Nigeria and Mexico.(1)
    A feature of the world petroleum trade which facilitated corporate cartel action during the pre-1945 period and encouraged a banding together of producer interests after 1945 was the large share conducted by multi-national corporations based in developed countries. The oil industry has been dominated by seven large oil companies, four of which (Exxon, Mobil, Texaco and Standard Oil) are US in nationality. These companies have exercised a strong degree of control over all aspects of oil exploration, production and marketing, a circumstance which has led to anti-trust legislation and nationalisation measures in their turn, in addition to generating a substantial literature.(2)
    A further aspect which has increased its suitability for cartelisation has been the inelasticity of demand for petroleum, particularly in the short run, and the limited possibilities for substitution. Whereas substitution was rapid to petroleum and away from coal after the First World War and, notably, after the Second, the switch away from oil has been slow since the price rises of the early 1970s. In 1979, for example, oil still provided about half of the

world's energy needs from a peak of 53 per cent in 1973 although there is some evidence to suggest that the shift away from oil has accelerated since then.(3)

b. Controls before 1945

It was the international nature of world petroleum production and marketing which created the conditions for cartel action during the late 1920s in the face of a stream of new discoveries which depressed prices. Following a price war between Shell and Standard Oil in 1927, three companies, Shell, Standard Oil and Anglo-Persian, held secret meetings in 1928 which culminated in an agreement to set up an oil cartel. This covered the world outside the US and the USSR. The cartel aimed in the first instance to divide the Indian market between participants. In 1929, it extended its coverage to the European market in an attempt to avoid price cuts (Chapter 4).

Although attempts were made to keep the cartel in operation during the 1930s - in 1932, for example, the cartel was extended to Romanian producers with the aim of maintaining production at the existing level by production and export quotas - this was never completely successful since there was always a degree of leakage of supplies through non-participants. The cartels were important, however, in formulating the Gulf pricing system under which the price of oil was established as being the same in every export centre of the world as in the American ports along the Gulf of Mexico. The final price at the point of delivery varied in accordance with the distance from the Gulf of Mexico and whether or not the purchaser was a member of the cartel.(4)

c. Controls to 1970

Early attempts to coordinate the policies of countries (as opposed to corporations) producing oil began in the mid-1940s with the establishment of the Arab League. Iraq and Saudi Arabia signed an agreement for cooperation on oil matters and in 1959 called an Arab Petroleum Conference in Cairo under the sponsorship of the Arab League. In 1960, when the US imposed a mandatory import quota system, many of the independent oil companies, shut off from the US market, cut posted prices of Middle Eastern oil with a view to improving their profit margins. These cuts, which meant an aggregate loss of US $231 million for Kuwait, Iran, Iraq and Saudi Arabia, encouraged the establishment of OPEC in the same year, with those four countries and Venezuela as founder members. The aim of OPEC was to restore prices to the level prevailing before the reduction and OPEC's founder members held 67 per cent of world oil reserves and accounted for about 38 per cent of world oil production and nearly 90 per cent of internationally traded oil. (By 1973, OPEC

250

included amongst its members Qatar (1961), Indonesia and Libya (1962), Abu Dhabi (1967), Algeria (1969), Nigeria (1971) and Ecuador and Gabon (1973).(5))

In its first ten years, OPEC's main actions were defensive and centred on attempting to prevent a further erosion in posted prices. In 1964, agreement was also reached with the major oil companies to change the method by which oil company profits were calculated, the net effect of which was to lead to some increase in the revenues of oil-producing countries. By 1968, OPEC was also urging its members to undertake the production and processing of crude oil themselves and to revoke the traditional export licences granted to foreign firms, a system which had itself replaced long-term concessions from the late 1940s. In the same year, a second association of oil-exporting countries, the Organization of Arab Petroleum Exporting Countries (OAPEC), was established following the 1967 Arab-Israeli War. Its main purpose was to create an effective instrument of political rather than economic policy although OAPEC members were required to respect OPEC resolutions even if they were not OPEC members.

On balance, the defensive period of OPEC's operations to 1970 did not achieve the success that had been envisaged in respect of its pricing objectives. In 1970, for example, the real price of oil was 47 per cent below the 1955 level. However, in the 1960s the coordinated action of OPEC not only prevented any further cuts in posted prices but also separated the payment of royalties from taxes and restored to the producer control of unexploited territories.

d. Controls after 1970

The 1970s, in contrast, heralded two dramatic rises in oil prices, the first from 1971 to 1974 and the second from 1979 to 1981 (Figure 14:1). The first rise was triggered by Libya, a relatively new oil exporter supplying about a quarter of Western Europe's oil, which in 1970, under the revolutionary government of Qadaffi, demanded and achieved a 13 per cent rise in prices. In conditions of short supplies and strong demand, Libya's move was followed by several other countries, including Iraq, Iran and Kuwait, and at its twenty-first conference in December 1970, OPEC advocated formally higher posted prices and higher minimum rates of taxation on oil company profits. Members resolved to undertake 'concerted and simultaneous action' in pursuit of these goals.(6)

The gradual upward trend in prices continued between 1971 and 1973 accompanied by nationalisation measures in Libya, Iraq and Algeria and moves in Iran and Saudi Arabia to increase their equity stakes in oil production. It was not until October 1973, however, following the move in the market price of oil above the posted price (for the first time in OPEC's history) and the outbreak of the fourth

251

Figure 14:1: Crude Petroleum Prices, 1965-1982
(annual average, official price, Arabian light, $ per barrel)

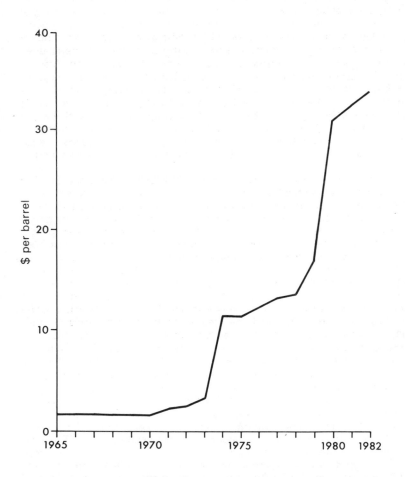

Source: IMF, International Financial Statistics (IMF, Washington, various issues).

Arab-Israeli War, that OPEC members decided to raise prices - to $5.12 a barrel -and to restrict output. This was accompanied by the imposition by some countries of an embargo on oil shipments to the US. A combination of continued supply shortages and speculative buying then enabled OPEC, led by Iran, to push the posted price further to $11.65 per barrel. At the beginning of 1974, in the words of Sampson,

'The Western nations . . . found themselves, to their bewilderment, confronted with a cartel, not of companies, but of sovereign states'.(7)

In order to control over 80 per cent of oil exports and 45 per cent of global production, OPEC had to obtain the cooperation of twelve producers. As Brown has noted, however, the ability of OPEC to quadruple royalties in 1973 did not lie only in the concentration of supply but also in the inelasticity of demand, the limited possibilities for substitution and the lack of organised response from consumers.(8) It is also important to note that the gains made were far less spectacular than they appeared at first since for a number of years prior to 1971 the tax and royalty per barrel for oil exporters had remained unchanged and oil prices had declined in real terms.

Nevertheless, the implications of the oil price hike, as outlined in Chapter 1, were far-reaching. Oil-exporting countries emerged as a new category in international trade, with additional earnings of $60 billion a year, more than six times concessional flows from developed to developing countries in 1973 and more than three times global financial flows between the two groups. This represented one of the largest and most rapid shifts in world income, equal in magnitude to two per cent of world GNP. A second result was that oil price rises added to existing inflationary pressures and invoked a restrictive policy response from major industrialised countries. Thirdly, the rise in oil prices generated a strong ripple effect, both in terms of strong speculative movements in the prices of other primary commodities and in terms of the difficult environment it created for the negotiation of international commodity agreements.(9)

In these circumstances, and after a four year period in which the price of crude oil remained comparatively steady in nominal terms -although falling by almost twenty per cent in real terms - the second oil price surge, which took place towards the end of 1978, was viewed by many as a second oil crisis. Although the revolution in Iran and the consequent reduction in Iranian output provided a trigger mechanism, the sharp rises in the official Middle East price - from US $13.5 per barrel in the first quarter of 1979 to US $34 in the fourth quarter of 1981 - were associated with an increased speculative demand for inventories.(10) Bi-lateral sales between consumer and producer governments doubled in two years and the spot market, formerly the locus only of marginal sales, became a more important avenue for transactions.(11)

By the beginning of 1983, however, this situation had altered markedly: with a glut in world oil supplies and slack world demand, relations within OPEC came under increasing strain. On the one hand, producers found difficulty in agreeing on the allocation of individual quotas to achieve a targeted output of 17.5 million barrels a day. On the other, divisions existed on the appropriate differentials to be charged over the official reference price of $34 per barrel for some premium grades of crude oil. With a cut in prices triggered by the British National Oil Corporation in February, it appeared to some commentators that OPEC had lost, at least for the time being, its ability to determine world oil prices.(12)

The potential impact of the apparent reverse in OPEC's fortunes was considered to be as far-reaching as its rise to power. Concern was expressed, for example, that if oil prices fell substantially, the strain placed on heavily indebted oil-producing countries, such as Mexico, Venezuela, and Nigeria, would pose a serious problem for the world banking system, which had expanded rapidly partly on the basis of the re-cycling of petro-currency flows. The uncertainty created was also felt as an important influence in the foreign exchange markets. Thus, from its role as a model for developing country producers of primary commodities, OPEC had by 1983 substantially diminished in stature.

e. Conclusion

The case of oil suggests that raw material cartels may vary substantially in terms of participation (corporate in the pre-War period and governmental afterwards), in objectives (market division, the prevention of price falls, price stabilisation, the raising of prices, increasing national control, nationalisation and so on) and in methodology (the exchange of information, measures concerning royalties and production restraints). Oil represented a special case, however, as a leading and strategic world commodity and OPEC, similarly, must be viewed as an extraordinary example of cartelisation. Although OPEC's control over prices was weakened by divisions between members, the emergence of important non-member producers and some structural shifts away from oil as a result of conservation and substitution, particularly in the late 1970s, its impact on the world oil import bill, nevertheless, was substantial, especially between 1973 and 1974. The countries mostly seriously affected by OPEC's activities were the lowest income developing countries with little or no oil of their own.

3. Copper
a. General

As a major item in world trade and a core commodity under UNCTAD's Integrated Programme, copper, with its long association with cartelisation, offers a good second example for consideration. Until 1800, Europe was the centre of the world's copper industry. However, with the decline in British output, Chile and, later, the US emerged as leading producers. In the 1970s, the US retained a dominant position and the USSR, Chile, Canada, Zambia and Zaire were also important producers; Zambia and Chile stood out as countries with a high degree of dependence on copper for their export earnings.(13)

Like the oil industry, the world's copper industry is highly integrated; in 1970, for example, only eleven companies, a consortium and three government corporations controlled 81 per cent of non-centrally planned ore production and thirty-four companies and government corporations controlled 94 per cent of world refining capacity. The degree of concentration may be explained in terms of the capital-intensive nature of the industry; it survived, in varying degrees, despite nationalisation policies set in place in several developing countries during the 1960s and 1970s.(14) An important feature of world copper production is the wide range which exists between the costs of producers; production costs are cheapest where copper is produced as a by-product of other metals, such as in the Sudbury Basin in Canada where the main commodity produced is nickel. Another feature is the producer-consumer contract which forms the basis for most international trade in primary copper. The producer price, on which US companies are the most important influence, changes infrequently and, as in the case of sugar, the world market price is applied only to a small part of total production.(15)

Owing to the length of time taken to set a new mining project in place - between five and ten years - copper mining and metallurgy are slow to respond to increased demand. Before the Second World War, the price of copper tended to reflect the trade cycle. Since then, demand for copper has continued to follow the trend of industrial activity fairly closely, although copper has suffered some competition, notably from aluminium. Mention should also be made of the important market which exists for secondary or reclaimed copper.(16)

b. Controls to 1945

The first major cartel established by copper producers dated back to 1887 and was associated with Pierre Secrétan, head of the largest European copper-buying association, Société Industrielle et

255

Commerciale des Métaux, backed by French bankers. The cartel gained control of four-fifths of world copper production and contracted supply on fixed terms or on terms which included a share of any profit over a fixed price. In 1887 when the cartel began, the price of copper on the London Metal Exchange stood at £40 per ton. By early 1888, it had risen to almost double. However, by the end of 1888, declining industrial demand meant that the syndicate was forced to buy increasing quantities of copper in order to sustain prices. When in 1889 one of the supporting banks collapsed, the price of copper fell back sharply to its 1887 level.(17)

The Secrétan cartel was followed by several attempts by producers' associations to restrict output in times of abundant supplies and falling prices. The first example of this action was in 1892 when the American Producers' Association agreed to restrict production and exports, with limited success. Subsequent attempts to control prices were made by US interests in 1900 and in 1907; and a Copper Exports Association was formed after the First World War (following the relaxation of US anti-trust laws for export associations) with a view to raising prices by restricting output and accumulating stocks. After a period of successful cooperation, the cartel faded and the association dissolved in 1923 as a result of dissent between those producers with purely domestic and those with foreign interests.

In 1926 the same (US) producers formed another association, Copper Exporters Inc, which included foreign firm participation and was estimated to cover over 85 per cent of world production. The aim of the organisation was to stabilise prices and, according to the League of Nations, to eliminate middlemen (Table 4:2). The tactics adopted, which included price fixing by two central offices, helped to push prices from US 13 cents per pound in 1926 to US 24 cents per pound at the beginning of 1929. A further repercussion, however, was the hostility aroused among UK financial interests and consumers; in 1929, for example, the high level of prices prevailing led to a buyers' strike which forced a reduction in prices to US 18 cents per pound. Even this lower level was sustained only until April 1930 when, in the face of substantially reduced demand and increased production from non-participants - notably Zambia (Northern Rhodesia) -the cartel lost control and prices fell dramatically.(18)

Two interesting points emerge from a consideration of the copper cartels before 1931. First, they were all designed to raise prices; and, secondly, with the exception of the Secrétan cartel, they all reflected the dominant position held in the world copper market by US producers. By 1931, however, this situation had changed markedly owing to the expansion of production outside the US. As a result, interest was evinced from US producers in negotiating a (producers') arrangement which was more international in nature. A short-lived agreement was reached at the end of 1931 between twenty-four producers. This involved a commitment to restrict output to 20 per cent of capacity. In practice, however, the generous quota allocations granted to Zaire and Zambia, in order to secure their support, meant that the US continued to shoulder the main burden of restraint.

By 1932, the US share of world copper production had fallen to only 23 per cent from 47 per cent in 1929 and the serious financial difficulties faced by the copper states of Montana, Arizona and Michigan led to increased pressure for protection. As a result, a tariff of 4 cents per pound was imposed on US copper imports in May 1932, affording domestic producers in effect complete protection in their home markets.

In 1935, a further international conference was called by producers in the face of continued low prices, although US interests were represented only in respect of mines outside the US. In what amounted to a new cartel, producers, representing 70 per cent of total output outside the US, agreed to restrict production to certain specified quantities. The impact of the cartel was not judged to have been large owing partly to the exclusion of US production and partly to the expansion of supplies of secondary copper. The cartel ended with the outbreak of war.(19)

c. Controls since 1945

By the time trade in copper had resumed on the London Metal Exchange in 1953, the US had become a net importer of copper, which was included as an item in its strategic stockpile. Limited cartel action in the form of reduced output was resumed in Africa in 1956 in the face of a price decline associated with declining world consumption. However, only partial support was obtained and the experiment ended in 1956. Further voluntary production cut-backs were introduced in 1960 by companies in Africa and North America and these continued until the mid-1960s when support weakened in the face of conflicting long-term policy goals.(20) The debate was continued, however, at a meeting of developing country copper producers in Lusaka in 1967. The only formal decision of the conference was to establish a permanent organisation, the Conseil Intergouvernemental des Pays Exportateurs de Cuivre (CIPEC), to monitor developments in the world copper market and to collect data.

A philosophy underlying CIPEC's foundation was that increased cooperative action would help to improve conditions for major copper exporting countries and that a greater degree of national control over mining was desirable. Accordingly, following the lead of Zaire in its nationalisation of Belgium's Société Générale des Minerais in 1966, Zambia, Chile and Peru pursued nationalisation policies, in varying degrees, between 1970 and 1974. It was only in 1974, however, that

257

CIPEC intervened actively in the world copper market in an effort to raise prices. As Nappi has outlined, the impact of its intervention, which took the form of reduced exports, was modest and despite the cutback, the price of copper on the London market was 70 per cent lower in 1975 than it had been in 1973.

There are several explanations for CIPEC's lack of success in raising prices in this period. On the one hand, its control was far less strong than that of the copper cartels before the War, extending only to 60 per cent of world exports and to a far smaller proportion of world copper ore production. On the other, the consumption of secondary copper and of copper substitutes such as aluminium and plastics increased after the Second World War, and CIPEC exercised no control over these developments. As Sir Ronald Prain commented in his history of the copper industry:

> '... not even CIPEC's most enthusiastic supporters can claim that it had much influence on the market which continued to act according to time-honoured laws of supply and demand, tempered only by political considerations, strikes and stockpiles, wars and rumours of wars'.(21)

As a result of the failure of a further cutback in 1976 to bring the desired impact on copper prices, the leading developing country producers turned instead to UNCTAD's Integrated Programme and a formal international commodity agreement as an alternative approach. The first UNCTAD preparatory meeting on copper was held in November 1976. However, by a seventh preparatory meeting in March 1980 little advance had been made toward international agreement, divergent views between developing and developed country producers and producers and consumers providing major obstacles. Whereas representatives of several developing country producers urged that a negotiating conference be held to discuss such issues as the appropriate size of a buffer stock, an (unspecified) developed country representative stated discouragingly that it was still far from clear whether or not an international stabilisation agreement was feasible or desirable.(22) The meeting ended in an impasse with a failure to agree even upon the form to be taken by an international commodity organisation for copper.(23)

In contrast to the pre-War period, developing country producers were thus the prime motivating forces behind the negotiation of international controls on copper after the War. In both periods, it was the sensitivity of copper prices to changes in business conditions which awakened interest in international controls. After the War, the failure of uni-lateral producer action to bring about the desired outcome stimulated interest in a formally negotiated international agreement. The commitment of consumer interests to this concept, however, was far from wholehearted and the wide range of production costs, the existence of a secondary market for copper and strong substitute products made the failure to reach agreement far from surprising.(24)

4. Mercury

Whereas the cases of oil and copper are fairly well-known examples of cartelisation, that of mercury, a very minor commodity in world trade, is not. And yet, as outlined in Part II, mercury has been the object of regular cartelisation since 1928 and as such, it offers a further interesting example for analysis.

Mercury is a silvery-white metallic chemical, the only metal to be liquid at ordinary temperatures. Production costs are subject to wide variation owing to the varying quality and density of the ore. Until the beginning of the 1960s, most world demand for mercury was met by Spain, Italy, the US, the USSR and Mexico. Although overall production has continued to be dominated by a relatively small number of producing countries and companies, higher mercury prices during the 1960s and 1970s encouraged the development of lower grade deposits in Algeria, Canada, Turkey, Peru and the Philippines and larger sales from China and the USSR.(25)

Mercury has a variety of uses which include its traditional use in barometers and thermometers. Several special factors have influenced the level of demand for mercury. These have included the development of alternative and substitute products, such as nickel-cadmium battery systems following a period of high prices during the 1960s, the limit imposed on the use of mercury in the production of paint, agricultural and pharmaceutical products on environmental grounds from the 1960s and increased supplies owing to the recycling of mercury formerly discharged into waterways. As a result of these influences, the price of mercury declined from a peak in 1966 until the mid-1970s.(26)

The first major controls on mercury production were imposed in 1928 by the main Spanish and Italian government-owned mines (Table 4:2). The controls, set for an initial ten-year period, were introduced when the price of mercury had reached a plateau and they established a production quota system, uniform prices and a common sales organisation. (This eventually gave one firm, Roura and Forgas in London, the exclusive sales agency for all exports.) The cartel, known as Mercurio Europeo, was not generally regarded as having succeeded either in its pricing objective or in its aim of monopolising the world market for mercury. And, as the League of Nations pointed out, it did not prevent prices from halving between 1930 and 1933 and probably encouraged the growth of mercury production in the US and Mexico, neither of which were members. The cartel's actions were halted in 1936, when Spanish supplies became subject to severe governmental restrictions during the Spanish Civil War, but were resumed in 1939, as prices rose rapidly reflecting increased military requirements.(27)

The Mercurio Europeo cartel continued in operation until 1949 with the Italian mines supplying Europe and the North-American market reserved for Almadén, the major Spanish producer. It disintegrated only when Amiata, the major Italian producer, made large sales to the US in 1949, and, even then, reappeared briefly between 1958 and 1962 to operate on a similar basis. It was disbanded when challenged by EEC anti-trust legislation in 1962.

It was production in new areas and the declining level of demand which encouraged Spanish and Italian producers to attempt coordinated action again in 1972. This took the form of setting a floor price of $ 170 per flask (of 76 pounds), equivalent to the prevailing New York price but slightly above that current in London. Support was also obtained from Mexican producers to defend a $ 200 per flask floor price in the US. This intervention brought some recovery in the price of mercury in the second half of 1972 and with continued intervention and the support of Algeria, Yugoslavia and Peru, the rise in prices was sustained until 1974. In 1975, however, prices fell to well below the average 1972 level in the face of declining consumption levels and producers from Spain, Italy, Algeria, Peru, Turkey and Yugoslavia banded together formally as the International Association of Mercury Producers (ASSIMER), with a view to promoting new uses for mercury and to sustaining a price of $ 350 per flask, twice the existing level.

It is hardly surprising, given its ambitious objectives, that the cartel should fail in its pricing goals. In 1976, the annual price for mercury averaged only $ 124.25 per flask, despite reduced output, and it edged up only gingerly to an average of $ 139.70 in 1977. It was not until the late 1970s, with the resurgence of demand, that a substantial rise in prices was witnessed and even then the rise was by no means secure, since high stock levels existed in both producing and consuming countries.(28)

The case of mercury offers another example of the way in which the policies of producers with respect to short-term pricing objectives could be counter-productive by leading to the development of new sources of supply and the use of substitute products. Despite their comparatively strong degree of control over output, mercury producers were not able to achieve their short-term pricing objectives when market conditions worked strongly in counterpoint. In the mid-1970s, as in the early 1930s, it was forces beyond the control of producers which called the tune in establishing the level of mercury prices.

5. Bauxite

Bauxite, a minor item in world trade, is the ore from which alumina is extracted. Aluminium is subsequently produced from alumina by the use of an electrolytic process. The production of bauxite is therefore linked directly to the demand for aluminium in key industries such as construction and transportation and subject to the same influences, such as the supply of recycled aluminium and comparative energy costs.(29)

The nature of the bauxite-alumina-aluminium industry has led to a large degree of vertical integration with six multi-national companies dominating both the mining and refining aspects of the industry until the 1960s. However, key sources of bauxite were located in developing countries (notably, Jamaica, Guyana and Surinam) and it was the desire of these countries to exercise more control over the transformation and conversion processes which led to the formation of the International Bauxite Association (IBA) in 1974.

Within the industry as a whole, such a move was far from unprecedented. Five cartels for aluminium were formed in the first half of the century, the first of any importance in 1926 (Chapter 4).(30) The 1974 Association broke new ground, however, in that it applied to the mining as opposed to the processing side of the industry, it was led by developing rather than developed country interests and it was given strong government rather than corporate support. As such, it reflected a deliberate move away from the integrated system of production which had been reinforced by cartelisation between the Wars.

Jamaica was a key force behind coordinated producer action on bauxite with its call in 1968 for the establishment of an association to coordinate information and production policy. In 1972, Jamaica was joined in its endeavours by Guyana - which had nationalised Demba, a subsidiary of Alcan, in 1971 - and by Surinam. A preliminary meeting established the IBA with seven countries - Jamaica, Guyana, Australia, Guinea, Sierra Leone, Surinam and Yugoslavia - adhering to a twenty-eight article text setting out the aims and regulations of the association. These were drafted in the spirit of UNCTAD II and stipulated that the production, transformation and marketing of bauxite should permit producers a 'just and reasonable' real income. An executive office for the IBA was established in Kingston, Jamaica.(31)

Initial action on the part of participants in the IBA, which, by the end of 1974, covered over 70 per cent of world production, centred on mining policy and, in particular, on mining taxation. Jamaica, for example, increased royalty and export levies on a specified level of production by 700 per cent. The action of Jamaica was followed by other countries, including Surinam, Guyana, the Dominican Republic and, to a lesser extent, Australia.(32) However, although a net increase in revenues for producing countries was achieved in the first instance, this was not without its cost in the medium term. The policy pursued by Caribbean producers in

261

particular was reported to have encouraged the major corporations to expand their investment outside the Caribbean. And the creation of the IBA, coinciding as it did with a period of rising energy prices, probably did little to discourage the search for alternative ores and the use of cheaper substitutes for aluminium.(33) A second stage in the IBA's activities was the announcement in December 1977 of a minimum price of $ 24 per ton for bauxite sold to the US market. In practice this was of little importance since prices charged were above that level and rising. As a gesture of intent, however, the announcement was of more significance and such was the credible public face of the IBA that in 1980, in an unprecedented move, a meeting was held between the largest aluminium companies and the IBA to discuss the current state and future prospects of the industry and other general issues of mutual interest, such as energy and shipping. At this meeting, the IBA sought to reassure the companies that the association did not intend to become a price fixing cartel like OPEC but rather to work towards a fair and equitable price for bauxite.(34)

Even a brief review such as this is sufficient to show that the IBA did not accord to the standard pattern of cartelisation in contrast to the aluminium cartels of the 1930s and to OPEC and CIPEC in the 1960s and 1970s. On the contrary, with formal regulations and consultative meetings with consumer interests (as represented by the multi-nationals), the IBA was in some respects a hybrid which fell between the classification of cartel and international commodity agreement which has been used in this study. It is interesting to note in this context that bauxite producers appear to have felt that little could be gained from the inclusion of bauxite as a core commodity under UNCTAD's Integrated Programme. In their view, the main problems they faced were structural in nature and international commodity agreements in their traditional form could offer little in the way of solution.(35)

6. Uranium

Unlike OPEC, whose actions have been fairly well plotted, the Uranium Cartel, which operated between 1972 and 1976, has been only partly documented despite extensive US anti-trust hearings. It offers an interesting example, nonetheless, of a cartel in which developed countries and their governments were active members.

Uranium production on a large scale was initiated only in the late 1940s when the US and the UK sought to increase their supplies for military reasons. Production was encouraged by a broad range of exploration incentives in the US, Canada, South Africa and, to a lesser extent, Australia. This led to a ten-fold increase in output to a peak of 44,000 short tons in 1959. However, the peak was reached just as military requirements were saturated and during the course of the 1960s the uranium industry experienced a period of prolonged contraction. This was reflected in the declining prices reported by the US Atomic Energy Commission which itself threatened further to depress demand by selling its excess stock of uranium. Commercial demand for uranium developed slowly but was in no way sufficient to take up the slack.(36)

It was the long period of depressed market conditions which provided the background to the Uranium Cartel of the early 1970s. Cartelisation was facilitated by the high degree of concentration of production with four countries, the US, Canada, France and South Africa, accounting for over 90 per cent of Western output and six companies alone for about two-thirds. On the purchasing side, the enrichment service was entirely in public ownership whereas conversion and fuel fabrication were provided by private firms. The structure of the uranium industry meant that there was a considerable degree of intra-trade and spot transactions constituted only a marginal share of total trade.(37)

The first reported cartel action for uranium pre-dated the 1972 Cartel by almost fifty years. In 1925, an arrangement between Zaire, Czechoslovakia and, later, Canada, established a common sales agency in Brussels which was alleged to have set common export prices.(38) The 1972 Cartel, in contrast, applied to a commodity which had new strategic and environmental associations and achieved a far more dramatic record in terms of price movements. Action was precipitated by the closure of the US market to foreign sources in the context of surplus domestic supplies. It was reported to have been instigated by Canada with the aim of safeguarding the survival of the Canadian uranium industry. Government support was also judged to have been given by France and South Africa whereas in the US itself several leading companies were implicated.

Data on the terms of reference of the Cartel and of its operations are partial. The initial aim was to establish minimum prices, set at $ 7.7 per pound, a little above the prevailing world level, and to divide the world market between participants. Later, the available evidence suggests that $ 40 per pound was set as a goal, a level reached and exceeded in 1976. Dramatic rises in the price of uranium were achieved by supply restrictions, although producers were assisted in their action by a sharp increase in demand in the US in 1973 associated with enrichment policies. The general speculative wave which swept through world commodity markets in this period was probably also an additional contributory factor to the Cartel's success.(39)

The Cartel appeared to halt its activities in 1976. Although prices remained above the $ 40 per pound level in 1978 and 1979, producers experienced a substantial erosion of real prices and, by 1981, the price of uranium had fallen to $ 25 per pound. This was the result of over-production, following the high prices of the early

1970s, and of reduced demand, stemming from the cancellation of reactor projects. Environmental factors and a tightening of the regulations surrounding nuclear energy associated with the Three Mile Island incident offer some explanation for the cancellations, although high interest charges were also important.(40)

The Uranium Cartel enjoyed success in meeting its pricing objectives thus only in the short-term. In the medium term, a range of influences, including the encouragement of new production following the period of high prices and government policy, served to reverse some of the gains made and to suggest that a repetition of the Cartel's earlier success would not easily be achieved.

7. Iron Ore

Trade in iron ore, described as the most useful and common of the metallic elements, evolved in response to rising post-War demand and to the discovery of high grade deposits in developing countries such as Brazil. Whereas only 17 per cent of iron ore production was traded internationally in 1950, in 1974 this proportion had risen to 55 per cent. Although the production of iron ore is well dispersed throughout the world, with the USSR by far the most important producer (accounting for 28.5 per cent of the total, for example, in 1977), its trade has been concentrated in a small number of countries. In addition to the USSR, Canada, Sweden, Australia and Brazil are all important exporters(41) and Japan, the US, the Federal Republic of Germany, Belgium and the UK are major importers.

World demand for iron ore is a derived demand depending mainly on that for steel, produced historically in developed countries such as the US, UK, Canada, France and Sweden.(42) Although intra-company trade forms an important method of procuring supplies, notably in the US, where it was reported to account for four-fifths of company requirements in 1977, the proportion of total trade conducted via this route has declined rapidly since the Second World War and iron ore is marketed also under short-term purchase agreements (notably in Western Europe) and under long-term contracts (notably in centrally planned countries). The variety of marketing arrangements, the comparative stability of iron ore prices (Chapter 1) and its low value-weight ratio distinguish iron ore from other metals which have been considered in this study.(43)

It was only with the growth of international trade in iron ore and the entry of a growing number of developing country producers that interest in the coordination of policy on iron ore production and trade flourished. In the period before the Second World War, in contrast, international steel concerns frequently produced their own iron ores.(44) The main stimulus to producer cooperation was the downward drift in prices from an annual peak of $ 15.1 per metric ton of Swedish ore in 1957 to a low point of $ 8.4 in 1968. This reflected the over-stimulation of iron ore exploitation in the 1950s in response to the rapid growth in demand in industrialised countries.

In the face of declining export receipts, a group of developing countries met in Caracas in 1968 to consider the formation of a producers' association with a view to securing 'fair and remunerative returns' from the mining, processing and marketing of iron ore. This and a subsequent meeting in 1969 brought no firm agreement and, with prices remaining very low, UNCTAD called an ad hoc meeting of producer and consumer interests in January 1970 to discuss the possibility of forming an international commodity agreement. However, no agreement was reached in the course of discussions and producers again reverted to the idea of forming their own association.(45)   After further meetings in 1973 and 1974, accordingly, an Association of Iron Ore Exporting Countries (AIEC) was established in 1975 with Algeria, Australia, Chile, India, Mauritania, Peru, Sierra Leone, Sweden, Tunisia and Venezuela as participants.   Canada remained outside the organisation on the grounds that it excluded consumer representations and Brazil refused to join due, reportedly, to ambitious expansion plans which depended on capital imported from the major consuming countries.(46)

The aims of AIEC coincided with those of several other of the cartels which have already been discussed.   Cooperation and the exchange of information to assist members to secure 'fair and remunerative returns' and to improve their export earnings and terms of trade were the guiding principles on which policy was to be based. AIEC also planned to encourage 'further processing of iron ore in member countries'.   However, the mechanisms specified were much more limited than those applied in the case of other raw material cartels.   Individual decisions by governments were to form the basis for action and policies on pricing, output, exports and stocks were not contemplated.   The association showed a realistic awareness, in sum, that economic action would be severely handicapped by its inadequate coverage - 33 per cent of world iron ore production, 51 per cent of world iron ore exports and 3.2 per cent of steel production in 1974 - and by the wide range of sources and types of ores available.(47)

It was a similar recognition of the problems involved in attempting to apply pricing policies to the complex world iron ore market and the lack of interest on the part of some developing country producers which led to the failure of discussions on iron ore under UNCTAD's Integrated Programme.   At the first meeting in 1977, AIEC rejected the concept of price stabilisation by buffer stock action.   Three further conferences on the same subject also ended without issue.   As a result, the question of an international agreement for iron ore was shelved owing to the inability of consumers and producers to establish that such an agreement would bring tangible benefits.(48)

One clear outcome of the formation of a producers' association for iron ore was the articulation by AIEC (mainly developing country) producers of doubts regarding the suitability of iron ore for international commodity agreement action as proposed under UNCTAD's Integrated Programme. Another was their realistic recognition that the many sources and the variety of types of iron ore made any cooperative production or pricing provisions very difficult to implement and potentially counter-productive in impact. A third result was that producers were forced to a certain extent to put their cards on the table. Brazil, for example, by failing to participate, made it clear to other producers that it would continue in its programme of iron ore expansion. By doing so, it may have deterred AIEC participants from attempting to adopt simplistic solutions to complex structural problems.

8. Conclusion

The examples of cartelisation examined in this chapter do not suggest that such arrangements were more successful than international commodity agreements in meeting their objectives. For those with pricing provisions, OPEC probably came closest to doing so, followed by the short-lived Uranium Cartel of the early 1970s, although in both instances the results were not sustained and unforeseen repercussions such as substitution and over-production were also experienced. In contrast, neither the mercury nor the copper cartels met with long-term success in their repeated attempts to raise prices before and after the Second World War; and the IBA cartel announced a minimum price to the US market only in 1977 when prices had already risen above the level set.

Slightly more success was achieved by cartels than by their international commodity agreement equivalents in respect of their broader structural goals. The action of OPEC, for example, substantially increased the control of producers over royalty levels. And the existence of OPEC and the IBA probably encouraged producers in their endeavours to increase national control over production. However, such actions were not without their costs. In the case of bauxite, for example, the increased royalties achieved in Jamaica probably encouraged the diversion of corporate investment elsewhere; and the greater insecurity of oil supplies and higher oil prices were instrumental in encouraging consumers to investigate alternative sources of energy, particularly after 1979. In addition, although producers increased their influence over the supplies of oil, copper and bauxite in the 1970s, multi-national companies remained for each of these three commodities the decisive influence in terms of marketing and distribution.

It seems fair to conclude that cartelisation or uni-lateral producer action were only realistic alternatives to international commodity agreements when the commodity in question was subject to several important conditions such as a relative high concentration of supply and relative inelasticity of demand - conditions which help to explain why minerals rather than agricultural commodities provided the outstanding examples of cartelisation. Even in cases when these conditions were met, the lack of consultative framework in general and the absence of consumer participation in particular may have limited the sustainability of such arrangements, particularly when policy goals were altered and allegiances wavered. Cartels, in sum, offered few instant cures to the problems facing the producers of primary commodities. Like international commodity agreements, they were forced to work within the constraints of prevailing market conditions.

Notes

1   Lamartine Yates, Commodity Control, Chapter IX and P. Odell, Oil and World Power: Background to the Oil Crisis (Penguin, Baltimore, 1974).

2   For examples see N. Jacoby, Multinational Oil (Macmillan, New York, 1974), A. Sampson, The Seven Sisters (Hodder & Stoughton, Sevenoaks, 1975), M.A. Adelman, The World Petroleum Market (Johns Hopkins University Press, Baltimore, 1972) and C. Tugendhat, Oil: the Biggest Business (Eyre and Spottiswoode, London, 1968).

3   International Atomic Energy Agency, Bulletin, vol. 13 (1973) and Y.S. Park, Oil Money and the World Economy (Wilton House Publications, London, 1976). In 1925, petroleum represented 13 per cent of world consumption of primary energy, coal 82 per cent, natural gas 3 per cent and hydro-electric power 2 per cent. The literature on price elasticities is copious. See, for example, M. Kennedy, 'An Economic Model of the World Oil Market', Bell Journal of Economics and Management Science (Autumn 1974), R.V. Mancke, 'The Long-Run Supply Curve of Crude Oil produced in the United States', Antitrust Bulletin (Winter 1970) and H.S. Houthakker, 'The World Price of Oil: A Medium-Term Analysis' (American Enterprise Institute for Public Policies Research, Washington, 1976).

4   See Tugendhat, Oil: the Biggest Business, pp. 99-104, Lamartine Yates, Commodity Control, Chapter IX and United Nations, International Cartels, Table 1.

5   A.A. Kubbah, OPEC: Past and Present (Petro-Economic Research Centre, Vienna, 1974), p. 13, Park, Oil Money and the World Economy, pp. 18-19 and Z. Mikdashi, The Community of Oil Exporting Countries: A Study in Governmental Cooperation (Cornell University Press, 1972).

6   Park, Oil Money and the World Economy and see Tugendhat, Oil: The Biggest Business, for the chronology.

7   Sampson, The Seven Sisters, p. 272.

8   Brown, The Political and Social Economy of Commodity Control, pp. 56-7.

9   See for example D.M.G. Dewbery, 'Oil Prices, Cartels and the Problem of Dynamic Inconsistency', Economic Journal, vol. 91 (September 1981), J. Cremer and M. Weitzman, 'OPEC and the monopoly price of world oil', European Economic Review, vol. 8 (1976) and M. Radetzki, 'The Potential for Monopolistic Commodity Pricing by Developing Countries', in G.K. Helleiner (ed.), A World Divided: the Less Developed Countries in the International Economy (Cambridge University Press, London, 1976).

10 Petroleum Intelligence Weekly, 12 April 1982. The price refers to light crude.

11 B.P. Bosworth and R.Z. Lawrence, Commodity Prices and the New Inflation (Brookings Institution, Washington, 1982).

12 See for example Financial Times, 25 January 1983, Ibid., 10 February 1983 and Ibid., 19 February 1983.

13 See, for example, World Bureau of Metal Statistics, World Metal Statistics (World Bureau of Metal Statistics, London, February 1982), p. 35. In 1980, world mine production amounted to 7,801,100 metric tons of which the US produced 1,168,300, the USSR 1,150,000, Chile 1,067,700, Canada 708,400, Zambia 595,800 and Zaire 459,700.

14 As R.F. Mikesell, The World Copper Industry (Johns Hopkins University Press, Baltimore, 1979) pointed out, however, the share of the four major mining companies (Kennecott, Newmont, Phelps Dodge and Rio Tinto-Zinc) declined markedly from 1947, when they accounted for about 60 per cent of world output, to 1974, when these

companies had a majority interest in less than 19 per cent of the mine output of the market economy countries.

15 Ibid., pp. 81-93 offers a clear account of the pricing systems for copper.

16 Good general accounts of the world copper industry include Sir Ronald Prain, Copper: the Anatomy of an Industry (Mining Journal Books Ltd, London, 1975) and Mikesell, The World Copper Industry. See also F.E. Banks, The World Copper Market: an Economic Analysis (Ballinger Publishing Co, Cambridge, Mass., 1974) and Charles Rivers Associates, Economic Analysis of the Copper Industry, Report to the Property Management and Disposal Service (General Services Administration, US, March 1980).

17 For an account of the Secrétan episode, see Prain, Copper: The Anatomy of an Industry, pp. 103-4.

18 Ibid., pp. 104-6 and Lamartine Yates, Commodity Control, Chapter VIII.

19 See, for example, Mikesell, The World Copper Industry, p. 104, Lamartine Yates, Commodity Control, Chapter VIII, Nappi, Commodity Market Controls, p. 33 and pp. 38-9 and O.C. Herfindahl, Copper Costs and Prices: 1870-1957 (Johns Hopkins University Press, Baltimore, 1959), Chapters 4-6, which provides a detailed history of US and world copper prices in the 1870 to 1957 period and the numerous collusive arrangements and government activities designed to control them.

20 Prain, Copper: The Anatomy of an Industry, pp. 107-8 and Eckbo, OPEC and the Experience of Previous International Commodity Cartels. A major problem was the recognition that boom conditions, such as those prevailing in 1966 stimulated by the Vietnam War, encouraged substitution.

21 Nappi, Commodity Market Controls, Chapter 7 and Prain, Copper: The Anatomy of an Industry, p. 251.

22 UNCTAD, Report of the Seventh Preparatory Meeting on Copper on its First and Second Parts (mimeo, UNCTAD, Geneva, 1980, TD/B/IPC/COPPER/19).

23 Brown, The Political and Social Economy of Commodity Control, Mikesell, The World Copper Industry (which offers an interesting analysis of the various forms that copper price stabilisation could take and the pros and cons of national versus international controls and producer-led controls as opposed to controls with producer and consumer participants) and Charles Rivers Associates, The Feasibility of Copper Price Stabilization Using a Buffer Stock and Supply Restrictions from 1953 to 1976 (UNCTAD, Geneva, November 1977, TD/B/IPC/COPPER/AC/E:42).

24 For a detailed and critical account of the negotiations under UNCTAD auspices, see Brown, The Political and Social Economy of Commodity Control, Chapter 6.

25 The percentage shares of mercury production accounted for by the major producers in 1937 and 1977 are shown below:

	1937	1977
Italy[a]	45.1	0.2
Spain	29.6	17.6
US	11.6	14.2
USSR	5.5	29.1
Czechoslovakia	n.a.	3.0
Algeria	n.a.	15.3
Mexico	n.a.	4.8
Turkey	n.a.	2.3
China	n.a.	10.0

Note: n.a.   denotes not available
         a   share distorted by production restraint

Source: League of Nations, Raw Materials and Foodstuffs, p. 19 and Commodity
         Research Bureau, Commodity Yearbook 1981, p. 219.

26   For prices in this period see Commodity Research Bureau, Commodity Yearbook 1981,
     p. 220, which quotes annual averages.

27   League of Nations, International Cartels, Table 1 and Hexner, International Cartels,
     pp. 232-33.

28   For the prices see Commodity Research Bureau, Commodity Yearbook 1981, pp. 219-
     21. Nappi, Commodity Market Controls, Chapter 10, also offers a useful account.

29   R.M. Auty, 'Transforming Mineral Enclaves: Caribbean Bauxite in the Nineteen-
     Seventies', Tijdschrift voor Economische en Sociale Geografie vol. lxxi, no. 3 (1980),
     pp. 170-72 and N. Girvan, The Caribbean Bauxite Industry (University of the West
     Indies, Jamaica, 1967). The aluminium industry was reported to have higher energy
     and capital costs, on balance, than close substitutes.

30   The aluminium cartels of this period attracted much interest. See, for example,
     D.H. Wallace, Market Control in the Aluminium Industry (Cambridge, Mass., 1937) and
     League of Nations, International Cartels, Table 1. Hexner, International Cartels, also
     offers a useful summary. The 1926 cartel introduced sales quotas for all markets
     outside the US, and in a revised form in 1931, with North American participants,
     established a company to administer the agreement; shares in the company were
     allocated according to the aluminium productive capacity of participants. Production
     quotas were also introduced and, in an unusual provision, the cartel was authorised to
     confiscate property without compensation if the production quotas were exceeded by
     more than 5 per cent a year. Surplus stocks were pooled and disposed of by the
     company at prices set by the cartel. The cartel was successful in gaining the active
     participation of three-fifths of world production of aluminium and of almost all
     exports: only Alcoa of the major companies remained outside it. The cartel also
     succeeded in reducing costs by cutting the number of middlemen and by lowering
     customs duties between participating countries. Although prices were rigidly set, the
     evidence suggests that they declined on average between 1931 and 1939 due in part to
     problems faced by the cartel in 1936 when the quota system was virtually abandoned.

31   Nappi, Commodity Market Controls, Chapter 8, Brown, The Political and Social
     Economy of Commodity Control, pp. 60-2, UNCTAD, Second Session, Report and
     Annexes, Annex I and International Bauxite Association, 'International Congress of
     Bauxite Producing Countries: Final Act of the Conference' (mimeo, Jamaica, 1974).

32   Nappi, Commodity Market Controls, pp. 136-37 and C.F. Bergsten, 'A New OPEC in
     Bauxite', Challenge, vol. 19, no. 3 (July-August 1976).

33   Nappi, Commodity Market Controls.

34   Financial Times, 16 December 1980, D.W. Woods, 'Current Price and Investment
     Trends in the World Aluminium Bauxite Market: their Effect on the US Economy', in
     Denoon (ed.), The New International Economic Order: a US Response and R.S. Pindyck,
     'Cartel Pricing and the Structure of World Bauxite Market', The Bell Journal of
     Economics, vol. 8, no. 2 (Autumn 1977).

35   Brown, The Political and Social Economy of Commodity Control, p. 62 reported that
     only Jamaica of major bauxite producers favoured talks on bauxite within the
     Integrated Programme in 1977.

36   For good general sources see M. Radetzki, Uranium: A Strategic Source of Energy
     (Croom Helm, London, 1981) and J.W. Griffith, The Uranium Industry, its History,
     Technology and Prospects (Canada, Department of Energy and Mines, Ottawa, 1967).

37 Radetzki, Uranium: A Strategic Source of Energy, Chapter 7. See also The Uranium
    Institute, The Balance of Supply and Demand 1978-1990 (The Uranium Institute,
    London, 1979).

38 Hexner, International Cartels, p. 237.

39 Radetzki, Uranium: A Strategic Source of Energy, pp. 116-21.

40 Commodity Research Bureau, Commodity Yearbook 1981, p. 358.   M.   Gillis and
    R.E. Beals, Tax Investment Policies for Hard Minerals (Ballinger Publishing Co.,
    Cambridge, Mass., 1980), pp. 225-41 noted the considerable uncertainty surrounding
    government policy on uranium in the 1970s.

41 UNCTAD, 'Consideration of International Measures on Iron Ore: Iron Ore: Features of
    the World Market' (mimeo, UNCTAD, Geneva, 1977, TD/B/IPC/IRON ORE/2), p. 18,
    Commodity Research Bureau, Commodity Yearbook 1981, p. 195 and G. Manners, The
    Changing World Market for Iron Ore, 1950-1980:   An Economic Geography (Johns
    Hopkins University Press, Baltimore, 1981).

42 UNCTAD, 'Consideration of International Measures on Iron Ore', pp. 4 and 18.

43 Ibid., p. 16 and pp. 19-20.

44 Hexner, International Cartels, pp. 203-5.

45 UNCTAD, International Action on Commodities in the Light of Recent Developments:
    Problems of the Iron Ore Market (UNCTAD, Geneva, 1969, TD/B/C.a.60), Ibid.,
    International Action on Commodities in the Light of Recent Developments: Problems
    of the World Market for Iron Ore (UNCTAD, Geneva, 1971, TD/B/C.1/104), Ibid.,
    Report of the Ad Hoc Meeting on Iron Ore held at the Palais des Nations Geneva from
    19 to 23 January 1970 (UNCTAD, Geneva, 1970, TD/B/C.1/75) and Ibid., Report on
    Consultations on Iron Ore held at the Palais des Nations, Geneva, 24 and 25 February
    1972 (UNCTAD, Geneva, 1972, TD/B/C.1/125).

46 IBRD, Commodity Trade and Price Trends, p. 108, Nappi, Commodity Market Controls,
    pp. 146-47 and Canada, Department of Energy, Mines and Resources, Iron Ore
    (Ministry of Supply and Services, Ottawa, 1976).

47 Canada, Department of Energy, Mines and Resources, Iron Ore.

48 Ibid., Chapter 9 and Brown, The Political and Social Economy of Commodity Control,
    pp. 202-5.

271

CONCLUSION AND APPRAISAL

> 'Would you tell me, please, which way I go from here?'
> 'That depends a good deal on where you want to get to.'

(Alice in Wonderland)

This study has sought to shed some light on the guiding principles, the frequency, the mechanics and the operation of international commodity control within the context of the changing world environment of trade and institutional developments. There remains the task of summarising the main conclusions, assessing the strengths and weaknesses of international commodity controls in the past and attempting to suggest their prospects for the future.

1. International Commodity Agreements

It is international commodity agreements rather than cartels which have formed the central object of this enquiry owing to their more open terms of reference, their recurrent role as an instrument of trade policy and the central position that they have occupied in UNCTAD's Integrated Programme. Before the Second World War, interest in such agreements sprang from the failure of cartelisation in the 1920s and the plummetting of raw material prices during the Depression; producers or their colonial authorities were the main moving forces. After the War, similarly, the impetus for controls came from producers rather than consumers in periods of low or falling prices although consumer interests were also represented on a regular basis. Only in a few cases, such as the 1962 Coffee Agreement, did consumers take the leading role in pressing for controls to be negotiated.

A range of common characteristics may be distinguished in commodities which have been covered by international commodity agreements. Key amongst them was that all but tin were agricultural in nature, and that of these, over half (rubber, coffee, cocoa, tea and olive oil) had comparatively long gestation periods. Secondly, trade in all but wheat and olive oil was led by developing rather than developed countries, although only sugar and coffee of these commodities attracted a high degree of dependency on the part of individual developing countries as a source of export earnings. Thirdly, the production of five of the commodities - tin, rubber, wheat, cocoa and olive oil - was concentrated in the hands of relatively few major producing countries. A characteristic common to four of the commodities ((natural) rubber, coffee, cocoa and tea) was that they could be produced only in tropical climates. Finally, the status of several of the commodities considered was challenged by synthetic substitutes (synthetic for natural rubber, artificial sweeteners for sugar) or by competing alternative goods (aluminium for tin, substitutes based on the shorea species, the carob and on natural oils for cocoa, corn syrup for sugar and other soft oils for olive oil).

The coincidence of these common characteristics was by no means fortuitous. Seasonal fluctuations in the supply of agricultural crops often contributed to sharp movements in prices and awakened interest in international controls. Similarly, long gestation periods complicated the planning of output and stimulated interest in measures to stabilise prices. The major role played by developing countries in formulating international commodity agreements is also understandable in view of the importance of such commodities in their export portfolios. The negotiation of agreements, likewise, was facilitated when production was concentrated in a small rather than a large number of countries and when producers faced strong competition from substitute or alternative goods. As noted in Chapter 1, the rank of the commodity in question in world trade, in contrast, was not an important factor in determining the incidence of international commodity agreements.

As the case-by-case analysis has shown, the impact of international commodity agreements varied markedly over time, from commodity to commodity and even for the same commodity. It is impractical, therefore, to seek neat conclusions regarding their operational success or failure. What follows, instead, is an appraisal of their strengths and weaknesses in meeting the common objectives set. (For conclusions relating to individual commodities, see Part III.)

The success or failure of the agreements in their most common objective, the balancing of the supply of the commodity with the demand for it, may be measured, broadly, in terms of their ability to avoid large surplus and deficit positions. The evidence suggests that few of the agreements exercised a strong positive influence in this regard. In the pre-Second World War period, the reduction of large stock levels under the 1933 Tin Agreement was due more to special factors, such as short supplies from Bolivia and the recovery in world demand, than to action taken under the Agreement. In the case of the 1934 Rubber Agreement, similarly, the upward phase in the business cycle was the main influence in enabling stock levels to be reduced sharply. Post-War experience suggests a similar trend. Under the 1968 Coffee Agreement, for example, it was special factors, notably variations in supplies from Brazil, rather than the operation of the Agreement, which permitted a substantial drawing down of stocks and brought the demand for and supply of coffee into better balance. Likewise, the substantial reduction of large stock levels under the 1962 Wheat Agreement resulted from weak supply conditions and a rising level of demand rather than to the salutary influence of the Agreement itself.

However, although the agreements did not exert, on average, a strong positive influence on stock positions, their influence does not appear either to have been a negative one. With the exception of the wheat agreements between 1949 and 1959 and the 1937 Tin Agreement, most worked towards reducing large surpluses and avoiding deficit positions. Mounting surpluses under the former fell outside the terms of reference of the agreements, which covered only a small proportion of world trade. In the case of the 1937 Tin Agreement, over-expansionary increases in quota allocations resulted from an over-estimate of the strength of demand.

The success or failure of the agreements in addressing their second recurrent policy goal, the stabilisation of prices, has already been considered indirectly in Chapter 1, together with the definitional and methodological problems involved in any such assessment. To recapitulate, the average level of price volatility for the commodities considered did not alter markedly between 1901 to 1951 and 1952 to 1972 although it increased sharply when the 1970s were included in the calculation. It is difficult to attribute causality, particularly in cases such as tin and wheat, when out-of-agreement periods are not available for comparison. It is interesting to note, however, that only the price of coffee of the commodities considered became very much less volatile between 1965 and 1981; in contrast, the price of tin, wheat, rubber and tea became more volatile and sugar stood out as the commodity with the most unstable prices on average during the periods covered, followed by cocoa, rubber and tin. The results obtained from an examination of real commodity prices for the sub-periods 1965 to 1972 and 1973 to 1981 are even less encouraging: whereas dollar prices in the two periods displayed no clear trend, real commodity prices, in contrast, showed a clear tendency to become more variable.

It is perhaps not reasonable, however, to judge the performance of the agreements against long-term trends since, on the one hand,

275

few operated without interruption for long periods and, on the other hand, goals were usually set in terms of keeping prices moving in a specified direction or within a given range in the short rather than long-term. Against these objectives, the agreements may be judged to have enjoyed a greater degree of success, although performances varied substantially from agreement to agreement and even within the life of the same agreement. During the course of the operation of the economic provisions of the 1954 Tin Agreement between 1956 and 1960, for example, the price of tin moved both above the ceiling (1956) and below the floor (1958). On average, however, prices remained within the target band established (which was raised in March 1957) despite a number of unpredictable influences, such as USSR sales of tin and US stockpile policy. Another interesting example is provided by the 1953 Sugar Agreement: prices remained within the specified price range for about half of the Agreement's duration despite a number of special factors pushing prices both above and below the target range.

Although only four of the agreements may be viewed as having met their pricing objectives on a consistent basis (the wheat agreements of 1949 to 1959), only eight (the 1960 and 1975 Tin Agreements, the 1933 Wheat Agreement, the 1967 Grains Arrangement, the 1958 and 1977 Sugar Agreements and the 1972 and 1975 Cocoa Agreements), conversely, may be deemed to have failed in this regard. In the case of the latter, unpredictable influences contributed to failure in several instances. The 1933 Wheat Agreement, for example, was thwarted by a bumper crop in Argentina, the 1958 Sugar Agreement by the dramatic shift in the pattern of world trade in sugar following the reduction by the US of Cuba's preferential quota and the 1972 Cocoa Agreement by unusually volatile international economic conditions.

It is difficult to gauge precisely the success of the agreements with regard to their third common policy goal, that of increasing the export earnings of producers (a goal included in the tin agreements from 1965, the coffee agreements, the sugar agreements, the cocoa agreements and the 1979 Rubber Agreement). The value of the export earnings of (developing) countries deriving from tin, coffee, sugar and cocoa all rose during the 1964 to 1979 period but by substantially less on average than the value of the total export earnings of developing countries. In real terms, the value of tin, coffee and cocoa exports also rose in the same period, whereas that of sugar exports fell, despite a rise in volume terms. Comparable figures are not yet available for the early 1980s. However, falls in the real prices of sugar, rubber, cocoa and tin and the weakness of industrial activity suggest strongly that the export earnings of developing countries from these sources fell rather than rose in the years to 1982.(1)

Although many of the international commodity agreements included the aim of increasing the consumption of, or trade in, the commodity to which they applied, only a few, the 1958, 1973 and 1977 Sugar Agreements, the coffee agreements, the cocoa agreements and the olive oil agreements, made specific provisions for promotional activities. None of the agreements achieved conspicuous success in raising the level of consumption of the commodity concerned. In the case of the olive oil agreements, for example, structural factors, such as wide fluctuations in supplies, contributed to the substitution of other soft oils for olive oil. Cocoa consumption, in contrast, was affected by factors beyond the agreements' control such as the growth in popularity of competing end-products. In each of the examples, the room for manoeuvre was limited by the scale of the resources available. In the case of the coffee agreements, it was also reported that funds had been mis-allocated to the North-American market where saturation points in coffee consumption had already been reached.

There is no clear example, finally, of action taken under the agreements in pursuit of non-economic goals such as the prevention or alleviation of unemployment, the fostering of reconstruction and development or the maintenance of fair labour standards. It seems to have been the hope that such goals would be realised as a result of the general increase in welfare stemming from the operation of the economic provisions of the agreements. At the beginning of the 1980s, however, there were few signs that such increases in welfare had been effected. On the contrary, sharp declines in farm income in North America, attributable in part to reduced levels of grain sales, and the structural surplus faced by olive oil producers suggested that the opposite was the case. In no instance, in sum, did the evidence point to an unambiguous link between the action taken under an agreement and the achievement of the non-economic goals considered in Part II.

If some explanation is sought for the failure of the agreements to fulfil their objectives on a consistent basis, the over-ambitious nature of the objectives must be the starting-point for any discussion. As outlined in Chapter 4, expectations tended to be great as to what such agreements could achieve, both in the short and the long term. The objectives included were often couched in such broad and ill-defined terms as to be meaningless in practice. And the non-economic aims were included more usually as gestures of intent than because it was thought that they might realistically be met.

A second factor which helps to explain their shortcomings was that the mechanisms incorporated in the agreements were limited in scope and geared towards the short rather than long-term time horizon. Many of the problems faced by primary commodity producers, in contrast, in developed and developing countries alike, were either structural in nature or arose from special factors outside

277

the relevant agreement's control. The agreements could do little, for example, to reverse structural problems such as the secular decline in the demand for a commodity resulting from technical innovation (the electrolytic process in the case of tin and tea bags in the case of tea), changes in preferences (the growing popularity of soft drinks in the beverages market and of animal oils instead of olive oil) or the development of viable alternative goods (aluminium for tin and synthetic for natural rubber). Responses such as the establishment of monitoring services by the international commodity organisation concerned (the tin and olive oil agreements), attempts to improve the quality of the product (the olive oil agreements) and the promotion of consumption by means of advertising (the coffee agreements), were essentially cosmetic measures which did little to address the fundamental questions involved.

Similarly, the agreements offered little in the way of relief to the problems associated with long gestation periods, such as a tendency to over-invest in periods of high prices. This was a recurrent problem in the agreements relating to tropical beverages, despite considerable variation in the mechanisms used. Their failure to deal resolutely with the structural problems involved was demonstrated most clearly in the case of coffee where the tendency for production to exceed demand was as much a problem in the early 1980s as it had been in 1906 when (national) controls were first introduced, this despite the increasing sophistication of the agreements and their provision of measures to increase consumption and to facilitate diversification away from coffee production.

The agreements could do little, likewise, to avoid pressures resulting from cyclical movements in world economic activity. The sensitivity of rubber and tin prices to movements in the business cycle, for example, contributed to the operational difficulties faced by the rubber and tin agreements, particularly during the 1930s. Similarly, the depth of the recession in the world economy at the beginning of the 1980s exercised such a dampening influence on the prices of a number of commodities that the standing and credibility of the agreements in operation were severely undermined.

It was not only the gearing of the mechanisms to short-term rather than to long-term goals which limited their operational ability; their narrow focus on pricing objectives was also a serious constraint. Examples are provided in the operation of the post-War tin and wheat agreements. In the case of the former, the main control mechanisms, the buffer stock and the export quota, were designed to fulfil pricing rather than other of the specified economic objectives and it was expected that the balancing of supply and demand, for example, would 'fall out' from the attainment of pricing goals. As outlined above, there are few examples of the positive influence of the agreements in this respect. In the case of the wheat agreements, the pricing commitments were related to specified quantities of wheat traded and no provision was made to control trade in wheat outside the terms of the agreements. The impact of both the post-War tin and wheat agreements on structural questions, accordingly, was minimal. It could even be argued that their focus on pricing objectives contributed to existing structural problems since in the case of tin the prices set in the agreements may have encouraged a move to use alternative, cheaper products and the operation of the wheat agreements during the 1950s, with the guarantee of a given volume of sales at a specified price, may have contributed to mounting wheat surpluses in North America.

Deficiencies in the mechanisms also handicapped the operation of the agreements. The assessment of export quotas, for instance, was often a major bone of contention between participants vying for limited market shares. Examples include the allocative problems of the tin agreements before 1945 (associated with the under-shooting by Bolivia of its export quota), the 1934 Rubber Agreement (which was strongly criticised for the alleged preferential treatment it accorded to European producers) and the 1962 Coffee Agreement (under which new African producers pressed for generous quota allotments). The competing claims of established and new producers in the tea industry, similarly, was a factor which contributed to the failure of negotiations for a new international agreement during the 1970s.

Secondly, the buffer stock was made redundant in several cases by a price range which bore little relation to market prices. Examples include the 1975 Cocoa Agreement and the 1979 Rubber Agreement. In other cases, notably the post-War tin agreements, the buffer stock was considered to have been too small to exercise a decisive influence on prices and equipped asymmetrically, with the supporting export quota, to protect the floor rather than the ceiling price. Overall, in sum, international stock policy does not emerge from this analysis as the effective instrument of trade policy suggested by the degree of international acceptability conferred upon it since the 1930s and its prominent role in UNCTAD's Integrated Programme.

Thirdly, the conferral of preference included in many of the agreements brought its own difficulties. In periods of short supply it was difficult to honour supply commitments owing to the administrative problems involved (the 1968 Sugar Agreement) or to the lead-time before new output could come on stream (the 1960 Tin Agreement). Conversely, in periods of ample supplies none of the agreements provided adequate policing of the commitments of consumers. In most cases, little provision was made for enforcement. In those which did contain such provisions, such as the 1962 Coffee Agreement, infringements were frequent owing to the inadequate powers of the international commodity organisation concerned. An example of the magnitude of the problems faced by the commodity

279

authorities was provided by the tea agreements, in which smuggling was an important element.

A further critical factor in the operation of the agreements was the extent to which they depended, necessarily, on judgement. This reliance extended from the drafting process - the establishment of an appropriate price range and buffer stock - to the allocation of quotas/preferences and the operation of the control mechanisms. Examples of errors in judgement are easy to highlight - the over-expansion in output sanctioned in the 1937 Tin Agreement, the ill-timed introduction of export controls in the 1965 Tin Agreement, the disregard for the build-up of large national stocks during the 1950s in the life of the 1953, 1956 and 1959 Wheat Agreements. It is less easy to identify how such errors might have been prevented. Even the most sophisticated of forecasters could not have been expected to predict accurately wide seasonal variations in output or factors such as the timing of sales of US stockpiled tin or USSR purchases of wheat. The most in such circumstances that an agreement could be expected to do was to adjust flexibly to changing market forces and to attempt to attenuate potentially destabilising influences.

The over-ambitious nature of the aims of the agreements, the gearing of their control mechanisms toward pricing rather than to other of the economic objectives, the technical deficiencies in their mechanisms and the reliance they placed on judgement for their administration offer only part of the explanation for their overall lack of success in meeting their economic goals. Of at least as much if not more importance were the policies pursued by individual countries and trading blocs in respect of commodity trade which meant that the administrators of the agreements were often faced with the difficult task of reconciling widely divergent interests or of dealing with unpredictable influences outside their authority.

The US offers the most conspicuous example of a country whose policies were a critical-influence in this regard. In the case of tin, for example, the building up of the strategic stockpile after the Second World War encouraged over-production; and subsequent sales of tin from the stockpile generated speculative uncertainty. In the case of wheat, domestic policy led to mounting surpluses during the 1950s, a move to bi-lateral sales from the 1960s and the embargo on sales to the USSR in 1980. Each of these influences fell outside the terms of reference of the agreement in question and tended to work counter to its aims.

There are several other examples of the negative impact of US policy on the operation of international commodity agreements: these include the case of sugar (the change in policy toward Cuba and the protection of domestic sugar production) and cocoa (the failure of the US to accede to the 1980 Cocoa Agreement). Examples of its positive influence are less easy to identify. Although the US took on the burden of stock withdrawal of wheat during the 1950s, for instance, and led negotiations for the 1962 Coffee Agreement, these actions were something of a mixed blessing, the former because the US did nothing to address the root of the problem, namely domestic over-production, and the latter because US initiatives sprang from political rather than economic motives and may have encouraged subsequent over-production.

Although the US offers the clearest example of the way in which policy adopted at the national level could bear on international controls, it was by no means unique in this respect. Further important countervailing forces were provided by the EEC and the USSR. In the case of the former, the increasingly prominent role played by the EEC in world trade in primary commodities has been a repeated theme of this study. In terms of the commodities which were the object of international commodity agreements, the countervailing influence of the EEC was felt most strongly in respect of the subsidising of wheat and sugar production under the CAP and the EEC's failure to participate in the 1968 and 1977 Sugar Agreements. In the case of the latter, the periodic entry of the USSR into the international commodity markets as a major purchaser (of wheat, for example, in 1972/73) or exporter (of tin, for example, in the late 1950s) was another strong and unpredictable influence which seriously weakened the ability of the agreements to achieve their specified objectives.

Mention should be made, finally, of the important role played by many other countries in respect of individual agreements. These are too numerous to itemise separately and have already been considered in Part III of this study. It is sufficient to note here that in general it was the unsupportive policies of individual countries and country groups rather than their failure to participate which militated most against the successful operation of the agreements. The inclusion in the 1975 Tin Agreement of the US and the USSR as leading consumers, for example, seemed to reduce rather than to increase the Agreement's operational efficiency by adding further complicating elements. Although the absence of major producers or consumers could on occasion undermine the credibility of an agreement, this was by no means necessarily the case.

From the early 1970s, finally, it is possible to point to a wider malaise in attempting to explain the failure to re-negotiate economic provisions for the wheat agreements, the lull in the economic provisions of the sugar agreements between 1973 and 1977, the move toward uni-lateral action by tin producers, the teething problems faced by the 1979 Rubber Agreement, the range of difficulties experienced by the coffee agreements and, finally, the poor performance of the cocoa agreements. These broader influences, which included the increased instability of the international financial and economic system and a greater concern by policy makers to reduce inflationary pressures, at once heightened interest in international commodity controls whilst, paradoxically, lessening substantially their chances of success.

2. Raw Material Cartels

Raw material cartels were more numerous, more frequent and broader in their commodity coverage than international commodity agreements, with some overlap of commodities to which both applied. In the inter-War period, the aims of and mechanisms employed by cartels closely resembled those of international commodity agreements with the main focus on stabilising rather than on raising prices. After the Second World War, the similarities became far less pronounced since cartels relied largely on exclusive producer rather than on producer and consumer participation, aimed more frequently to raise rather than simply to stabilise prices and addressed a wider range of structural issues than their international commodity agreement counterparts. However, cartelisation was used instead of international commodity agreements in their absence - both when negotiations to formulate agreements failed to bear fruit (such as those for tea in 1968), and when agreements broke down (the 1975 Cocoa Agreement) - and also to supplement their action (the Geneva and Otras Suaves Coffee Agreements). To be effective cartels required a high concentration of production, relatively inelastic demand for the commodity in question and a cost advantage over outside sources. This combination of factors helps to explain why minerals rather than agricultural products have provided the outstanding examples of cartel action. Although producers of agricultural commodities have reverted to cartelisation when it appeared to them that the international agreement in operation did not represent their interests to the full, such action has not provided a sustainable alternative in view of the possibility of increased production from other sources.

Any consideration of the cartel as an alternative to international commodity agreements might do well to recall their association with the restriction rather than the expansion of world trade. At the 1927 World Economic Conference, for example, a comprehensive network of international cartels was proposed to replace tariffs. The proposal was not adopted on account of the perceived undesirable effects of cartelisation -high prices, restricted output and exploitation of the consumer - and the difficulty of supervision. The same points apply equally in the 1980s. The benefits to the producer resulting from cartel action must also be questioned from the examples considered in this study. Even OPEC, considered generally to have been the most successful of cartels in this regard, enjoyed only limited and unsustained success in meeting its pricing objectives. The hidden costs, such as the search for substitutes, the disaffection of consumers and the search for more secure sources of supply, emerged only with the passage of time.

APPRAISAL

Perhaps the clearest point to emerge from an examination of past experience with international commodity controls is that they did not operate in a vacuum. Each depended on supporting measures at the national level; and each, correspondingly, could be rendered ineffective by countervailing national measures. Similarly, international controls could not immunise their participants from changes in business conditions - a sharp downturn in output, for example, often awakened interest in the formulation of controls whilst simultaneously lessening their chances of success. Thirdly, speculative flows, associated with special factors such as strategic requirements (the Korean War boom) or exchange rate instability (the breakdown of the Bretton Woods system of fixed exchange rates in 1970) fell outside the influence of international commodity control measures.

A second conclusion is that international commodity controls were as effective or as ineffective as their mechanisms and participants. Thus, the olive oil agreements, which aimed to reduce fluctuations in supplies but provided no mechanisms for doing so were doomed to failure in this regard. Similarly, the detailed technical specifications of the 1977 Sugar Agreement were brought to nothing by the failure of the EEC, an increasingly important exporter, to adhere to its provisions. Although there was scope, then, for an improvement in the mechanisms used, this would have been of little avail in the absence of political support for the agreement in question. Strong support, conversely, would have counted for little in the absence of effective control mechanisms.(2)

International controls, in sum, whether in the form of international commodity agreements or cartels, worked best when based on a realistic appraisal of current operating conditions, when provided with mechanisms enabling flexible responses to changes in such conditions, when they secured adequate levels of support of both producers and consumers and when they limited their objectives to goals which were non-structural in nature. It is worth noting also that the definition of 'adequate' levels of support could vary markedly from agreement to agreement, but that, in this context, international commodity agreements, with consumer participation, offered an advantage over cartels. In the case of both, the effectiveness of the control measures depended also on the judgement and sensitivity of their administrators.

Given past experience, then, what are the prospects for the operation of international commodity controls in the future?

The long-standing nature of problems in primary commodity trade and the recurrence of attempts to seek their solution suggests that the history of international commodity control will not end in the early 1980s. International commodity agreements rather than cartels are likely to continue to be sanctioned as instruments of trade policy on account of their more open and consultative nature, although cartels will probably continue to exert a strong appeal to producers when international commodity agreements break down. However, the viability of international commodity agreements as a development tool designed to raise the export earnings of developing countries must be strongly questioned. On the one hand, it is difficult to assert with any certainty that such agreements led in the past to more stable, still less higher prices than would otherwise have been the case. On the other, higher prices did not necessarily lead to higher export earnings for the commodity in question. In cases where they did (such as for crude petroleum), higher export earnings for one developing country often meant a higher import bill for another. On balance, past experience suggests that the performance of international commodity agreements has been too unreliable and their distributive effects too uneven to secure the development goals they have been set.

The recognition of the shortcomings of international commodity agreements has led to a growing disenchantment with them on the part of primary producers in recent years. A key example is offered by Malaysia, the leading world exporter of rubber, tin, palm oil and tropical timber of the commodities included in UNCTAD's Integrated Programme. Disillusionment with the operation of the 1979 Rubber Agreement and the 1980 Tin Agreement led Malaysia, formerly a strong advocate, to question the value of the Common Fund and to consider seriously taking uni-lateral producer action in support of tin and rubber prices.

A parallel lack of enthusiasm with international commodity agreements was reflected in the slow progress in the negotiation of new agreements under UNCTAD's Integrated Programme. Of the eighteen commodities included, only six, tin, sugar, rubber, coffee, cocoa and jute, were covered by such agreements in early 1983. Of these, the 1977 Sugar Agreement was recognised as a failure (largely due to the stance of EEC policy on sugar), the Rubber and Cocoa Agreements had enjoyed little clear success, the long-standing Tin Agreement was being threatened by uni-lateral producer action and the Jute Agreement, which lacked economic provisions, had yet to be tested. Of the remainder, only vegetable oils were covered by an international commodity agreement, and then to a very limited extent (by the Olive Oil Agreement, which lacked economic provisions).

The prospects for the successful completion of international commodity agreements for the other eleven commodities in the Integrated Programme seem bleak despite a considerable volume of research and discussion. The hurdles are of various shapes and forms. In the case of some, such as iron ore, hard fibres, bauxite and phosphates, lack of interest on the part of some developing countries appears to have been a major stumbling block. In the case of others, such as cotton and copper, the lack of developed country interest has posed a major obstacle. Some negotiations, such as those for iron ore and tea, foundered on the question of the appropriate mechanism; whilst, in the case of others, such as hard fibres, some participants were reported to favour an agreement without economic provisions. For several, including cotton, iron ore and manganese, the very complexity of the commodity market concerned made the negotiation of an agreement extremely difficult.

Although there will probably continue to be a role for international commodity agreements as an important instrument of trade policy, it is unlikely, therefore, to be the central price stabilising and raising role envisaged under UNCTAD's Integrated Programme nor based necessarily on the buffer stock mechanism. Instead, other strands of the Integrated Programme, such as research and development, improved marketing and more flexible compensatory financing provisions, are likely to occupy a more prominent position. Examples of this trend are already available. Negotiations under the auspices of UNCTAD on bananas, for example, reached agreement on cost-cutting and promotional activities whereas, in contrast, price stabilisation measures have not yet been brought to fruition. Proposed measures for meat, similarly, centred on research and marketing, with a view to enhancing the development of livestock rearing and meat production in developing countries rather than on the conventional international commodity agreement model. And discussions on tropical timber, likewise, reached agreement on plans to increase investment in developing countries, to create a market research and intelligence system and for co-operation between producers and consumers to facilitate long-term planning whereas plans to establish an international commodity agreement have yet to bear fruit.

It is worth pointing out that such functions as these have been carried out under international commodity agreements in the past and, indeed, represent some of their most positive achievements. Examples are plentiful. Most of the agreements established international commodity organisations which exercised an important influence in stream-lining the collection of statistics and other data concerning the commodity in question. The watching briefs they held on market conditions and trends probably served also to assist in the assessment of current problems and, in some cases, to highlight potential problem areas. The Olive Oil Council, by standardising the quality of the product and improving its labelling, contributed positively to an improvement in its marketability. Perhaps most important of all, however, was the role played by the international commodity organisations in acting both as channels of communication and as consultative fora. The net benefits deriving from this function are unquantifiable. However, in providing a means by which different

285

views could be presented, the way was opened in some instances for reconciliation and in others, at least a public airing of the main points of discord.

A further positive aspect of international commodity agreements which seems likely to be carried forward in the future was the special function of the wheat agreements after 1967 in acting as a channel for a steady stream of 'special' exports of wheat. Although variable in quantity and, in the minds of some commentators, insufficient to meet the needs concerned, such an innovation was a move forward in the complex international wheat trade. It may well be that the value of the machinery set up will prove itself even more fully at some future date.

To sum up, past experience suggests that the strengths of international commodity agreements lie in their broader functions of data collection and dissemination, research, quality control and, above all, in providing a framework for communication and discussion rather than in the economic functions on which such great emphasis has been laid in recurrent trade negotiations, even though, on occasion, agreements have achieved some success with regard to the latter. This is likely to continue to be the case in the future, particularly if the main problems facing primary commodity producers remain similar to those outlined in Chapter 1. It is these broader functions which have distinguished international commodity agreements from cartel action and which have rendered them more acceptable as policy instruments. This is also likely to be a feature of future developments.

There are many ways, however, in which it would be possible to build on existing strengths. Although this subject merits a study in its own right, three key areas emerge from this analysis as worthy of further investigation and may be mentioned here briefly. The first, in the spirit of UNCTAD, would be for a more integrated approach between international commodity organisations, the IMF and the IBRD for policy concerning the same commodities, for commodities covering similar markets (such as tropical beverages) or competing for similar land use (such as rice and jute). Such an approach could be applied at many levels including data collection and dissemination, promotion and the allocation of development finance. A directory of investment in primary commodity projects, for example, might be of value to individual producer and institutional investor alike. It is interesting to note in this context that UNCTAD was pressing in 1983 for a new programme of loans from the IBRD to encourage structural adjustments, including diversification.

A second way in which international commodity agreements might be further refined would be if they took specific account of domestic measures, whether supporting or countervailing, instead of leaving them to the auspices of GATT. The importance of regional and national controls has been a recurrent theme in this study. And

286

yet, as outlined in Part I, they have tended to be treated as separate entities instead of different sides of the same coin. In the case of tariff concessions, agricultural goods, which have formed the major object of international commodity controls, have not been covered by GATT. It would be naïve to expect that farm policy could be radically altered by action taken under the terms of an international commodity agreement. And yet, if international commodity agreements included some coverage and appraisal of domestic measures, inconsistencies in approach would be revealed and the implications of non-adherence by certain countries would clearly be demonstrated.

Finally, international commodity agreements might benefit from a shift in emphasis away from narrow economic and, specifically, pricing provisions toward a wider range of functions. There is no obvious reason, for instance, why international commodity organisations should not be authorised to take more active part in other strands of the Integrated Programme such as improved research, development and marketing. Similarly, such institutions would be well placed to assess the viability of new projects, particularly if these might conflict with the objectives of an existing international commodity agreement. Whilst such organisations would not necessarily bring solutions to problems of a structural nature, by careful monitoring and assessment, they might exercise a valuable function in contributing to avoiding their exacerbation in the future.

Notes

1   The export earnings calculations are derived from IBRD, <u>Commodity Trade and Price Trends</u>, Tables 7 and 8.

2   For a pioneering study of a means of improving the mechanisms used, by allocating quotas on the basis of export earnings rather than in terms of volumes, see L. de Silva, 'International Commodity Trade: A Scheme for Export Earnings Entitlements', <u>Verfassung und Recht in Ubersee</u>, vol. 14 (1981). The relative merits of the economic mechanisms of the agreements is discussed in an interesting recent study, A. Maizels, <u>Selected Issues in the Negotiations of International Commodity Agreements: An Economic Analysis</u>.

APPENDIX : INTERNATIONAL COMMODITY AGREEMENTS : A SUMMARY OF KEY FEATURES

(For full sources for this Appendix, see the Bibliography, Section I.)

1. INTERNATIONAL TIN AGREEMENTS

Date/Year	Duration (years)	Administrative Body	Aims
28.2.31	2	an international committee	to balance supply and demand; to stabilise prices
27.10.33	3	International Tin Committee	as in 1931; also to absorb surplus stocks
5.1.37	4	International Tin Committee with invited consumer representation	to balance supply and demand; to stabilise prices; and to maintain reasonable stocks
9.9.42	5	"	"
1.3.54	5	International Tin Council	to prevent unemployment; to stabilise supply, demand and prices; to promote 'more economic' production; and to ensure fair labour standards
24.6.60	5	"	"
14.4.65	5	"	to stabilise demand, supply and prices; to ensure fair labour standards; to help to maintain and increase export earnings from tin, especially from developing countries; to prevent unemployment; and to review the disposal of non-commercial stocks
1970	5	"	to stabilise supply, demand and prices; to ensure fair labour standards; to increase export earnings from tin; to accelerate economic development; to prevent unemployment; and to review the disposal of non-commercial stocks
21.6.75	5	"	as in 1970; also to encourage 'wider participation' in processing
26.6.80	5	"	"

289

TIN (cont'd)

Date/Year	Production Quotas	MECHANISMS		Price Range Specified	OTHER FEATURES
		Export Quotas	Stocks		
28.2.31	✓	✓	-	-	proposed research to stimulate consumption
27.10.33	✓	✓	-	-	required national legislation to be passed in support; proposed research to stimulate consumption; buffer stock established as an adjunct in 1934; research scheme formalised in 1938
5.1.37	✓	✓	maximum: 25% of production quota	-	-
9.9.42	✓	✓	"	-	-
1.3.54	-	✓	buffer stock of 25,000 tons; national stocks limited to 25% of permitted exports	£640 - £880 per ton	-
24.6.60	-	✓	buffer stock of 20,000 tons; national stocks limited to 25% of permitted exports	£730 - £880 per ton	-
14.4.65	-	✓	"	that in force at end of 1960 Tin Agreement	-

TIN

Date/Year	Production Quotas	MECHANISMS Export Quotas	Stocks	Price Range Specified	OTHER FEATURES
1970	-	✓	buffer stock of 20,000 metric tons; national stocks specified	that in force at end of 1965 Tin Agreement	provided that a country disposing of tin from a non-commercial stockpile should consult the Council
21.6.75	-	✓	buffer stock of 20,000 metric tons; national stocks specified	that in force at end of 1970 Tin Agreement specified in currency of Council's choice	"
26.6.80	-	✓	buffer stock of 30,000 metric tons; national stocks specified	that in force at end of 1975 Tin Agreement	"

2. INTERNATIONAL WHEAT AGREEMENTS

Date/Year	Duration (years)	Administrative Body	Aims
25.8.33	2	Wheat Advisory Committee	to balance supply and demand; to eliminate abnormal surpluses; and to bring about a rise in and a stabilisation of prices
1.9.49	4	International Wheat Council	to assure supplies and markets at equitable and stable prices
13.4.53	3	"	"
1956	3	"	"
1959	3	"	as in 1956; also to promote the expansion of trade in wheat and the freest flow of such trade and to encourage the consumption of wheat in order to improve health and nutrition
1962	3	"	"
1967	4	"	as in 1962; also to carry out a programme of food aid
1971	3	"	as in 1967; also to provide a framework for the negotiation of provisions relating to the price of wheat

292

WHEAT (cont'd)

Date/Year	Quotas	Exports Guaranteed Sales	Recording of Transactions	MECHANISMS Provision of Special or Concessionary Transactions	Imports: Guaranteed Purchases	Price Range Specified	Stocks	OTHER FEATURES
25.8.33	✓	-	-	-	-	-	-	favoured lower tariffs on wheat
1949	-	✓	✓	-	✓	minimum and maximum prices specified	'adequate' stocks to be maintained	multi-lateral contract
13.4.53	-	✓	✓	-	✓	"	"	"
1956	-	✓	✓	-	✓	"	"	"
1959	-	✓	✓	✓	✓	"	-	"
1962	-	✓	✓	✓	✓	"	-	"
1967	-	✓	✓	✓ Food Aid Convention attached	✓	"	-	"
1971	-	-	-	✓ Food Aid Convention attached	-	-	-	no economic provisions

3. INTERNATIONAL SUGAR AGREEMENTS

Date/Year	Duration (years)	Administrative Body	Aims
6.5.37	5	International Sugar Council	to assure adequate supplies at reasonable prices including 'a reasonable profit of efficient producers'; and to promote sugar consumption
October 1953	5	"	to balance supply and demand at equitable and stable prices; to increase consumption; to maintain the purchasing power of areas dependent on sugar production or exports; and to maintain fair labour standards
1.12.58	5	"	"
December 1968	5	International Sugar Organization	to increase trade in sugar and the export earnings of developing countries deriving from sugar; to stabilise prices so as not to encourage the expansion of production in developed countries; to increase consumption; to stabilise supply and demand; to increase access to the markets of developed countries; to monitor developments in substitutes; and to foster fair labour standards
7.5.73	2	"	"
7.10.77	5	"	"

SUGAR (cont'd)

Date/Year	Production Quotas	Export Quotas	MECHANISMS Measures concerning Imports	Price Range Specified	Stocks	OTHER FEATURES General	Promotion Committee
6.5.37	production restraint implied and specified for UK	✓	major importers agreed to maintain 1937 import levels	(prevention of large price rises an aim)	limited to 25% of annual production levels	-	-
October 1953	general commitment to adjust production so as not to exceed domestic and external requirements	✓	limited from non-participants	✓	maximum of 20% of annual production levels; minimum of 10% of export quota	participants required to notify the Council of grants or subsidies on sugar	-
1.12.58	"	✓	"	✓	maximum of 20% of annual production; minimum of 12% of export quota	"	-
December 1968	not specified	✓ Certificates of origin also permissible	"	✓	maximum of 20% of annual production; minimum of 10% of exports for developing countries, 15% for developed countries	-	✓

SUGAR (cont'd)

Date/Year	Production Quotas	Export Quotas	MECHANISMS Measures concerning Imports	Price Range Specified	Stocks	OTHER FEATURES General	Promotion Committee
7.5.73	-	-	-	-	-	International Sugar Council to prepare a new international sugar agreement with economic provisions	✓
1977	-	✓	limited from non-participants	✓	'special stocks' introduced up to 2.5 million metric tons; maximum national stocks set at 20% of production in previous years; a Stock Financing Fund also provided	-	✓

4. INTERNATIONAL RUBBER AGREEMENTS

Date/Year	Duration (years)	Administrative Body	Aims
7.5.34	4	International Rubber Regulation Committee	to stabilise supply and demand; to maintain fair prices; and to reduce world stocks
1979	5	International Natural Rubber Organization	to balance supply and demand; to alleviate surpluses and shortages; to stabilise prices from natural rubber; to stabilise and to increase export earnings; to accelerate economic growth; to improve market access for natural rubber and increase its competitiveness; to facilitate promotion; to maintain fair labour standards; and to encourage the 'efficient development' of the natural rubber economy

| Date/Year | MECHANISMS | | | Price Range Specified | Stocks |
	Production Restraint	Exports Quotas	Certificate of Origin	Imports limited from non-members		
7.5.34	✓	✓	✓	✓	-	maximum, 20% of annual production; minimum, 12½% of export quota
1979	-	-	-	-	range specified	nationally held buffer stock of 550,000 metric tons

297

5. INTERNATIONAL COFFEE AGREEMENTS

Date/Year	Duration (years)	Administrative Body	Aims
September 1962	5	International Coffee Organization	to balance supply and demand; to stabilise prices; to alleviate burdensome surpluses; to promote employment in member countries; to foster fair labour standards; to increase the purchasing power of exporters; and to encourage consumption
1968	5	"	"
1976	6	"	as in 1968 except for the clause relating to surpluses

	MECHANISMS						OTHER FEATURES	
Date/Year	Production Controls	Exports Quotas	Recording of Transactions	Measures concerning Imports	Stocks	Price Range Specified	Promotion Committee	Diversification Fund
September 1962	general commitment to adjust output to meet objectives of the agreement; production goals to be set	✓	certificates of origin and re-export	limited from non-member sources	policy not specified	(lower limit only)	✓	- (but established in 1966)
1968	"	✓	"	"	-	"	✓	✓
1976	✓	✓	"	"	-	to be specified	✓	-

6. INTERNATIONAL COCOA AGREEMENTS

Date/Year	Duration (years)	Administrative Body	Aims
20.10.72	3	International Cocoa Organization	to balance supply and demand; to prevent excessive price fluctuations; to stabilise and to increase export earnings for producers; to accelerate economic growth; and to facilitate the expansion of consumption
10.11.75	3	"	as in 1972; also to raise labour standards
27.10.80	3	"	"

| | MECHANISMS | | | | | OTHER FEATURES | |
Date/Year	Measures concerning Production	Exports Quotas	Certificate of Origin	Measures concerning Imports	Price Range Specified	Stocks	Promotion Committee
20.10.72	✓	✓	✓	✓	✓	buffer stock of a maximum of 250,000 metric tons	optional
10.11.75	✓	✓	✓	✓	✓	"	optional
27.10.80	✓	-	✓	✓	✓	"	optional

7. INTERNATIONAL TEA AGREEMENTS

Date/Year	Duration (years)	Administrative Body	Aims
9.2.33	5	International Tea Committee	to balance supply and demand; and to recommend methods of increasing consumption
25.8.38	5	"	"
1948 (Interim Agreement)	2	"	"
1950	5	"	"

Date/Year	Production Restraint	MECHANISMS Exports Quotas	Licences	OTHER FEATURES
9.2.33	✓	✓	✓	No pricing provisions
25.8.38	✓	✓	✓	"
1948 (Interim Agreement)	✓	✓	✓	"
1950	✓	✓	✓	"

8. INTERNATIONAL OLIVE OIL AGREEMENTS

Date/Year	Duration (years)	Administrative Body	Aims
1956	5	Olive Oil Council	to ensure fair competition among countries producing and exporting olive oil; to reduce fluctuating supplies; and to maintain fair labour standards
June 1963	4	"	to ensure fair competition; to extend the production and consumption of and international trade in olive oil; and to reduce supply fluctuations
March 1979	n/a	"	to increase consumption and to improve processing methods

MECHANISMS

Date/Year	Certificate of Origin	OTHER FEATURES Promotion	Other
1956	✓	Publicity Fund	Olive Oil Council briefed to standardise grading and labelling
June 1963	✓	"	"
March 1979	n/a	"	as in 1963; fund also established to improve production and processing methods

BIBLIOGRAPHY

The Bibliography is limited to those publications to which reference is made in the text. It excludes references to newspaper articles and weekly journals.

I.   PRIMARY SOURCES

1.   International Commodity Agreements

a.   Agreements to 1943

The agreements to 1943 were published in a useful compendium, International Labour Office, Intergovernmental Commodity Agreements (International Labour Office, Montreal, 1943), as follows:

Tin

'Agreement on the International Tin Control Scheme' (28 February 1931), pp. 73-5.

'Agreement for the International Tin Control Scheme' (27 October 1933), pp. 75-9.

'Agreement for the Tin Buffer Stock Scheme' (10 July 1934), pp. 80-1.

'Agreement on the International Tin Control Scheme' (5 January 1937), pp. 81-6.

'Agreement on the Tin Buffer Stock Scheme' (20 June 1938), pp. 90-4.

'Agreement for the International Control of the Production and Export of Tin' (9 September 1942), pp. 95-103.

Wheat

'Final Act of the Conference of Wheat Exporting and Importing Countries' (25 August 1933), pp. 1-6.

'Memorandum of Agreement concerning Draft Wheat Convention' (22 April 1942) and 'Draft Convention' (22 April 1942), pp. 10-25.

Sugar

'Agreement concerning the Regulation of Production and Marketing of Sugar' (6 May 1937), pp. 26-43.

'Protocol to enforce and to prolong after August 31, 1942, the International Agreement regarding the Regulation of Production and Marketing of Sugar' (22 July 1942), pp. 45-6.

Rubber

'Agreement for the Regulation of Production and Export of Rubber' (7 May 1934), pp. 104-13.

'Annex II. Revised Text of the Agreement of 7 May 1934', pp. 118-31.

Tea

'The International Tea Agreement 1933-1938' (9 February 1933), pp. 47-51.

'The International Tea Agreement 1938-1943' (25 August 1938), pp. 52-8.

b.   Agreements since 1943

There is no single source for the agreements since 1943.   The following have been used in the course of this study:

Tin

'International Tin Agreement, 1953' in United Nations Tin Conference 1950 and 1953: Summary of Proceedings (United Nations, New York, 1954 II.D.4).

'Second International Tin Agreement' (HMSO, London, 1961, Cmnd. 1332).

'Third International Tin Agreement' in United Nations Tin Conference, 1965: Summary of Proceedings (United Nations, New York, 1965, II.D.2), pp. 29-48.

'Fourth International Tin Agreement' (HMSO, London, 1970, Cmnd. 4493).

'The Fifth International Tin Agreement' (International Tin Council, London, 1976).

'Sixth International Tin Agreement' (UNCTAD, Geneva, 1981, TD/TIN.6/14).

Wheat

'International Wheat Agreement, Washington, 6 March 1948', _International Journal of Agrarian Affairs_, vol. I, no. 3 (September 1949).

'International Wheat Agreement' (US, Department of State, Washington, 1949).

'Agreement Revising and Renewing the International Wheat Agreement' (Washington, 1953).

'International Wheat Agreement, 1956' (International Wheat Council copy, no date or place reference).

'International Wheat Agreement and Rules of Procedure' (HMSO, London, 1960, Cmnd. 1074).

'International Wheat Agreement, 1962' (HMSO, London, 1962, Cmnd. 1709).

'International Grains Arrangement 1967' (International Wheat Council, London, 1968).

'International Wheat Agreement, 1971 incorporating the Wheat Trade Convention and the Food Aid Convention' (HMSO, London, 1971, Cmnd. 4643).

Sugar

'International Agreement for the Regulation of the Production and Marketing of Sugar (1953)' (HMSO, London, 1956, Cmd. 9004).

'International Sugar Agreement of 1958' (US, Department of State, Washington, 1958).

'International Sugar Agreement' (HMSO, London, 1969, Cmnd. 3887).

'Text of the International Sugar Agreement, 1973' (mimeo, UNCTAD, Geneva, 1973, TD/SUGAR.8/4).

'International Sugar Agreement, 1977' in _United Nations Sugar Conference 1977_ (United Nations, New York, 1978, TD/SUGAR.9/12).

Rubber

'International Natural Rubber Agreement, 1979' (United Nations, New York, 1980, TD/RUBBER/15/Rev.1).

Coffee

'International Coffee Agreement, 1962' (US, Department of State, Washington, 1962).

'International Coffee Agreement, 1968' (International Coffee Organization, London, 1968).

'International Coffee Agreement 1976' (HMSO, London, 1976, Cmnd. 6505).

Cocoa

'International Cocoa Agreement, 1972' in United Nations, International Cocoa Conference, 1972 (United Nations, New York, 1973, TD/COCOA.3/9).

'International Cocoa Agreement, 1975' (HMSO, London, 1976, Cmnd. 6448).

'International Cocoa Agreement, 1980' (UNCTAD, Geneva, 1980 TD/COCOA.6/7).

Tea

The key features of successive agreements on tea between 1943 and 1950 were reported in the International Tea Committee's Bulletin of Statistics.

For the tea producers' arrangement, see 'Report of the Meeting of Tea Exporting Countries' (Mauritius, 1969).

Olive Oil

'Draft Intergovernmental Agreement prepared by the Working Party on Olive Oil' in United Nations, Food and Agriculture Organization, The Stabilization of the Olive Oil Market (United Nations, Food and Agriculture Organization, Rome, 1955).

'International Agreement on Olive Oil' (modified by the Protocol of 3 April 1958) (HMSO, London, 1960, Cmnd. 954).

'International Olive Oil Agreement 1963' (HMSO, London, 1963, Cmnd. 2155).

'International Olive Oil Agreement 1979' (UNCTAD, Geneva, 1979, TD/OLIVE OIL 7/7).

2.   Other Official and Semi-Official Publications

a.   International

Bank for International Settlements, Oil-Related Payments Imbalances (Basle, 1975).

Commonwealth Economic Committee, A Review of Commonwealth Agriculture (London, 1952).

Commonwealth Secretariat, Terms of Trade Policy for Primary Commodities (London, 1976).

General Agreement on Tariffs and Trade (HMSO, London, 1948, Cmnd. 7258).

General Agreement on Tariffs and Trade, Part IV: Trade and Development (HMSO, London, 1965, Cmnd. 2618).

(---) 'Arrangement regarding International Trade in Textiles' (Geneva, 1974).

(---) A Study on Cotton Textiles (Geneva, 1966).

(---) Documents relating to the First Session (HMSO, London, 1948, Cmd. 7376).

(---) 'Extension of Multifibre Arrangement Agreed' (December 1981).

(---) GATT Activities in 1973 (Geneva, 1974).

(---) GATT Activities in 1976 (Geneva, 1977).

(---) GATT Activities in 1978 (Geneva, 1979).

(---) GATT Activities in 1979 (Geneva, 1980).

(---) 'GATT Information' (Geneva, February 1981).

(---) 'Long Term Arrangement regarding International Trade in Cotton Textiles' (Geneva, 1963).

(---) The Role of GATT in relation to Trade and Development (Geneva, March 1964).

(---) Trends in International Trade: A Report by a Panel of Experts (Geneva, 1958).

(---) 'What it is; What it Does' (Geneva, October 1977).

General Agreement on Tariffs and Trade, Committee on Trade and Development, 'Tropical Products: Information on the Commercial Policy Situation and Trade Flows' which includes 'Coffee and Coffee Products' (12 March 1981), 'Oilseeds, Vegetable Oils and Oilcakes' (3 July 1981), 'Cocoa and Cocoa Products' (13 March 1981), 'Rubber and Rubber Articles' (10 July 1981) and 'Tea and Instant Tea' (13 March 1981).

Independent Commission on International Development Issues, North-South: A Programme for Survival: The Report of the Independent Commission on International Development Issues under the Chairmanship of Willy Brandt (Pan Books, London, 1980)

International Bank for Reconstruction and Development (IBRD), Commodity Trade and Price Trends (Johns Hopkins University Press, Baltimore, August 1981)

(---) The Problem of Stabilization of Prices of Primary Products (IMF and IBRD, Washington, 1969)

(---) World Development Report 1982 (Oxford University Press, New York, 1982)

International Bauxite Association, 'International Congress of Bauxite Producing Countries: Final Act of the Conference' (mimeo, January 1976)

International Cocoa Organization, 'International Cocoa Organization' (London, 1977)

(---) 'Study of Cocoa Production and Consumption Capacity' (London, various issues and dates)

International Coffee Organization, Annual Coffee Statistics (London, various issues)

(---) 'International Coffee Organization' (London, 1982)

(---) Quarterly Statistical Bulletin (London, various issues)

(---) 'Quotas' (London, October 1981)

(---) 'Statement by the Executive Director' (London, November 1981)

International Labour Office, First Annual Meeting 1919 (Geneva, 1919)

(---) Food Control in Great Britain (Montreal, 1943)

(---) Intergovernmental Commodity Agreements (Montreal, 1943)

(---) Studies in War Economics (Montreal, 1941)

International Monetary Fund, Compensatory Financing of Export Fluctuations (Washington, 1963)

(---) International Financial Statistics (Washington, various issues)

(---) IMF Survey (Washington, various issues)

(---) World Economic Outlook: A Survey by the Staff of the International Monetary Fund (Washington, 1982)

International Rubber Study Group, Rubber Statistical Bulletin (London, various issues)

(---), World Rubber Statistics Handbook 1946-1974 (London, 1974)

International Sugar Council, The World Sugar Economy Structure and Policies (London, 1963)

International Tea Committee, Annual Bulletin of Statistics (London, various issues)

International Tin Council, Annual Report 1975-1976 (London, 1976)

(---) Monthly Statistical Bulletin (London, various issues)

(---) Statistical Yearbook (London, various issues)

(---) 'The International Implications of the United States Disposal of Stockpiled Tin' (London, n.d.)

(---) Tin Production and Investments (London, 1979)

(---) Tin Statistics 1968-1978 (London, n.d.)

(---) Trade in Tin 1960-1974 (London, n.d.)

International Tin Study Group, Statistical Yearbook (London, various issues)

International Wheat Council, Annual Report of the Council for the Crop-Year 1953/54 (London, 1954)

(---) 'International Wheat Agreements: A Historical and Critical Background' (International Wheat Council Report EX/74/74, 2/2, London, October 1974)

(---) International Wheat Prices (London, 1961)

(---) Problems in Grain Handling and Transportation (London, 1980)

(---) Review of the World Wheat Situation (London, various issues)

(---) Tables and Charts of Wheat Prices (London, May 1958)

(---) The World Wheat Situation (London, 1954)

(---) Trends and Problems in the World Grain Economy 1950-1970 (London, 1966)

(---) World Wheat Statistics 1970 (London, 1971)

League of Nations, Commercial Policy in the Interwar Period: International Proposals and National Policies (Geneva, 1942, II.A.6)

(---) Commercial Policy in the Post-War World (Geneva, 1945, II.A.7)

(---) Food, Famine and Relief 1940-1946 (Geneva, 1946)

(---) Food Rationing and Supply 1943/44 (Geneva, 1944)

(---) Industrialisation and Foreign Trade (Geneva, 1945)

(---) International Cartels (published subsequently by the United Nations, New York, 1947, II.D.2)

(---) International Sugar Conference held in London from 5 April to 6 May 1937. I: Text of the Agreement; II: Proceedings and Documents of the Conference (Geneva, 1937, C.289.M.190.II.B.8)

(---) International Trade Statistics 1938 (Geneva, 1939, II.A.21)

(---) Monetary and Economic Conference, London 1933, Report of the Economic Commission of the London Monetary and Economic Conference on the Work relating to the Coordination of Production and Marketing (Geneva, 1933, C.435, M220, 1933, II. Conf. ME 22(1))

(---) Raw Materials and Foodstuffs (Geneva, 1939, II.A.24)

(---) Report of the Committee for the Study of the Problem of Raw Materials (Geneva, 1937, A.27, II.B)

(---) Report of the Proceedings of the World Economic Conference (Geneva, 1927, C.356, M.129)

(---) Sugar: Memoranda prepared for the Economic Committee by Dr. H.C. Prinsen Geerligs, Messrs F.O. Licht and Dr. Gustav Mikusch (Geneva, 1929, C.148.M.127)

(---) The Course and Phases of the World Economic Depression (Geneva, 1931, II.A.2)

(---) The Network of World Trade (Geneva, 1942, II.A.3)

(---) The Statistical Yearbook of the League of Nations (Geneva, various issues)

(---) The World Economic Conference, Geneva, 1927 Final Report (Geneva, 1927, CEI 44 (1))

(---) Economic Committee, Consideration on the Present Evolution of Agricultural Protectionism (Geneva, 1935, II.B.7)

Organization for Economic Co-operation and Development (OECD), Export Cartels (Paris, 1974)

The Uranium Institute, The Balance of Supply and Demand 1978-1990 (London, 1979)

Tin Producers' Association, Tin World Statistics 1939 (London, n.d.)

United Nations, A Study of Trade Between Latin America and Europe (Geneva, 1953)

(---) Commodities: A Select Bibliography 1965-1975 (New York, 1975)

(---) Commodity Trade and Development (New York, 1953, E.2519, II.B.1)

(---) Commodity Trade and Economic Development (New York, 1956)

(---) 'Declaration on the Establishment of a New International Economic Order', Resolution 3201 (S-VI) (1 May 1974) in Resolutions Adopted by the General Assembly during its Sixth Session

(---) Instability in Export Markets of Underdeveloped Countries (New York, 1952, II.A.1)

(---) International Cocoa Conference, 1972 (New York, 1973, TD/COCOA.3/9)

(---) 'Programme of Action on the Establishment of a New International Economic Order', Resolution A/RES/3202 (S-VII) (16 May 1974) in Resolutions Adopted by the General Assembly during its Sixth Special Session

(---) 'Report of Working Party I on Prices and Quotas' (New York, March 1966, TD/COCOA.1./WP 1/2)

(---) Resolutions Adopted by the General Assembly during its Sixth Special Session (New York, 1974, A/9559)

(---) The Maritime Transportation of Natural Rubber (New York, 1970, TD/B/C.4/60 Rev. 1)

(---) United Nations Cocoa Conference 1975 (New York, 1976, TD/COCOA 4/10)

(---) United Nations Conference on Olive Oil, 1973 (New York, 1973, TD/OLIVE OIL 5/6 Rev. 1)

(---) United Nations Conference on Olive Oil, 1978 (New York, 1978, TD/OLIVE OIL 6/10)

(---) United Nations Sugar Conference 1977 (New York, 1978, TD/SUGAR.9/12)

(---) United Nations Tin Conference 1950 and 1953: Summary of Proceedings (New York, 1954, II.D.4)

(---) United Nations Tin Conference: 1960 Summary of Proceedings (New York, 1961, 61.II.D.2)

(---) United Nations Tin Conference, 1965: Summary of Proceedings (New York, 1965, 65.II.D.2)

(---) United Nations Tin Conference 1970: Summary of Proceedings (New York, 1970, E.70.II.D.10)

United Nations, Coffee Study Group, The World Coffee Problem: Present Status of the Industry and Future Prospects (Washington, April 1961)

United Nations Conference on Trade and Development (UNCTAD), A Common Fund for the Financing of Commodity Stocks: Suitability for Stocking of Individual Commodities: Country Contributions and Burden Sharing, and some Operating Principles (Geneva, 1975, TD/B/ C.1/1969)

(---) 'Agreement establishing the Common Fund for Commodities' (mimeo, Geneva, 1980, TD/IPC/CF/CONF/24)

(---) 'Considerations of International Measures on Iron Ore: Iron ore: Features of the World Market' (mimeo, Geneva, 1977, TD/B/IPC/ IRON ORE/2)

(---) Final Act (HMSO, London, 1964, Cmnd. 2417)

(---) Handbook of International Trade and Development Statistics: Supplement 1980 (New York, 1980, TD/STAT.9)

(---) International Action on Commodities in the Light of Recent Developments: Problems of the Iron Ore Market (Geneva, 1969, TD/B/C.a.66)

(---) International Action on Commodities in the Light of Recent Developments: Problems of the World Market for Iron Ore (Geneva, 1971, TD/B/C.1/104)

(---) Marketing and Distribution System for Cocoa (Geneva, 1975, TD/B/C.1/164)

(---) Official Records of the General Assembly, Thirty-first Session: Supplement No. 15 (Geneva, 1976, A/31/15)

(---) Operation and Effects of the Generalized System of Preferences: Selected Studies submitted to the Seventh Session of the Special Committee on Preferences for its Third Review (Geneva, 1974, TD/B/C.5/15, E. 78.II.D.2)

(---) Proceedings of the First Session of UNCTAD, Geneva (New York, 1964, 64.II.B.11. Conf. 46/141)

(---) Proceedings of the Second Session of UNCTAD, New Delhi, 1 February - 29 March, 1968 (New York, 1968, E.68.II.D.14/15.TD/ 197)

(---) Proceedings of the Third Session of UNCTAD, Santiago de Chile, 13 April to 12 May 1972 (New York, 1972, TD/180, E.73.II.D.4)

(---) Proceedings of the UNCTAD Fourth Session, Nairobi 5 - 31 May 1976 (New York, 1977, TD/218, E.76.II.D.10)

(---) 'Prospective Supply/Demand Balance for Tea and the Implications for an International Buffer Stock Arrangement and for an Export Quota Scheme for the Period 1980-84' (mimeo, Geneva, 1979, TD/B/IPC/TEA/AC/8).

(---) Report of the Ad Hoc Meeting on Iron Ore held at the Palais des Nations, Geneva, from 19 to 23 January 1970 (Geneva, 1970, TD/B/ C.1/75)

(---) Report of the Secretary General: Towards a New Trade Policy for Development (Geneva, 1964, E/Conf. 46)

(---) 'Report of the Seventh Preparatory Meeting on Copper on its First and Second Parts' (mimeo, Geneva, 1980, TD/B/IPC/COPPER 19)

(---) 'Report of the United Nations Negotiating Conference on a Common Fund under the Integrated Programme for Commodities on its Fourth Session 5-27 June 1980' (mimeo, Geneva, 1980, TD/IPC/ CF/CONF/26)

(---) 'Report of the UNCTAD on its Fifth Session held at the Philippine International Convention Center from 7 May to 3 June 1979' (mimeo, no place ref., 1979, TD/268/Add. 1)

(---) Report on Consultations on Iron Ore held at the Palais des Nations, Geneva 24 and 25 February 1972 (Geneva, 1972, TD/B/C.1/ 125)

(---) The Generalized System of Preferences and the Multilateral Trade Negotiations (New York, 1978, TD/B/C.5/52 Rev. 1 E.78.II.D.6)

United Nations, Economic Commission of Europe, Economic Survey of Europe, 1960 (Geneva, 1961)

United Nations, Food and Agriculture Organization, An Enquiry into the Problems of Agricultural Price Stabilisation and Support Policies (Rome, 1960)

(---) A Strategy for Plenty: the Indicative World Plan for Agricultural Development (Rome, 1970)

(---) Cocoa (Rome, 1977)

(---) Commodity Review and Outlook (Rome, 1979-80)

(---) Monthly Bulletin of Agricultural Economics, various issues

(---) 'New Protectionism and Attempts at Liberalization in Agricultural Trade' in Commodity Review and Outlook (Rome, 1979-80)

(---) Processing of Raw Cocoa for the Market (Rome, 1963)

(---) Report of the Fourth Session of the FAO Group on Grains to the Committee on Commodity Problems (Rome, 1959)

(---) Report of the Preparatory Commission on World Food Proposals (London, 1947, Cmd. 703)

(---) The Stabilization of International Trade in Grains: An Assessment of Problems and possible Solutions (Rome, 1970)

(---) The Stabilization of the Olive Oil Market (Rome, 1955)

(---) Things to Come: the World Food Crisis - the Way Out (Rome, 1974)

(---) Trade Yearbook 1980 (New York, 1981)

(---) World Coffee Supply (Rome, 1968)

United Nations, Industrial Development Organization, Textile Industry (New York, ID/40/7, E.69)

b.   Regional and National

Brazil, Ministry of Agriculture, Industry and Commerce, O Brasil Actual (Rio de Janeiro, 1930)

Brazil, Ministry of Foreign Affairs, Brasil 1933 (Rio de Janeiro, 1934)

314

(---) <u>Brasil 1943</u> (Rio de Janeiro, 1943)

(---) <u>Brasil, 1940-42</u> (Rio de Janeiro, 1942)

Canada, Department of Energy, Mines and Resources, <u>Iron Ore</u> (Ministry of Supply and Services, Ottawa, 1976)

European Economic Communities (EEC), 'Background Report: Lomé II: Terms of the New Convention' (London, September 1979, ISEC/ B33/79)

(---) <u>Memorandum on Reform of Agriculture in the European Communities</u> (European Communities Information Service, London, 1968)

(---) <u>Official Journal of the European Communities</u>

(---) 'Proposals for the Working out and Putting into Effect of the Common Agricultural Policy in Application of Article 43 of the Treaty establishing the European Economic Community' (Brussels, 1960)

European Free Trade Association (EFTA), <u>The European Free Trade Association: Structure, Rules and Operation</u> (Geneva, 1976)

Great Britain, Department of Overseas Trade, Garnett Lomax, J., <u>Economic Conditions in Brazil December, 1930</u> (HMSO, London, 1931)

(---) <u>Economic Conditions in Brazil December, 1931</u> (HMSO, London, 1932)

(---) Hambloch, E., <u>Report on the Economic and Financial Conditions in Brazil September, 1925</u> (HMSO, London, 1925)

(---) <u>Report on the Economic and Financial Conditions in Brazil October, 1926</u> (HMSO, London, 1927)

(---) Murray Harvey, E. and Garnett Lomax, J., <u>Economic Conditions in Brazil December, 1932</u> (HMSO, London, 1933)

Great Britain, House of Commons, <u>Accounts and Papers</u>, various papers (London)

Great Britain, House of Lords, <u>Select Committee on the European Community</u> (HMSO, London, 19 March 1980)

Great Britain, Ministry of Agriculture and Fisheries, Report on the Beet Sugar Industry at Home and Abroad (HMSO, London, 1931)

Great Britain, Ministry of Food, Second Review of the World Food Shortage July 1946 (HMSO, London, Cmd. 6879)

Great Britain, National Board for Prices and Incomes, 'Tea Prices' (HMSO, London, 1970, Cmnd. 4456)

Great Britain, Parliamentary Report, World Economic Interdependence and Trade in Commodities (HMSO, London, 1975, Cmnd. 6061)

US, Commission on Foreign Economic Policy, Report to the President and the Congress (The Randall Commission) (US Government Printing Office, Washington, 1954)

US, Council on International Economic Policy, Special Report: Critical Imported Materials (Washington, December 1974)

US, Department of Agriculture, see Bohall, R.

US, Department of the Treasury, Department of the Treasury News (Washington, 9 June, 1976)

US, Federal Preparedness Agency, The Strategic and Critical Materials Stockpile (General Services Administration Fact Sheet, Washington, October 1976)

II.   SECONDARY SOURCES

Abbot, G.C., International Indebtedness and the Developing Countries (Croom Helm, London, 1979)

Adams, F.G. and Klein, S.A. (eds.), Stabilizing World Commodity Markets, Analysis, Practice and Policy (D.C. Heath & Co., Lexington, Mass., 1978)

Adelman, M.A., The World Petroleum Market (Johns Hopkins University Press, Baltimore, 1972)

Adler, J., 'The Quest for a Stabilization Policy in Primary Producing Countries', KYKLOS (1958.2)

Agostini, B.B. see Grilli, E.R. and Hooft-Welvaars, M.J. 't

Agricultural Adjustment Unit, University of Newcastle, Stability and the Beef Market (Agricultural Adjustment Unit, Newcastle, 1970)

Aguilar, L.E., Cuba 1933 (Cornell University Press, Ithaca, 1972)

Ahlfeld, H., 'The International Sugar Agreement of 1977: Problems of Regulating the Free World Market' in F.O. Licht, International Sugar Report (F.O. Licht, Ratzeburg, Germany, n.d.)

Ainely, E.M., The IMF: Past, Present and Future (University of Wales Press, Bangor, 1979)

Al-Chalabi, F.J., OPEC and the International Oil Industry: a Changing Structure (Oxford University Press, London, 1980)

Ali, L., 'The Regulation of Trade in Tea', Journal of World Trade Law vol. 4 (July:August 1970)

Allen, G.C. and Donnithorne, A.G., Western Enterprise in Indonesia and Malaya (Allen & Unwin, London, 1957)

Allen, H.W., 'The International Tin Agreement, Why It Works', Tin International (London, December 1975)

Allen, P.W., Natural Rubber and the Synthetics (Crosby Lockwood, London, 1972)

Allen, P.W., Thomas, P.O. and Sekhar, B.C., The Techno-Economic Potential of Natural Rubber in Major End-Uses (Malaysian Rubber Research and Development Board, Kuala Lumpur, 1973)

Alston, P., 'Commodity Agreements - As Though People Don't Matter', Journal of World Trade Law vol. 15, no. 5 (September: October 1981)

Anderson, J.G., 'The Rubber Manufacturers' Choice: Natural or Synthetic Rubber?', Plastics and Rubber International (July/August 1977)

Ashworth, W., A Short History of the International Economy since 1850 (Longman, London, 1975)

Auty, R.M., 'Transforming Mineral Enclaves Caribbean Bauxite in the Nineteen Seventies', Tijdschrift voor Economische en Sociale Geografie vol. lxxi, no. 3 (1980)

317

Bairoch, P., The Economic Development of the Third World since 1900 (Methuen, London, 1975)

Balaam, D.N. and Carey, M.J., Food Politics: The Regional Conflict (Croom Helm, London, 1981)

Balassa, B. (ed.), European Economic Integration (North-Holland Publishing Co., Amsterdam, 1975)

Balassa, B., Studies in Trade Liberalisation (Johns Hopkins University Press, Baltimore, 1967)

(---) The Structure of Protection in Developing Countries (Johns Hopkins University Press, Baltimore, 1971)

(---) 'Trade Creation and Trade Diversion in the European Common Market', Economic Journal vol. 77 (March 1967)

(---) 'Trade Creation and Trade Diversion in the European Common Market: An Appraisal of Evidence', The Manchester School vol. XLII, no. 2 (1974)

Baldwin, R.E., Non-Tariff Distortions of International Trade (Allen & Unwin, Washington, 1971)

Baldwin, R.E. (ed.), Trade Growth and the Balance of Payments: Essays in Honour of Gottfried Haberler (North-Holland Publishing Co., Amsterdam, 1966)

Banks, F.E., The World Copper Market: an Economic Analysis (Ballinger Publishing Co., Cambridge, Mass., 1974)

Bardan, B., 'The Cotton Textile Agreement 1962-1972', Journal of World Trade Law vol. 7, no. 1 (January:February 1973)

Barton, D.B., A History of Tin Mining and Smelting in Cornwall (D.B. Barton, Truro, 1967)

Bauer, P.T., The Rubber Industry: A Study in Competition and Monopoly (Longmans, Green & Co., London, 1948)

Bauer, P.T. and Paish, F.W., 'The Reduction of Fluctuations in the Incomes of Primary Producers', Economic Journal (December 1952)

Bauer, P.T. and Yamey, B., Markets, Market Control and Marketing Reform (Weidenfeld and Nicolson, London, 1968)

(---) The Economics of Under-developed Countries (Cambridge University Handbook, Cambridge, 1957)

Beals, R.E. see Gillis, M.

Behrman, J.R., International Commodity Agreements: an Evaluation of the UNCTAD Integrated Commodity Programme (Overseas Development Council, no place ref., October 1977)

(---) 'Monopolistic Cocoa Pricing', American Journal of Agricultural Economics vol. 50, no. 3 (August 1968)

Bello, J.M., História da República, 1889-1954 (São Paulo, 1959)

Bennett, M.K., International Commodity Stockpiling as an Economic Stabilizer (Stanford University Press, Stanford, 1949)

Berge, W., Cartels: Challenge to a Free World (Public Affairs Press, Washington, 1948)

Bergsten, C.F., 'A new OPEC in Bauxite', Challenge vol. 19, no. 3 (July-August 1976)

Bhagwati, J., 'On the Equivalence of Tariffs and Quotas' in R.E. Baldwin (ed.), Trade, Growth and the Balance of Payments: Essays in Honour of Gottfried Haberler

Bhaskar, K., The Future of the World Motor Industry (Kogan Page, London, 1980)

Bidwell, P., Raw Materials: A Study of American Policy (Harper, New York, 1958)

Blau, G., 'International Commodity Agreements and Policies' in United Nations Food and Agriculture Organization, Monthly Bulletin of Agricultural Economics no. 12 (1963)

(---) 'Some Implications of Tin Price Stabilisation', Malayan Economic Review vol. 17, no. 1 (April 1972)

Bloomfield, G., The World Automotive Industry (David and Charles, Newton Abbott, 1978)

Bohall, R., 'The Sugar Industry's Structure, Pricing and Performance' (US Department of Agriculture Report, Washington, 1977)

Bosworth, B.P. and Lawrence, R.Z., Commodity Prices and the New Inflation (Brookings Institution, Washington, 1982)

van Brabant, J.M.P., Bilateralism and Structural Bilateralism in Intra-CMEA Trade (Rotterdam University Press, Rotterdam, 1979)

Bracewell-Milnes, B., Economic Integration in East and West (Croom Helm, London, 1976)

Brandow, G.E., 'American Agriculture's Capacity to Meet Future Demands', American Journal of Agricultural Economy vol. 56, no. 1 (December, 1974)

British Sugar Corporation, Home Grown Sugar: Rise and Development of an Industry (London, 1961)

Brown, C.P., The Political and Social Economy of Commodity Control (Macmillan, London, 1980)

Burford-Brandis, R., A Short History of US Textile Import Quotas (American Textile Manufacturers' Institute, Washington, 1974)

Burger, S.H., 'The Fifth International Tin Agreement', Law and Policy in International Business vol. 9 no. 2 (1977)

Caine, S., 'Instability of Primary Product Prices: A Protest and A Proposal', Economic Journal vol. 44 (September 1954)

Carey, M.J. see Balaam, D.N.

Carone, E., A Segunda República, 1930-1937 (Difusão Européia do Livro, São Paulo, 1973)

Caves, E., 'Organisation, Scale and Performance of the Grain Trade', Food Research Institute Studies vol. XVI, no. 3 (1977-78)

Chan, F., 'A Preliminary Study of the Supply Responses of Malayan Rubber Estates between 1948 and 1951', Malayan Economic Review vol. 7 (1962)

Chapman, A., 'Trade of Brazil for the Year 1907' in Great Britain, House of Commons, Accounts and Papers (London, 1908, Cd. 3727-137), vol. CIX

Charles Rivers Associates, Economic Analysis of the Copper Industry, Report to the Property Management and Disposal Service (General Services Administration, US, March 1980)

(---) The Feasibility of Copper Price Stabilization Using a Buffer Stock and Supply Restrictions from 1953 to 1976 (UNCTAD, Geneva, November 1977, TD/B/IPC/COPPER/AC/E:42)

Chisholm, M., Modern World Development: A Geographical Perspective (Hutchinson & Co., London, 1982)

Cline, W.R., Kawanabe, N., Kronsjo, T.O.M. and Williams, T., Trade Negotiations in the Tokyo Round: A Quantitative Assessment (The Brookings Institution, Washington, 1978)

Club of Rome, The Limits to Growth (Potomac Associates Books, Earth Island Ltd, London, 1972)

Cochrane, W.W., 'International Commodity Management as a Policy Problem for the United States: The Grains Case' in Denoon (ed.), The New International Economic Order: a US Response

(---) see also Tomek, W.G.

Coffey, P., The External Relations of the EEC (Macmillan, London, 1976)

Cohen, S.D., The Making of the United States International Economic Policy (Praeger Publishers, New York, 1977)

Colebrook, J., 'The Cost of Stocking Primary Commodities', Journal of World Trade Law vol. 11, no. 4 (July:August 1977)

Commodity Research Bureau, Commodity Yearbook (New York, various issues)

Coppock, J.D., International Economic Instability (McGraw-Hill, New York, 1962)

Corden, W.M., The Theory of Protection (Oxford University Press, London, 1971)

Corden, W.M. see Scott, M.F.G.

Cottrell, R.H., Beet-Sugar Economics (The Caxton Printers Ltd, Caldwell, Idaho, 1952)

Courtenay, P.P., 'International Tin Restriction and its Effects on the Malayan Tin Industry', Geography vol. 46 (1961)

Cremer, J. and Weitzman, M., 'OPEC and the monopoly price of world oil', _European Economic Review_ vol. 8 (1976)

Curzon, G., _Hidden Barriers to International Trade_ (Trade Policy Research Centre, London, 1971)

(---) _Multilateral Commercial Diplomacy; GATT_ (Michael Joseph, London, 1965)

Curzon, G. and V., _Hidden Barriers to International Trade_ (Trade Policy Research Centre, London, 1971)

Curzon, V., _The Essentials of Economic Integration: Lessons of EFTA Experience_ (Macmillan, London, 1974)

Dale, R., _Anti-Dumping Law in a Liberal Trade Order_ (Macmillan, London, 1980)

Dam, K.W., _The GATT: Law and International Economic Organization_ (University of Chicago Press, Chicago, 1970)

(---) see also Schultz, G.P.

Daniels, P., 'The Inter-American Coffee Agreement', _Law and Contemporary Problems_ vol. VII (Autumn 1941)

Davis, J.S., 'New International Wheat Agreements', _Wheat Studies of the Food Research Institute_ (November 1942)

Deerr, N., _The History of Sugar_ (Chapman and Hill Ltd, London, 1950)

Dell, S., _A Latin American Common Market?_ (Oxford University Press, London, 1966)

Denoon, D.B. (ed.), _The New International Economic Order_ (Macmillan, London, 1979)

Dewberry, D.M.G., 'Oil Prices, Cartels and the Problems of Dynamic Inconsistency', _Economic Journal_ vol. 91 (September 1981)

Donnithorne, A.G. see Allen, G.C.

Duignan, P. and Rabushka, A. (eds.), _The United States in the 1980s_ (Croom Helm, London, 1980)

Eckbo, P.L., OPEC and the Experience of Previous International Commodity Cartels (Massachusetts Institute of Technology, Cambridge, Mass., 1975)

Edwards, C., Economic and Political Aspects of International Cartels (US Government Printing Office, Washington, 1944)

Einzig, P., Economic Warfare 1939-1940 (Macmillan, London, 1941)

El-Agraa, A.M. (ed.), The Economics of the European Community (Philip Allan, Oxford, 1980)

Ellsworth, P.T., 'The Terms of Trade between Primary Producing and Industrial Countries', Interamerican Economic Affairs (Summer 1956)

Emery, R.F., 'The Relation of Exports to Economic Growth', KYKLOS vol. 20 (1967)

Enoch, C.A. and Panić, M., 'Commodity Prices in the 1970s', Bank of England Quarterly Bulletin (March 1981)

Erb, G.F. and Schiavo-Campo, S., 'Export Instability, Level of Development and Economic Size of Less Developed Countries', Oxford Bulletin of Economics and Statistics (31 May 1969)

Evans, J.W., The Kennedy Round in American Trade Policy (Harvard University Press, Cambridge, Mass., 1971)

Eyre, S.R., The Real Wealth of Nations (Arnold, 1978)

Farnsworth, H.C., 'Imbalance in the World Wheat Economy', Journal of Political Economy vol. LXX (February 1958)

(---) 'International Wheat Agreements and Problems, 1949-56', The Quarterly Journal of Economics vol. LXX, no. 2 (May 1956)

Fawcett, J., International Economic Conflicts: Prevention and Resolution (Europea Publications Ltd., London, 1977)

Fennell, R., The Common Agricultural Policy of the European Economic Community (Granada, St Albans, 1979)

Ferrell, R.H., American Diplomacy in the Great Depression (Yale University Press, New Haven, 1957)

Fetter, F.A., The Masquerade of Monopoly (Harcourt Brace, New York, 1931)

Finger, J.M., 'GATT Tariff Concessions and the Exports of Developing Countries: United States' Concessions at the Dillon Round', Economic Journal vol. 84 (September 1974)

Finger, S. see Kreinin, M.

Fisher, B., The International Coffee Agreement: A Study in Coffee Diplomacy (Praeger Publishers, New York, 1972)

Ford, D.J., 'Commodity Market Modelling and the Simulation of Market Intervention: the case of Coffee' in Adams, F.G. and Klein, S.A. (eds.), Stabilizing World Coffee Markets, Analysis, Practice and Policy

Ford Foundation Agricultural Production Team, Report on India Food Crises and Steps to Meet It (Government of India, New Delhi, April 1959)

Fox, D.J., Tin and the Bolivian Economy (Latin American Publications Fund, London, 1970)

Fox, W., The Working of a Commodity Agreement: Tin (Mining Journal Books, London, 1974)

Freeman, C. and Jahoda, M. (eds.), World Futures: The Great Debate (Robertson, 1978)

Friesen, C.M., The Political Economy of East-West Trade (Praeger Publishers, New York, 1976)

Garland, J.S., Financing Foreign Trade in Eastern Europe: Problems of Bilateralism and Currency Inconvertibility (Praeger Publishers, New York, 1977)

'GATT: Third Multifibre Arrangement', Journal of World Trade Law vol. 16, no. 2 (March:April 1982)

Geer, T., 'The Post-War Tin Agreements: A Case of Success in Price Stabilization of Primary Commodities', Schweizerische Zeitschaft für Volkwirtschaft und Statistic no. 2 (1970)

Gill & Duffus, Cocoa Market Report (London, various issues)

(---) Cocoa Statistics (London, various issues)

Gillis, M. and Beals, R.E., Tax Investment Policies for Hard Minerals (Ballinger Publishing Co., Cambridge, Mass., 1980)

Gillis, M. et al, Taxation and Mining: Non-Fuel Minerals in Bolivia and Other Countries (Ballinger, Cambridge, Mass., 1978)

Girvan, N., The Caribbean Bauxite Industry (University of the West Indies, Jamaica, 1967)

Gittinger, J.P., North American Agriculture in a New World (Canadian-American Committee, US, 1970)

Golay, F.H., 'The International Wheat Agreement of 1949', The Quarterly Journal of Economics vol. LXIV, no. 3 (August 1950)

Golt, S., 'World Trade and the Developing Countries' in Johnson, H.G. (ed.), The New Mercantilism (Basil Blackwell, Oxford, 1974)

Goodwin, G. and Mayall, J. (eds.), A New International Commodity Regime (Croom Helm, London, 1979)

Gordon-Ashworth, F., 'Agricultural Commodity Control under Vargas in Brazil, 1930-1945', Journal of Latin American Studies vol. 12, part 1 (May 1980)

(---) 'International and National Commodity Control, 1930 to 1945: Sugar and the Brazilian Case', unpublished PhD thesis, University of Southampton, 1978

Goreux, L.M., Compensatory Financing Facility (IMF, Washington, 1980)

Green, C. and Kirkpatrick, C. 'The IMF's Food Financing Facility', Journal of World Trade Law vol. 16, no. 3 (May:June 1982)

Grey, R. de C., The Development of the Canadian Anti-dumping System (Private Planning Association of Canada, Montreal, 1973)

Griffith, J.W., The Uranium Industry, its History, Technology and Prospects (Canada, Department of Energy and Mines, Ottawa, 1967)

Grilli, E.R., Agostini, B.B. and Hooft-Welvaars, M.J.'t., The World Rubber Economy: Structure, Changes and Policies (IBRD, Johns Hopkins University Press, Baltimore, 1980)

Groom, A.J.R. see Taylor, P.

Grubel, H.G., 'The Case against the New International Economic Order', Weltwirtschaftliches Archiv, band 113, heft 2 (1977)

Gunnarsson, C., Malaysian Rubber Production: Patterns of Growth 1900-1975 (Ekonomisk-Historiska Institutionen, Lund University, 1979)

(---) 'The Gold Coast Cocoa Industry, 1900-1939: Production, Prices and Structural Change' (mimeo, Lund, 1978)

Habakkuk, H.J. and Postand, M. (eds.), The Cambridge Economic History of Europe vol. 6 (Cambridge University Press, Cambridge, 1965)

Haberler, G., International Trade and Economic Development (National Bank of Egypt, Cairo, 1959)

Hagelberg, G.B., 'International Sugar Agreements, 1864-1977' in F.O. Licht, International Sugar Report: Problems and Prospects of a New International Sugar Agreement

Hague, D.C. (ed.), Stability and Progress in the World Economy (London, 1958)

Hallett, G., The Economics of Agricultural Policy (Basil Blackwell, Oxford, 1981)

Hallwood, P., Stabilization of International Commodity Markets (Jai Press, Connecticut, 1979)

Halsay Holloway, T., 'The Brazilian Coffee Industry and the First Valorisation Scheme of 1906-7', unpublished MA thesis, University of Wisconsin, 1971

Hansson, G., Social Clauses and International Trade (Croom Helm, London, 1983)

Harler, C.R., The Culture and Marketing of Tea (Oxford University Press, London, 1964)

Harris, S. and Smith, I., World Sugar Markets in a State of Flux (Trade Policy Research Centre, London, 1973)

Harvey, H.J., Consultation and Co-operation in the Commonwealth (Oxford University Press, London, 1952)

Haslemere Declaration, Coffee: The Rules of Neo-Colonialism: A Study of International Coffee Trade and the International Coffee Agreement (Haslemere Declaration, London, n.d.)

Haviland, W.L., International Commodity Agreements (Private Planning Association, Montreal, 1963)

Hedges, J.L. see Wright, C.B. and Hedges, J.L.

Heidhues, T., Josling, T.E., Ritson, C. and Tangermann, S., Common Prices and Europe's Farm Policy (Trade Policy Research Centre, London, 1978)

Helleiner, G.K. (ed.), A World Divided: the Less Developed Countries in the International Economy (Cambridge University Press, Cambridge, 1976)

Helleiner, G.K., International Trade and Economic Development (Penguin, Middlesex, 1972)

Helmberger, P. and Weaver, R., 'Welfare Implications of Commodity Storage under Uncertainty', American Journal of Agricultural Economics vol. 59 (November 1977)

Herfindahl, O.C., Copper Costs and Prices 1870-1957 (Johns Hopkins University Press, Baltimore, 1959)

Heuser, H., Control of International Trade (George Routledge, London, 1939)

Hexner, E., International Cartels (Sir Isaac Pitman & Sons, London, 1946)

(---) 'International Cartels in the Postwar World', Southern Economic Journal (October 1943)

Hooft-Welvaars, M.J.'t. see Grilli, E.R. and Agostini, B.B.

Hoong, Y.Y., The Development of the Tin Mining Industry of Malaya (University of Malaya Press, Kuala Lumpur, 1969)

Hoover, C.B. (ed.), Economic Systems of the Commonwealth (Duke University Press, Durban, 1962)

Houthakker, H.S., 'The World Price of Oil: A Medium-Term Analysis' (American Enterprise Institute for Public Policies Research, Washington, 1976)

Hudoc, R.E., The GATT Legal System and World Trade Diplomacy (Praeger Publishers, New York, 1975)

327

Hughes, H. and Singh, S., 'Economic rent: incidence in selected metals and minerals', Resource Policy vol. 4, no. 2 (1978)

Hulley, J.C. see Singh, S., de Vries, J., Hulley, J.C. and Yeung, P.

Humpbert, R.P., The Growing of Sugar Cane (Elsevier Publishing Co., London, 1968)

Hurni, B.S., The Lending Policy of the World Bank in the 1970s: Analysis and Evaluations (Westview Press, Colorado, 1980)

Hurstfield, J., The Control of Raw Materials (HMSO, London, 1953)

Jacoby, N., Multinational Oil (Macmillan, New York, 1974)

Jahoda, M. see Freeman, C.

Johnson, D.G. (ed.), Food and Agricultural Policy for the 1980s (American Enterprise Institute for Public Policy Research, Washington, 1981)

Johnson, H.G. (ed.), The New Mercantilism (Basil Blackwell, Oxford, 1974)

(---) Trade Strategy for Rich and Poor Nations (Toronto University Press, Toronto, 1971)

Josling, T., Burdens and Benefits of Farm-Support Policies (Trade Policy Research Centre, London, 1972)

(---) see also Heidhues, T.

Kaldor, N., 'Stabilising the Terms of Trade of Underdeveloped Countries', Economic Bulletin for Latin America vol. 8, no. 1 (March 1963)

Kaser, M., Comecon: Integration Problems of the Planned Economies (Oxford University Press, London, 1967)

Kawanabe, N. see Cline, W.R.

Keesing, D.B. and Wolf, M., Textile Quotas against Developing Countries (Trade Policy Research Centre, London, 1980)

Keesing's Publications Ltd, Treaties and Alliances of the World (Keesing's Publications Ltd, Bristol, 1968)

Kelly, W.B. (ed.), Studies in the United States Commercial Policy (The University of North Carolina Press, Chapel Hill, 1963)

Kemp, T., Industrialisation in Nineteenth Century Europe (Longman, London, 1976)

Kenen, P.B. and Lubitz, R., International Economics (Prentice-Hall, New Jersey, 1971)

Kennedy, M., 'An Economic Model of the World Oil Market', Bell Journal of Economics and Management Science (Autumn 1974)

Keynes, J.M., 'The Control of Raw Materials by Government', The Nation and the Athenaeum vol. XXXIX (June 1926)

(---) The Economic Consequences of the Peace (Macmillan, London, 1920)

(---) 'The International Control of Raw Materials', Journal of International Economics no. 4 (1974) (UK Government (Treasury) Memorandum of 1942)

(---) 'The Policy of Government Storage of Foodstuffs and Raw Materials', Economic Journal vol. 48 (1938)

de Keyser, E. (ed.), Guide to World Commodity Markets (Kogan Page, New York, 1977)

Kidron, M. see Robinson, E.A.G.

Kindleberger, C.P., The World in Depression, 1929-1939 (Allen Lane, London, 1973)

Kirkpatrick, C. see Green, C.

Kirkpatrick, C.H., 'Lomé II', Journal of World Trade Law vol. 14, no. 4 (July:August 1980)

Klein, S.A. see Adams, P.G.

Knorr, K.E., Tin Under Control (Stanford University Press, Stanford, 1945)

Kofi, T.A., World Trade in Cocoa (Third World Forum, Occasional Paper no. 10, Switzerland, 1977)

Kottke, F., The Promotion of Price Competition Where Sellers are Few (D.C. Heath, Lexington, Mass., 1978)

Kreinin, M. and Finger, S., 'A New International Economic Order: A Critical Survey of its Issues', Journal of World Trade Law vol. 10 (1976)

Kronsjo, T.O.M. see Cline, W.R.

Kronstein, H., The Law of International Cartels (Cornell University Press, Ithaca, 1973)

Kubbah, A.A., OPEC: Past and Present (Petro-Economic Research Centre, Vienna, 1974)

Kullemann, U., 'Fair labour standards in International Commodity Agreements', Journal of World Trade Law vol. 14, no. 6 (November: December 1980)

Labys, W.C., Optional Portfolio Analysis of Multicommodity Stocking Arrangements (University of West Virginia Press, Morgantown, 1976)

Lamartine Yates, P., Commodity Control: A Study of Primary Products (Jonathan Cape, London, 1943)

Latham, A.J.H., The Depression and the Developing World, 1914-1939 (Croom Helm, London, 1981)

Law, A.D., International Commodity Agreements (Lexington Books, Lexington, Mass., 1975)

Lawrence, R.Z. see Bosworth, B.P.

Leeds, A., 'Economic Cycles in Brazil: The Persistence of Total Culture Patterns - Cacao and Other Cases', unpublished PhD thesis, University of Columbia, 1967

Licht, F.O., International Sugar Report: Problems and Prospects of a New International Sugar Agreement (F.O. Licht, Ratzeburg, Germany, 1977)

Lichtblau, J.H., 'OPEC Now at an Historic Turning Point', Petroleum Intelligence Weekly (8 June 1981)

Little, I.M.D. see Scott, M.F.G.

Lloyd, P., Anti-dumping Actions and the GATT System (Trade Policy Research Centre, London, 1977)

London Corn Trade Association, Grain Trade Lectures (Northern Publishing Company Ltd, Liverpool, 1946/47)

Luard, E., International Agencies: The Emerging Framework of Interdependence (Macmillan, London, 1977)

Lubitz, R. see Kenen, P.B.

Luttrell, C., in Federal Reserve Bank of St Louis Review (September 1980)

Mabro, R., 'OPEC's Future Pricing Role may be at Stake', Petroleum Intelligence Weekly (19 April 1982)

MacBean, A.I., Export Instability and Economic Development (Allen & Unwin, London, 1966)

MacBean, A.I. and Nguyen, D.T., 'Commodity Concentration and Export Earnings Instability: A Mathematical Analysis', Economic Journal vol. 90 (1980)

MacBean, A.I. and Snowden, P.N., International Institutions in Trade and Finance (Allen & Unwin, London, 1981)

MacGibbon, D.A., The Canadian Grain Trade 1931-1951 (University of Toronto Press, Toronto, 1952)

Madden, A.C.B., 'International Wheat Agreements', International Journal of Agrarian Affairs vol. 1, no. 3 (September 1949)

Maizels, A., Exports and Economic Growth of Developing Countries (Cambridge University Press, Cambridge, 1968)

(---) Selected Issues in the Negotiation of International Commodity Agreements: an Economic Analysis (UNCTAD, Geneva, 1982, TD/B/C.1/224)

Mancke, R.V., 'The Long Run Supply Curve of Crude Oil produced in the United States', Antitrust Bulletin (Winter 1970)

Manners, G., 'Our Planet's Resources', Geographical Journal vol. 147 (1981)

(---) The Changing Market for Iron Ore 1950-1980: An Economic Geography (Johns Hopkins University Press, Baltimore, 1981)

Massell, B.F., 'Export Concentration and Fluctuations in Export Earnings: a Cross-Section-Analysis', American Economic Review vol. 54, no. 2 (1964)

(---) 'Export Instability and Economic Structure', American Economic Review vol. 60 (September 1970)

Maxcy, G., The Multinational Motor Industry (Croom Helm, London, 1981)

Mayall, J. see Goodwin, G.

Mayes, D.G., 'The Effects of Economic Integration on Trade', Journal of Common Market Studies vol. 17, no. 1 (September 1978)

McFadyean, A., The History of Rubber Regulation 1934-1943 (Allen & Unwin, London, 1944)

McNicol, D.L., Commodity Agreements and Price Stabilization (Lexington Books, Lexington, Mass., 1978)

Meade, R. see Spencer, G.L.

Medlicott, W.N., The Economic Blockade (HMSO, London, 1959)

van Meerhaeghe, M.A.G., A Handbook of International Economic Institutions (Martinus Nijhoff, The Hague, 1980)

Meier, G.M., 'US Foreign Economic Policies', see Duignan, P. and Rabushka, A. (eds.), The United States in the 1980s

Meyer, F.V., International Trade Policy (Croom Helm, London, 1978)

(---) The European Free Trade Association: An Analysis of 'The Outer Seven' (Praeger Publishers, New York, 1960)

Mikdashi, Z., The Community of Oil Exporting Countries: A Study in Governmental Cooperation (Cornell University Press, 1972)

Mikesell, R.F., The World Copper Industry (Johns Hopkins University Press, Baltimore, 1979)

Milward, A. and Saul, S.B., The Economic Development of Continental Europe (Allen & Unwin, London, 1973)

Morgan, D., Merchants of Grain (Weidenfeld & Nicolson, London, 1979)

Morgan, D.J., The Official History of Colonial Development (Macmillan, London, 1980)

Myers, L., 'Analysing Sugar Price Trends', Commodity Year Book 1977 (Commodity Research Bureau, New York, 1977)

Myrdal, G., An International Economy: Problems and Policies (Routledge & Kegan Paul, London, 1956)

Nappi, C., Commodity Market Controls (Lexington Books, Lexington, Mass., 1979)

Netto, A.D., 'Foundation for the Analysis of Brazilian Coffee Problems' in Peláez, C.M. (ed.), Essays on Coffee and Economic Development

Newberry, D.M.G., 'Oil Prices, Cartels and the Problems of Dynamic Inconsistency', Economic Journal vol. 91 (September 1981)

Nguyen, D.T. see MacBean, A.I.

Normano, J.F., Brazil: A Study of Economic Types (Chapel Hill, 1965)

Noys, S., 'Fluctuations in Export Earnings and Economic Patterns of Asian Countries', Economic Development and Cultural Change (July 1973)

Nurkse, R. and Singer, H. (eds.), 'The Quest for a Stabilization Policy in Primary Products', KYKLOS vol. 11 (1958)

(---) 'Stabilization and Development of Primary Producing Countries', KYKLOS vol. 12 (1959)

Odell, P., Oil and World Power: Background to the Oil Crisis (Penguin, Baltimore, 1974)

O'Neill, H., A Common Interest in a Common Fund (United Nations, New York, 1977)

Ormsby Gore, Report on Malaya, Ceylon and Java during the Year 1928 (HMSO, London, 1928, Cmd. 3235)

Oualid, W., International Raw Materials (Paris, 1939)

Paish, F.W. see Bauer, P.T.

Pan American Coffee Bureau, Annual Coffee Statistics (New York, 1966)

Paniĉ, M. see Enoch, C.A.

Park, Y.S., Oil Money and the World Economy (Wilton House Publications, London, 1976)

Parry, J.H., Europe and a Wider World 1415-1715 (Hutchinson, London, 1977)

Patterson, G., Discrimination in International Trade: the Policy Issues (Princeton University Press, Princeton, 1966)

Pearce, I.F., International Trade (Macmillan, London, 1970)

Pearson, L.B., Partners in Development (Praeger Publishers, New York, 1969)

Peck, A.E., 'Implications of Private Storage of Grains for Buffer Stock Schemes to Stabilise Prices', Food Research Institute Studies vol. XVI, no. 3 (1977-78)

Peláez, C.M., 'Análise económico do Programa Brasileiro de Sustentação do Café, 1906-1945: Teoria, Política e Medição', Revista Brasileira de Economia vol. 25 (1971)

Peláez, C.M. (ed.), Essays on Coffee and Economic Development (Rio de Janeiro, 1973)

Pertot, V., International Economics of Control (Oliver and Boyd, Edinburgh, 1972)

Phegan, C., 'GATT Article XVI.3: Export Subsidies and 'Equitable Share", Journal of World Trade Law vol. 16, no. 3 (May:June 1982)

Pindyck, R.S., 'Cartel Pricing and the Structure of the World Bauxite Market', The Bell Journal of Economics vol. 8, no. 2 (Autumn 1977)

Postand, M. see Habakkuk, H.J.

Prain, Sir Ronald, Copper: the Anatomy of an Industry (Mining Journal Books Ltd, London, 1975)

Prest, A.R., War Economics of Primary Producing Countries (Cambridge University Press, Cambridge, 1948)

Rabushka, A. see Duignan, P.

Radetzki, M., 'The Potential for Monopolistic Commodity Pricing by Developing Countries' in Helleiner, G.K. (ed.), A World Divided: the Less Developed Countries in the International Economy

(---) Uranium: A Strategic Source of Energy (Croom Helm, London, 1981)

Rangarajan, L.N., Commodity Conflict: the Political Economy of International Commodity Negotiations (Croom Helm, London, 1978)

Reynolds, P.D., International Commodity Agreements and the Common Fund: A Legal and Financial Analysis (Praeger Publishers, New York, 1978)

Ritson, C. see Heidhues, T.

Robertson, W., Tin: Its Production and Marketing (Croom Helm, London, 1982)

Robinson, E.A.G. and Kidron, M. (eds.), Economic Development in South Asia (Macmillan, London, 1970)

Roll, E., The Combined Food Board: A Study in Wartime International Planning (Stanford University Press, Stanford, 1956)

Rom, I.M., UNCTAD and the Problem of Preferences for Export of Manufactures from Developing Countries (Tel Aviv Export Institute, Tel Aviv, November 1965)

Rom, M., The Role of Tariff Quotas in Commercial Policy (Macmillan, London, 1979)

Rostow, W.W., 'The Terms of Trade in Theory and Practice', Economic History Review vol. III (1950)

(---) The World Economy: History and Prospect (Macmillan, London, 1978)

Rowe, J.W.F., Markets and Men (Cambridge University Press, Cambridge, 1936)

(---) Primary Commodities in International Trade (Cambridge University Press, Cambridge, 1965)

(---) The World's Coffee (HMSO, London, 1963)

Roy, H., 'Some Observations on a New International Tea Agreement', Economic Affairs vol. 17 (1972)

Sampson, A., The Seven Sisters (Hodder & Stoughton, Sevenoaks, 1975)

Sarkar, G., The World Tea Economy (Oxford University Press, London, 1972)

Saul, S.B. see Milward, A.

Scammell, W.M., International Trade and Payments (Macmillan, London, 1974)

Schiavo-Campo, S. see Erb, G.F.

Schink, G.R. see Smith, G.W.

Schneider, W., Food, Foreign Policy and Raw Material Cartels (National Strategy Information Center, New York, 1976)

Schuh, G.E., 'US Agriculture in an Interdependent World Economy: Policy Alternatives for the 1980s' in Johnson, D.G. (ed.), Food and Agricultural Policy for the 1980s

Schultz, G.P. and Dam, K.W., Economic Policy Beyond the Headlines (W.W. Norton, New York, 1977)

Scott, M.F.G., Corden, W.M. and Little, I.M.D., The Case Against General Import Restrictions (Trade Policy Research Centre, London, 1980)

Sekhar, B.C. see Allen, P.W., Thomas, P.O. and Sekhar, B.C.

Shephers, G., Industrial Adjustment and Intervention: Textiles and Clothing in Britain and Germany (University of Sussex, Brighton, 1979)

Sidhu, B., Land Reform, Welfare and Economic Growth (Bombay, 1976)

de Silva, L., 'Cocoa, Coffee and Tea: Producer Co-operation for Structural Change', Marga vol. 6, no. 3 (January 1982)

(---) 'Commodity Export Policy and Technical Assistance', Development Policy Review vol. 1 (forthcoming, 1983)

(---) 'International Commodity Trade: A Scheme for Export Earnings Entitlements', Verfassung und Recht in Ubersee vol. 14 (1981)

Singh, M., 'The Economics of an International Tea Agreement: a Study of Some Aspects of Stabilization of Commodity Prices', Indian Economic Journal vol. 4 (1970)

Singh, S. see Hughes, H.

Singh, S., de Vries, J., Hulley, J.C. and Yeung, P., Coffee, Tea and Cocoa: Market Prospects and Development Lending (IBRD, New York, 1977)

Sitterson, J.C., Sugar Country: the Cane Sugar Industry in the South, 1753-1950 (University of Kentucky Press, Lexington, 1953)

Smith, G.W., 'US Commodity Policy and the Tin Agreement', in Denoon (ed.), The New International Economic Order

Smith, G.W. and Schink, G.R., 'International Tin Agreement: A Reassessment', Economic Journal vol. 86 (1970)

Smith, I. see Harris, S.

Snowden, P.N. see MacBean, A.I.

Sorenson, V.L., International Trade Policy: Agriculture and Development (Michigan State University, Michigan, 1975)

de Sousa, E., A Crise da Borracha (Rio de Janeiro, 1913)

Spencer, G.L. and Meade, R., Cane-Sugar Handbook (New York, 1945)

St Clare Grondona, L., Australia in the 1960s (Anthony Blond, London, 1962)

Stevenson, J., Rubber Situation in the British Colonies and Protectorates 1922 (HMSO, London, 1922, Cmd. 1678)

Stewart, I.M.T., Information on the Cereals Market (Hutchinson, London, 1970)

337

Streeten, P., 'The Case for Export Subsidies', Journal of Development Studies vol. 5, no. 4 (1969)

Strong, L., The Story of Sugar (Weidenfeld and Nicolson, London, 1954)

Swann, D., The Economics of the Common Market (Penguin, Middlesex, 1970)

Swerling, B., International Control of Sugar, 1918-1941 (Stanford University Press, Stanford, 1949)

(---) 'The International Sugar Agreement of 1958', The American Economic Review vol. XLIV, no. 5 (December 1954)

Swerling, B. see Timoshenko, V.P.

Szuprowicz, B.O., How to Avoid Strategic Material Shortages (John Wiley & Sons, New York, 1981)

Tangermann, S. see Heidhues, T.

Taunay, A., História do Café no Brasil (Departamento Nacional do Café, Rio de Janeiro, 1939)

Taylor, P. and Groom, A.J.R., International Organisation: A Conceptual Approach (Francis Pinter, London, 1978)

Thoburn, J.T., Primary Commodity Exports and Economic Development : Theory, Evidence and a Study of Malaysia (John Wiley & Sons, London, 1977)

Thomas, H., Cuba or the Pursuit of Freedom (Eyre and Spottiswoode, London, 1971)

Thomas, P.O. see Allen, P.W., Thomas P.O. and Sekhar, B.C.

Tilton, J.E., The Future of Nonfuel Minerals (The Brookings Institution, Washington, 1977)

Timoshenko, V.P. and Swerling, B., The World's Sugar: Progress and Policy (Stanford University Press, Stanford, 1957)

Tisdell, C., 'Price Instability and Average Profit', Oxford Economic Papers vol. 22 (1970)

Tomek, W.G. and Cochrane, W.W., 'Long-run Demand: A Concept and Elasticity Estimate for Meat', Journal of Farm Economics vol. 43 (August 1962)

Toplin, R.B. (ed.), Slavery and Race Relations in Latin America (Greenwood Press, Westport, Connecticut, 1974)

Treydte, K.P., 'The Stabilisation of Export Earnings: Two Years' Experience in STABEX', Intereconomics, vol. 11/12 (1977)

Tsadik, T.W., 'The International Sugar Market: Self Sufficiency or Free Trade', Journal of World Trade Law vol. 16, no. 3 (1982)

Tugendhat, C., Oil: the Biggest Business (Eyre and Spottiswoode, London, 1968)

Turner, T., The Marketing of Sugar (Irwin Inc, Homewood, Illinois, 1955)

Twitchett, C.C., A Framework for Development: The EEC and the ACP (Allen & Unwin, London, 1981)

US Beet Sugar Association, 'What is the US Sugar Program?' (Washington, March 1966)

Vannerson, F., 'An Econometric Analysis of the Postwar United States Wheat Market', unpublished PhD thesis, Princeton University, Princeton, 1969

Vargas, G., A Nova Política do Brasil (José Olympio, Rio de Janeiro, 1938-1947)

Vargas-Hidalgo, R., 'The Crisis of the Andean Pact: Lessons for Integration Among Developing Countries', Journal of Common Market Studies vol. 17, no. 3 (March 1979)

Vastine, J.R., 'United States International Commodity Policy', Law and Policy in International Business vol. 9, no. 2 (1977)

Venkataratnam, M., 'The Coffee Agreement', Planters' Chronicle (November 1980)

Viner, J., Dumping: A Problem in International Trade (University of Chicago Press, Chicago, 1973)

Viner, T., 'Stability and Progress: The Poorer Countries' Problems' in Hague, D.C. (ed.), Stability and Progress in the World Economy de Vries, J., 'Structure and Prospects of the World Coffee Economy' (IBRD Working Paper 208, Washington, 1975)

de Vries, J. see Singh, S., de Vries, J., Hulley, J.C. and Yeung, P.

de Vries, M.G., The International Monetary Fund 1966-1971 (IMF, Washington, 1976)

Wallace, D.H., Market Control in the Aluminium Industry (Cambridge, Mass., 1937)

Walworth, G., Feed the Nation in Peace and War (Allen & Unwin, London, 1940)

Warley, T.K., Agriculture in an Interdependent World: US and Canadian Perspective (Canadian-American Committee, C.D. Howe Research Institute, US, 1977)

Wasserman, U., 'Breakdown of International Cocoa Agreement', Journal of World Trade Law vol. 14, no. 4 (July:August 1980)

(---) 'Commodities in UNCTAD: Rubber', Journal of World Trade Law vol. 11, no. 3 (May:June 1977)

(---) 'Jakarta Natural Rubber Agreement 1976', Journal of World Trade Law vol. 11, no. 3 (May:June 1977)

(---) 'UNCTAD: International Olive Oil Agreement 1979', Journal of World Trade Law vol. 13, no. 5 (September:October 1979)

Watts, N.G.M. (ed.), Economic Relations between East and West (Macmillan, London, 1978)

Weaver, R. see Helmberger, P.

Weitzman, M. see Cremer, J.

Weymar, F.H., The Dynamics of the World Cocoa Market (Massachusetts Institute of Technology Press, Cambridge, Mass., 1968)

(---) 'The Supply of Storage Revisited', American Economic Review vol. 56 (December 1976)

White, L.J., The Automobile Industry since 1945 (Harvard University Press, Cambridge, Mass., 1971)

Whittlesey, C., Governmental Control of Crude Rubber: The Stevenson Plan (University of Princeton Press, Princeton, 1931)

Wickizer, V.D., Coffee, Tea and Cocoa (Stanford University Press, Stanford, 1951)

(---) The World Coffee Economy with Special Reference to Control Schemes (Stanford University Press, Stanford, 1943)

Williams, T. see Cline, W.R.

Wolf, M. see Keesing, D.B.

Wood, G.A.R., Cocoa (Longman, London, 1975)

Woods, D.W., 'Current Price and Investment Trends in the World Aluminium Bauxite Market: their effect on the US Economy' in Denoon (ed.), The New International Economic Order: a US Response

World Bureau of Metal Statistics, World Metal Statistics (World Bureau of Metal Statistics, London, various issues)

Wright, C.B. and Hedges, J.L., 'Price Stability in Commodity Markets' (Bank of England unpublished working paper, October 1982)

Yamey, B.S. see Bauer, P.T.

Yeung, P. see Singh, S., de Vries, J., Hulley, J.C. and Yeung, P.

341

Note: Names of organisations abbreviated in the text are indexed under that abbreviation. Material on specific commodities relating to a particular country is indexed under the name of the country.

345

quotas, and production controls

copper 7-8, 15, 45, 58, 101n, 249, 255-59, 285; cartels 57, 84-88, 255-59, 266; CIPEC 257-58; Copper Exports Association 256; dependence on 16, 255; industry structure 255; prices 16-17, 255, 258; producer-consumer contract 255; producers' associations 256; substitutes 255, 258

copra 14

core commodities, UNCTAD 73

cotton 8-9, 16, 27, 44-5, 58; agreements 73, 285

cotton seeds 58

cotton yarns 44

crop diversion 66

crude petroleum 7, 9, 11, 14, 101n; Arab Petroleum Conference (1959) 250; cartels 84, 86-88, 249-54; 1928 cartel 250; companies 249, 266; demand for 249-50, 253; dependence on 16; Gulf pricing system 250; as a non-renewable resource 19; price rise (1973-74) 19, 191-92, 251, 253; price rise (1979) 19, 251, 253-54; prices 252; as primary commodity 8 see also OPEC

Cuba 97; missile crisis 183, 212; sugar and 166-67, 169-71, 175-76, 181

currants 50n

currency realignment 19, 151

currency restrictions 26

customs tariffs 30

customs unions 30, 39

customs valuation practices 100n

Czechoslovakia 62, 165, 263

dairy products 33-5, 40, 52n; International Dairy Arrange-ment 34, 40; International Dairy Products Council 34

debt rescheduling 40, 42

defence related materials 67

Denmark 31, 43, 148, 161n

dependence on commodities 15-16, 49, 74, 164, 173, 219n, 255; IMF funds and 46

developed countries 11

development finance 36, 286

developing countries 11; clothing exports from 38-9; CMEA and 63; coffee and 205, 218; commodity processing and 36; dependence on commodity trade 14-16, 74, 274; dependence on imports 16; effect of price instability on 17-18; export earnings 276; external debts xv; foreign capital in 44; GATT and 31-2, 40; iron ore and 264; share of world trade 11-14; sugar and 177; tea and 233; UNCTAD and 40-6; wheat and 151

diversification of output 44; of coffee 83, 214, 216-18; projects financed by IBRD 48; provided for in agreements 76

Dominican Republic 261

dumping 98; of sugar 169-70, 181; of wheat 138

East Africa: coffee and 206, 210, 212, 216; tea and 234, 238

economic growth, price instability and 17-18

ECOSOC 51n

Ecuador 61; cocoa and 223; oil and 251

Edwards, J. 163

EEC 11, 52n, 59-61; CAP 59-60, 98, 168; cocoa and 230; coffee and 35; colonial

346

348

cartels 283; aimed at increasing producers' purchasing power 25; aims of 74-6, 246, 277-80; commodity characteristics and 274; conditions for success of 274-75; disenchantment with 284; failures 277-78; frequency of, and coverage of 72-4; Havana Charter and 29; importers' and exporters' representation in 31; monitoring of 285-86; oil prices and 253; policing of 84; regulatory techniques 76-84; US policy and 64-5; wider role for 287 see also specific commodities

international commodity organisations 285-86 see also under specific commodities

international commodity trade: (1938) 4-8; colonial groupings and (1928-38) 9; new trading groups formed 11-12; participation in 8-15; post-War growth of 11-15; post-War policy development 27-30; primary and manufactured exports compared 14; problems of 15-19; value and volume of 11-14; value of exports (1938) 6; value of exports (1977) 7

International Development Association 48

International Finance Corporation 48

international monetary system 36, 281

international trade: decrease in 94; growth of 20; independent policies for 35

intervention points (for stocks) 79

intra-bloc trade 11

Iran 250-51, 253

Iraq 250-51

iron ore 7-8, 15, 44, 58, 249; AIEC 88, 265-66; cartels 88, 264-66; dependence on 16

iron ore agreements 73, 284-85

Italy 169, 247n; mercury and 259-60

ITO 28-9

Ivory Coast: cocoa and 57, 206, 223, 229-30, 232n; coffee and 206, 215

Jamaica 89, 261-62, 266

Japan: iron ore and 264; rubber and 191-92; sugar and 170; tea and 234; textiles and 38; tin and 107, 117; wheat and 148, 151

Java 170, 172; tea and 234

jute 14, 44-5; agreements 73, 284

Kenya: tea and 233-34, 237, 240

Keynes, J.M. 27

Kissinger, H. 56, 65

Korean War price boom 15, 113, 173, 183, 198, 238, 283

Kuwait 250-51

LAFTA 61-2

lamb 8, 11

Latin America 11

lead 84, 86-88

League of Nations 24-5; Monetary and Economic Conference (1932-33) 25; survey of world trade (1942) 4-6

liberalisation of trade 29, 40, 62; balance of payments problems and 46

Liberia 190

Libya 251

Licht, F.O. 178

liquidity squeeze 20

Lomé Convention (1975) 58, 168